Protestant Nonconformity in the Twentieth Century

Protestant Nonconformity in the Twentieth Century

Edited by

Alan P.F. Sell

and

Anthony R. Cross

PATERNOSTER PRESS

British Library Cataloguing in Publication Data
A catalogue record for this book is available from the British Library

ISBN 1–84227–221–7

Contents

Contributors

David Bebbington Professor of History, University of Stirling

Clyde Binfield Professor Associate in History, University of Sheffield

Hugh R. Boudin Formerly Pastor of the French Protestant Church, Canterbury

David Cornick General Secretary of the United Reformed Church and Fellow of Robinson College, Cambridge

David J. Jeremy Professor of Business History, Manchester Metropolitan University Business School

D. Densil Morgan Reader in Theology, University of Wales, Bangor

John A. Newton Associate Tutor in Church History, Wesley College, Bristol

Keith Robbins Vice-Chancellor, University of Wales, Lampeter

Alan Ruston Editor of the *Transactions of the Unitarian Historical Society*

Alan P.F. Sell Visiting Professor of Theology, Acadia University College of Divinity

Norman Wallwork Superintendant Minister of the Weston-super-Mare Methodist Circuit and Associate Tutor in Liturgy, Wesley College, Bristol

John Tudno Williams Principal of The United Theological College, Aberystwyth, and former Moderator of the Free Church Federal Council

Preface

Following two exploratory meetings the Association of Denominational Historical Societies and Cognate Libraries was formally constituted on 28 October 1993. Among its objects is the following: 'To encourage research into the several traditions, with special reference to projects which relate to more than one tradition.' In other words, part of the Association's mission is to attempt to overcome that tunnel vision which can all too easily overtake denominational history, and this it does through an annual lecture, a publishing programme and occasional conferences.

The title of the Association's second conference, held at Westhill College, Birmingham, 26-29 July 2000, was 'Protestant Nonconformity in England and Wales in the Twentieth Century: A Retrospect'. Speakers representative of most of the Association's member traditions were invited to address subjects in such a way as to bring out their trans-denominational import. This volume comprises fuller versions of the papers presented in Birmingham. While a variety of subjects is reviewed, the coverage is not quite as wide as originally envisaged. Leonard Smith, principal of the Unitarian College, Manchester, was unable through indisposition to prepare and deliver his paper on the socio-political contribution of twentieth-century Nonconformists. Happily, a Unitarian presence was maintained among the speakers thanks to the willing co-operation of Alan Ruston who, at considerably shorter notice than that enjoyed by others, worked up material for his paper which is here published. A paper on the Nonconformists and overseas mission was read at the conference, but is not available for publication.

What we have are four papers on the Nonconformist contribution to some of the classical disciplines of divinity; two papers concerning the content and physical environment of Nonconformist worship; four papers on several types and spheres of witness; a paper on those Protestants whose roots lie across the English channel; and a concluding paper on the contribution of Nonconformists to the modern ecumenical movement.

While the papers will speak for themselves, some running themes emerge, not least the numerical decline of mainline Nonconformity during the twentieth century, the not unrelated impact of the First World War, and relations between Nonconformity and the wider church.

It is hoped that as well as comprising a stock-taking exercise of interest to present-day Nonconformists and others, this volume will provide a marker to scholars fifty or a hundred years hence, who may wish to know how some of their forebears assessed Nonconformity's contibution to a variety of fields during the century leading up to Christianity's third millennium.

I should like to thank the authors for their attendance at the Birmingham conference, and for their papers; and Howard Gregg, secretary of the Association, and E. Dorothy Graham for their stalwart assistance in arranging the event.

Alan P.F. Sell

Milton Keynes

The Contribution of Protestant Nonconformists to Biblical Scholarship in the Twentieth Century

John Tudno Williams

There are a number of parameters and disclaimers which need to be set out at the beginning of this brief survey of scholarship. Protestant Nonconformity is assumed to embrace Baptists, Congregationalists, Presbyterians, Unitarians and Methodists as well, although, traditionally, some Methodists have jibbed at the label 'Nonconformist',[1] and also F.F. Bruce, a member throughout his life of the Brethren. The disclaimers include omitting scholars worthy of discussion whose sphere of service has taken them to other continents although they hailed originally from either England or Wales. My fellow-countryman, W.D. Davies, is a good case in point. However, his first major work, *Paul and Rabbinic Judaism*, will be considered since it was written while he was still in England, a tutor at the Yorkshire United Independent College, Bradford. There are also those who originated from other parts of the British Isles, notably Scotland, whose main contributions to scholarship have emanated from their activities in England or Wales, and I have deemed it proper to include them amongst those to be discussed.

The field of biblical scholarship is vast and the number of Nonconformist scholars of repute within it considerable. Lest this survey become little more than a catalogue of names I have had to confine myself to a consideration of the contributions of a relatively small number of scholars. Naturally the choice is a very personal one and one would be hard-pressed to find complete unanimity amongst today's scholarly community as regards such a comparatively short list.

Beginning with the Bible as a whole, I propose to proceed by way of a thematic route. The nineteenth century had experienced a surge in historical-critical scholarship in the study of the Bible. By the beginning of the twentieth century the results of all this research needed to be

---

1 Cf. C.K. Barrett, '1662 and 1962', *Expository Times* 73 (1961–62), p. 291.

conveyed to a wider public. Who better to do this for non-specialists than Nonconformist scholars? And so our survey ought to commence with the contribution of the Primitive Methodist, A.S. Peake. Indeed his first book, *A Guide to Biblical Study* (1897), sought to do precisely this.[2] In this context, it is salutary to note that in a review of it in *The Times* there occurred the comment: 'The line of study suggested by it cannot well be neglected if the Church of England is to maintain herself at least upon a level with Nonconformist bodies in theological learning'.[3] Peake, says Ian Sellers in a recent reassessment of his work, 'saw the dichotomy in church life as that between fundamentalist ignorance and modern learning'.[4] Indeed, it was said of Peake's predecessor at the Lancashire Independent College in the 1890s that: 'His mind was hermetically sealed against modern scientific views in criticism. One quaint manifestation of his love for his students was his borrowing the translation of Wellhausen's *History of Israel* from the college library and steadily declining to return it—it was safer with him; to him it could do no harm!'[5] As in every generation since, and increasingly so, the need to bridge the gap between the lecture room and the pulpit and the pews was sorely felt and had to be addressed.[6] In his biography of him, J.T. Wilkinson writes of 'his unflinching conviction that the fruits of his scholarship must be made available for ordinary intelligent folk who were seeking after the truth of the Bible'.[7] Yet in his day and age this was not a popular task for a leading churchman. He was accused in a letter to *The Christian Herald* of being 'the Truth Controller', 'our new and infallible pope', 'the light of the world'.[8] However, the contemporary Anglican, F.C. Burkitt, described him as 'a peace-maker between the old and the new—one who said in an age of transition and changing values "This is the way; walk ye in it"'.[9] And a modern Anglican, John Rogerson, writes of him as a proponent of biblical criticism in a climate of 'ignorance of Scripture'.[10]

---

2   Cf. John T. Wilkinson, *Arthur Samuel Peake: A Biography* (London: Epworth, 1971), pp. 86-88.

3   *The Times* 21 October 1897, quoted by Wilkinson, *Peake*, p. 88.

4   Ian Sellers, 'A.S. Peake Reconsidered', *Epworth Review* 24.4 (October, 1997), p. 83.

5   Quoted by James D.G. Dunn, 'A Word in Time: Understanding the Bible Today' (The Peake Memorial Lecture, 1991), *Epworth Review* 119.2 (May, 1992), p. 27.

6   On Peake's efforts in this respect, see Wilkinson, *Peake*, pp. 91-96.

7   Wilkinson, *Peake*, p. 92.

8   Quoted by Sellers, 'Peake', p. 84.

9   Quoted by Sellers, 'Peake', p. 84.

10   John W. Rogerson, 'Progressive Revelation: Its History and its Value as a key to Old Testament Interpretation' (The A.S. Peake Memorial Lecture, 1981), *Epworth Review* 9.2 (May, 1982), p. 73.

An anonymous writer quoted in the Peake commemoration volume wrote in 1929: 'Perhaps it was Peake's greatest service, not merely to his own communion but to the whole religious life of England, that he helped to save us from a fundamental controversy such as that which had devastated large sections of the church in America. He knew the facts which modern study of the Bible had brought to light. He knew them and was frank and fearless in telling them, but he was also a simple and consistent believer in Jesus, and he let that be seen too'.[11]

Peake was 'throughout his writings, almost without exception', 'directly or indirectly, the interpreter of Scripture... His task of biblical interpretation falls into two categories—the interpretation of the Bible in terms of an understanding of the Bible *as a whole*; the interpretation of the *text* in terms of truth by way of exact exegesis, and, therefore, as a commentator of Scripture... The life-work he set for himself was to make known far and wide a sound understanding of the *nature* and *content* of Scripture'.[12] Thus his mass of publications include works on the Bible as a whole and also commentaries on a number of Biblical books drawn from both Testaments.[13] He lay equal stress on *both* history and experience as significant in the process of revelation.[14] For him the Bible was the *record* of revelation. It was not the revelation itself. That was given through history and experience, in life and personality.[15] He was also a proponent of 'progressive revelation': 'The Bible is the record of this progressive revelation of the character and purpose of God in the history and experience of man'.[16] This is a notion that has its weaknesses, especially so in that it does not do justice to more modern ideas about the formation of the Old Testament. It also tends, theologically, to downgrade the Old Testament itself.[17] It was, nevertheless, taken up by Peake's immediate successor in the John Rylands Chair of Biblical Criticism and Exegesis in the University of Manchester—the only theological chair in England open at the time to Nonconformity.[18]

---

11   John T. Wilkinson (ed.), *A.S. Peake, 1865–1929: Essays in Commemoration* (London: Epworth, 1958), p. 12.

12   Wilkinson, *Peake*, p. 86.

13   Cf. the Select Bibliography in Wilkinson, *Peake*, pp. 198-207.

14   Wilkinson, *Peake*, p. 94.

15   Cf. A.S. Peake, *The Bible: Its Origin, Its Significance and Its Abiding Worth* (London: Hodder & Stoughton, 1913), pp. 290-95. Cf. also Rogerson, 'Progressive Revelation', p. 79.

16   Wilkinson, *Peake*, p. 93.

17   Cf. James Barr, *The Bible in the Modern World* (London: SCM Press, 1973), p. 146, and Rogerson, 'Progressive Revelation', p. 74.

18   Elaine Kaye, *Mansfield College, Oxford: Its Origin, History, and Significance* (Oxford: Oxford University Press, 1996), p. 177.

Indeed, Charles Harold Dodd, a Congregationalist, born and brought up in Wrexham, North Wales, concerned himself in his first major publication with *The Authority of the Bible*. In it he devoted a chapter to 'progressive revelation'.[19] He maintained that its main point was 'the work and influence of Jesus Christ' which was 'the climax of what [he called] that whole complex process' which can be traced in the Bible, this process being 'of the highest spiritual worth' so that 'we must recognize it in the fullest sense as a revelation of God'.[20] Thus it was Jesus Christ 'who gave to the whole biblical process its absolute meaning, and it is He who shapes and controls its remoter issues down to our own day'.[21]

Dodd played with the possibility that we are really concerned with progressive *discovery* rather than with progressive revelation,[22] but finally plumps for the latter term. For one thing, he says, 'before we can discover, something has revealed itself',[23] and similarly 'if we would discover life, we must allow life to reveal itself'.[24] And then, secondly, after all, the concept of revelation within the biblical context is the natural one to use in order to make a positive linkage between Jesus and the religious history of Israel as revealed in the Old Testament. Thus he feels justified in employing the term 'progressive revelation': 'Whether we say that men progressively discovered a revelation which in God's intention is eternally complete and unalterable, or that God Himself proportioned the measure of His revelation to the stages of human progress, is perhaps no more than a matter of verbal expression. That progress is there, and in the progress revelation, is the double fact we wish to establish'.[25]

G.B. Caird identified the *leitmotif* or principle of unity running through Dodd's work as 'the conviction that God is Lord of history, and that the Word of God spoken in scripture is so inextricably interwoven into the fabric of historical events that it can be let loose into the modern world in the fullness of its relevance and power only through historical

---

19   C.H. Dodd, *The Authority of the Bible* (London: Fontana, rev. edn, 19..), pp. 248-63. He demonstrated his approval of the term 'progressive revelation' in a later book, *The Bible Today* (Cambridge: Cambridge University Press, 1956), p. 98.

20   Dodd, *Authority*, p. 263.

21   Dodd, *Authority*, p. 263.

22   Dodd, *Authority*, p. 248.

23   Dodd, *Authority*, p. 249.

24   Dodd, *Authority*, p. 250.

25   Dodd, *Authority*, p. 255. Although Barr has noted points in favour of this standpoint (see *Old and New in Interpretation* [London: SCM Press, 1966], p. 21, and *The Bible in the Modern World*, p. 146), he has also expressed his unease with this approach, concluding that it is ultimately confused and unsuitable (*The Bible in the Modern World*, pp. 145-46).

criticism exercised with the utmost integrity and thoroughness'.[26] Throughout *The Authority of the Bible*, Dodd laid heavy stress on the importance of the historical element in the Bible, and in particular on the way it relates to the life and ministry of Jesus Christ: 'The peculiar historical situation in which Jesus lived and taught was such that the questions it raised and He answered were of decisive significance not for that age alone but for all history'.[27] In *History and the Gospel* (1938) he stressed the need to ask the historical question about the life, death and resurrection of Jesus. He recoiled from the nineteenth-century Quest of the Historical Jesus with its seeking after the bare facts of history. The Gospels were written 'from faith to faith' he reminds us.[28] However, he refused to follow Bultmann and his disciples in denying the importance of the historical Jesus for faith: 'We need not be so sceptical as some recent critics have shown themselves of the possibility of getting behind the early church to the real Jesus of history'.[29] Again he claimed: 'Neither Mark nor any other evangelist had any idea that in setting forth "the Jesus of history" he was doing other than illuminate "the Christ of faith"'.[30] His belief in the fundamental trustworthiness of the Synoptic traditions (and in part those of the Fourth Gospel as well) is nowhere better exemplified than in his last published work called *The Founder of Christianity* (1970). This little volume embodied his assured results in setting forth the 'Historical Jesus'.

In his work he embraced many of the insights of form-criticism, albeit in a much less negative way than that of such German pioneers of this method of studying the Gospels as Bultmann.[31] Dodd turned their

---

26   George B. Caird, 'C.H. Dodd', in M.E. Marty and D.G. Perman (eds), *A Handbook of Christian Theologians* (Cambridge: Lutterworth, 1984), p. 321.

27   Dodd, *Authority*, p. 224.

28   C.H. Dodd, *History and the Gospel* (London: Nisbet, 1938), p. 14.

29   Dodd, *Authority*, p. 215; cf. also his *The Apostolic Preaching and Its Developments* (London: Hodder & Stoughton, new ed, 1956), p. 56.

30   Dodd, *Authority*, p. 212.

31   For Dodd's remarks on form-criticism see *The Present Task in New Testament Studies* (Cambridge: Cambridge University Press, 1936), pp. 19-22; *History and the Gospel*, pp. 91-103; *The Parables of the Kingdom* (London: Nisbet, rev. edn, 1953), p. 40 n. 2; and *Historical Tradition in the Fourth Gospel* (Cambridge: Cambridge University Press, 1963), pp. 5-6. His use of this method is seen in the following studies: 'The Appearances of the Risen Christ: An essay in form-criticism of the Gospels', in D.E. Nineham (ed.), *Studies in the Gospels: Essays in Memory of R.H. Lightfoot* (Oxford: Blackwell, 1955), pp. 9-35 (reprinted in C.H. Dodd, *More New Testament Studies* [Manchester: Manchester University Press, 1968], pp. 102-33); 'The Beatitudes: a form-critical study', *Melanges Bibliques rediges en l'honneur de Andre Robert* (Paris: Bloud & Gay, 1955) (reprinted in Dodd, *More New Testament Studies*, pp. 1-10); and his treatment of John 11.47-53 according to form-critical categories as a 'pronouncement story' in 'The Prophecy of Caiaphas: John xi.47-53', in *Neotestamentica et Patristica: O.*

methods, as Caird put it, 'to more constructive use'.[32] In his essay on 'The Framework of the Gospel Narrative', he countered the arguments of the form-critics who had propounded the view that no credence could be placed on the Marcan order of events as regards the ministry of Jesus with the view that 'in broad lines the Marcan order does represent a genuine succession of events within which movement and development can be traced'.[33]

A similar position is also found in the work of other leading Nonconformist scholars of the twentieth century, such as the Methodist, Vincent Taylor, who can be credited with introducing the methods of form criticism into Britain and indeed with refining them.[34] It was he who coined the appropriate appellation 'pronouncement stories' to describe what Martin Dibelius had called *Paradigmen* ('models') and Rudolf Bultmann *Apophthegmata* ('pointed sayings'), that is, miracle and other narratives which climax in a significant pronouncement of Jesus. Similarly, the English Presbyterian, T.W. Manson, believed that the Gospel tradition could be used as dependable historical material and that eye-witness tradition could still be relied upon in assessing the value of the Gospel narratives as history.[35] He also, in a justly famous lecture entitled 'The Quest of the Historical Jesus—Continued', reaffirmed the need for such a quest in the second half of the century.[36] Later the Methodist, C. Kingsley Barrett,[37] and George Caird followed a similar path. Indeed, the latter has been called the pioneer of the so-called 'Third Quest' of the historical Jesus.[38] It is a description coined by Tom Wright in 1992 of a quest that regards Jesus as an eschatological prophet and emphasizes his location in first-century Judaism.[39] The respective

---

Cullmann Freundesgabe (*Novum Testamentum* Supplement, 6; Leiden: Brill, 1962), pp. 134-43 (reprinted in *More New Testament Studies*, pp. 58-68).

32   Caird, 'Dodd', p. 324.

33   C.H. Dodd, 'The Framework of the Gospel Narrative', *Expository Times* 43 (1932), p. 400 (reprinted in C.H. Dodd, *New Testament Studies* [Manchester: Manchester University Press, 1953], p. 11).

34   See Vincent Taylor, *The Formation of the Gospel Tradition* (London: Macmillan, 1933).

35   Thomas W. Manson, *Studies in the Gospels and Epistles* (ed. Matthew Black; Manchester: Manchester University Press, 1962), pp. 6, 40-42. Similarly, as regards eye-witnesses, see V. Taylor, *The Gospel According to St. Mark* (London: Macmillan, 1952), p. 102.

36   The lecture is reproduced in Manson, *Studies*, pp. 3-12.

37   C. Kingsley Barrett, *Jesus and the Gospel Tradition* (London: SPCK, 1967).

38   Cf. Mark A. Powell, *The Jesus Debate: Modern Historians Investigate the Life of Christ* (Oxford: Lion, 1999), p. 200 n. 35.Cf. also James Barr, 'Obituary of G.B. Caird', in *Proceedings of the British Academy* 71(1985), pp. 504-505.

39   N. Tom Wright, 'Quest for the Historical Jesus', in D.N. Freedman (ed.), *Anchor Bible Dictionary* (6 vols; New York: Doubleday, 1992), III, pp. 796-802.

reactions of Barrett and Caird to Bultmann, undoubtedly the leading continental European *Neutestamentler* of the century, are instructive. Whereas the former showed sympathy, indeed some accommodation to his views, notably as regards the extent of Gnostic influence on New Testament Christianity,[40] Caird 'repeatedly cited the Bultmannian positions as evidence of how far biblical scholarship could go wrong and had gone wrong'.[41] Caird summed up the matter: 'A gospel means news about historical events, attested by reliable witnesses, and having at their centre, an historical person'.[42]

Such contributions by Dodd, like those we have already alluded to, were undoubtedly precursors of a trend, indeed many would claim it to be a movement, a number of features of which were characteristic of the so-called Biblical Theology Movement which flourished in the forties and fifties of the twentieth century: 'The idea of revelation through history was basic to most or all biblical theology in a period like 1945–60. It was in many ways the focal point of the entire idea of biblical theology and summarized its values: revelation through history was supposed to be characteristic of Hebrew thought..., common to the entire Bible, and thus the underlying basis of its inner unity'.[43] This movement embodied a reaction to the liberal theology of the earlier part of the century and to the way biblical scholarship had behaved in the era of liberal theology.[44] In his critique of the movement in North America, Brevard S. Childs notes that 'there were certainly significant groups within Britain—particularly from the Free Churches—which shared many of the goals and attitudes of the American Biblical Theology Movement'.[45] It is claimed that the influence of the neo-orthodox theologian, Emil Brunner, in particular, is to be discerned on the biblical theology of Dodd, and also other leading Nonconformist scholars such as T.W. Manson, Vincent Taylor and Norman Snaith.[46]

---

40   Cf. Richard G. Jones, 'Profile: The Preacher-Scholar of Durham, C. Kingsley Barrett', *Epworth Review* 20.1 (January, 1993), p. 26, and J. Painter, 'Barrett, C(harles) K(ingsley)', in Donald K. McKim (ed.), *Historical   Handbook of Major Biblical Interpreters* (Leiccstcr: Inter-Varsity Press, 1998), p. 429.

41   Barr, 'Caird', p. 516; cf. also pp. 507, 513, 516-17.

42   G.B. Caird, *Our Dialogue with Rome: The Second Vatican Council and After* (Oxford: Oxford University Press, 1967), p. 49.

43   J. Barr, *Explorations in Theology. 7: The Scope and Authority of the Bible* (London: SCM Press, 1980), pp. 4-5.

44   Cf. Brevard S. Childs, *Biblical Theology in Crisis* (Philadelphia: Westminster Press, 1970), p. 15, and Barr, *Explorations*, p. 2.

45   Childs, *Biblical Theology*, p. 26.

46   Cf. L.D. Hurst, 'Caird, G(eorge) B(radford)', in McKim (ed.), *Historical Handbook*, p. 457, and J. Munsey Turner, 'Preaching, Theology and Spirituality in Twentieth-Century British Methodism', *Expository Times* 111 (1999–2000), p. 115.

A notable feature of the Biblical Theology Movement was its stress on the unity of the Bible. Similarly, a hallmark of Dodd's interpretation of the New Testament writings was his search for their unity,[47] and indeed it was his emphasis on the kerygmatic unity of the New Testament which provided a major impetus to the growth of biblical theology itself.[48] This has to be seen as his personal reaction to the older liberal criticism with its emphasis on the search for sources and analysis of the material. 'In the end', he said of it, 'we were presented with a New Testament of bits and pieces. Each separate constituent was characterised and appreciated in depth, often to its great illumination, but they scarcely seemed to form a whole. The relation they bore to one another was obscure'.[49] It was thus that Dodd sought for a principle of unity for the New Testament material.

In *According to the Scriptures* (1952), Dodd tried to show how the writers of the New Testament made use of the Old Testament scriptures. He demonstrated that they selected certain sections of the Old Testament, especially from the prophetical books and the psalms, and although they often quoted or alluded to certain verses only or even just phrases from these sections, the total context of such passages was always held in view by the various New Testament authors and formed the basis of their argument. (We note in passing that more recent studies have tended to confirm the pattern of biblical exegesis in the early church which Dodd elucidated.[50]) This treatment of the Old Testament scriptures led to the formulation of a whole body of material which was common to all the main portions of the New Testament. Thus the application of Old Testament prophecies to events in the life of Jesus was the earliest form of Christian theology.[51] In particular, this treatment of the Old Testament provides the formation of the theological edifices built upon it by the great theologians of the New Testament, Paul, John and the author of the Epistle to the Hebrews.[52] In this way Dodd claimed to have discovered

---

47   Cf. J.A.T. Robinson, 'Theologians of our Time: xii. C.H. Dodd', *Expository Times* 75 (1963–64), pp. 100-101.

48   Cf. W.D. Davies' tribute to Dodd, 'In Memoriam Charles Harold Dodd, 1884–1973', *New Testament Studies* 20 (1973–74), p. iii.

49   C.H. Dodd in his Introduction to P. Gardner-Smith (ed.), *The Roads Converge: A Contribution to the Question of Christian Reunion* (London: Edward Arnold, 1963), p. 4.

50   Cf. G.N. Stanton, *Jesus of Nazareth in New Testament Preaching* (Cambridge: Cambridge University Press, 1974), p. 74. See Dodd, *According to the Scriptures: The Sub-structure of New Testament Theology* (London: Fontana, 1965), p. 126. Cf. also Barnabas Lindars, *New Testament Apologetic: The Doctrinal Significance of the Old Testament Quotations* (London: SCM Press, 1961), p. 14.

51   Cf. Dodd, *History and the Gospel*, p. 60.

52   Dodd, *According to the Scriptures*, pp. 12-13.

what he termed 'the substructure of all Christian theology' and 'its chief regulative ideas'.[53]

He also approached the question of the existence of a common tradition within the early church underlying the whole of the New Testament from another angle: 'Reflection on the epistles', he wrote, 'will show that for all the individuality of the writers and their creative power in the realm of theological and ethical thought, their work presupposes everywhere a common tradition of the centre, by which they and their readers are bound, however boldly and freely they may interpret and apply it in the rapidly changing situations of an expanding Church'.[54] He went on: 'Broadly speaking, we may recognise two aspects of this central tradition. On the one hand, it is a preaching or proclamation (*kerygma*) about God's action for the salvation of men, by which the church was called into existence, and which it announces to all men everywhere as the ground of faith and hope. On the other hand, it embodies an ethical ideal for a corporate and individual life. The most general term for this is "teaching" (*didache*)'.[55] Dodd himself called the *kerygma* the 'ground-plan of New Testament theology'.[56] Thus the original Christianity was not a message about 'the Fatherhood of God and the Brotherhood of man', as Adolf von Harnack (whose lectures in Berlin he had attended[57]) had stated,[58] but rather a proclamation by the apostles of the life, death and exaltation of Jesus as Christ and Lord.[59] In his pioneering work, *The Apostolic Preaching and its Developments* (1936),[60] he set out the main elements in the preaching or proclamation (*kerygma*) of the early church, which he reconstructed on the basis of the relevant contents of Paul's epistles,[61] the pattern being repeated, it was claimed, in the early speeches of the Book of Acts.[62] In addition, he

---

53   Dodd, *According to the Scriptures*, p. 127; cf. p. 27.

54   Dodd, *History and the Gospel*, pp. 50-51; cf. *Present Task*, p. 37, and *The Founder of Christianity* (London: Fontana, 1973), p. 27.

55   Dodd, *History and the Gospel*, p. 50; cf. further pp. 51-53 and 85; and *Apostolic Preaching*, pp. 7-8; *Bible Today*, pp. 74-79; *Gospel and Law: The Relation of Faith and Ethics in Early Christianity* (Cambridge: Cambridge University Press, 1951), pp. 8-10; and *According to the Scriptures*, pp. 11-27, 61-62.

56   Dodd, *According to the Scriptures*, p. 12; cf. also p. 27.

57   F.W. Dillistone, *C.H. Dodd: Interpreter of the New Testament* (London: Hodder & Stoughton, 1977), p. 54.

58   Adolf von Harnack, *What is Christianity?* (London: Williams & Norgate, 1901), lecture vi, pp. 63-74.

59   Cf. Robinson, 'Dodd', p. 101.

60   According to C.F. Evans, 'The Kerygma', *Journal of Theological Studies* 7 (1956), p. 25 n. 3, a number of German scholars had also pioneered this theory.

61   Dodd, *Apostolic Preaching*, p. 17.

62   Dodd, *Apostolic Preaching*, pp. 21-26.

proposed the view that the written Gospels were based on the *kerygma*, the spoken gospel.[63]

It was, according to Dodd, thoroughly characteristic of the Christian mission that the proclamation—the *kerygma*—should be followed by the beginning of instruction in morals—the *didache*.[64] As he had earlier discovered a pattern of proclamation common to many parts of the New Testament, so now he discerned a common practice of ethical teaching in the New Testament: 'It appears, then', he claimed, 'that the ethical portions of the epistles are based upon an accepted pattern of teaching which goes back to a very early period indeed, and whose general form and content can be determined with considerable probability'.[65] Whilst Dodd's thesis has often been assailed in subsequent years,[66] it is still under frequent discussion in the context of contemporary New Testament scholarship and has always to be addressed. However, the contemporary Methodist scholar, James Dunn, has urged us to speak of *kerygmata* in the plural rather than of a single *kerygma* in the New Testament, and finds the answer to the problem of variety in the New Testament in lines that converge backward to the historical Jesus.[67]

Throughout the twentieth century, Old Testament studies in England and Wales have been heavily influenced, if not indeed dominated, by Baptist scholars, and this is recognized in the dedication by one of the most eminent Old Testament scholars of the century, the German, Otto Eissfeldt, of his standard introduction to the Old Testament 'to the Representatives of three generations of British Old Testament Scholarship, Theodore H. Robinson, Harold H. Rowley, and Aubrey R. Johnson', Baptists to a man.[68]

---

63   Cf. Dodd, *Apostolic Preaching*, pp. 47-52.

64   Dodd, *Gospel and Law*, p. 10.

65   Dodd, *Gospel and Law*, p. 20. For its form see pp. 20-21. On this matter Dodd acknowledged his indebtedness to the work of the Anglicans, P. Carrington (later Archbishop of Canada), *The Primitive Christian Catechism* (Cambridge: Cambridge University Press, 1940), and E.G. Selwyn (Dean of Winchester), *The First Epistle of St. Peter* (London: Macmillan, 1946): cf. Dodd, *Gospel and Law*, p. 22 n. 4.

66   The following critics may be noted: H.J. Cadbury, 'Acts and Eschatology', in W.D. Davies and D. Daube (eds), *The Background of the New Testament and Its Eschatology* (Studies in Honour of C.H. Dodd) (Cambridge: Cambridge University Press, 1954), pp. 313-20; Evans, 'The Kerygma', pp. 26-41, and J.P.M. Sweet, 'Second Thoughts: viii. The Kerygma', *Expository Times* 76 (1964–65), pp. 143-47.

67   James D.G. Dunn, *Unity and Diversity in the New Testament: An Inquiry into the Character of Earliest Christianity* (London: SCM Press, 1977).

68   Otto Eissfeldt, *The Old Testament: An Introduction* (Oxford: Blackwell, 1965).

Since he was a proponent of the Biblical Theology Movement, the unity of the Bible was a recurring theme in Rowley's publications,[69] as was the need to recover a theological dimension to the Bible allied with the need to restate its contemporary relevance for modern man.[70] 'No single word seems more cogently to express Rowley's belief in the evangelical message of the Old Testament, or the purpose of the scholar's task, than does this one word *relevance*'.[71] 'Honest' or 'veiled' biblical criticism was for him a handmaiden to Biblical Theology rather than an opponent,[72] and he wrote that the new direction must not be 'less scholarly than we have known but more profoundly theological'.[73] His works were usually of a popular or semi-popular nature where the themes covered often overlapped and repetition of material was a feature of them. However, 'Rowley was at his best in the disentangling of complex critical problems where the proliferation of rival views had tended to obscure the essentials'.[74] He was 'beyond question the most accomplished biblical bibliographer of this century in the English-speaking world', says G.W. Anderson in his obituary for the British Academy.[75] His many critical surveys of outstanding Old Testament problems 'were notable for their lucid analysis of the issues involved, their comprehensive documentation, their unbiased presentation of the views of other scholars, and the combination of caution and sound judgement with which the conclusions were presented'.[76] He was not deemed to have been a scholar of great originality: 'Rowley may not have flown many kites, but he pricked many balloons'.[77]

---

69   Cf. Harold H. Rowley, *The Unity of the Bible* (London: Carey Kingsgate Press, 1953). Cf. also Henning Graf Reventlow, *Problems of Biblical Theology in the Twentieth Century* (trans. John Bowden; London: SCM Press, 1986), pp. 4-5.

70   Cf. H.H. Rowley, *The Relevance of the Bible* (London: James Clarke, 1942), and *The Re-discovery of the Old Testament* (London: James Clarke, 1945). Cf. also Childs, *Biblical Theology*, p. 15.

71   Ronald E. Clements, 'The Biblical Scholarship of H.H. Rowley (1890–1969)', *Baptist Quarterly* 38.2 (April, 1999), p. 77.

72   Childs, *Biblical Theology*, p. 35.

73   H.H. Rowley, 'The Relevance of Biblical Interpretation', *Interpretation* 1 (1947), p. 11.

74   George W. Anderson, 'Obituary of Harold Henry Rowley, 1890–1969', *Proceedings of the British Academy* 56 (1970), p. 316.

75   Anderson, 'Rowley', p. 312.

76   Anderson, 'Rowley', p. 314. See Rowley's three volumes of collected essays: *The Servant of the Lord and Other essays on the Old Testament* (London: Lutterworth, 1952); *From Moses to Qumran: The Authority of the Bible and Other Major Issues in Old Testament Studies* (London: Lutterworth, 1963), and *Men of God: Studies in Old Testament History and Prophecy* (London: Nelson, 1963).

77   Anderson, 'Rowley', p. 316.

Childs discerns a greater degree of continuity between successive generations of scholars in England, and notes that Rowley understood his work to be in direct continuity with that of his mentor, Wheeler Robinson.[78] Indeed, the doyen of them all was undoubtedly Henry Wheeler Robinson, whose concept of 'corporate personality' coloured not only studies of the Old Testament, but also topics in New Testament studies such as the concept of the church in Paul. He first used the phrase 'corporate personality' in his book *The Christian Doctrine of Man* (1911), and his early essay entitled 'Hebrew Psychology in Relation to Pauline Anthropology'[79] contained *in nuce* some of the ideas later developed in his influential paper 'Corporate Personality',[80] which has been called 'a classic of British Old Testament scholarship'.[81]

He defined what he meant by it thus: 'Corporate personality means for us in this place the treatment of the family, clan, or the nation, as the unit in place of the individual. It does not mean that no individual life is recognized, but simply that in a number of realms in which we have come to think individualistically, and to treat the single man as the unit, e.g. for punishment or reward, ancient thought envisaged the whole group of which he was part'.[82] Thus the concept 'recognized the social solidarity of the ancient Hebrew people in their relation to God, emphasizing the singular identity of individual, family, clan and nation. Corporate personality means that in community the individual has meaning only in relation to the group'.[83] Thus the conception 'largely removes the sharp antithesis between the collective and the individualistic views'.[84]

In his work Wheeler Robinson drew attention to four aspects of the concept of corporate personality:

1.   the unity of its extension both into the past and into the future;

---

78   Childs, *Biblical Theology*, p. 24.

79   Published in W.B. Selbie (ed.), *Mansfield College Essays: Presented to the Reverend Andrew Martin Fairbairn, D.D., on the occasion of his seventieth birthday* (London: Hodder & Stoughton, 1909), pp. 265-86.

80   Cf. John Reumann in 'Introduction' to the second edition of *Corporate Personality* (Edinburgh: T&T Clark, 1981), p. 20.

81   By Cyril S. Rodd in 'Introduction' to the second edition of *Corporate Personality*, p. 7.

82   H. Wheeler Robinson, 'Hebrew Psychology', in A.S. Peake (ed.), *The People and the Book: Essays on the Old Testament* (Oxford: Clarendon, 1925), p. 376.

83   R.A. Coughenour, 'Henry Wheeler Robinson', in McKim (ed.), *Historical Handbook*, p. 516.

84   Wheeler Robinson, *Corporate Personality*, p. 38. Cf. the earlier publication 'The Hebrew Concept of Corporate Personality', in *Werden und Wesen des Alten Testaments* (Beihefte zur Zeitschrift fur die Alttestamentliche Wissenschaft, 66; Berlin: Topelmann, 1936), pp. 49-62.

2.   the characteristic 'realism' of the conception, which distinguishes it from 'personification', and makes the group a real entity actualised in its members;
3.   the fluidity of reference, facilitating rapid and unmarked transition from the one to the many, and from the many to the one;
4.   the maintenance of the corporate idea even after the development of a new individualistic emphasis within it.[85]

Finally, he indicated three outstanding types of application of the concept to the Old Testament:

1.   the representation of the nation by some outstanding figure belonging to it;
2.   the individual–collective nature of the 'I' of the Psalms and of the 'Songs of the Servant of Yahweh';
3.   the character and content of Hebrew morality as the right relation of individual members of the group to one another.[86]

In this way, along with J. Pedersen and A.R. Johnson, 'he opened up a new vista on the Old Testament world that proved immensely exciting to his contemporaries'.[87] However, in recent years Wheeler Robinson's treatment of the concept has been subjected to severe criticism notably by the Anglicans, J.R. Porter and J.W. Rogerson.[88] The latter's criticisms are twofold: firstly, that Robinson's use of the term contained much ambiguity, and, secondly, that the anthropological theories of Levy-Bruhl, on which he drew, were flawed. Nevertheless, it is unlikely the term 'corporate personality' will be dropped in the near future as easily as Rogerson hopes and disappear without trace from basically scholarly writing.[89]

The concept of corporate personality attracted the attention of New Testament scholars as well, and in particular T.W. Manson. 'Where the tendency to think of the social group as a single social organism ("one flesh") is powerful', he wrote, 'there is often also a strong tendency to see the corporate personality as embodied or expressed in an individual. The king is apt to be thought of as embodying the corporate personality of his subjects. It is at this point that the transition from Son of Man as a

---

85   Wheeler Robinson, *Corporate Personality*, pp. 27-34.
86   Wheeler Robinson, *Corporate Personality*, pp. 35-44.
87   Rodd, *Corporate Personality*, p. 14.
88   Joshua R. Porter, 'The Legal Aspects of the Concept of "Corporate Personality" in the Old Testament', *Vetus Testamentum* 15 (1965), pp. 361-80, and John W. Rogerson, 'The Hebrew Conception of Corporate Personality: A Re-Examination', *Journal of Theological Studies* n.s. 21 (1970), pp. 1-16.
89   Cf. Rodd, *Corporate Personality*, pp. 8 and 14.

name for the people of the saints of the Most High to Son of man as a messianic title becomes possible'.[90] Thus the corporate interpretation of the expression most commonly found on the lips of Jesus in the Gospels, Son of man, is usually associated with Manson, although he was by no means the first scholar in history to have adopted it.[91] It is based on the portrayal of the 'one like a son of man' in Daniel 7.13, who is generally understood to be a symbolic figure representing the 'saints of the Most High', that is, the kingdom or people of God.[92] For Manson, the Son of Man is 'an ideal figure and stands for the manifestation of the Kingdom of God on earth in a people wholly devoted to their heavenly king'.[93] The term becomes a designation of Jesus alone when his mission to create the Son of man, the kingdom of God's people, succeeds neither among the people nor among his disciples. Then he stands alone, embodying in his own person the perfect response to the regal claims of God.[94] Dodd commented: 'He makes his thesis, perhaps, more acceptable to some who have their doubts, by a fuller recognition of the idea of "corporate personality", and by allowing for an "oscillation" between the corporate and the individual senses'.[95] However, a very recent assessment of Manson's position is less amenable to it: 'The weakness of this interpretation is that none of the Son of Man sayings require it, while most demand a reference to Jesus alone. It can only be adopted, therefore, on the assumption that most or all of the sayings have been modified to reflect a more individual reference'.[96]

Wheeler Robinson also contributed substantially to our understanding of the primitive semitic idea of man. In it 'there is', he wrote, 'no distinction of the psychical and ethical from the physical, so that the actual breath of man can be thought of as his "soul", and the reek of hot blood identified with this "breath-soul"'.[97] 'This breath-soul is conceived as the animating principle of man's life, its essential

---

90   Thomas W. Manson, *The Servant–Messiah* (Cambridge: Cambridge University Press, 1953), p. 74.

91   Cf. Delbert Burkett, *The Son of Man Debate: A History and Evaluation* (Society for New Testament Studies Monograph Series, 107; Cambridge: Cambridge University Press, 1999), pp. 35-37.

92   Cf. T.W. Manson, 'The Son of Man in Daniel, Enoch and the Gospels', in *Studies*, pp. 126-27. Cf. already Wheeler Robinson, *Corporate Personality*, pp. 29-30.

93   T.W. Manson, *The Teaching of Jesus: Studies of its Form and Content* (Cambridge: Cambridge University Press, 1935), p. 227.

94   Manson,*Teaching*, p. 228.

95   C.H. Dodd, 'T.W. Manson and His Rylands Lectures', *Expository Times* 73 (1961–62), p. 303.

96   Burkett, *Son of Man Debate*, p. 37.

97   Wheeler Robinson, 'Hebrew Psychology', p. 353.

constituent'.[98] Thus 'there is no trichotomy in Hebrew psychology, no triple division of human personality into body, soul and spirit'.[99] Man, he wrote in his early paper in Mansfield College Essays, is no 'immortal soul, imprisoned in a body', but an interreaction of 'breath-soul, spirit and the body with its various organs', that is in short, 'an animated body',[100] a phrase which entered into common parlance whenever the Hebrew conception of man was subsequently discussed.

Most important of all, according to Rex Mason's recent assessment of his contribution, was Wheeler Robinson's notion of how divine inspiration works: the 'invasion' of the human personality by the Spirit of God.[101] His representation of corporate personality inevitably led, as has been noted, to a blurring of the distinction between a person *qua* individual and *qua* member of the larger, collective unity such as family or clan. This presented 'an understanding of human personality which is open at the edges, or has ill-defined frontiers'.[102] Thus it is wide open to outside influences, as Wheeler Robinson himself put the matter: 'The most important aspect of [the individual's] personality is its constant accessibility to "spiritual" influences from without'.[103] As a consequence, it 'more easily enabled the Hebrew mind to regard itself as the vehicle of divine revelation'.[104] Thus Hebrew psychology 'which has directly developed from Semitic animism provides the cardinal conception of God's means of contact with man—the idea of the Spirit of God, together with the idea of human personality as a unity of soul and body, entirely dependent upon God'.[105] He developed his ideas about revelation through the Spirit in his *The Christian Experience of the Holy Spirit* (1928),[106] and concluded that the only real spiritual authority was intrinsic, an intuitive response to the inward working of the Spirit: 'However transcendent God is, the point at which He reveals Himself to us must be a point at which He becomes intelligible to us, that is, a point at which there is kinship between His nature and ours'.[107]

---

98   Wheeler Robinson, 'Hebrew Psychology', p. 357.

99   Wheeler Robinson, 'Hebrew Psychology', p. 362.

100   Wheeler Robinson, 'Hebrew Psychology in Relation to Pauline Anthropology', p. 277. Cf. also 'Hebrew Psychology', p. 362.

101   Rex A. Mason, 'H. Wheeler Robinson Revisited', *Baptist Quarterly* 37.5 (January, 1998), p. 220.

102   Mason, 'Wheeler Robinson', p. 219.

103   Wheeler Robinson, 'Hebrew Psychology', p. 366.

104   Wheeler Robinson, 'Hebrew Psychology', pp. 371-72.

105   Wheeler Robinson, *The Religious Ideas of the Old Testament* (London: Duckworth, 1913), p. 48.

106   (London: Nisbet, 1928).

107   Wheeler Robinson, *Redemption and Revelation in the Actuality of History* (London: Nisbet, 1942), p. 165. Cf. Mason, 'Wheeler Robinson', p. 222.

It is with the University of Wales' Semitics Departments that two of the dedicatees of Eissfeldt's volume were associated throughout their academic careers, whilst the third, H.H. Rowley, taught for fifteen years at both Cardiff and Bangor. Of the former, Theodore Henry Robinson is known for a number of textbooks in particular. In co-operation with the Anglican, W.O.E. Oesterley, he produced *Hebrew Religion: Its Origin and Development* (1930); *A History of Israel* in two volumes, he himself being responsible for the first volume: *The Exodus to the Fall of Jerusalem* (1932), and *An Introduction to the Books of the Old Testament* (1934). Not unexpectedly, Old Testament studies had by later in the century superseded a number of the standpoints set forth in these volumes. We shall note an example or two only here: the first part of *Hebrew Religion*, heavily influenced by the theories of Julius Wellhausen about the evolution of religion from the primitive to the sublime and by W. Robertson Smith's theories about the early religion of the Semites, portrayed the religion of the Israelites as a development from animism.[108] (It should, however, be noted that it was actually Oesterley who was responsible for the first part of the volume.) However, in the 1940s and subsequently, as indeed Rowley has tabulated in one of his famous bibliographical lectures given at the John Rylands Library, Manchester,[109] the religion of Abraham and his descendants was treated with a greater respect and admiration. Yet by the end of the century Old Testament scholars had become more reticent regarding the possibility of knowing much about the character of this early form of Israelite religion, and indeed about the very notion of a 'history of Israel'. In the first volume of *A History of Israel*, Robinson hazarded a date in the fifteenth century BC, namely 1440, for the Exodus, following the supposed discovery a little earlier by the archaeologist Garstang of what he claimed was evidence for the fall of Jericho.[110] Subsequently, it became much more fashionable to date the event some two centuries later.

---

108 W.O.E. Oesterley and Theodore H. Robinson, *Hebrew Religion: Its Origin and Development* (London: SPCK, 1930), pp. 21-28, 32-37, 41-7, 62-75, 116-22 and 124, in particular. Such views were also held by Wheeler Robinson: cf. Mason, 'Wheeler Robinson', pp. 219-21.

109 Harold H. Rowley, 'Recent Discovery and the Patriarchal Age', reproduced in *The Servant of the Lord*, pp. 269-305. Cf. also Rowley's positive view of the history of the Exodus period in *From Joseph to Joshua: Biblical Traditions in the Light of Archaeology* (The Schweich Lectures for 1948; London: British Academy, 1950), and Clements' comments on it in 'Biblical Scholarship of Rowley', pp. 80-81.

110 Theodore H. Robinson, *A History of Israel* (2 vols; Oxford: Clarendon, 1932), I, pp. 77-79.

Undoubtedly T.H. Robinson's most important contribution was to the study of the prophets.[111] Indeed, Rowley, in a survey of the study of Old Testament prophecy, states that no contemporary British scholar had contributed more towards an understanding of the prophets.[112] Indeed he pioneered two aspects of these studies in particular by emphasizing the ecstatic element in prophecy and by suggesting how the prophetic oracles were transmitted and committed to writing in the literature of the Old Testament. In the preface to his volume *Prophecy and the Prophets in Ancient Israel* (1923), he claimed that it was he, along with John Skinner of Westminster College, Cambridge, in his book on Jeremiah, *Prophecy and Religion* (1922), who had presented the new ideas from Germany to the English-speaking world about the psychology of the prophets, although, he claimed, 'some of the greatest of British Old Testament scholars still deny that there was any ecstatic element in the life of the canonical prophets'. The volume itself lays great store by this element in prophecy. Indeed, if this element were denied, three important facts about the prophets would be inexplicable. Firstly, the fact that the Hebrew word for prophet, *nabi*, is used as often to describe classical prophets such as Amos, Hosea, Isaiah and Jeremiah as it is used of the prophets of Baal.[113] Secondly, a notable feature of theirs was that they, like the earlier prophets, possessed the gift of second sight and second hearing.[114] Thus, too great a contrast between the two categories of prophets, the early and the so-called classical ones, should not be drawn, in as much as both types experienced ecstasy.[115] Moreover, it was the ecstasy which was 'both to the Prophet and to his hearers...a guarantee of Yahweh's presence and message'.[116] The commonest expression used by the prophets to introduce their oracles, 'Thus said Yahweh', 'suggests an ecstatic experience now past, which is being reported to the audience' in the

---

111 When a *Festschrift* was presented to him in 1946 on the occasion of his retirement at the age of 65 from the secretaryship of the Society for Old Testament Study, its title was significantly *Studies in Old Testament Prophecy*, edited by H.H. Rowley (Edinburgh: T&T Clark, 1950).

112 Rowley, 'The Nature of Old Testament Prophecy in the Light of Recent Study', in *Servant of the Lord*, p. 92 n. 6.

113 T.H. Robinson, *Prophecy and the Prophets in Ancient Israel* (London: Duckworth, 1923), p. 40. According to Rowley, *Servant of the Lord*, p. 97, the term *nabi* cannot be used as an argument for the ecstatic nature of the later prophets. See also O. Eissfeldt, 'The Prophetic Literature', in H.H. Rowley (ed.), *The Old Testament and Modern Study* (Oxford: Clarendon, 1951), p. 142.

114 T.H. Robinson, *Prophecy and the Prophets*, p. 41.

115 Rowley, *Servant of the Lord*, p. 107.

116 T.H. Robinson, *Prophecy and the Prophets*, p. 46.

present.[117] There is little doubt, however, that Robinson exaggerated the ecstatic element in prophecy.[118]

In addition Robinson did as much as anyone to try to explain how the prophetical books were composed.[119] Three stages in their growth are set out: firstly, that which the prophet himself said, usually in short sayings dealing with contemporary events. These were then transmitted orally by his hearers and subsequently, often after the death of the prophet, they were formed into small collections and written down. Additional material that did not in fact emanate from the prophet himself was added. Finally, everything was gathered by editors to form the prophetical books as we know them today.[120] On the whole, he doubted whether the prophet himself could have been responsible for writing or collecting the bulk of the oracles attributed to him.[121] This tendency of his to divide the prophetical books into small units drew adverse reactions later on.[122]

T.H. Robinson was succeeded in the Semitics chair in Cardiff by one of his former pupils, Aubrey R. Johnson. His main contribution to Old Testament scholarship lies in the study of the Psalms. Following on from the innovative work of H. Gunkel and S. Mowinckel in interpreting the Psalms in the context of worship, liturgy and the cult of the Jerusalem temple, Johnson gave his attention to the place of the king in the worship, naming the main festival 'the Festival of Kingship'. After delineating the close connection between the king in Israel and the cult, as it is portrayed in the historical books of the Old Testament,[123] he followed Gunkel in demonstrating that some Psalms, namely the 'Royal Cult-Songs', portray particular happenings in the Enthronement Festival of the King.[124] However, Mowinckel and Johnson went further in their researches and

---

117   T.H. Robinson, *Prophecy and the Prophets*, pp. 43-45.

118   Cf. Rowley, *Servant of the Lord*, pp. 96-102.

119   Cf. C.R. North, 'Living Issues in Biblical Scholarship: The Place of Oral Tradition in the Growth of the Old Testament, *Expository Times* 61 (1949–50), p. 293, and Eissfeldt, 'Prophetic Literature', p. 126.

120   T.H. Robinson, *Prophecy and the Prophets*, pp. 50-59, and 'The Methods of Higher Criticism', in *People and the Book*, pp. 181-82.

121   T.H. Robinson, *Prophecy and the Prophets*, p. 55.

122   Cf. Eissfeldt, 'Prophetic Literature', pp. 128-34, and Herbert F. Hahn, *The Old Testament in Modern Research* (London: SCM Press, 1956), p. 146.

123   Cf. Aubrey R. Johnson, 'Living Issues in Biblical Scholarship: Divine Kingship and the Old Testament', *Expository Times* 62 (1950-51), p. 37, and 'Hebrew Conceptions of Kingship', in S.H. Hooke (ed.), *Myth, Ritual and Kingship: Essays on the Theory and Practice of Kingship in the Ancient Near East and in Israel* (Oxford: Clarendon, 1958), pp. 204-35.

124   Cf. Johnson, 'Divine Kingship', pp. 36-37; 'The Psalms', in *The Old Testament and Modern Study*, pp. 167-68; *Sacral Kingship in Ancient Israel* (Cardiff: University of Wales Press, 1955, 2nd edn, 1967), *passim*, and 'Hebrew Conceptions', pp. 204-35.

sought to uncover a form of divine or 'sacral' kingship in Israel. Johnson himself preferred the neutral term 'sacral kingship' to the more common term 'divine kingship'.[125] He described the ritual drama in which the kings or nations of the earth who represent the forces of darkness and death oppose the representatives of light and life, the king of Israel and his people. The king is sometimes referred to as the Son, the Servant and the Messiah of the Lord, and it is upon him that all the nation depends for its welfare as a whole. At first the ritual appears to represent him as being humiliated and beaten and nearly swallowed by the forces of chaos; nevertheless, later because of his faithfulness and justice he is rescued by Yahweh from the jaws of death. This revival in the case of the king corresponds to the revival of life in the case of the whole nation. It denotes that the Suffering Servant and the humble Messiah have once more been adopted as the Son of the Most High.[126] On the other hand, Johnson refused to go as far as some Scandinavian scholars who suggested that Yahweh was to be considered as a dying and rising God like the fertility gods of the ancient world, and that the king of the house of David assumed the role of the High God or some other God in this ritual as a type of the divine king.[127]

R.E. Clements, another in this distinguished line of Baptist scholars, comments in his review of *A Century of Old Testament Study*,[128] that a result of such studies as those of Johnson into the meaning of kingship as expressed in the Psalms 'has been a better understanding of the nature and significance of a number of passages in the prophetic books which refer to a future king, and which have loosely been regarded as messianic'. Johnson's standpoint was not without its critics amongst whom was the Methodist, C.R. North, who concluded: 'There is little evidence for the conception of "the divinity of the king" in ancient Israel; indeed, such evidence as we have seems definitely to point against it'.[129]

Following Mowinckel again, Johnson sought to show what was the role of cultic prophets in Israel. (T.H. Robinson had, by the way, made no mention of such a class of prophets.) Johnson claimed they were present at all the sanctuaries of Yahweh, but especially in the Jerusalem Temple. They stood side by side with the priests and played as important a part as they there. They would receive and proclaim the Lord's oracles to the people, and as representatives of the people before God they would bring

---

125 Johnson, 'Divine Kingship', p. 41.

126 Johnson, 'Psalms', pp. 196-97; cf. also 'Divine Kingship', pp. 37-40.

127 Johnson, 'Divine Kingship', p. 40, and 'Psalms', p. 197.

128 R.E. Clements, *A Century of Old Testament Study* (Cambridge: Lutterworth, rev. edn, 1983), p. 108.

129 Christopher R. North, *The Old Testament Interpretation of History* (London: Epworth, 1946), p. 123.

their needs before him in prayer. Later these communities of cultic prophets became choirs of singers mentioned in the Priestly Code and the Books of Chronicles. This came about as a result of the weakening of the influence of the cultic prophets after the fall of Jerusalem in 587 BC because they had misled the people into believing that they would be secure in the face of that disaster.[130] However, Johnson did not discuss the important question to what extent, if at all, the classical prophets should be regarded as members of the cultic prophets' communities.[131] We could accept that cultic prophets served on the staff of the Temple,[132] but would suggest that they should be clearly differentiated from the canonical prophets.[133] In his final published work, *The Cultic Prophet and Israel's Psalmody* (1979),[134] Johnson tried to reconstruct the activities and aims, with their setting in a festival, of the cultic prophets, deriving the picture from a detailed study of many psalms. This work, which was a long time in gestation, has not on the whole been favourably received.[135]

Stimulated by the work of the Danish scholar, J. Pedersen,[136] Johnson contributed extensively to our understanding of the psychology of the Israelites. In the monograph, *The One and the Many in the Israelite Conception of God* (1942, 2nd edn, 1961), a work greatly influenced also by Wheeler Robinson's notion of 'corporate personality', he described the natural movement from the individual to the group or the many in common parlance about man and about God. There is an 'extension of a person's personality in the spoken word; in a similar way a 'name' carries on living after the person has died. A similar extension in his personality is found in his representatives—his servants, his property and his household. The social unit is regarded as a 'corporate personality'.[137] However, Johnson was careful to point out that he himself, while deriving

130 A.R. Johnson, *The Cultic Prophet in Ancient Israel* (Cardiff: University of Wales Press, 1944, 2nd edn, 1962). Rowley disagreed with this position: cf. *Worship in Ancient Israel: Its Forms and Meaning* (London: SPCK, 1967), pp. 171-72.

131 Cf. Johnson, *Cultic Prophet* (2nd edn), p. v.

132 Cf. Rowley, *Worship*, pp. 150-54.

133 This was precisely what G. Holscher, who first presented this theory, did. Cf. also G. von Rad, *Old Testament Theology* (2 vols; trans. D.M.G. Stalker; Edinburgh: Oliver & Boyd, 1965), II, pp. 52-53 and 55.

134 (Cardiff: University of Wales Press, 1979).

135 Cf. Clements, *Century*, p. 117.

136 And, indeed, Johnson conceded that it had to be used critically and with caution: cf. *The Vitality of the Individual in the Thought of Ancient Israel* (Cardiff: University of Wales Press, 2nd edn, 1964), p. 1 n. 3.

137 A.R. Johnson, *The One and the Many in the Israelite Conception of God* (Cardiff: University of Wales Press, 1942), pp. 5-17. See further the critique of Rogerson, 'Hebrew Concept', pp. 1-16, on the whole idea as it is used by H. Wheeler Robinson and Johnson, and in particular pp. 11-13.

inspiration from Levy-Bruhl, Wheeler Robinson and others, drew his understanding of Hebrew psychology from the evidence of the Old Testament itself and from writings from the ancient near east.[138] A similar situation arises in relation to God.[139] An extension in his personality is found in the Spirit, the Word, the Name, and the Ark. There are also examples in stories in the Old Testament of the rapid oscillation from the Lord to his angels or messengers.[140] Indeed, it would at times be difficult to distinguish between Yahweh and one of his prophets. The latter was his representative speaking his words. He was the 'extension' of his personality, and, as such, was Yahweh in 'his Person'.[141] At the same time this should not be regarded as an expression of the mystical experience of being absorbed into the Godhead.[142] At the end of this study Johnson recommended its value as a new way towards the doctrine of the Trinity.[143]

In his preface to the only other study of a similar nature published by him, *The Vitality of the Individual in the Thought of Ancient Israel* (1949, 2nd edn, 1964), Johnson stated that it was to be preparatory for a Biblical Theology. It was to be in fact the first of a series intended to explain the saying in Habakkuk 2.4b, 'The righteous shall live by his faith', which is a fundamental principle in the Bible.[144] In this study he discussed every example in the Old Testament of terms relating to man:[145] *nephesh* first of all;[146] *ruach*;[147] and lastly various parts of the body.[148] Such a study could have been tedious to read, but in reality the author succeeded in making it remarkably lively and interesting, especially as he associated

---

138 Cf. Rodd, *Corporate Personality*, p. 11. Contrast Johnson's uncritical standpoint in *The One and the Many* with his more critical position in *Sacral Kingship*, pp. 2-3; *Vitality*, pp. 1-2, and *Cultic Prophet and Israel's Psalmody*, pp. 10-11.

139 Johnson, *One and the Many*, pp. 17-26.

140 Johnson, *One and the Many*, pp. 32-37.

141 Johnson, *One and the Many*, p. 37.

142 Cf. Rowley, *Servant of the Lord*, p. 120.

143 Johnson, *One and the Many*, p. 41.

144 The titles of the second and third in the projected series are referred to here as *The Vitality of Society in the Thought of Ancient Israel* (see Johnson, *Vitality*, pp. 82 n.1 and 104 n.5), and *The Vital Importance of the Covenant in the Thought of Ancient Israel* (see *Vitality*, pp. 86 n.7, and 105 n.2). In his contribution to *Congress Volume* (Copenhagen, 1953) (*Vetus Testamentum* Supplement, 1; Leiden: Brill), entitled 'The Primary Meaning of G'L', pp. 67-77, we find a preview of what can be expected in the next volumes.

145 Wheeler Robinson had carried out a similar exercise in 'Hebrew Psychology', pp. 354-66.

146 Johnson, *Vitality*, pp. 3-22.

147 Johnson, *Vitality*, pp. 23-37.

148 Johnson, *Vitality*, pp. 37-87.

the Hebrew words and expressions with English colloquialisms.[149] In the final section of the work the various Israelite ways of thinking of life and death were considered.[150] Throughout these discussions Johnson sought, in the tradition of Wheeler Robinson, to picture the Hebrew notion of man as a psycho-somatic unity rather than in dualistic terms as a body and soul: 'True life is only to be found in that ordered functioning of the whole personality which reveals itself in well-being of body and circumstance. Disorder is weakness, and weakness is death; unity is power, and power is life'.[151] We note, in conclusion, that he was very reluctant to date his Old Testament examples.[152]

In 1970 the German Old Testament scholar, Klaus Koch, wrote a book entitled in German, *Ratlos vor der Apokalyptik* (which might be rendered 'Clueless or Perplexed with regard to Apocalyptic'), which points to the comparative neglect of apocalyptic literature in German circles especially over a large part of the century. The English translation of this work became *The Rediscovery of Apocalyptic*.[153] H.H. Rowley has been credited with reviving interest in this form of literature. Indeed, his book on the subject was entitled, *The Relevance of Apocalyptic* (1944).[154] It is remarkable that this literary form was so long neglected by biblical scholars during the twentieth century, especially when one recalls how the century had begun in a blaze of interest in the subject. In particular Johannes Weiss and Albert Schweitzer had set the agenda for New Testament study by the very first decade of the century. At this time there was universal agreement among scholars that the kingdom was central to the teaching of Jesus. Harnack had recognized that fact, although for him the kingdom had no connection with apocalyptic. Indeed, he would have removed every eschatological connotation from it: for him it was a spiritual kingdom, one present to the individual, that Jesus had proclaimed. It was Johannes Weiss in his volume *Die Predigt Jesu vom Reiche Gottes* (1892) who led the opposition against such a standpoint. The kingdom of God was not to be regarded as something present in the world nor as something which grew as a part of the history of the world, but as eschatological, that is, the kingdom was above and beyond the present historical order. It would not come about through the moral efforts of men, but solely through a supernatural act of God himself. It was he who would bring the world and history to a sudden end and would bring a new world into being, a world of eternal blessing.

---

149 See, e.g., Johnson, *Vitality*, pp. 25-26.

150 Johnson, *Vitality*, pp. 87-109.

151 Johnson, *Vitality*, p. 100.

152 See, e.g. Johnson, *Vitality*, p. 31.

153 (Studies in Biblical Theology, 2nd series, 22; London: SCM Press, 1972).

154 H.H. Rowley, *The Relevance of Apocalyptic: A Study of Jewish and Christian Apocalypses from Daniel to the Revelation* (London: Lutterworth, 1944).

It must be remembered, however, that Weiss and Schweitzer had emphasized one side of the Jewish hope about the kingdom, namely the supernatural element.[155] There was indeed another tradition, a strong one, which stressed that the kingdom would be an earthly one.[156] It was as a reaction to Schweitzer's views that Dodd developed his ideas about eschatology. It must be admitted (indeed he didn't hide the fact) that some aspects of apocalyptic were abhorrent to him: for example, he considered the Book of Revelation to be sub-Christian.[157] He rejected traditional Jewish apocalyptic because it devalued the present order of the world in all its aspects, and indeed was not relevant to the present.[158]

It was in the context of his study of the parables of the kingdom that Dodd set out his evidence regarding the concept which is indissolubly linked with him, namely 'realised eschatology'. Indeed, the term was first used by him in his book, *The Parables of the Kingdom* (1935).[159] There are passages in the Synoptic Gospels, he claimed,[160] which demonstrated that 'in the earliest tradition Jesus was understood to have proclaimed that the Kingdom of God the hope of many generations, had at last come. It is not merely imminent, it is here... Whatever we make of them the sayings which declare the Kingdom of God to have come are explicit and unequivocal. They are moreover the most characteristic and distinctive of the Gospel sayings on the subject. They have no parallel in Jewish teaching or prayers of the period. If therefore we are seeking the *differentia* of the teaching of Jesus upon the Kingdom of God, it is here that it must be found'.[161]

It would be inappropriate in this paper to enter into a technical discussion as to whether the Greek verb *eggizo*, which usually means 'to draw near' or 'to be at hand' in the Synoptic Gospels, should be translated, as Dodd averred, 'has come' or 'has arrived', implying that the kingdom had already arrived.[162] Suffice it to say that Dodd's

---

155 Cf. Owen E. Evans, 'Kingdom of God', in G.A. Buttrick (ed.), *The Interpreter's Dictionary of the Bible* (4 vols; Nashville: Abingdon, 1962), III, p. 20.

156 Cf. G. Lundstrom, *The Kingdom of God in the Teaching of Jesus* (Edinburgh: Oliver & Boyd, 1963), p. 75, and T.F. Glasson, 'Schweitzer's Influence—Blessing or Bane?', *Journal of Theological Studies* 28 (1977), pp. 289-90.

157 Dodd, *Apostolic Preaching*, pp. 39-41, 64.

158 C.H. Dodd, 'The Mind of Paul: II', in *New Testament Studies*, pp. 113, 126-28.

159 Dodd, *Parables*, p. 51.

160 See the passages cited in Dodd, *Parables*, pp. 43-48. He acknowledged his indebtedness to Rudolf Otto's *Reich Gottes und Menschensohn* (Munich, 1934) on this question: cf. *Parables*, pp. 38 n. 1 and 49 n. 1. Actually, T.W. Manson, 'The Life of Jesus: Some Tendencies in Present-day Research', in *Background of the New Testament*, p. 218 n. 2, believed the two works were quite independent of one another.

161 Dodd, *Parables*, p. 49.

162 It is interesting to note the ambiguity of *The New English Bible* on this point: see e.g. Mt. 5.17; 10.7; Mk. 1.15; Lk. 10.9. It does not wholeheartedly support Dodd's

linguistic arguments did not go unchallenged.[163] Indeed, we may rightly claim that in countering the over-emphasis of Johannes Weiss[164] and Albert Schweitzer[165] upon the futurist element in the eschatological teaching of Jesus, Dodd went too far in the opposite direction in emphasizing that the kingdom had come with power. He did in fact at one time appear to lose sight of the real futurist element in Jesus' teaching. Thus in stressing the 'realised eschatology' in Jesus' teaching, he stated that those sayings which imply a future kingdom of God did not refer to a future coming in this world, but rather to something beyond time and space.[166] Later, in *The Coming of Christ* (1951), he talked of expectation passing into realization and of realization in turn kindling fresh expectancy: 'There is always more to hope for', he claimed.[167] Furthermore, the second coming refers to 'a coming beyond history: definitely, I should say, *beyond* history, and not a further event *in* history, not even the last event'.[168] Yet he remained typically undogmatic on this point: 'I certainly cannot profess to give an authoritative solution', he declared.[169] Thus we conclude that it is not true to say that Dodd in his later work left no room for a future hope. He may well have overstated his case at first by denying that either Jesus or his immediate followers looked forward to any ultimate consummation. 'But', says G.B. Caird, 'he soon made the necessary adjustments and declared his belief that the New Testament eschatology was summed up in the Johannine

---

views on this matter; interesting indeed in view of Dodd's being Director of the *NEB* project.

163 Cf. Norman Perrin's verdict on this matter: 'Dodd's interpretation has not established itself, nor has it been driven from the field' (*The Kingdom of God in the Teaching of Jesus* [London: SCM Press, 1963], p. 66). Cf. also his summary of the linguistic arguments, pp. 64-66, and also R.H. Fuller, *The Mission and Achievement of Jesus* (Studies in Biblical Theology, 12; London: SCM Press, 1954), pp. 20-27; W.G. Kümmel, *Promise and Fulfilment: The Eschatological Message of Jesus* (Studies in Biblical Theology, 23; London: SCM Press, 1957), pp. 19-25; and R.F. Berkey, '*Eggizein, phthanein,* and Realized Eschatology', *Journal of Biblical Literature* 82 (1963), pp. 177-87.

164 Weiss' views are summarized by Perrin, *Kingdom*, pp. 16-23.

165 Likewise a summary of Schweitzer's views appears in Perrin, *Kingdom*, pp. 28-35.

166 Dodd, *Parables*, p. 56.

167 C.H. Dodd, *The Coming of Christ* (Cambridge: Cambridge University Press, 1951), p. 10.

168 Dodd, *Coming*, p. 17; cf. *Parables*, pp. 108-109; *Apostolic Preaching*, p. 36; and *History and the Gospel*, pp. 170-78.

169 Dodd, *Coming*, p. 12; cf. *Parables*, pp. v-vi; and *The Interpretation of the Fourth Gospel* (Cambridge: Cambridge University Press, 1953), p. 447 n. 1. See also the remarks of Berkey, '*Eggizen*', pp. 72-73.

phrase "the time is coming and now is"'.[170] So, despite the many criticisms of his concept of a 'realised eschatology', nothing can detract from the fact that, in the words of one of the most radical of twentieth-century Nonconformist scholars, the Baptist, Norman Perrin, his has been deemed 'the most important single contribution made to the Anglo–American discussion of Kingdom of God in the teaching of Jesus'.[171]

'Dodd was greatest as a Johannine scholar', said *The Times* obituary of him,[172] and this is probably a correct judgement. John Robinson once wrote of 'The New Look on the Fourth Gospel' with particular reference to the rediscovered emphasis during the second half of the twentieth century on the historicity of the Fourth Gospel.[173] Whilst this particular phase in Johannine study is not to be attributed directly to Dodd, his influence was, nevertheless, considerable in the development and support of this kind of view. His second *magnum opus* on John's Gospel, *Historical Tradition in the Fourth Gospel* (1963), published, incidentally, in his eightieth year, greatly influenced this trend.[174] In an appendix to his earlier volume, *The Interpretation of the Fourth Gospel* (1953), he had set out 'Some Considerations upon the Historical Aspect of the Fourth Gospel'. In this section he had dismissed any attempt at writing a life of Jesus without using John's Gospel,[175] and in fact he put this principle into practice in his *The Founder of Christianity* (1971).[176] His main conclusion from a detailed study of *Historical Tradition in the Fourth Gospel* was that behind this Gospel there 'lies an ancient oral tradition independent of the other gospels, and meriting serious consideration as a contribution to our knowledge of the historical facts concerning Jesus Christ'.[177] John is thus said not to have read Mark—a fact which the Methodist scholar C. Kingsley Barrett, in particular, has

---

170 G.B. Caird, 'The Study of the Gospels. iii. Redaction Criticism', *Expository Times* 87 (1975-76), p. 170. Cf. Dodd, *According to the Scriptures*, p. 74.

171 Perrin, *Kingdom*, p. 58.

172 *The Times* 24 September 1973. Contrast C.L. Mitton, who, writing at the time of his death, as the editor in the *Expository Times* 85 (1973–74), p. 66, expressed his personal feeling that 'he was more surely at home in the synoptic gospels'.

173 Cf. J.A.T. Robinson, *Twelve New Testament Studies* (Studies in Biblical Theology, 34; London: SCM Press, 1962), pp. 94-102.

174 (Cambridge: Cambridge University Press, 1963).

175 Dodd, *Interpretation*, p. 446; cf.also *History and the Gospel* , pp. 99-103.

176 (London: Collins, 1971).

177 Dodd, *Historical Tradition*, p. 423; cf. *Interpretation*, p. 449; and 'The Appearances of the Risen Christ', pp. 20 and 24.

disputed over the years.[178] Yet Dodd constructed a formidable edifice which has, on the whole, successfully withstood major assaults upon it.[179]

In Dodd's wide-ranging description of the Gospel's background in *The Interpretation of the Fourth Gospel* the Hellenistic element is particularly prominent. This element would, we presume, have been explained by him as a later accretion to the original tradition in a non-Jewish environment.[180] In an article published some years before *The Interpretation of the Fourth Gospel* appeared he had written: 'The Evangelist shows himself to be deeply versed in Judaism... His mind moves with equal freedom in the Jewish and in the Hellenistic ways of thought...as though both were native to him, so that they are deeply fused into a theology that is neither Jewish nor Greek, but intelligible from both sides'.[181] It has been aptly said that Dodd's 'writings are a mirror of the transition which has marked our time from a predominantly Hellenistic to a more Semitic approach to the New Testament'.[182]

That was a tribute to him by W.D. Davies, whose own contribution needs to be mentioned here. It would be true to claim that the majority of contemporary Pauline scholars would want to stress the apostle's Jewishness and that he has to be understood against the background of the Old Testament and of the Judaism of his time. Indeed, no one has done more since the Second World War to stress this aspect than the Welsh Congregationalist, W.D. Davies. In his first major study, *Paul and Rabbinic Judaism*, published while he was still in Britain and at the time a tutor at the Yorkshire United Independent College, Bradford, before he emigrated to the United States, he set Paul firmly in his Jewish identity.[183] More recently one of Davies' American disciples, E.P. Sanders, has inaugurated, or more accurately, has redefined the so-called 'New Perspective on Paul'. Amongst other matters, this entails a reappraisal of the portrayal of contemporary Judaism that has traditionally, that is at least since Luther's time, claimed to be derived from the Pauline letters. Indeed, Sanders in his striking work *Paul and Palestinian Judaism* (1977), argued that the picture of that Judaism derived from the apostle's

---

178 Cf. C.K. Barrett, 'John and the Synoptic Gospels', *Expository Times* 85 (1973–74), pp. 228-33.

179 Cf. D. Moody Smith, *John Among the Gospels: The Relationship in Twentieth-Century Research* (Minneapolis: Fortress, 1992), pp. 53-84.

180 Cf. Dodd, *According to the Scriptures*, p. 136, and *Historical Tradition*, pp. 426-27.

181 C.H. Dodd, 'The History and Doctrine of the Apostolic Age', in T.W. Manson (ed.), *A Companion to the Bible* (Edinburgh: T&T Clark, 1939), pp. 411-12.

182 W.D. Davies' tribute in *New Testament Studies* 20 (1973–74), p. iv.

183 *Paul and Rabbinic Judaism* (London: SPCK, 1948).

polemic against it is in fact a parody of the real thing.[184] Another modern scholar who has taken up the theme of this 'new perspective', the Methodist, James D.G. Dunn, has summed up the historical tradition in scholarship on this matter thus: 'Luther himself made the explicit link: the Church was tarnished with "Jewish legalism"; the Catholics' "rules and regulations remind me of the Jews, and actually very much was borrowed from the Jews"; the Catholic understanding of the sacraments is essentially the same as the Jewish view of circumcision; on faith and works, the doctrine of the church was a variation of the Jewish error that mere acts can win favour in God's sight'.[185]

The sticking point for Paul as far as Judaism was concerned, and specifically in relation to the Law, according to Dunn, consisted of what he termed 'the badges' of Judaism, and not the Jewish Law as a whole. The Pauline expression 'works of the law' is equated by Dunn with these 'badges', which separated Jews from Gentiles, and in effect frustrated the Gentile mission of the early church. They consisted of circumcision, food and ritual requirements as well as the keeping of the Sabbath.[186]

It was the Lutheran scholar (and later bishop), Krister Stendahl, who had argued in a seminal paper for two decisive positions: firstly, that the usual (Lutheran) interpretation of Paul's view of righteousness by faith is historically erroneous, since it understands the doctrine as freeing one from the guilt of an 'introspective conscience', while Paul had not in fact suffered from such a dilemma, and, secondly, that in any case the centre of Pauline theology is not righteousness by faith but the history of salvation described especially in Romans 9–11.[187] James Dunn applauds Stendahl's thesis that Paul's doctrine of justification by faith should not be understood primarily as an exposition of the individual's relation to God, but in the context of Paul the Jew wrestling with the question of how Jews and Gentiles stand in relation to each other within the covenant purpose of God which has now reached its climax in Jesus Christ.[188]

In the letter dedicatory in the *Festschrift* presented to him in 1954, Dodd was called 'a prince of exegetes', and he clearly had the great preacher's gift of exposition.[189] Nowhere are these exegetical gifts better exemplified than in his attempts to draw out the teaching of the apostle

---

184 E.P. Sanders, *Paul and Palestinian Judaism: A Comparison of Patterns of Religion* (London: SCM Press, 1977).

185 J.D.G. Dunn, 'The Justice of God', *Journal of Theological Studies* 43 (1992), p. 7 n. 19.

186 J.D.G. Dunn, *Jesus, Paul and the Law* (London: SPCK, 1990).

187 Cf. Krister Stendahl, *Paul Among Jews and Gentiles and other Essays* (Philadelphia: Fortress, 1976), pp. 1-96.

188 J.D.G. Dunn, 'New Perspective on Paul', *Bulletin of the John Rylands Library* 65 (1983), p. 121.

189 See, e.g., Dodd, *Gospel and Law*, p. 76.

Paul. The title of his earliest published volume, *The Meaning of Paul for Today* (1920), shows his constant concern to make the New Testament relevant to modern contemporary life. 'A Gospel such as that experienced by Paul', he wrote in the preface to a later edition of the book (1957), 'so deeply personal and so widely human can survive the intellectual vicissitudes of centuries, and bear re-interpretation for a new age without losing its vital force'.[190] 'My main concern', he continued, 'has been to bring out what I conceive to be the permanent significance of the apostle's thought, in modern times, and in relation to the general interests and problems which occupy the mind of our generation. I find here a religious philosophy orientated throughout to the idea of a society or commonwealth of God. Such a philosophy finds ready contact with the dominant concerns of our own day'.[191] Likewise, his lucid commentary on *The Epistle of Paul to the Romans* (1932) in the Moffatt New Testament Commentary series exhibited a similar concern to make the scripture relevant: 'The task of the commentator', he maintained, is 'to try to discover as exactly as possible what Paul meant, in his own terms'.[192] In his inaugural lecture at Cambridge in 1936 he had presented a description of the ideal interpreter: '[He] would be one who has entered into that strange first-century world, has felt its strangeness, has sojourned in it until he has lived himself into it, thinking and feeling as one of those to whom the Gospel first came; and who will then return into our world, and give to the truth he has discovered a body out of the stuff of our own thought.'[193]

Nonconformity has throughout the century produced Pauline scholars of the very highest order: besides Dodd, we would name George B. Caird, C. Kingsley Barrett, F.F. Bruce and the Methodist, Morna Hooker, who has produced a series of distinguished papers elucidating various topics and texts in the Pauline corpus, in particular the concept of 'interchange'.[194] Barrett and Bruce, in particular, produced major commentaries on the Pauline corpus of letters and in addition volumes on the apostle's thought and circumstances.[195] More recently James Dunn has produced a massive study of his thought: *The Theology of Paul the*

---

190   C.H. Dodd, *The Meaning of Paul for Today* (London: Collins, 1957), p. 9.

191   Dodd, *Meaning*, p. 11.

192   C.H. Dodd, *The Epistle of Paul to the Romans* (London: Hodder & Stoughton, 1932), p. xxxiv.

193   Cf. Dodd, *Present Task*, pp. 37-41.

194   Morna D. Hooker, *From Adam to Christ: Essays on Paul* (Cambridge: Cambridge University Press, 1990).

195   C.K. Barrett, *Paul: An Introduction to his Thought* (London: Chapman, 1994), and F.F. Bruce, *Paul: Apostle of the Free Spirit* (Exeter: Paternoster, 1977).

Apostle (1998).[196] Indeed, the very concept of a 'Theology of Paul' has often been questioned, and in the opening chapter of his volume, entitled 'Prolegomena to a Theology of Paul', as well as in earlier studies,[197] Dunn has given close attention to the matter. Apart from his epistle to the Romans, his letters do not appear to be orderly, theological compositions, but rather examples of his reactions to various situations, which arose during the course of his missions as an apostle. Thus any treatment of his theology needs to take into consideration practical and dynamic elements.[198] We are also drawn into a living dialogue with his theology as we recognize our need to question ourselves regarding our theological standpoints vis-a-vis those discovered in his epistles. Thus Dunn locates himself within the dialogue of Paul's theology in Romans itself because this epistle is the most sustained and reflective statement of Paul's own theology, and so the framework employed for his setting out of the apostle's theology is that supplied by Romans.[199] 'Paul is never simply theologian', he says, 'he is always at one and the same time Paul the theologian, missionary, and pastor, or simply Paul the apostle'.[200]

A necessary preliminary to the doing of theology is a close study of the text of the New Testament. At the beginning of his Preface to *Jesus and His Sacrifice* (1937), Vincent Taylor wrote: 'After devoting something like twenty-five years to the study of the problems of literary and historical criticism in connection with the Gospels, and especially the minutiae of source criticism, I am conscious of a strong desire to investigate some more vital issue, arising out of these studies, which bears intimately upon Christian life and practice'.[201] Thus there came about his trilogy expounding the New Testament teaching about the death of Christ and its consequences, followed by a further trilogy on what it has to say about his person.[202] As regards the former, he concluded that the essence and aim of Jesus' sacrifice on the cross was to restore fellowship by

196   James D.G. Dunn, *The Theology of Paul the Apostle* (Edinburgh: T&T Clark, 1998).

197   J.D.G. Dunn, 'Prolegomena to a Theology of Paul', *New Testament Studies* 40 (1994), pp. 407-32, and 'In Quest of Paul's Theology: Retrospect and Prospect', in D.M. Hay and E.E. Johnson (eds), *Pauline Theology:* 4 (Atlanta: Scholars Press, 1997), pp. 95-115.

198   Cf. Dunn, *Theology*, p. 21.

199   Dunn, 'In Quest of Paul's Theology', p. 105. See also Dunn's *Romans 1–8* and *Romans 9–16* (Word Biblical Commentary, 38A and 38B; Dallas: Word, 1988).

200   Dunn, 'In Quest of Paul's Theology', p. 99.

201   V. Taylor, *Jesus and His Sacrifice* (London: Macmillan, 1937), p. vii.

202   See V. Taylor, *The Atonement in New Testament Teaching* (London: Epworth, 1940); *Forgiveness and Reconciliation: A Study in New Testament Theology* (London: Macmillan, 1941); *The Names of Jesus* (London: Macmillan, 1953); *The Life and Ministry of Jesus* (London: Macmillan, 1954); and *The Person of Christ in New Testament Teaching* (London: Macmillan, 1958).

means of a representative offering, which is closely co-ordinated with
'the attitude of the worshipper': 'Whatever that death has achieved stands
outside ourselves until there is a believing response which makes the
achievement a vital element in our approach to God'.[203] In his studies of
christology, he firmly rehabilitated a 'kenotic' element in any adequate
doctrine of the incarnation: 'Christology...is incurably kenotic... The
reason must be that self-limitation is an essential form of the divine
manifestation. God is God when He stoops no less than when He reigns.
He is a God who in revelation hides Himself'.[204] Brevard Childs has
written with disdain of Taylor's *magnum opus*, his commentary on *The
Gospel According to St. Mark* (1952) (dubbed by generations of
Methodist students: 'The fifty-shilling Taylor'), that 'it combines a
cautious form-critical analysis with an older form of liberal, free church
theology which, in my judgment, often badly obscures the biblical
text'.[205] James Barr's riposte is apposite: 'Well, why should he not have a
free church theology?'[206]

It has not been of the nature of British scholars, unlike their
counterparts in Germany, to form themselves into schools of followers of
a particular scholar or viewpoint.[207] However, if, as has frequently been
said, Bultmann's influence has been the dominating one in New
Testament scholarship in Germany and the United States over the greater
part of the century, it can legitimately be claimed that it was C.H. Dodd's
influence which was the guiding one in these islands.

Outside the world of scholarship he will probably be most remembered
for his work in connection with *The New English Bible*. He was appointed
General Director of the project in 1947 and held this position for over
twenty years, seeing the task through from inception to completion. The
New Testament was published in 1961 and the Old Testament with the
Apocrypha in 1970. In a tribute to him published in *The Times* after his
death, Donald Coggan, who became Chairman of the Joint Committee,
recalled what he had written in his preface to the complete Bible: 'As
director, Dr. Dodd gave outstanding leadership and guidance to the
project, bringing to the work scholarship, sensitivity, and an ever watchful
eye'. 'The words', he added, 'were carefully chosen, and were amply
justified... He had the gift of conveying the nuance of one language into

---

203 Cf. C.L. Mitton, 'Vincent Taylor: New Testament Scholar', in Vincent Taylor,
New Testament Essays (London: Epworth, 1970), p. 19, referring to Taylor,
Forgiveness, passim.

204 Taylor, *Person of Christ*, pp. 272, 276.

205 Brevard S. Childs, *The New Testament As Canon: An Introduction* (London:
SCM Press, 1984), p. 548.

206 James Barr, *The Concept of Biblical Theology: An Old Testament Perspective*
(London: SCM Press, 1999), p. 394.

207 Cf. Painter, 'Barrett', in McKim (ed.), *Historical Handbook*, p. 428.

another'.[208] We ought also at this point to record the considerable contribution of other Nonconformist scholars from England and Wales to *The New English Bible* project. Of the eleven members of the Old Testament panel, six were Nonconformists, two out of seven of the Apocrypha panel, and three out of nine members of the New Testament panel.[209]

The middle part of the century has been termed by J. Munsey Turner 'the golden age of Free Church scholarship', and he continued: 'The glory of our theology is the ability of scholars to be "middle men" between research work and the preacher, teacher and worshipper. Peake and Dodd were supreme here'.[210] And so we end, as we began, with the Rylands Chair in Manchester, as has been intimated already, the oldest theological one in England open to a non-Anglican. The holder of the chair between 1959 and 1978 was the Scotsman, Frederick Fyvie Bruce, who made an immense contribution in writing over the whole span of the Bible for a popular audience as well as for scholars. Coming as he did from a religiously conservative background it was his particular contribution to demonstrate 'to his fellow-evangelicals that biblical criticism can help them understand the Bible better and lead to positive conclusions as well as negative ones'.[211] Howard Marshall goes on to claim: 'It is not too much to say that [Bruce's commentary on the Greek text of Acts[212]] marked the real beginning of conservative evangelical scholarship'.[213] 'In all this Bruce was something of a bridge-builder between different schools of scholarship'.[214] Unlike two of his Nonconformist predecessors in Manchester, Dodd and Manson, 'his gifts were...perhaps more akin to those of the first holder of the Rylands Chair, A.S. Peake, who was also responsible for the high level of mediation of biblical scholarship to the Christian church'.[215] 'Far too often the accusation is heard that the pulpit is fifty years behind the teacher's rostrum, and the pew even further out-of-date. Some of the blame for this situation undoubtedly rests on a scholarship which does not trouble to communicate with both pulpit and pew in a way that both can

---

208 D. Coggan, *The Times* 26 September 1973.

209 B.J. Roberts, A.R. Johnson, L.H. Brockington, N.H. Snaith, H.H. Rowley and T.H. Robinson (OT); W.H. Cadman and G.B. Caird (Apocrypha); and C.H. Dodd, W.F. Howard and T.W. Manson (NT).

210 J. Munsey Turner, 'The Free Church Traditions—Treasures Old and New', *Free Church Chronicle* 41.2 (Summer, 1986), p. 24.

211 I. Howard Marshall, 'Obituary of F.F. Bruce', *Proceedings of the British Academy* 80 (1991), p. 251.

212 F.F. Bruce, *The Acts of the Apostles* (London: Tyndale Press, 1951).

213 Marshall, 'Bruce', p. 254.

214 Marshall,' Bruce', p. 251.

215 Marshall, 'Bruce', p. 258.

understand'.[216] In conclusion, we submit that there is abundant evidence that the leading Nonconformist biblical scholars of the twentieth century were acutely aware of this danger, and strove might and main to play their part in transmitting the word of God to their fellow-countrymen and women, thereby confronting them with it with an evangelical zeal.

---

216 Marshall, 'Bruce', p. 249.

CHAPTER 2

The Theological Contribution of Protestant Nonconformists in the Twentieth Century: Some Soundings[1]

Alan P. F. Sell

'Vote for the man who promises least; he'll be the least disappointing.' These words of Bernard Baruch have haunted me over the months as I have contemplated the vast theme on which I agreed to write. I cannot fail to disappoint. Almost certainly I shall omit somebody's favourite theologian, somebody else's pet doctrinal skirmish. Rigorous selection has been the only way of avoiding the creation of a mere bibliographical list.[2] I intend no disrespect to other Nonconformists in restricting my attention to those of the Congregational, Baptist, Presbyterian, Unitarian, Methodist and United Reformed traditions. My omission of theologians who have concentrated upon biblical, moral, pastoral, liturgical and ecumenical theology implies no lack of interest in those fields, some of which will be treated elsewhere in this volume. In what follows I propose first to single out some of the theological excitements of the twentieth century; then to introduce a specific theological topic on which Free Church people might have been expected to wax lyrical; and finally to offer some reflections upon the state of Nonconformist theology as Christianity's third millennium gets under way.

The fact that most of my references will be to those of the Congregational way does not indicate partisanship. Having reviewed as much of the twentieth-century Nonconformist theological corpus as possible, it does appear that the Congregationalists made the largest contribution to the fields with which I am concerned. Statistically, this is

---

1   As this volume was in the final stages of preparation, the sudden and unexpected death of Colin Ewart Gunton was announced. I dedicate this paper to the memory of one who was a deeply committed church member, an internationally-known theologian, a good friend.

2   In preparing this paper I gathered sufficient material for a book, which I hope in due course to write.

not surprising given that they were second only to the totality of Methodists in size, and considerably more numerous than the Unitarians and the English Presbyterians. But it also appears that whereas the Methodists spawned a number of church historians and not a few biblical scholars, and the Baptists all but cornered the market in Old Testament studies in the middle decades of the twentieth century, the Congregationalists, though not lacking biblical scholars and historians, were more prone to produce theologians. This may have something to do with the fact that at the beginning of the century their prominent theological teachers included A.M. Fairbairn and Robert Mackintosh, who received their theological education in Scotland where the tradition of systematic, dogmatic and apologetic theology was strong; and P.T. Forsyth and A.E. Garvie, who read Arts at Aberdeen and Glasgow respectively, and the latter of whom studied under Fairbairn in Oxford. All of these Scots thoroughly identified themselves with the English Nonconformity into which they came and, in turn, they trained a number of English and Welsh Congregational theological college principals and professors including the theologians W.B. Selbie, Robert Franks, Thomas Rees, D. Miall Edwards, J.D. Vernon Lewis, Sydney Cave, H.F. Lovell Cocks and George Phillips.[3]

While I shall concentrate upon published works, it should not be forgotten that most theologizing has been done in quite other ways. When A.J. Grieve prepared a bibliography of Congregational theology he inserted the following footnote, which applies to other denominations as well:

---

3   There was a long-standing link between Scotland and Old Dissent. Excluded from the universities of Oxford and Cambridge, a number of eighteenth- and nineteenth-century divines received some of their theological education in Scotland. Some of these, together with others—the Independent Philip Doddridge, the Baptist John Gill and the Presbyterian Arian John Taylor among them—were awarded the degree of Doctor of Divinity by Scottish universities. We should also note that a number of Nonconformist theologians studied abroad; for example, A.M. Fairbairn, R. Mackintosh and A.E. Garvie, the Baptists Arthur Dakin, Leondard G. Champion in Germany and W. Morris S. West in Zurich, the Congregationalist/United Reformed John Heywood Thomas and the Welsh Presbyterian Stephen N. Williams in the United States. I shall not supply biographical references to the many to whom I shall here refer. Among sources for these are *The Dictionary of National Biography*; *The Dictionary of Welsh Biography*; R.S. Robson, *Our Professors* (London: Presbyterian Historical Society, 1956); Alan Ruston, 'Obituaries of Unitarian Ministers 1900–1999', *Supplement to Transactions of the Unitarian Historical Society* 22.2 (April, 2000), pp. 164-246; John Vickers (ed.), *A Dictionary of Methodism in Britain and Ireland* (Peterborough: Epworth Press, 2000); obituaries in denominational year books; Charles Surman's card index at Dr Williams's Library, London.

While one is naturally expected and obliged to keep to literary contributions, it is imperative to remember that these, so far from exhausting the subject, are probably but a small part of it. The teachers in our Academies and Colleges have not always reduced their instruction to the printed page;[4] our preachers for 350 years have delivered more sermons than they have published; and perhaps as effective contributions to theology as any, if theology is a knowledge of God, have been those made one to another by members of the household of faith, the fellowship of the saints, in one generation after another.[5]

To all of which, we shall not be surprised to discover, the Welsh Presbyterian J. Young Evans added hymns: 'Modern Welsh theology is no less the product of Welsh hymnody than of catechisms and sermons...'[6]

To reduce a complicated story to a few sentences, we may say that during the last quarter of the nineteenth century a mood of optimism prevailed in many Nonconformist circles. There was a feeling of relief and satisfaction that some of what were regarded as the rougher edges of Calvinism had been smoothed out; that shriller exponents of the higher biblical criticism had not after all scuppered the faith; and that the idea of evolution had been cashable in terms of God's providential and progressive way of going about his creative work. All of this notwithstanding, there were some who expressed grave disquiet, especially concerning the state of systematic theology as such. In his address to the Congregational Union of England and Wales in 1873, Eustace Conder asked: 'is it not true that whatever place systematic Theology may maintain in the studies of our pastors, it has been for many years in steady course of disappearance from our pulpits; and that the number has

---

4   In this category should be placed the greatly respected and fondly remembered George Phillips of Lancashire Independent College. A few fugitive articles, from one of which I shall make a point of quoting in due course, may be tracked down by the diligent; but his self-effacing nature and his characteristic mode of expression are epitomized in his reply to my youthful query concerning his literary output. In deep, fruity, tones he cheerfully expostulated: 'Bless my soul, Alan! Who on earth would wish to read anything I might write?' Again, J.D. Vernon Lewis of the Congregational Memorial College, Brecon, who succeeded D. Miall Edwards as professor of Christian doctrine and ethics, and was subsequently professor of Old Testament and, for two years, principal, published on biblical and devotional themes, but published no purely theological work. Yet he did as much as any to introduce Barth to Wales.

5   A.J. Grieve, 'Congregationalism's Contribution to Theology: Some Material for a Bibliography,' in Albert Peel (ed.), *Essays Congregational and Catholic issued in Commemoration of the Centenary of the Congregational Union of England and Wales* (London: Congregational Union of England and Wales, [1931]), p. 359 n. 1.

6   J. Young Evans, 'The New Theology in Wales,' in T. Stephens (ed.), *Wales: To-day and To-morrow* (Cardiff: Western Mail, 1907), p. 30.

been continually increasing among our hearers who account this disappearance a blessed riddance?'[7]

Little could Conder have known that in the first twenty years of the twentieth century a relative explosion of Nonconformist theological activity was to occur, associated with the such names as those of the Congregationalists P.T. Forsyth and A.E. Garvie, the Presbyterian John Oman, the Methodist J. Scott Lidgett, and the Unitarian S.H. Mellone.

I

The twentieth century provided Nonconformist theologians with both inner-family and external stimuli to theological endeavour. As the century opened the Wesleyans were earnestly debating the question of eternal life. The particular question at issue was the final fate of the impenitent. Discussion of this topic had been rumbling on at least since the eighteenth century, and R.W. Dale had specified the options in 1877. There are, he said, those who cannot make up their minds on the subject: 'They cannot warn men against eternal condemnation, because they are not sure that any man will be eternally condemned.' There are those who hold that the impenitent are to be condemned to suffering, whilst hoping that 'there may be some transcendent manifestation of the Divine grace in reserve, of which as yet we have no hint.' There are those who believe that the Christ who came to seek and to save the lost will persist in this effort even though, because of the invincibility of human freedom, it cannot be affirmed that all will in fact be saved. There are those who believe that God's love cannot finally be thwarted, and hence all will finally be saved; those who hold that the impenitent will nevertheless enjoy an eternal life on a lower plane than the saved; and those who deny that the impenitent can finally be restored.[8]

It was J. Agar Beet, of Richmond College, who lit the touch paper among the Wesleyans by advancing yet another option into which some read 'the annihilation of the wicked'. In 1897 he published *The Last Things*, a work concerning the second coming of Christ and the doom of the wicked. It was his position on the doom of the wicked which caused a stir. He argued that the Bible affirms that those who come to Christ will be saved, and that those who continue, impenitently, in wickedness will suffer ruin. But, on biblical grounds, he did not feel able to affirm that the suffering of the wicked will be endless. Indeed, he argued that the idea of immortality—the endless permanence of all human souls—was a

---

7   E.R. Conder, 'The Decay of Theology,' *Congregational Year Book* (1874), pp. 70-71.

8   R.W. Dale, 'On Some Present Aspects of Theological Thought among Congregationalists', *The Congregationalist* 6 (1877), pp. 13-15.

Greek importation into Christian theology, and one unsupported from scripture. At the same time, he did not claim that annihilation of the wicked was actually taught in the Bible. His book was commended by the Methodist press; when some of the godly went after Beet's scalp the Theological Institution Committee, by a vote of thirty-one to five with two abstentions, resolved to take no action against him; and the Second London Synod unanimously supported him. Despite this, efforts were made to suppress his book, and he was removed from his post at Richmond. In 1901 he published a follow-up work, *The Immortality of the Soul: A Protest*, in which he reiterated his position and found the celebrated Dr William Burt Pope guilty of holding to the human being's natural immortality whilst failing to prove it.[9] In 1902 he was reappointed to Richmond on condition that he would not republish his views without the consent of the Methodist Conference. In 1904 he sought that consent, but such was the furore that he gave twelve months' notice of his resignation with a view to republishing his book thereafter. In 1905 the revised version appeared. In the new Preface Beet urges the free discussion of theological differences over against inquisitorial attitudes; claims that no-one had attempted to refute him; shows in an appendix that the respected scholar W.T. Davison, his successor at Richmond, and the Rev. George Jackson are, respectively, expressing views similar to and identical with his own; and regrets that the theme of the doom of the lost has vanished from the pulpits because preachers no longer know what to say about it.[10]

In saying that nobody had formally responded to him, Beet overlooks his opposite number at Headingley College, J.S. Banks, who published a critique of *The Immortality of the Soul* in 1902. He faults Beet with attempting to place the onus of proof on his opponents in that Beet grants that scripture does not positively affirm the annihilation of the wicked, and invites others to say that the Bible repudiates the doctrine. In fact, Banks claims, the biblical passages which teach eternal punishment imply unlimited immorality. In passing he repudiates the doctrine of conditional immortality on the ground that it implies that human beings have a capacity for immortality but are not actually immortal. He appreciates the motives of those who opt for annihilation, but 'If we could know sin in its nature and effects as God does, what penal consequences should we think too great?'[11] Banks further makes it clear that he deprecates caricatures of eternal punishment, and declares that 'Our main business is to preach the certainty, the freeness, the

---

9   See J.A. Beet, *The Immortality of the Soul: A Protest* (London: Hodder & Stoughton, 1901), pp. 58-63. Note the non-Methodist publisher of this volume.

10   See J.A. Beet, *The Last Things* (London: Hodder & Stoughton, rev edn, 1905), Preface and pp. 313-15.

11   J.S. Banks, *Words on Immortality* (London: C.H. Kelly, 1902), p. 28.

completeness of salvation in Jesus Christ—doom reversed, anger turned away, hell's curse changed into heaven's blessing.'[12]

In 1907 R.J. Campbell, minister of London's City Temple, caused a fluttering in Congregational dovecotes, and ripples elsewhere, with the publication of his book, *The New Theology* (how risky the terms 'new' and even 'recent' are in book titles). Repudiating both bibliolatry and ecclesiolatry, Campbell understands his new theology to represent 'an untrammelled return to the Christian sources in the light of modern thought. But since its starting-point is a re-emphasis of the Christian belief in the Divine immanence in the universe and in mankind',[13] modern thought—especially in its post-Hegelian immanentist form—seems to be the controlling factor. By 'God' Campbell means 'the one reality I cannot get away from, for whatever else it may, it is myself'.[14] In a variety of other ways he blurs the Creator-creature distinction which is so prominent in 'the Christian sources' and, notwithstanding the tradition that Jesus Christ is our Saviour from sin, he declares that Jesus 'came to show us what we potentially are'.[15] Indeed, when his spirit becomes ours, 'we, like Him, become saviours of the race'.[16] All of this is laid against the background of God's Fatherhood: 'God is not a fiend, but a Father... Why should we be required to be saved from Him?'[17]

Many took up their pens against Campbell—Bishop Charles Gore among them.[18] From within the ranks of Congregationalism C.H. Vine gathered a collection of essays under the title, *The Old Faith and the New Theology* (1907). Among the theologians who contributed papers are W.F. Adeney, D.W. Simon, R. Vaughan Pryce and P.T. Forsyth, principal of Hackney College. Of these the last, himself an erstwhile theological liberal, is the most pungent. He argues that the concept of immanence, on which the New Theology turned, is an inheritance from Greek and pagan thought, and that it has little to do with evangelical Christianity: it is monistic and evolutionary, and 'It does not go to the depths. It speculates about a Christ made flesh, but it never gauges the true seat of

---

12   Banks, *Words on Immortality*, p. 32.
13   R.J. Campbell, *The New Theology* (London: Chapman and Hall, 1907), p. 4.
14   Campbell, *New Theology*, p. 18.
15   Campbell, *New Theology*, p. 84.
16   Campbell, *New Theology*, p. 174.
17   Campbell, *New Theology*, p. 175.
18   See C. Gore, *The Old Religion and the New Theology* (London: John Murray, 1907). For more on the intellectual context see Alan P.F. Sell, *Theology in Turmoil: The Roots, Course and Significance of the Conservative–Liberal Debate in Modern Theology* (Eugene, OR: Wipf & Stock, 1998 [1986]), ch. 1, and *Philosophical Idealism and Christian Belief* (Cardiff: University of Wales Press/New York: St Martin's Press, 1995), chs 1 and 2.

Incarnation—a Christ made sin. It is not a theology of Incarnation.'[19] In the same year the Scottish Congregationalist W.L. Walker, who had sojourned among the Unitarians between 1886 and 1893, published, *What about the New Theology?* This temperate, judicious, work ran to two editions in 1907, and contained some incisive criticisms. Opinion in Wales, as represented by T. Charles Williams of Menai Bridge and J. Young Evans, was mutually contradictory. The former, explaining that Wales was intensely theological and tolerant, agrees with one in 'high authority' that 'the attitude of the Welsh public to the New Theology, as it is called, is much more liberal than the English.' The latter declares, 'The New Theology, as enunciated in the City Temple, the Welsh Nonconformists will reject'.[20]

Campbell subsequently espoused a more orthodox position, reverted to the Church of England in which he had been raised, finally becoming canon and chancellor of Chichester Cathedral. With hindsight we can see that the affair was little more than a nine days' wonder. It did, however, demonstrate the lengths to which liberal attenuations of the gospel could go; and it is not fanciful to suppose that such a scholarly liberal theologian as the Congregationalist C.J. Cadoux had the unreconstructed Campbell in mind when he admitted and regretted that there were liberals who emphasized the self-sufficiency of human beings, ignored sin and evil and denied the Lordship, divinity and saving power of Jesus, and also his incarnation and resurrection.[21]

Liberal optimism in humanity (though not all liberals were equally optimistic), the notion that we are bringing in the kingdom, the doctrine of God's Fatherhood-gone-sentimental: all of these ideas suffered a severe jolt with the onset of the First World War. Prompted by this dire stimulus from without, in the light of which squabbles over the New Theology must have seemed domestic indeed, a number of theologians— Nonconformists among them—turned their thoughts to theodicy. Had they a prophetic word to address to a nation at war, and to a people many of whom were asking how could there be a loving and just God when such devastation was permitted? Three principals and one former principal rose to reply: E. Griffith-Jones of Yorkshire United Independent College, W.F. Adeney, who had retired from Lancashire College in 1913, S.H. Mellone of Manchester Unitarian College, and P.T. Forsyth of Hackney (Congregational) College.

---

19   P.T. Forsyth, 'Immanence and Incarnation', in C.H. Vine (ed.), *The Old Faith and the New Theology* (London: Sampson, Low, Marston, 1907), p. 48.

20   T.C. Williams, 'The Influence of Higher Criticism upon Welsh Preaching' and J. Young Evans, 'The New Theology in Wales', in Stephens (ed.), *Wales To-day and To-morrow*, pp. 21 and 30 respectively.

21   C.J. Cadoux, *The Case for Evangelical Modernism* (London: Hodder & Stoughton, 1938), pp. 8-9.

Griffith-Jones's book of 1915 is thoughtful and wide-ranging. Entitled *The Challenge of Christianity to a World at War*, Griffith-Jones discusses the challenge of faith in the divine providence, which poses the question, 'what has the world of civilised men been doing with its God-given liberty that this calamitous war has come to pass?'[22] The challenge to civilization consists in showing the inadequacy of materialism; the challenge to morality consists in the demonstration that human beings are related to the Father-God revealed in Jesus Christ; the challenge to the home is to revive a healthy family sentiment; the challenge to nationalism is a regeneration of true patriotism; the challenge to militarism is the elevation of faith, hope and love as the solvents of all rivalries and the only secure bases of peace; and the challenge to religion is to recover its spiritual vision, to manifest unity in Christ, and to work for the healing not only of relations between the nations, but of those social ills which disfigure our own society.

W.F. Adeney was keen that people should sort out their ideas on this most perplexing question. To say that a calamity is a punishment is not to say that is is 'planned, and purposed, and produced by God'.[23] To think otherwise would be to fall into pagan anthropomorphism. This is not to deny that God is transcendent, it is to affirm that he is also immanent. But in the latter connection the peril is that of pantheism, and 'To say that everything that happens is a deed of God is pantheistic.'[24] The present war is directly contrary to God's will, and was not sent or ordered by him. Why, then, did he permit it? God does not give permission to war's promoters: it is an absurdity to speak of God's permitting an evil. Why, then, does he not prevent it? This would deny us the gift of freedom; there could be no sin; and nontheistic determinism leaves us with no moral order at all. Faith in God's providence is historically justified, and in our own lives we have experienced many blessings at his hand. But these appeals will not suffice the doubter. Our final appeal is to Christ for an assurance of God's goodness in the world. In his life, death and resurrection we have a redemptive gospel: 'It comes to us as a redemptive power offering this deliverance from evil by its own specific grace.'[25] As for the practical question of the action to be taken in time of war: we have to accept the paradox that while our faith repudiates war, it encourages people to participate in it. To be a warmonger is utterly unchristian; to counteract the mischief of war is not an unworthy act.

S.H. Mellone approaches the question from a different direction. He thinks it idle to speculate upon an alleged failure of Christianity as the

---

22   E. Griffith-Jones, *The Challenge of Christianity to a World at War* (London: Duckworth, 1915), p. 24.

23   W.F. Adeney, *Faith Today* (London: James Clarke, 1915), p. 18.

24   Adeney, *Faith Today*, p. 21.

25   Adeney, *Faith Today*, p. 71.

cause of the war, though it is because people and nations are 'imperfectly Christianized' that such calamities as war descend upon us. War places substantial moral demands upon individuals and the nation, and in addition to the physical shock of war, there is the mental and spiritual shock. Thus

> in the agony of war, we are learning the full horror of many things which were commonplaces in peace. We know now something of what it means to the nation that the most unholy trinity of mammon, strong drink, and lust should grind away the lives of unnumbered helpless children. We made progress a watchword, though all history cries out against the notion of a gradual upward and onward movement of man... We made an idol of science; but now, many know what a few knew before— that science can do nothing but fulfil purposes set by human wills... Science proves herself the obedient and efficient servant of the will to destroy, as she is of the will to save. In religion, we had rejoiced at the departure of the 'age of dogma.' We supposed that a few broad and simple principles, the 'religion of all sensible men,' would suffice. We had lost the God of the old covenant, the God of the fire, of the cloud, and of the thick darkness; and the God of the Cross of Calvary we had not found. Knowing that we must labour even for daily bread, we thought that faith in God would be cheap![26]

But perhaps the bravest words on the subject were uttered by P.T. Forsyth in *The Justification of God.* By 'brave' I mean that when many were wondering how God could be good and loving if all these disasters were happening, Forsyth came thundering out with the point: if God is holy love, and if human beings are as wicked as they are, what else should you expect but all this calamity? His reliance throughout is upon the redemptive and reconciling cross which alone both saves us and satisfies God's violated holy love. A collage of his sentences will make his point:

> Our faith did not arise from the order of the world; the world's convulsion, therefore, need not destroy it... All is well with the world, since its Saviour has it finally and fully in hand. Victory awaits us because victory is won... The anomoly [here is his theological courage when many were perishing] is not that a God of love should permit such things as we see. In the egoist conditions of Europe and of civilisation everywhere, and with a God of holy love over all, the scandal and the stumbling block would have been if such judgments did not come... That God spared not His own Son is a greater shock to the natural conscience than the collapse of civilisation in blood would be. For civilisation may deserve to collapse, if only because it crucified the Son of God, and crucifies Him afresh. But if God spared not His own Son, He will spare no historic convulsion needful for His kingdom. And if the unspared Son neither complained nor challenged, but praised and hallowed the Father's name, we may worship and bow the head... It is a vanquished world where men play their devilries. Christ has overcome it. It can make tribulation, but

---

26   S.H. Mellone, 'The Moral Equivalent of War', in J. Estlin Carpenter (ed.), *Ethical and Religious Problems of the War* (London: Lindsey Press, 1916), pp. 166-67.

desolation it can never make... The thing is done, it is not to do. 'Be of good cheer, I have overcome the world.'[27]

In some quarters the older liberal optimism died hard. As late as 1923 the Congregational historian Albert Peel was confidently proclaiming the progress of the human race;[28] and the Welsh Congregational theologian D. Miall Edwards, a former student under Fairbairn at Mansfield, published a number of books and articles, including *Crist a Gwareiddiad* (*Christ and Civilization*, 1921) and *Crefydd a Diwylliant* (*Religion and Culture*, 1934) of which his continuing commitment to liberal theology and to social reform were among the inspirations. By now, however, other voices were beginning to be heard, and some felt that they could not ignore the prophetic word of the Swiss theologian Karl Barth, whose *Romans* was published in 1919. As is well known, Barth, nurtured in Calvinism, taught by Harnack and Herrmann, became convinced that neither the scholastic conservative theology of his youth nor the anthropocentric liberal theology of his mentors had a word for a world shattered by World War I. Hence his recourse to the God who addresses his Word to human beings in such a way as to demand a 'Yes' to it, and a 'No' to all attempts to translate theology into language about ourselves and our condition. According to Barth, we cannot any longer embark upon the enterprise of natural theology, for this would entail elevating our human intellectual constructions into interpretative norms; and in any case there is no analogy of being between ourselves and God; rather, there is an impassable gulf. This bold position gave rise to Barth's hostile reception of Emil Brunner's 'softer' position on natural theology;[29] and it also caused concern in a number of Nonconformist circles as we shall see.

Among early respondents to the early Barth was the Methodist Charles J. Wright of Didsbury College. It is his conviction that the Barthian challenge to religious experience derives from the sceptical view that 'man cannot by the constitution of his own spiritual, moral and rational nature come to know God', and that 'Any theology which begins by denying the bond which unites God and man condemns itself to a perpetual inability to say anything about the Transcendent who is the

27   P.T. Forsyth, *The Justification of God* (London: Independent Press, 1948 [1917]), pp. 57, 78, 119, 194, 223, 166-167. The following works betoken a revival of interest in Forsyth's theology: Trevor Hart (ed.), *Justice the True and Only Mercy* (Edinburgh: T. & T. Clark, 1994); Leslie McCurdy, *Attributes and Atonement: The Holy Love of God in the Theology of P.T. Forsyth* (Paternoster Biblical and Theological Monographs; Carlisle: Paternoster Publications, 1999); Alan P.F. Sell (ed.), *P.T. Forsyth: Theologian for a New Millennium* (London: United Reformed Church, 1999).

28   A. Peel, 'Progress', *Congregational Quarterly* 1 (1923), pp. 229-33.

29   Emil Brunner and Karl Barth , *Natural Theology* (London: Geoffrey Bles, 1946).

object of religion.'[30] Another Methodist, J. Arundel Chapman, who taught at Handsworth, Didsbury and Headingley colleges, also had reservations concerning the early Barth: 'Barth', he writes, 'is scornful when he speaks of "religious experience"; God is the "Wholly Other"; "God in us" implies arrogance. Most of the religious seers of the past will, then, have to be convicted of this "arrogance", not excluding our Lord.'[31]

In 1940 C.J. Cadoux published *Christian Pacifism Re-examined*, one of the most learned volumes on its theme, though not without an occasional pugilistic, undefended, broadside of the kind to which some pacifists are on occasion strangely inclined: 'A theology like Barthianism', he declared, 'which professes independence of philosophy, is bound to be arbitrary and unconvincing.'[32] Take that! In fairness to Cadoux, however, it must be noted that two years previously he had published *The Case for Evangelical Modernism*, in which, more temperately, he lodges complaints against Barthianism. While not unappreciative of its strengths, he nevertheless regards the phenomenon as a blind-alley. In particular he dislikes the Barthian passion for discontinuities rather than for distinctions: 'Natural Theology is one thing, revelation through Christ something totally other; and the difference between them is fundamental.'[33] He finds 'truly surprising' the way Barthians speak about religion: 'For them, religion is what man thinks about God; revelation is what God says to man—and the distinction between the two must be rigidly maintained.'[34] He further finds the Barthian emphasis upon sin morbid. Without at all denying the weight given to sin in the Synoptic Gospels, Cadoux feels that God's Fatherhood there takes precedence, and that 'The son's normal position is that, not of a sinner, but of a beloved child and member of the family circle; and when he sins, his sin is dealt with on that basis... Jesus' great utterance that the Kingdom of God belonged to the childlike contradicts in my judgment any view of humanity which makes sin the principal item in the relation between man and God.'[35] More generally, 'If there is no way from man to God, why did Jesus bid men ask, seek, and knock, as the

---

30   Charles J. Wright, *The Meaning and Message of the Fourth Gospel: A Study in the Application of Johannine Christianity to the Present Theological Situation* (London: Hodder & Stoughton, 1933), pp. 193-94.

31   J. Arundel Chapman, *Modern Issues in Religious Thought* (London: Epworth Press, 1937), p. 56.

32   C.J. Cadoux, *Christian Pacifism Re-examined* (Oxford: Basil Blackwell, 1940), p. 46.

33   C.J. Cadoux, *The Case for Evangelical Modernism* (London: Hodder & Stoughton, 1938), p. 45.

34   Cadoux, *Case for Evangelical Modernism*, p. 46.

35   Cadoux, *Case for Evangelical Modernism*, p. 47.

condition of receiving, finding, and having the door opened to them...?'[36] Cadoux further rebukes the inconsistency which he detects in the fact that on the one hand Barthians acknowledge the immanence of God, his presence in nature, and the inner witness of the Holy Spirit, whilst on the other hand they declare that God is revealed, not supremely but solely in Christ. As if all this were not enough, despite all that Barthians say about the historical character of God's revelation, they are comparatively indifferent to the historical facts of the earthly life of Jesus. The upshot is that Barthianism 'is not only paradoxical, but self-contradictory; it is needlessly dualistic, and bristles with false antitheses; it displays strong tendencies to obscurantism'.[37]

Gentler treatment of Barth flowed from other Congregational quarters. In his book, *By Faith Alone* (1943), H.F. Lovell Cocks, principal of Western College, Bristol, showed himself sympathetically critical of Barth. His general view is that the earlier 'humanist theology is now in its decline, not so much because it has been shaken by the frontal attack of Barth and his school as for the reason that the harsh climate of our contemporary world has blighted it'.[38] He parts company with Barth most decisively in relation to the question of apologetics. He agrees that

> the best apologetic is in the end the proclamation of the Word, but is Barth wholly right in claiming that there is no room for any other?... We know the Gospel cannot be made acceptable to the natural man by any argument of ours, but some of his rationalizations of his refusal of grace can be exposed... Here natural faith, remaining discontinuous with saving faith, can yet be baptized into Christ and made to render valuable service to the cause of the Word among men... Not to establish saving truth but to clear away irrelevancies is the function of a legitimate Christian apologetic.[39]

This theme was resumed later by the Congregationalist Herbert Hartwell in *The Theology of Karl Barth* (1965).[40]

Though by no means uninfluenced by Barth, Hubert Cunliffe-Jones, professor at Yorkshire United Independent College, Bradford, subjected Barth's strictures against natural theology to close attention in *The Authority of the Biblical Revelation* (1945). He first states Barth's objective: 'He is contending primarily that the God of Biblical faith is

---

36   Cadoux, *Case for Evangelical Modernism*, p. 48.

37   Cadoux, *Case for Evangelical Modernism*, p. 54.

38   H.F. Lovell Cocks, *By Faith Alone* (London: James Clarke, 1943), p. 9. For Lovell Cocks see Alan P.F. Sell, *Commemorations: Studies in Christian Thought and History* (Calgary: University of Calgary Press and Cardiff: University of Wales Press, 1993, reprinted Eugene, OR: Wipf & Stock, 1998).

39   Lovell Cocks, *By Faith Alone*, pp. 118-119.

40   See H. Hartwell, *The Theology of Karl Barth* (London: Duckworth, 1965), p. 184.

our sovereign Lord and that He remains free even in His Revelation to act towards us according to His will. God never in any way becomes an object of our mind so that we can take Him captive and bend Him to the service of our own desires.'[41] Cunliffe-Jones is the first to agree that there is an absolute claim of Christ upon us, 'but we do not honour that absolute claim by representing it as discontinuous at all points with the rest of human life'.[42] Admitting that in contrast with the light of the Christian gospel, natural theology is 'a poor, frail, weak thing', Cunliffe-Jones nevertheless insists that natural theology is 'the sign that man has been created in God's image and that God has mercy on man in never leaving him to be content with a godless existence'. Accordingly, 'it is the duty of Christian theology to implant a limited confidence in natural theology where none exists'.[43] In a word, Barth is 'over-emphatic in a good cause... The motive is a right one, but the contention is wrong. Indeed, if Jesus Christ is indeed Lord, there must be some natural theology... If man could repudiate entirely the claim of God upon him he would not be human.'[44]

In 1971 the Welsh Presbyterian Huw Parri Owen, professor of Christian Doctrine at King's College, London, published *Concepts of Deity*. In his section on Barth he welcomes the way in which 'Barth consistently unites the ideal of God as Being with the idea of him as personal; ...maintains a true balance between the ideas of transcendence and immanence; ...[reconciles] belief in God's creative love with belief in God's *aseitas*; ...[and] Although Barth holds that we can know God only through Christian revelation, he makes a sustained attempt to articulate this knowledge in rational terms.'[45] But among a number of characteristically crisp negative comments is one in which Owen claims against Barth that even if it is true that Christianity differs in kind, not only in degree, from all other religions, and that a saving knowledge of God can occur only through Christ, these positions 'do not entail the view that all non-Christian concepts of God are totally false'—indeed many resemblances between Christian and non-Christian concepts of deity can be traced.[46] To Barth's underlying presuppositions (a) that if non-Christians cannot prove God's existence and have full knowledge of him they are idolatrous; and (b) that the doctrine of original sin entails total ignorance of God, Owen objects that one may hold that non-Christians 'possess a (logically) non-probative and partial knowledge of God', and that all the

---

41   H. Cunliffe-Jones, *The Authority of the Biblical Revelation* (London: James Clarke, 1945), p. 80.

42   Cunliffe-Jones, *Authority of the Biblical Revelation*, pp. 81-82.

43   Cunliffe-Jones, *Authority of the Biblical Revelation*, p. 82.

44   Cunliffe-Jones, *Authority of the Biblical Revelation*, pp. 83, 88.

45   H.P. Owen, *Concepts of Deity* (London: Macmillan, 1971), pp. 104-105.

46   Owen, *Concepts of Deity*, p. 107.

doctrine of original sin entails is 'that apart from Christ no man can have a perfect knowledge of God's nature or render perfect obedience to God's will.'[47]

Despite all the dissuasives, the Barthian leaven worked its way into a number of Nonconformist pamphlets and articles, but few Nonconformists in the second half of the twentieth century have shown themselves as indebted to it as the United Reformed minister, Colin E. Gunton, of King's College, London. Like his Nonconformist predecessors, he has learned from Barth, but he is not a clone of Barth. It would seem that since his early work, *Becoming and Being*, in which he contrasts the process theology of Charles Hartshorne with that of Barth, he has tempered his Barthian zeal as influences as various as those of S.T. Coleridge, John Owen, John Zizioulas and Michael Polanyi have worked upon him. I shall return to his Hartshorne–Barth book shortly, but for the present I note the modification of his position in his own words. In the preface to his *Theology Through the Theologians* (1996) Gunton writes: 'I have over the years attained a measure of distance from Barth's theology', a claim which is borne out in the ensuing essays; and in the Preface to the second edition of *The Promise of Trinitarian Theology* (1997) he refers to his discussion in *Becoming and Being* of the logic of Barth's move from revelation to eternal God, and comments: 'I now believe that [Barth] failed to give adequate account of the distinction of the persons'[48] of the Trinity: a remark which suggests the increasing influence of a particular reading of the Cappadocian Fathers upon Gunton's thought.

The upshot is that while some Nonconformist theologians—Cadoux among them—were convinced that Barth's method was faulty, others were more sympathetic to his work. Even these, however, did not for the most part swallow him whole: Lovell Cocks and Cunliffe-Jones, for example, found Barth's opposition to natural theology too drastic, while Gunton has become progressively dissatisfied with Barth at certain doctrinal points. F.W. Camfield, a student under Forsyth and later a DD of London University, came nearest to being a dyed in the wool Barthian, but he became an Anglican. W.A. Whitehouse, on whom Barth was a formative influence, was one of the United Reformed Church's most respected theologians.

The nineteen-sixties, with their swinging theologies—J.A.T. Robinson's *Honest to God*, Harvey Cox's *The Secular City*, and the disparate offerings of the Death of God theologians (some of them

---

47   Owen, *Concepts of Deity*, p. 107.

48   Colin E. Gunton, *The Promise of Trinitarian Theology* (Edinburgh: T. & T. Clark, 2nd edn. 1997), p. xxv n. 29. The reference is to *Becoming and Being: The Doctrine of God in Charles Hartshorne and Karl Barth* (Oxford: Oxford University Press, 1978), pp. 127-30.

erstwhile Barthians)—did little to prompt Nonconformist theologians to enter these lists, though the Methodist philosopher of religion, David A. Pailin, in *A New Theology?* (1965), produced an account of the philosophical tributaries from Kant and Schleiermacher onwards which flowed into *Honest to God*, and the Baptist Keith Clements later provided an account of the debate surrounding that book in *Lovers of Discord* (1988). The Congregationalist Erik Routley wrote a jubilant review of Robinson's manifesto, which he soon said would have been more cautious had he read *The Observer*'s article published under the sensational title, 'Our image of God must go', before putting pen to paper.[49] The Methodist Gordon Rupp, esteemed by many for his Luther scholarship, wryly remarked:

> The Bishop of Woolwich sees a parallel between himself and Martin Luther, whose 95 Theses were also caught up in a publicity explosion. I wish him well. He has now only to be unfrocked, tried and condemned for high treason, to write four of the world's classics, to translate the Bible and compose a hymn book, and to write some 100 folio volumes which 400 years hence will concern scholars all over the world, and to become the spiritual father of some thousands of millions of Christians—to qualify as the Martin Luther of a New Reformation.[50]

For his part C. Leslie Mitton urged a balanced response to Robinson's tract.[51] But Routley and Rupp were primarily historians and Mitton was a New Testament scholar; the theologians were largely silent. Perhaps they endorsed the view expressed long before by E.R. Conder: 'the weathercock of fashion does but show which way the wind blows, not which way the world is moving. The real pioneers of progress are not always in the foremost ranks of change.'[52] But if that was their conclusion, one could wish that more of them had attempted to adjust the weathercock. It is not, of course, denied that some Nonconformist theologians paid considerable attention to Bonhoeffer and Tillich, on some of whose insights Robinson drew.[53] As for the secularization debate, the Presbyterian J.E. Lesslie Newbigin stands almost alone with his popular discussion of the secularization theme: *Honest Religion for Secular Man* (1966).

Towards the end of the following decade, *The Myth of God Incarnate* (1977) appeared. The general thrust of this collection of papers is that

---

49　See *British Weekly*, 21 March and 16 May 1963.

50　G. Rupp, *The Old Reformation and the New* (London: Epworth Press, 1967), p. 51.

51　See C.L. Mitton, 'Honest to God', *Expository Times* 74 (June, 1963), pp. 276-79.

52　Conder, 'Decay of Theology', p. 67.

53　See, for example, Daniel T. Jenkins, *Beyond Religion* (London: SCM Press, 1966); J. Heywood Thomas, *Paul Tillich: An Appraisal* (London: SCM Press, 1963).

incarnational language is a mythological or poetic way of speaking of Jesus's significance for us. The Nonconformist contributors are John Hick and the Methodist Frances Young. In a follow-up volume, *Incarnation and Myth: The Debate Continued* (1979) they are joined by Lesslie Newbigin and the New Testament scholar, Graham Stanton of the United Reformed Church. A further minister of the same Church, Robert Crawford, published *The Saga of God Incarnate*, the revised edition of which appeared in 1987. More than one of the Nonconformist critics, while appreciative of the sensitivity of the 'mythographers' to those of other faiths, and fully aware of the 'scandal of particularity', nevertheless asked how far it is viable to dissociate Incarnation from Atonement in the way that their colleagues seemed to be doing.[54] Hick returned to the theme in *The Metaphor of God Incarnate* (1993).

In more recent years Newbigin was at odds with his fellow churchman John Hick over the question of the heart of the gospel in relation to religious pluralism. It is not the case that no earlier Nonconformist theologians had reflected upon the relations between Christianity and other faiths, but many of them had done so with the assumptions of Christendom in their minds, and under the inspiration of a post-Hegelian idealism which encouraged them to think of truth as one, of all religions having some glimpse of it, and of Christian truth as that to which all others pointed with greater or lesser degrees of clarity. Such, in brief, was the approach of A.M. Fairbairn, Mansfield College's first principal, among others. A change of key is noticeable in twelve small pages in *What Shall We Say of Christ?* published in 1932 by Sydney Cave, then president of Cheshunt College and subsequently principal of New College London, who had served for ten years in India, and who had already published *Redemption, Hindu and Christian* (1919) and *Christianity and Some Living Religions of the East* (1929).[55] Eschewing the condemnation by Christians of other faiths, Cave finds the decisive difference between them in the character of the god or gods they worship. He points out that the apparent modesty of the view that each race has the religion best suited to its needs can be a cover for racial superiority, but recognizes that serious thinkers also entertain the view that Christianity can no longer accord an unique pace to Christ. He answers: 'It is not arrogance or ignorance which impels us to give to

---

54   I may perhaps mention that after the dust had settled I was myself emboldened to make a few remarks along this line in *Aspects of Christian Integrity* (Calgary: University of Calgary Press/Louisville: Westminster John Knox, 1990, reprinted Eugene, OR: Wipf and Stock, 1998), pp. 42-45.

55   The former work is Cave's London DD thesis. He declined the opportunity of study in one of the ancient universities in order to sit under P.T. Forsyth at Hackney College. He was not the last Nonconformist to decline Oxbridge, a choice inexplicable to some—at least in England.

Christ a unique place. It is the conviction, born of faith and confirmed by knowledge, that in Him and Him alone has the character of God been fully manifested.'[56] Eleven years later, Hubert Cunliffe-Jones was even blunter: 'Whatever use God makes of the world's religions, in the last resort their witness to the nature of God is false, while the witness of the Bible to Jesus Christ is true.'[57]

In 1954 John Hick's (and Newbigin's) own teacher, the Presbyterian H.H. Farmer, made no bones about stating his assumptions thus: first, 'God has made a unique and final revelation of Himself as personal in history through Jesus Christ and through the personal relationship to Himself which that revelation makes possible and calls into being.'[58] Secondly, there is a common defining essence underlying all genuinely religious phenomena. Thirdly, the Christian view of the living essence of religion is determined by what Christians believe to be 'God's self-disclosure in the Incarnation and in particular by His disclosure therein of His personal nature and His personal purpose towards man.'[59] Fourthly, 'whenever religion arises with some degree of spontaneous, creative, living power, it does so because at that point ultimate reality is disclosing itself as personal to man'.[60]

In a number of works[61] Hick has taken with the utmost seriousness the reality of multi-faith societies and the difficulties posed when religious believers make exclusive truth claims for their own religion—in particular, the claim that it is the only way of salvation. Can it be, he asks, that God has created millions of people whom he knows will forfeit salvation, often as a result of the accident of having been born in areas where the alleged truth is not known, or is not widely acknowledged? Deeming such a possibility objectionable, Hick turns towards a pluralistic solution. He builds upon a distinction (whose philosophical father is Kant) between the Real in itself and the Real as conceived and

---

56   S. Cave, *What shall we say of Christ?* (London: Hodder & Stoughton, 1932), pp. 222-23.

57   H. Cunliffe-Jones, *The Holy Spirit* (London: Independent Press, 1943), p. 21. We may also note that in his apologetic work, *The Christian Belief in God in Relation to Religion and Philosophy* (London: Hodder & Stoughton, 1932), A.E. Garvie had in mind throughout 'two dangers which the Christian theologian must avoid: (1) the isolation of Christianity from all other religions, and (2) the isolation of religion from the other interests and activities of human personality', p. 25.

58   H.H. Farmer, *Revelation and Religion* (London: Nisbet, 1954), p. 23.

59   Farmer, *Revelation and Religion*, p. 27.

60   Farmer, *Revelation and Religion*, p. 28. See further, Christopher H. Partridge, *H.H. Farmer's Theological Interpretation of Religion: Towards a Personalist Theory of Religions* (Lampeter: Edwin Mellen Press, 1998).

61   See John Hick, *God and the Universe of Faiths* (London: Macmillan, 1974), *God has Many Names* (London: Macmillan, 1982), *Problems of Religious Pluralism* (London: Macmillan, 1985), and *An Interpretation of Religion*, (London: Macmillan, 1989).

experienced by human beings; and he proposes that the truth claims of the several religions do not really conflict because they are claims about the way the Real is diversely manifested and experienced. This proposal constitutes what he calls his Copernican revolution in theology, a revolution which entails that we 'shift from the dogma that Christianity is at the centre to the realisation that it is God who is at the centre, and that all the religions of mankind, including our own, serve and revolve round him'.[62] He recognizes that the price of this hypothesis (his word) is the forfeiture on the part of all religions of absolute truth claims; and that the standing challenge to his proposal is that it does not accord with the way in which the several religions perceive themselves, and is thus more of a recommendation that perceptions should change than a description of the intellectual or convictional *status quo* among the religions.

For his part, Newbigin understands the motivation which urges people to seek a basis of unity among the world's religions, but he repudiates Hick's approach, just managing, one feels, to stop short of using the word 'arrogant' to describe it. He writes,

> What claims to be a model for the unity of all religions turns out in fact to be the claim that one theologian's conception of God is the reality which is the central essence of all religions. This is the trap into which every program for the unity of the religions is bound to fall. There is no real encounter. Hick's conception of God simply is the truth and there is no possibility that one of the world's religions can challenge it.[63]

Whereas the Christian's 'basic commitment is to a historic person and to historic deeds', Newbigin continues: 'The other stance takes as its point of reference Transcendent Being.'[64] In this idealistic construction Hick places his faith, and no Christian can enter into dialogue with those who first propose that they surrender their own commitment to Jesus Christ for that of the idealist.

It cannot be said that other Nonconformist theologians have addressed this matter with the same amount of publicity as Hick and Newbigin (though it may be said that the criticisms of Hick levelled by the Welsh Presbyterian H.P. Owen are more incisive than those of Newbigin[65]); but it reflects a certain credit upon the United Reformed Church that from its ranks have come two very different thinkers who have between them so

---

62   Hick, *God and the Universe of Faiths*, p. 131.
63   L. Newbigin, *The Open Secret* (London: SPCK, 1978), pp. 184-85.
64   Newbigin, *Open Secret*, p. 187.
65   See the Appendix 'John Hick on Christianity and other religions' to his *Christian Theism: A Study in its Basic Pinciples* (Edinburgh: T. & T. Clark, 1984), pp. 141-45.

clearly set the terms of what shall surely be one of the critical theological debates of the twenty-first century.

As I conclude this bird's-eye-view of the twentieth century's theological excitements, I would simply remark that to date ordained Nonconformist theologians (I speak cautiously because since the laicizing of theology there may be theologians of whose denominational allegiance I am unaware) have not notably been inspired to advance, or respond to, feminist versions of theology, or to immerse themselves in the several theologies of liberation; and it would be a gross exaggeration to say that any of them has been a significant proponent, or critic, of postmodern views.

II

As we might expect, Nonconformist theologians have been much more active where their denominational distinctives were concerned; and those of the Congregational way scored a notable success with their *Declaration of Faith* of 1967[66]—surely one of the most substantial twentieth-century productions of its kind from within the Reformed family. But is there any theological topic distinctive of Free Churches as a whole and not of one denomination only, on which the Nonconformists might be expected to speak with a united voice? The obvious candidate is the establishment question. One may say that in the political circumstances in which they had to work out their polity, 'government by the Lord Jesus Christ alone' became for many of the Old Dissenters tantamount to a 'mark of the church' added to the classical confessional marks of the preaching of the word, the administration of the sacraments and the exercising of church discipline. By this reckoning the Church of England was a false church—even, to some, Antichrist. If Christ were the sole head of the church, then the monarch could not be its head as well. Neither republicanism on the one hand nor quietism on the other were necessary implications of this theological stance—very few members of Old Dissent adopted either position. Nor was it that Nonconformists denied the necessity of the state recognition of religion; it was, after all, the state which accorded religious toleration. They well understood the need for proper church–state relations, but were not persuaded that the Church of England's way of prosecuting them was theologically

---

66   *A Declaration of Faith* (London: Congregational Church in England and Wales, 1967), reprinted in David M. Thompson, *Stating the Faith, Formulations and Declarations of Faith from the Heritage of the United Reformed Church* (Edinburgh: T. & T. Clark, 1990).

appropriate.[67] Their point was ecclesiological and, depending upon prevailing circumstances, it was articulated with varying degrees of force (and sometimes scurrility) from the sixteenth century to the first half of the twentieth century.[68] Indeed, during the first fifty years of the latter century, numerous books and articles were published on the question, and if references to the Church of England as 'Antichrist' or a 'two-headed monster' became unfashionable, so distinguished a theologian as P.T Forsyth could still pack a punch with such a sentence as this: 'What we protest against is not the abuses but the existence, the principle, of a national Church.'[69] In the declining years of the nineteenth century Forsyth had been equally pungent in his book, *The Charter of the Church* (1896), in which he defined a state church as a monopolist church so constituted as to deny the catholicity of the church. Positively:

> However Establishment may seem to work at a given time, the thing is wrong... For my own part, any doubt of the truth of our Nonconformist priciples would mean doubt of the truth of what is most distinctive in Christianity itself—free faith, free action, and free giving, as the response of men who have been moved and changed and controlled by the free gift of God and grace in Jesus Christ.[70]

As the century opened, J. Courtney James published *The Philosophy of Dissent* (1900) in which he fuelled the argument not from the deeply ecclesiological side (he was a Methodist), but by invoking such considerations as liberty of conscience, the repudiation of secular control of the church, and the way in which an established and endowed church makes for inequality in the land.

Among more popular works of the early part of the century are J. Hirst Hollowell's *What Nonconformists Stand For* (1901), William Edwards's *A Handbook of Protestant Nonconformity* (1901), and *The Hope and Mission of the Free Churches* (n.d.) by Edward Shillito. Of these, that by

---

67   See further Sell, *Commemorations*, ch. 4; Nigel G. Wright, *Power and Discipleship: Towards a Baptist Theology of the State* (Oxford: Whitley Publications, 1996).

68   See further Sell, *Dissenting Thought and the Life of the Churches*, ch. 22, and *The Dissenting Witness Yesterday and Today* (London: Protestant Dissenting Deputies of the Three Denominations, 2002).

69   P.T. Forsyth, 'The Evangelical Basis of Free Churchism', *Contemporary Review* 81 (January–June, 1902), p. 693.

70   P.T. Forsyth, *The Charter of the Church: The Spiritual Principle of Nonconformity* (London: Alexander and Shepheard, 1896), p. 32. I have sometimes wondered whether there is any connection between the fact that this book by Forsyth was not republished when so many others were from the late 1940s to the 1960s. Is it conceivable that Forsyth's style and/or content on this issue were deemed ecumenically inappropriate at a time when inter-church relations were generally improving and the World Council of Churches had recently (1948) been formed?

Edwards, principal of the South Wales Baptist College, was 'designed mainly for young people'. In his opinion the establishment of religion 'is the child of the Dark Ages', and he enumerates no fewer than fifty theses against it, the last of which is that 'As the Welsh especially are a nation of Nonconformists, the presence of the Establishment is an anomaly and a grievous injustice'.[71] With the disestablishment of the church in Wales, effective from 1920, the Welsh Nonconformists had their reward and, according to some, an identity crisis now that that over against which they had defined themselves for so long had significantly changed its nature.

Much more substantial is the Congregationalist Henry W. Clark's two-volume *History of English Nonconformity*. Clark's objective is to trace the development and influence of what he understands as Nonconformity's spiritual principle, namely, that life takes precedence over organization. Though it was natural that it should be so, he laments that during the nineteenth century the forces of secular liberalism should have done more to marshall the troops against disabilities than the 'higher ground' of the 'ultimate ideal's inspiration'.[72] Moreover:

Nothing is more puzzling to the historian of Nonconformity than the comparative apathy with which the question of disestablishment was regarded by Nonconformists as a whole through a period when in other respects the struggle for Nonconformist rights was keen... [T]o a view of religion and the Church which makes the religion and the Church begin wholly in inward spiritualities and work themselves out from there, which makes the interior self-identification of the soul's life with the indwelling life of Christ the only true formative and constructive force behind whatever religious organisation may come into being— to such a view of religion and the Church the assumption of the State by right or power to direct, control, legislate for, a Christian Church implies dishonour to religion which ought not for an instant to be brooked...[73]

We reach a landmark in 1937, with the delivery by the 'Genevan' Congregationalist, John Whale, of the sermon commemorating the 250th anniversary of Emmanuel Congregational Church, Cambridge:

To us a State Church is a contradiction in terms... There can be no such thing as territorial Christianity, as though the faith were like the English Language or

---

71   W. Edwards, *A Handbook of Protestant Nonconformity...Designed mainly for Youg People* (Bristol: W. Crofton Hemmons, 1901), pp. 200, 206.

72   H.W. Clark, *History of English Nonconformity* (2 vols; London: Chapman and Hall, 1911–13), II, pp. 388-400.

73   Clark, *History of English Nonconformity*, II, p. 409. For R.W. Dale's disquiet at the thought that political pressure was taking precedence over churchmanship in Nonconformist minds, see A.W.W. Dale, *The Life of R. W. Dale of Birmingham* (London: Hodder & Stoughton, 1899), p. 378.

> English Common Law—an aspect or function of our national life. To us, State control of the deepest things by which Christendom lives would be a blasphemous betrayal of the Crown Rights of the Redeemer... [I]n asserting that His Church must necessarily be free from that Erastianism which is to us the supreme abomination, we are standing in a tradition of High Churchmanship which preserves and sets forth the true conception of the Church in all its spiritual nature and glory. We are asserting the Church's independence of the State and, if need be, her superiority to it; the utter inadmissibility of her being controlled and regimented by a secular power like King, Magistracy, Parliament, or Dictator; in short, her freedom, governance, and godly discipline under the sole lordship of Him whose service is perfect freedom.[74]

Such points were endorsed, in characteristically witty style, by that lover of the Church of England, Bernard Lord Manning, the Congregational lay historian, in his collection of papers, *Essays in Orthodox Dissent* (1939).

In 1949 the General Secretary of the Free Church Federal Council, Henry T. Wigley, wrote two sentences on the establishment question, in the first of which he sounded what may now seem to some to have been an unduly optimistic note; and calls to mind the as yet unrealized hope of the reconciliation of memories as between the Church of England and the heirs of the separatist martyrs and their Nonconformist partners:

> Most Anglicans now recognise that the present system of Establishment, which means the control of the Church by the State, is wrong in theory and in practice alike, and are seeking ways and means whereby, without disestablishment, supreme authority in the Church will be transferred from the King in Council to the official courts of the Church. What a lovely and gracious thing it would be if some responsible person in the Anglican Church were to acknowledge that our Free Church forefathers were right in standing, often at great cost to themselves, for the spiritual freedom of the Church of Christ, and were to pay public and ungrudging tribute to their insight and courage![75]

Wigley proceeds to quote the *Joint Reply of the Free Churches to the Lambeth Conference's Appeal of 1920*: 'Free Churchmen cannot be asked to consent that the civil power—which within its own sphere is called to be the servant of God—has any authority over the spiritual affairs of the Church.'[76]

In a more substantial volume entitled *The Claims of the Free Churches* (1949), Henry Townsend, principal of Manchester Baptist College, revealed himself as in the line of Forsyth with such a sentence as this:

---

74   J.S. Whale, 'Commemoration Sermon,' in *Congregationalism Through the Centuries* (London: Independent Press, 1937),pp. 106-107.

75   H.T. Wigley, *The Distinctive Free Church Witness Today* (Wallington, Surrey: Religious Education Press, 1949), p. 64.

76   Wigley, *Distinctive Free Church Witness Today*, p. 64.

'National Churches have arrested the universal ideas of the New Testament, and have thereby de-christianised the idea of God which was revealed by Jesus.'[77] He further addresses the claim, frequently advanced by members of the Church of England, not least in the Commission on Church and State of 1935, that establishment is a bulwark in society against secularism. Townsend attacks this utilitarian argument, declaring that 'the whole argument from Free Church history is a protest against the complacency of the principle of the utility of the Establishment'.[78] The same argument had, six years earlier, provoked even the self-effacing George Phillips into one of his rare appearances in print: 'The argument, heard so often in these days even from the mouths of Free Churchmen, that the Establishment should be preserved as a barrier against the spread of secularism, belongs to a class of deliberation so low in ethical principle that even the most unscrupulous politician might blush to hear it. Surely better things are expected of us than a juggling expediency! "Fiat iustitia, ruat coelum," though pagan in origin, is a loftier standard and a safer guide.'[79]

On 14 May 1952 Ernest Payne, the general secretary of the Baptist Union of Great Britain and Ireland, delivered a lecture to the Congregational Union Assembly entitled, 'The Free Churches and the State'. Holding staunchly to Free Church principles construed in an ecumenical manner, Payne nevertheless felt that the time was not ripe to press the establishment question: (a) because 'We are obviously in a dangerous transitional period in regard to the theory and activity of the State'; (b) because 'The Churches are engaged in a serious and sustained conversation regarding the nature of the Church... A sharp Church conflict would seriously endanger the growing mutual understanding and trust, and would certainly be a grave scandal in the eyes of the world'; and (c) because 'it would be disastrous at the beginning of a new reign to embark upon a religious controversy which would inevitably be complicated, prolonged and embittered, and which would, equally

---

77   H. Townsend, *The Claims of the Free Churches* (London: Hodder & Stoughton, 1949), p. 200.

78   Townsend, *Claims of the Free Churches*, p. 208.

79   G. Phillips, 'Freedom in Religious Thought,' in *The Fourth Freedom* (London: Independent Press, 1943), p. 60. Proponents of the utilitarian argument would do well to reflect upon the fact that the United States manages, in the absence of an established church, to be a more churchgoing nation, and perhaps a more Christian nation in some ways (some of them disturbing!) than England. That this point is not lost upon some Anglicans is clear from E.L. Mascall, *Up and Down in Adria: Some Considerations of Soundings* (London: Faith Press, 1963), p. 104.

inevitably, involve the status and powers of the crown.'[80] In the following year the Free Church Federal Council published the report entitled, *The Free Curches and the State: The Report of the Commission on Church and State appointed by the Free Church Federal Council in March, 1950.*

There the matter seems almost to have rested. The trickle of books and pamphlets by Nonconformists on the establishment question almost entirely dried up,[81] though in 1977 the Congregational ecumenist, John Huxtable, said that 'the Church–State relationship will have to be discussed and settled in whatever way eventually seems right'.[82] Not even the musings of the tabloid press—and of some of the broadsheets—on the question, Is prince Charles fit to be the temporal head of the Church of England? (than which no question could more completely miss the point), stimulated much by way of a Free Church response. Neither did the more serious publication by the Anglican John Habgood of his book, *Church and Nation in a Secular Age* (1983). When addressing objections to the establishment, he mentions none of the theologians of Nonconformity to whom I have here drawn attention; he appeals to the utilitarian argument which Townsend, Phillips and others trounced; and he gives the game away with his methodological statement: 'My defence of establishment...was based fundamentally on an assessment of the needs of the nation, and a view of the church as not confined to those whose religious commitment is most explicit and most ready to express itself in overt religious activity.'[83] Unless such pragmatism is qualified by serious consideration of those biblical and ecclesiological questions concerning the nature of the church and the due relations of church and state—and this with a view to honouring the crown rights of the Redeemer in his church (and who are the church?)—Free Church people and members of the Church of England will continue to talk past one another as they have

---

80   E.A. Payne, *The Free Churches and the State* (London: Independent Press, 1952), p. 28; reprinted in E.A. Payne, *Free Churchmen, Repentant and Unrepentant and Other Papers* (London: Carey Kingsgate Press, 1965), ch. 5.

81   Historians may be trusted to reflect upon why this might have been. Did the removal of almost all socio-political disabilities take the steam out of the debate? (Cf. Bernard Lord Manning, *The Protestant Dissenting Deputies* [Cambridge: Cambridge University Press, 1952], p. 403). Did the growing spirit of ecumenism foster reticence on matters deemed to be 'neuralgic'? Has the inreasing mobility of the population and the fact that people are less likely nowadays to find a 'church home' on grounds of traditional denominational loyalty had a stultifying effect upon the debate?

82   J. Huxtable, *A New Hope for Christian Unity* (London: Collins Fount, 1977), p. 78.

83   John Habgood, *Church and State in a Secular Age* (London: Darton, Longman and Todd, 1983), p. 176.

done for so long. The martyrs cry out for something better, and the reconciliation of memories is urgently required.[84]

But even as I write those words concerning the martyrs—those sixteenth-century harbingers of Congregationalism—and the reconciliation of memories, I am bound to acknowledge that it is not easy for the Free Churches as a whole to speak with one mind on the establishment question. The martyrs are not within the memory of those relative youngsters the Methodists—still less so in those of the Pentecostalists and black churches. Furthermore, there have always been those among the Methodists who are but reluctant Nonconformists.[85] All power, therefore, to those Anglicans and Free Churchpeople who, I understand, are currently engaged in fresh discussions of establishment. May their outlook be ecumenical and their thoughts in the first place theological.[86]

---

84   It must be admitted that Free Churchmen have not always been the best advocates of their cause. Too often 'Free' in 'Free Church' has been understood as 'freedom from state control', whereas such freedom is but a corollary of the primary freedom which is that of the risen and ascended Lord to be the only Lord of the church. Again, the emphasis has sometimes been too much upon the real or alleged privileges enjoyed by the established church: John Habgood is thus presented with a smoke-screen which, not surprisingly, he utilizes. Yet again, it is sometimes glibly said that 'We are all established now'. But this fails to recognize the important distinction between the state recognition of religion which is necessary from the point of view of the right to freedom of worship, trust laws and the like, and establishment theology, which at its theologico-political root in the sixteenth century teaches that national cohesion, especially over against Roman Catholic Spain, is required; this is best achieved by religious conformity induced by legislation the violation of which can lead to death; to be a true English person is to be a member of the Church of England—non-members are very likely to be traitors against the nation. I do not think that a single Anglican today believes any of this. But if memories are to be reconciled, this needs to be acknowledged. There can also, of course, be smoke-screens perpetrated by Anglicans. For example, it is not impossible that the pragmatists in their midst will make hay over the current issue of the reform of the House of Lords, whilst overlooking more serious theological points.

85   For sociological and other factors which may perhaps conduce to the tying of Free Church tongues see David M. Thompson, 'The Free Churches in Modern Britain', in Paul Badham (ed.), *Religion, State and Society in Modern Britain* (Lampeter: Edwin Mellen Press, 1989), pp. 99-117.

86   Preliminary conversations took place on 30 November 1998. As one who has been urging engagement in such talks for at least a quarter of a century, I am delighted that there is some movement on this front. See reports in *The Sunday Times*, 10 January 1999 (the *ST* at its most tabloid-like); *The Tablet*, 16 January 1999; and *Church Times*, 22 January 1999. For end-of-the-century inner-Anglican discussion of the matter see Wesley Carr, 'A Developing Establishment', *Theology* 102 (January–February, 1999), pp. 2-10, and (May–June, 1999), pp. 230-31; 'Editorial: The Big Issue: Is There a Third Way for "Establishment"?', *Modern Believing* 42.2 (1999), pp. 2-5; Paul Avis, 'Establishment and the Mission of a National Church', *Theology* 103 (January–February,

As I conclude this section concerned with the ecclesiological *raison d'être* of Nonconformity, I should like to place side by side two quotations, dredged up from the nineteenth century, which between them epitomize the tightrope which must ever be walked by those who know both that they must speak of what they have seen and heard and know with equal certainty that they have not seen everything. In 1834 Thomas Binney declared:

> I am a dissenter because I am a catholic; I am a separatist, because I cannot be schismatical; I stand apart from some, because I love all; I oppose establishments because I am not sectarian; I think little of uniformity, because I long for union; I care not about subordinate differences with my brother, for 'Christ has received him' and so will I...[87]

Exactly a century ago as I write, A.M. Fairbairn addressed the International Congregational Council in Boston in these terms:

> [T]here is the magnanimity of Christ,—he consents to live in communities that vainly call themselves Presbyterian or Independent, Baptist or Methodist, and there is a still greater humility in his being ready to dwell in proud communities which speak of themselves as imperial, infallible or apostolic. Oh, I sometimes think that the hardest text in Scripture is, 'He that sitteth in the heavens shall laugh.' If there be divine laughter, must it not often be at the follies of men who think that they hold God in their custody and distribute him to whomsoever they will?[88]

III

Among the many retrospective articles prompted by the approach of the end of the twentieth century is one by Ian Markham, in which he reflects upon British theology of the previous one hundred years. Admittedly his paper is short, and he concedes that there are exceptions to all his generalizations, but his work is myopic in two respects. First, apart from John Hick and Colin Gunton (and T.F. Torrance and George Newlands, who are invoked from north of the Border) those discussed are almost

---

2000), pp. 3-12. See further on church-state relations, Sell, *Commemorations*, ch. 4; on the ethics of establishment, Alan P.F. Sell, 'A Renewed Plea for "Impractical Divinity"', *Studies in Christian Ethics* 7.2 (1995), pp. 68-91.

87   T. Binney, *Dissent Not Schism: A Discourse delivered in the Poultry Chapel, December 11, 1834, at the Monthly meeting of the Associated Ministers and Churches of the London Congregational Union* (London: Joseph Ogle Robinson, 1835), p. 65.

88   A.M. Fairbairn, 'The Text and the Context,' *Proceedings of the International Congregational Council* (1899), p. 75.

entirely members of the Church of England—and even then we have John Milbank and Gareth Jones, but not William Temple, Leonard Hodgson and John Macquarrie. Secondly, Markham writes: 'It is worth noting that lectureships in systematic theology in English universities have only developed in the past twenty years. On the whole, writing in systematic theology came from those interested in patristics.'[89] This, of course, is completely to overlook the fact that for many decades significant contributions to theology have been made, and are still being made, to English universities by Nonconformist scholars whose institutions enjoyed a relationship with the universities, but who were not themselves on the university payroll. Many of these were founder-members of university theological faculties—indeed, deans of them, and it is indisputable that Forsyth, Garvie, Cave, Mackintosh, Franks, Drummond, Davison, Oman, Farmer and others were theologians of note. Having well-nigh exhausted myself in reading a considerable quantity of Nonconformist theology, I trust that present study may go some way towards balancing Markham's account of twentieth-century British theology.

In preparing this paper I placed myself under the self-denying ordinance of not entering into discussion with those whose views I was presenting and, difficult at times though it has been, I have done my best to bite my tongue. Looking back on the Nonconformist theological corpus (and by way of a reward for having waded through it!) I shall allow myself a few adjudications on what I have found, confining my attention to those who are deceased. I marvel at the range of A.E. Garvie: biblical studies, apologetics, systematic theology, ethics—all of these fell within his purview, and he dealt with them in a most orderly fashion, though employing a somewhat cumbersome style. I enjoy the sardonic wit of Robert Mackintosh as much as I value his perceptive judgements on thinkers and movements. I applaud Oman and Farmer even more for their grasp of the realities of the Christian life than for their theoretical positions. I greatly appreciate the integrity of Drummond and Mellone, and the urbanity of Jacks and Garrard. T. Vincent Tymms would be a stimulating intellectual sparring partner, while the scholarship of C.J. Cadoux and Robert Franks is humbling. Franks's work on *The Atonement* (1934) is among the most intellectually stimulating books I have reviewed, while Harold Roberts's paper of the Trinity covers much in brief compass,[90] and would aid many Christians and enquirers who wish to improve their understanding of that doctrine. Vincent Taylor's

---

89   I. Markham, 'Looking Back on the 20th Century. 3. Theological Reflections', *Expository Times* 110.12 (September, 1999), p. 384.

90   It is in a volume by the professors at Wesley College, Headingley, Leeds: Harold Roberts, 'The Holy Spirit and the Trinity', in *The Doctrine of the Holy Spirit* (London: Epworth Press, 1937), pp. 107-28.

The Cross of Christ (1956) remains a most helpful guide to its subject, while, nearly sixty years on from its year of publication, John Whale's *Christian Doctrine* (1941) is still the liveliest one-volume work of introduction to Christian teaching as a whole. H.F. Lovell Cocks is one of the most underrated of Nonconformist theologians, and every ecumenist should be required to read Bernard Lord Manning's *Essays in Orthodox Dissent* (1939). Of those more recently departed, I think with gratitude of the clarity combined with learning modestly borne which characterizes the work of Huw Parri Owen. But if I were forced to name one twentieth-century Nonconformist theologian who, more decisively than any other has driven to the heart of the gospel of God's holy love, my choice would fall upon P.T. Forsyth, in whose work there is currently a second revival of interest.[91]

Undeniably, the bulk of Nonconformist theological writings appeared during the first half of the twentieth century. Since then the denominations have declined significantly in numerical strength. News of rising educational standards notwithstanding, the remaining readers of Nonconformist newspapers are treated to less substantial theological articles than were their grandparents, while the readership for sermons has all but evaporated. Many Nonconformist theological colleges have been closed, or have amalgamated, and the universities have undertaken and paid for much teaching that was previously a charge upon denominational funds. In many cases the university teachers are church members, and increasingly—more perhaps in biblical studies, church history and philosophy of religion than in theology as such—they are laypeople. When at one and the same time Norman Snaith (Old Testament), Vincent Taylor (New Testament), H. Watkin-Jones (church history) and Harold Roberts (theology) were on the staff of Headingly Methodist College that was a vintage period indeed in terms of theological scholarship. By contrast, Paul Fiddes of Regent's Park College, Oxford (Baptist), is one of a declining number of Nonconformists who publish theological works from a base in a Nonconformist theological college.

But it is not simply that more Nonconformists, lay and ordained, are teaching theology in universities than taught in the theological colleges fifty years ago—if, indeed, that is the case; it is that as far as ministers are concerned some at least of the denominations do not have the 'critical mass' of scholarship that they once had. To take one example, which assumes that the earned English DD is indicative of world-class scholarship: from figures published in 1950 we learn that the Congregationalists had 1,968 ministers (including 407 retired ministers) of whom seven then in employment held the degree of DD. Of these six

---

91   See above n. 26.

were working under the auspices of the denomination, one (C.H. Dodd) under that of a university. At the same period there were two ministers of the Presbyterian Church of England in employment who held the earned DD. In 1999, out of 1,825 United Reformed Church ministers (including 759 retired and 193 non-stipendiary ministers), one only had an earned DD (Colin Gunton), and he was not employed by the denomination.[92] This difference is explained partly by the decline in the number of ministers in general, and partly by the demographic fact that more and more ministers are now second career people. However valuable these latter may be as preachers and pastors, it is unlikely that many of them will have the time or the inclination to become the church's scholars. I trust it is not necessary for me to explain that I am not pleading for elitism. I firmly believe that theologizing is the task of the church as a whole; but in the discharging of this task a leaven of deeply learned theologians—by which I mean theologians deeply learned in the things of God as well as technically competent—is a gift not to be despised.

Theological education has undergone considerable changes during the twentieth century, and these have implications for theological scholarship. While by no means all Nonconformist ministerial candidates received six years of training leading to the BA and BD degrees, a significant number did between the years 1900 and (roughly) 1970. But partly in response to financial difficulties, partly owing to calls for the increasing 'professionalization' of ministerial education, and, most recently, partly as a result of 'customer resistance'—students now being fee-payers, courses have been curtailed in length or otherwise modified, so that theological students are in many cases plunged into philosophy of religion without a background in philosophy, into church history without a background in history, and into biblical studies without a strong linguistic background. The foundations for theological study have thus to some extent (some would say to a considerable extent) been eroded.

No doubt theology will continue to be studied, and it will be for the churches to decide how they wish their ministerial candidates to be educated. Should they rely upon universities for the so-called 'academic' disciplines, which may be taught by persons lay or ordained, Christian or not, and then revert to the 'finishing school' model for the so-called 'practical' disciplines. Such a policy would be based upon an 'academic–practical' disjunction which I personally deplore; but if the

92   See the Congregational and Presbyterian year books for 1950; *The United Reformed Church Year Book* (1999). The present writer, though now returned to the United Reformed Church, was working under the auspices of the Presbyterian Church of Wales in 1999, when this paper was written.

academic teachers increasingly have no pastoral experience or even Christian allegiance, what are the alternatives?[93]

If it is impossible to predict what form theological education will take in fifty years' time, it is even more difficult to predict whether there will be any Nonconformist theology as we know it at the end of the twentieth-first century. Unless the End come, theology will surely be written, but by whom and under whose auspices? Will Nonconformity as we have known it dwindle away to nothing? Or will the Church of England? Or will the latter become disestablished? Or will the monarchy fall? Who can say? These would be the conditions for the demise of Nonconformist theology. Under whatever auspices they travel, theologians of the future as well as of today would do well to ponder some words of Eustace Conder, from whom I set out:

> The Theology of the future, as I venture to forecast it in my own mind, will not be the fruit either of the destruction of the past, or of a reproduction of the past, or of the fusing all doctrines into one featureless mass, where faith is replaced by feeling; although these three seem the prevailing theological tendencies of the present. It will be the fruit of deeper study of God's truth. Despising no ray of light from the past, it will fill its own lamp with fresh oil and kindle it with altar-fire. Its great instrument will be neither Controversy, which poisons, nor Criticism, which freezes all it handles (indispensable though these are in their place); but Interpretation, which, because it has to deal with the spirit as well as the letter, is impossible without faith, love, and reverence.[94]

---

93   It is not, of course, suggested that theology is the only discipline to have undergone such changes. A professor of Modern Languages has told me that when his career began mastery of the language was assumed on entry to university, whereas nowadays the language is still being taught in the third year of the degree course. An academic engineer once ruefully (if with some exaggeration) told me that he needs a year added to the BSc course because in the first term of the first year he has to teach basic English, in the second term, basic mathematics, and in the third term, how to close his door quietly! Only then can he proceed with engineering science. I cannot say how reliable such anecdotal evidence is, but it is conceivable that what one might call 'seed-corn' disciplines are at risk in more than one quarter.

94   Conder, 'Decay of Theology', pp. 79-80.

CHAPTER 3

Twentieth-Century Historians of English Protestant Nonconformity

David Cornick

Sylvester Horne was on his feet at the 1902 autumn meeting of the Congregational Union in Glasgow proposing an amendment to the official resolution that denounced the 1902 Education Bill. It was a fighting amendment, stating that the Union was prepared to advise its members not to pay their rates should the bill become law. Horne later confided to his diary his amazement that it was carried with only six against and continued: 'Anyhow, the Anti-Rate stand adopted by the Free Church Congress, as well as by the Baptist and Congregational Unions, is a note of fierce defiance to an unconventional and unjust Government without a parallel in our history. The battle will and must now go on to the bitter end.'[1]

However inadequate and pragmatic Balfour's administration might have been, it was hardly Stuart England *redevivus*. Horne's hyperbolic rhetoric was in itself clear evidence of dissonance. It has long been noted that the battle over the 1902 Education Act was the last skirmish in the nineteenth-century 'war' between church and chapel, a war that looked increasingly anachronistic as the tide continued to ebb on Dover beach. There was something touchingly absurd about passive resistance, and about Horne himself as he sallied forth to play an eloquent Sancho Panza to John Clifford's Don Quixote. The absurdity lay in the rhetoric of self-perception and in the mode of political operation, not in the justice of the cause.

Education was the one remaining part of English society where discrimination against Nonconformists was still clear. The 1902 bill contained much that was educationally worthy and sensible, indeed progressive, in its attempts to unify the school system under the control

---

1   W.B. Selbie, *The life of Charles Sylvester Horne* (London: Hodder & Stoughton, 1920), p. 131; for a narrative of the Education Bill and Passive resistance, see, e.g., James Munson, *The Nonconformists: In Search of a Lost Culture* (London: SPCK, 1991), pp. 244-89.

of Local Education Authorities. It met the needs of the nation's children, but it did so at the expense of the underlying issues. Asquith considered it to be reactionary, and his view was shared by most Liberals and not a few Unionists.[2] It was reactionary because it was sectarian. It continued the politics of privilege by incorporating denominational schools into the state system, provided one third of their management committees received nomination by the Local Education Authorities. Rate-payers would henceforth be footing the bill for denominational religious instruction. In Nonconformist eyes it was Rome and Canterbury on the rates. That meant, simply, that the Anglicans had preserved the advantages of the previous thirty years, and the Nonconformists had lost theirs. The bill, therefore, fuelled a fire of Nonconformist pain and anger.

Horne's *A Popular History of the Free Churches* was a tract for those troubled times. It was published in the spring of 1903. He wrote it the previous winter, combining writing with intense campaigning against the bill across the country, the chairmanship of the London Congregational Union, the not inconsiderable demands of his ministry at Kensington Chapel, and the painful realization that his time there was drawing to an end. He was at the height of his powers. He had been at Kensington for fourteen years. This was a congregation of the well-heeled and well-connected—Toms of Derry and Toms, Harrod of Harrods, together with a sprinkling of Spicers and Conders and Cozens-Hardys.[3] Well-heeled and well-connected, yet not afraid of risk, for they had called him from A.M. Fairbairn's unknown and untried Mansfield College, Oxford, after he had supplied the pulpit in 1887, and had waited eighteen months for him to finish training.[4] This was talent spotting at its most perceptive, and Horne had handled the transition with aplomb.

Yet there was always part of him that was uncomfortable in suburbia. 'My sympathies', he confided to his father whilst agonizing over his call, 'have always been with the working-class of people'.[5] An admirer of Baldwin Brown's work in Lambeth, it was unsurprising that in 1894 he guided the chapel to create a mission in Notting Dale. It was the same radical commitment that led him to accept a call to Whitfields Tabernacle in Tottenham Court Road in 1903, almost simultaneously with the publication of his history of the Free Churches. There is a sense in which his *A Popular History* can be read as a legitimation of that radicalism. He nailed his colours to the mast in the preface, hoping that his readers would perceive that their Puritan forbears 'stood for a spiritual

---

2   Roy Jenkins, *Asquith* (London: Collins, 1964), p. 134.

3   Clyde Binfield, *So Down to Prayers: Studies in English Nonconformity 1780–1920* (London: J.M. Dent, 1977), p. 201.

4   W.B. Selbie, *The Life of Charles Sylvester Horne* (London: Hodder & Stoughton, 1920), pp. 44-48.

5   Selbie, *Life of Charles Sylvester Horne*, p. 48.

interpretation of Christianity and the Christian Church. This spiritual interpretation, as Milton said, "it hath befallen us to assert, with God's assistance,...against regal tyranny over the State and State tyranny over the Church."' The former evil was no more, thanks to Puritan 'fidelity and fortitude'. However, a pale shadow remained in the form of 'an hereditary House of Peers, in which no single Free Churchman has a place'. The latter evil was enshrined in the establishment principle. Possibly the greatest danger for 'the Englishman of to-day' was 'Church tyranny over the State'. Those dangers would remain until the British constitution enshrined the fundamental principle—'Religious Equality for all, and Ecclesiastical Ascendancy for none.'[6]

Horne had been studying Free Church history for some years in his spare time. Although he made no pretence of being a professional historian or undertaking original research, he knew the subject well and was at ease in it. Reading the book, said an anonymous Presbyterian reviewer, was to 'give oneself up to unrestrained enjoyment...the story of English Nonconformity is one long romance'.[7] It certainly was in Horne's eyes. His work is full of tales of courage, heroism and derring-do, history for the Edwardian pulpit. Robert Browne, 'the half-deranged old man, borne on a feather bed in a cart to die in his last prison, he who in the freshness of youth, when young men see visions, had fastened on a great belief as to the simplicity and freedom of Church fellowship' would, Horne tells us, have been a fine theme for Browning's *Dramatis Personae*. The Milton of *Lycidas* and *Comus* is 'this young prophet of liberty and moral purity, who was to become the most eminent and consistent, and eloquent advocate, in his own or any age, of the ideal "a Free Church in a Free State." When the *Mayflower* encountered terrible storms, '...Some were for turning back even then, so desperate did the adventure appear, but the great majority were for battling on...'. Even Jesus is 'the young Revolutionist of Nazareth'.[8]

Macaulay sat on Horne's shoulder, or perhaps more accurately, was propped open on his desk with Carlyle ready to hand.[9] Facts might not be dross for Horne, but the past was clearly subservient to the present. This is the tale of the triumph of liberty, from Wyclif to the Education Bill, told with all the rhetorical flourish and Liberal passion of a radical Edwardian pulpiteer. This is the legitimation of the struggle. That is not to decry the book, simply to acknowledge the genre for what it is. This is the self-portrait of early twentieth-century Nonconformity. The genetic pool on which it draws includes Wyclif, Savonarola, Marsilius of Padua,

---

6   C. Sylvester Horne, *A Popular History of the Free Churches* (London: James Clarke, 1903), pp. vi-vii.
7   Review in *The Presbyterian* 10.22 (28 May 1903) p. 363.
8   Horne, *Popular History*, pp. 18, 103, 81 and 363.
9   Horne, *Popular History*, pp 205 and 220.

William of Occam, John Colet, Thomas More, Erasmus and Luther, all of whom were champions of religious freedom. That cardinal concept apart, the Reformation gets short shrift—the index records six references to Luther (all of them passing and comparative), one to Calvin (that he restrained the development of the hymn) and none to Zwingli. What matters is Free Churchmanship, not Protestantism. That is why Cromwell's army was 'the most comprehensive Church of England ever known in this country' and the church of the Protectorate 'truly catholic and apostolic'.[10] It was not simply that a remodelled army won the war, it was that it transformed the cry of 'Parliamentary privilege' into the irresistible clarion call 'liberty of conscience'. That, for Horne, is the pivot of the history of the Free Churches, indeed of the history of England. It was the Free Churches' passionate belief that God was on the side of freedom and the people. That freedom was positive as well as negative—freedom from the 'shackles' of theological confessions as well as freedom from state control. The future was bright. America was the shining ideal of the Free Church in a free state. That was a spiritual necessity for England too, for it was a precondition of the increase of religion. The fight for disestablishment was thus a political and moral duty. Horne concluded with pugnacious confidence: 'the Free Church ideal not only includes equal rights for all citizens, but it includes the nobler establishment of the Church of Christ in the affection and reverence of the people, and restitution of the privileges of the Christian commonality to govern and guide the affairs of the Christian Ecclesia. Towards the realisation of this ideal the nation is slowly but surely moving.'[11]

'[O]ne only has to read the preface [of Horne's work] to see what a gulf lies between his world and our own', wrote Ernest Payne in *The Free Church Tradition in the Life of England* in 1944.[12] This singular little book—159 pages, just over 45,000 words—was to take the place of Horne's work in the affections of Free Church men and women for more than a generation. Contemporary reviewers were slow to see its merits. The anonymous reviewer in the *Journal of the Presbyterian Historical Society of England* noted icily that 'In such a small book our Church must of necessity occupy only a minute amount of space',[13] and regretted that Payne skimped on both the Westminster documents and the savagery of the Clarendon Code. However, it ended with grudging acknowledgement that it was 'not a history of the Free Churches, but an estimate of their influence upon the life of England and it covers this

---

10   Horne, *Popular History*, pp. 177 and 118 respectively.

11   Horne, *Popular History*, pp 118,177, 121, 400, 416, 426

12   Ernest A. Payne, *The Free Church Tradition in the Life of England* (London: SCM Press, 1944), p. 7.

13   *Journal of the Presbyterian Historical Society* 8 (1944–47), p. 71.

ground admirably.' Payne's book was one of a rag-bag which fell under Geoffrey Nuttall's reviewing eye in two pages of short notices in the *Congregational Quarterly*.[14] Payne merited ten lines amidst studies of medieval recluses and German confessional witness, as well as biographies of Ghandi and King Haakon VII of Norway. Nuttall noted with approval Payne's attempt to bring Free Church principles into dialogue with historians and commentators like E.H. Carr and D.W. Brogan, and judged the work 'compact and business-like' written with 'clarity and conviction'.

This was a tract for very different times. 'I trust', Payne wrote in the preface, 'that nothing I have said will give offence or seem wilfully blind to those of other branches of the Christian Church who may read these pages.'[15] It is hard to imagine Sylvester Horne writing that. Both, of course, were Mansfield men, but Payne's Regent's Park College, Oxford, in 1942 was very different to Horne's Kensington in 1902. It was a new, uncomfortable world for the Free Churches. The rhetoric of hope and betterment had turned to ashes on the Somme. At home numerical growth had given way to sharp decline, and organized religion was being quietly but firmly pushed to the margins of English society. Payne's Baptist roots were deep, reaching back through his family into the eighteenth century, yet his growing ecumenical experience made him 'increasingly sure that [the Free Churches] are truly a part of the one, holy, catholic, apostolic church'.[16] So, as he sat at his tutor's desk in Regent's Park during 1942–43 Payne knew that it was time to take stock, to consider the inheritance. He had returned to Oxford from the offices of the Baptist Missionary Society at the behest of the Principal, H. Wheeler Robinson some two years earlier. As he settled down to write he knew that his aim was two-fold. First, he had to 'clear his own mind', and prove to himself that there was adequate reason for the Free Churches to continue their independent existence. Second, he wanted to set before his fellow Christians the contribution the Free Church tradition had made and was continuing to make.[17]

If Horne was a journalist, Payne was a serious scholar, abreast of the increasing professionalisation of history. This is a book with footnotes, the work of a scholar who had read Halévy and Knappen, Dakin and Peel, Jordan and Manning. It is, however, scholarship lightly worn in pursuit of his dual aim. More revealing is his chosen dialogue partner, Dennis Brogan, distinguished Americanist and Professor of Political Science at Cambridge. Brogan receives six citations in the index. One reference is a

---

14 Geoffrey Nuttall in *Congregational Quarterly* 23.1 (January, 1945), p. 92.
15 Payne, *Free Church Tradition*, p. 7.
16 Payne, *Free Church Tradition*, p. 8.
17 W.M.S. West, *To Be a Pilgrim: A Memoir of Ernest A. Payne* (Guildford: Lutterworth Press, 1983), pp. 59-60.

quotation at length, another forms a chapter heading. He served with the Intelligence Service during the war but still found time to publish *The English People, Impressions and Observations* in 1943. With characteristic insight he noted the decline of Nonconformity as one the greatest changes in English society since 1906 and attributed it partly to 'the comparative irrelevance of the peculiarly Nonconformist (as apart from Christian) view of the contemporary world and its problems'.[18] Here, Payne knew well, was a well-informed, shrewd commentator whose observations deserved serious treatment. The book is, in part at least, a conversation with him, for the charge of 'comparative irrelevance' invites 'a re-examination of the history and witness of the Free Churches and a consideration of their present position and future prospects.' This is, therefore, rather more than a work of history. It is an essay in self-examination.

First, Payne argues, a proper understanding of 'Englishness' should not be so captivated by the glamour of the parish church that it ignores the chapel. After rehearsing the classical contribution of Nonconformity to English culture, he suggests that 'most important of all has been the influence of the Nonconformist outlook and temperament on the average British citizen.' Three fairly recent studies are enlisted in support. He gives tacit approval to Halévy's theory that Methodism provided stability in the revolution and crises that produced a modern England which is 'anarchist but orderly, practical and businesslike, but religious and even pietist'; endorses Ernest Barker's judgement that English national development may best be understood as the struggle between Anglicans and Tories on the one hand and Whigs and the Free Church men and women on the other; and positively celebrates A.D. Lindsay's Troeltschian thesis that 'Democracy is the application to social life of the principle of the spiritual priesthood of all believers.' So, religious liberty, the limited state and 'our general temper of individual self-reliance', which are essential components of 'Englishness', are the product of the Nonconformist experience.[19]

If Brogan was right in writing Nonconformity's obituary Payne opined, 'then an end has come to a very rich and fruitful movement in English history and Christian history.'[20] Committed Baptist that he was, committed internationalist that he was, Payne was not convinced. From a war conscious Oxford, he faced his tradition with serious questions. The decline of the Free Churches was not simply distressing, it was dangerous. The replacement of 'the Nonconformist Conscience' by political corporatism did not necessarily improve social relations. The decline of

18   Payne, *Free Church Tradition*, p. 16.
19   Payne, *Free Church Tradition*, pp. 17-19.
20   Payne, *Free Church Tradition*, p. 19.

Free Church power was a complicating factor in Anglo–American relations as Brogan hinted. The suppression of the same tradition on the continent was a contributory cause of the rise of fascism. With that broad hint that the continued life of the Free Churches would be important to the well-being of a post-war state, Payne turned to history.

What follows is an impressive work of synthesis and compression as he guides us in chapter headings from protest through struggle to recognition and revival before occupation of the broad plains of expansion and confidence gives way to twentieth-century hesitancy. Traces of the Whig agenda remain, although now they are mediated through the work of Macauley's great nephew, G.M. Trevelyan, whose *History of England* (1926) and *British History in the Nineteenth Century* (1922) dominated cultural history in the inter-war years. Trevelyan's assumptions are Payne's—liberal, Protestant, alive to the 'forces of progress', lingeringly attached to a sense of English destiny.[21] So it is that the Free Churches are born in the 'stormy but exhilerating transition between the medieval and the modern world'; that the 1662 settlement paradoxically leads to greater freedom by denying freedom; that Judge Jeffreys epitomizes the cruelty of the Stuarts and the Glorious Revolution heralds a toleration more generous than the letter of the law.[22]

Emotive antipathy to the Stuarts was ingrained in the Dissenting soul. Payne was free from any revisionist instinct. James VI and I is accused of 'blundering and petulant obtuseness', his son of 'shifty scheming', and it is therefore only natural that 'the voice of England spoke judgement upon the Stuarts in the person of Oliver Cromwell' whose 'pleas for toleration, which were in advance of his time and even of his party, and his passionate desire for national righteousness, entered into the English heritage'. Like Horne before him, Payne understood his seventeenth-century forbears to be paradigms of Englishness. Owen and Baxter, Fox and Bunyan, Milton and Cromwell were 'great Englishmen, loyal Englishmen' whose 'faithfulness to their own consciences...broadened the whole conception of freedom in this country'. Take them away and what is left he asks. Jeremy Taylor, Sir Thomas Browne and the Cambridge Platonists—'fainter voices, whereas the others still speak directly to our modern need in language that the simplest may understand'.[23]

The echoes of the Whig agenda are faint though. History grew to maturity as a discipline between 1902–44, and the study of Free Church

---

21   For Trevelyan, see David Cannadine, *G.M. Trevelyan: A Life in History* (London: HarperCollins, 1992), especially pp. 113-19.

22   Payne, *Free Church Tradition*, pp. 24, 45, 47 and 48.

23   Payne, *Free Church Tradition*, pp. 42, 44 and 55.

history was similarly transformed.[24] Sylvester Horne had played a tiny part in that change, for in 1899 he had been a prime mover in the formation of the Congregational Historical Society.[25] The Methodists had been the first to establish an historical society in 1894. The Baptists followed the Congregationalists in 1906 and the Presbyterians created their society in 1913. All sought to preserve the treasures of the past and present them to a wider audience. By the time Payne wrote Free Church history was replete with the paraphernalia of academe—journals, learned societies, research students and publications. The vertical study of traditions remained important, but it was being complemented by the horizontal vision of the professional historian. Unlike Horne, Payne knew how to read horizontally with one finger placed firmly on the pulse of historical scholarship. He had read Manning on Wyclif, Garett on the Marian exiles, Jordan on toleration, Woodhouse on the Puritans, Maldwyn Edwards on Wesley and Wearmouth on Methodism and the working classes, and footnoted accordingly.

The writing of contemporary history is, as Payne acknowledged, 'both difficult and dangerous'.[26] That makes his final chapter, 'Hesitancy: 1900–1939' and his conclusion all the more remarkable. He treats the decline of the Free Churches in the inter-war period with unflinching honesty, and confesses that such turbulent times could herald revival or be a sign that the Free Churches have 'fulfilled their mission and...their day is over'. In company with many, he saw the new unity of a nation under pressure as evidence of a new beginning for church and state. 'Though the cloud on the Free Church horizon be but the size of a man's hand', he wrote, 'it is assuredly there as a sign of recovery and renewal'.[27]

That touching hope apart, Payne's acute reading of the signs of the times, gave him at least temporary membership of the guild of prophets. As an historian he forsaw the significance of sociology for his subject, making extensive use of Frank Tillyard's pioneering article 'The Distribution of the Free Churches in England' which had been published in the *Sociological Review* in 1935. He adopted as his own Ernest Barker's argument that tension between the Church of England and Nonconformity would be the chief interpretative feature of modern English history—a theme developed by such different historians as Alan Gilbert and Jonathon Clark. As a concerned pastor, he placed partial

---

24   See, for example, Arthur Marwick, *The Nature of History* (London: Macmillan, 1970), pp. 56-96.

25   Clyde Binfield, 'Transacting our History: The Congregationalists' Dimension', *Journal of the United Reformed Church Historical Society* 6.6 (May, 2000), pp. 384-98, at p. 389.

26   Binfield, 'Transacting our History', p. 121.

27   Binfield, 'Transacting our History', pp. 138-39.

blame for the decline of Nonconformity on its severence from the 'legitimate aspirations of the poor',[28] a theme later to be writ large in the work of liberation theology. As an English ecumenist he predicted a long and difficult journey before the Church of England and the Free Churches could be one. As a Christian statesman, he recognized that the ecumenical imperative was global, and with astonishing boldness predicted that by the end of the century the most significant Free Church movements might well be found in Russia and South America.[29] He saw the centre of gravity of the Christian world moving from north to south, from west to east.

Like Horne before him, Payne attempted to sum up the essential nature of the Free Church tradition. If freedom took precedence over Protestantism for Horne, Payne saw the anchor of freedom in the Protestant discernment of the primacy of the gospel. Faith came before order, the gospel came before the church. This was a tradition (to anticipate David Bebbington) which was part of a broader evangelical culture. Payne's four marks of the Free Churches—the necessity of a personal decision for Christ, a sense of the church as a company of believers gathered together, a commitment to the priesthood of all believers, and a striving to relate religion and life[30]—are not too distant from Bebbington's 'quadrilateral of priorities' that form the basis of evangelicalism.[31] Sobered by war, recalled to roots by Forsyth and the neo-orthodox, the Free Churches had changed.

In 1978 Michael Watts judged Payne's small book 'by far the best' brief survey of the history of Dissent. He did so in the preface to the first volume of his *The Dissenters*. This was the beginning of a Barcelona cathedral of a project which as yet, after little short of 1,500 pages has only reached 1859. Originally planned in two volumes, it will now encompass at least three. This is a different kind of book from Payne and Horne. Watts understands himself not to be the successor of Payne, but of H.W. Clark whose two volume *History of English Nonconformity* (1913) Watts considered 'no improvement' on Hubert Skeats and Charles Miall's *History of the Free Churches of England 1688–1891* (1891). He set himself the daunting task of producing a completely new study of the whole subject of English *and* Welsh Dissent which would take account of the 'changed perspective' of the late twentieth century and also 'synthesise and examine critically the work done by other scholars in the

---

28   Binfield, 'Transacting our History', p. 128.
29   Binfield, 'Transacting our History', p. 146.
30   Payne, *Free Church Tradition*, pp. 144-45.
31   The four are conversionism, activism, biblicism and crucicentrism, see D.W. Bebbington, *Evangelicalism in Modern Britain: A History from the 1730s to the 1980s* (London: Unwin Hyman, 1989), p. 3.

field over the last half-century, and...add the results of the author's own researches'.[32]

The perspective had certainly changed. Horne looked forward eagerly to the increasing influence of the Free Churches in the life of the nation. Payne regretted the passing of that influence and sensed that a chapter had closed and that the future was at best uncertain. Watts knew that the statistics told a story of 'uninterrupted decline' since the end of the first decade of the century. He announced his intention to analyse the causes in his second volume, promising to bring to bear on his subject the techniques of the social sciences. In other words, this was to be a deliberately empiricist work, concerned to 'recover what can be recovered about the lives, beliefs and religious practice of the ordinary lay men and women who constituted the overwhelming majority of English and Welsh Dissenters'.[33]

Watts's thoroughness is breathtaking. A twenty page appendix on the Evans List and Dissenting distribution in the early eighteenth century is to be found in volume one, but that is as nothing to the two hundred pages of statistics and maps which form two appendices in volume two. The first of these offers a re-evaluation of the 1851 religious census. The second analyses the reliability of baptismal registers as a source of information about the occupational structure of Nonconformist congregations. Similarly, his fresh and provocative analysis of conversion experiences between 1790–1850 is based on a sample of 670 accounts.[34] This is an empirical history of Dissent on a scale unseen before. Nothing is taken for granted. All one can do is stand astonished at such extraordinary labour and rigorous standards.

If there is one ghost that Watts is determined to lay to rest, it is that Nonconformity was essentially a middle-class movement. His team's work on baptismal and marriage registers has produced a significant revisionist reading of the class structure of Nonconformity in the first half of the nineteenth century. The work is deployed in various illuminating ways. A comparison of the proportion of men and women signing marriage registers with a mark between 1838–41 with Nonconformist chapel attendance according to the 1851 religious census proves a significant correlation between Nonconformist growth and illiteracy. That in turn is used to support the conclusions that Nonconformist expansion took place 'in the worst educated and most superstitious parts of England and Wales' and 'predominantly among

---

32   Michael R. Watts, *The Dissenters: Volume I. From the Reformation to the French Revolution* (Oxford: Clarendon Press, 1978), p. viii.

33   Watts, *Dissenters*, I, p. viii.

34   Michael R. Watts, *The Dissenters: Volume II. The Expansion of Evangelical Nonconformity 1791–1859* (Oxford: Clarendon Press, 1995), p. 50.

people who were poor, ill-educated, unsophisticated, and superstitious'.[35] So, Watts joins his voice to those of Hugh MacLeod, Jeremy Cox, Mark Smith and others to prove that the rural and urban poor were by no means alienated from organized religion in the mid-nineteenth century. However, as W.R. Ward has rightly said, this is 'a statistical sledgehammer to crack a social nut'.[36] It is comforting to know beyond reasonable doubt that the poor had not deserted the chapels, nor the chapels the poor—but such dramatic expansion would clearly have been impossible unless a large proportion of the membership base had been working class. It is equally comforting to know that there is hard statistical evidence that urban Congregationalists were upwardly socially mobile in the 1850s and 1860s, but that is scarcely a revelation. However, Watts's methodological thoroughness means that his work will be both a benchmark and a quarry for future historians of Nonconformity. No student of English or Welsh Dissent can afford to ignore him.

What, though, is his vision of the tradition he has spent so much of his life studying? At the conclusion of the introduction to his first volume he quotes with approval Macaulay's maxim that the true Dissenter 'prostrated himself in dust before his Maker, but he set his foot on the neck of his king'. The connecting thread he perceives between the Tudor Anabaptists and twentieth-century Free Churchmen and women is a refusal to accept state interference in matters of conscience—'The refusal to render to Caesar the things that are God's is of the very essence of Dissent'. The Toleration Act is thus their greatest achievement.[37] Its legacy of social apartheid stimulated the battle for religious and civil equality which occupied the nineteenth century. There is life in the old Whig tradition yet! That is why the architecture of volume one, in a manner reminiscent of Horne, is focused on the seventeenth century. There is little discussion of the continental Reformation. The English tradition is born of radicalism (both Lollard and Anabaptist) out of Calvinist Puritanism. In England Dissent is a marginalized, minority phenomenon, pushed to the edge of national culture—Rosencranz and Guildenstern to Anglicanism's Hamlet. In Wales, at least in the nineteenth century, it dominated and shaped the spirituality of the nation. For all that though, Watts is Horne's ancestor in his firm belief that American democracy and English toleration are results of the Dissenting traditions. Similarly, Dissent created an ethos which contained the radicalism that turned to revolution in France in 1789.[38] Simultaneously, it was a crucial component in the expansionism which exported Protantism around the

---

35   Watts, *Dissenters*, II, pp. 101-10 and 327.
36   W.R. Ward, review in *Journal of Ecclesiastical History* 48.1 (January, 1997), p. 187.
37   Watts, *Dissenters*, I, pp. 5, 3 and 2.
38   Watts, *Dissenters*, I, p. 4; and Watts, *Dissenters*, II, pp. 372-77.

world. Dissent helped 'to make Englishmen and Welshmen not perhaps what they are, but what they were until the middle of the twentieth century'.[39]

Volume III promises to be an obituary in the sense that Watts clearly believes a significant phase of Nonconformist life came to an end in the middle of the twentieth century. It is naturally impossible to predict its contents, but Watts's 1995 Dr Williams's lecture, *Why Did the English Stop Going to Church?* indicates the direction of his thinking. It is simple and compelling. First, church attendance was not a natural characteristic of the English before the nineteenth century, so what needs explaining is not twentieth-century decline but 'the extraordinarily high levels of church and chapel attendance in the nineteenth century'.[40] The explosive growth of Nonconformity during the Evangelical Revival was predicated on the fear of hell. The 670 conversion accounts so painstakingly analysed prove that the major factor which predisposed men and women to respond was fear—of death, judgement and the fires of hell. Second, church attendance held up until the 1880s. Thereafter the churches suffered from a recruitment crisis. They were not replacing the dying with the generations born in the 1860s and the following decades. 1859 was, of course, the year of the publication of Darwin's *Origin of Species*, soon to be followed by *Essays and Reviews* (1860). Contemporary anxiety about these two works, Watts argues, was focused not on evolution or higher criticism, but on the rejection of eternal punishment. The liberal re-scripting of Christianity as an agenda for the improvement of this life rather than a preparation for the next met its Armaggedon in the trenches of the First World War. Nonconformity had brought into it wholesale, and as a consequence fired its best recruiting sergeant, the doctrine of hell. All that was left, through a long, long century was decline. English popular religion transferred its allegiance from classical Nonconformity to those independent, charismatic, Pentecostal, Afro-Carribean and non-Union Baptist churches which have refused to soft-pedal on the doctrine of eternal punishment and the saving sacrifice of Christ.

The argument is so daring, so simple, that one is almost persuaded to believe it. Yet almost at every point, when one examines it closely, it is contentious. The jury is still out on the level of church attendance and religious observance before the nineteenth century. The Evangelical Revival stubbornly refuses to be reduced to one cause, notwithstanding the 670 conversion accounts and despite Robin Gill's work,[41] the starting

---

39   Watts, *Dissenters*, I, p. 5.
40   Michael R. Watts, *Why Did the English Stop Going to Church?* (London: Dr Williams's Library, 1995), p. 6.
41   Robin Gill, *The Myth of the Empty Church* (London: SPCK, 1993), *passim*.

point and the rate of church decline during the nineteenth century is uncertain, as Watts himself admits.[42]

Could the ebbing of the sea of faith on Dover beach have been turned by the retention of classical orthodoxy? Watts implies that it might, for conservative churches grow and liberal ones decline. Over the last twenty years in England new church evangelicalism has waxed as liberal Dissent, particularly Methodist and Reformed, has waned. However, evangelicalism has scant respect for denominational boundaries. It has also been re-shaping the older Dissenting denominations over the past twenty years. The picture of growth and decline is more nuanced than this thesis suggests. More significantly, the new churches have an increasing share of a decreasing market. So, would the English have continued going to Nonconformist churches if they had continued preaching the doctrine of eternal punishment?

If they had shared the same worldview as Watts's 670 converts they might well have done. But by 1914 hardly anyone did. In the early 1880s a Harrow schoolboy announced that 'Darwin had disproved the Bible'. Owen Chadwick commented: 'This is bringing us near the heart of the problem over secularization. When we come down to the axioms which intelligent schoolboys of fourteen years learn from less intelligent schoolboys of fifteen years, we come near to the point where the cloudy apprehensions of what is known as intellectual history...can be shown to affect the attitudes of a whole society'.[43] The re-alignment of Christian theology in the latter nineteenth century was an evangelical necessity as well as a matter of intellectual and spiritual integrity.

It is the seriousness of that challenge which suggests that simple models of continuity and decline, although superficially attractive, will fail to do justice to the complexity of the solutions. Dale Johnson has recently re-examined John Kent's proposal that 'renaissance' might offer richer possibilities in the study of late nineteenth century Nonconformity.[44] Kent chose it because he discerned 'a return to the human as the subject of value' within late nineteenth-century chapel culture, and he traced its emergence in 'art, liberal Christianity and many kinds of socialism'. Johnson widens the scope of the model to include the re-evaluation of ministry and its articulation of theology, which is the central concern of his monograph. As he does so he reminds us that Nonconformity was not hermetically sealed from wider cultural changes. As the quest for civil

---

42   Watts, *Why Did the English Stop Going to Church?*, p. 8.

43   Owen Chadwick, *The Secularization of the European Mind in the Nineteenth Century* (Cambridge: Cambridge University Press, 1975), p. 164.

44   Dale A. Johnson, *The Changing Shape of English Nonconformity 1825–1925* (Oxford: Oxford University Press, 1999), pp. 7-11; John Kent 'A Late Nineteenth-Century Nonconformist Renaissance', in Derek Baker (ed.), *Renaissance and Renewal in Church History* (Studies in Church History, 14; Oxford: Blackwells, 1977), pp. 351-60.

equality drew to a quietly triumphant conclusion, Nonconformist churches considered their identity anew—in relation to themselves, each other, the Church of England, and English culture. One product of that reflection was a renewed sense of identity and continuity as witnessed by the formation of historical societies. Another was a reconsideration of what it meant to be 'church', to be part of the catholic body of Christ. If the architectural expression of that reflection was Mansfield College chapel, its theological apotheosis was P.T. Forsyth's tart comment: 'I do not know which is the worst form of mischief, our neglect of priestly worship or the Catholic neglect of prophetic preaching.'[45]

Part of the late nineteenth-century Nonconformist renaissance was the realization that the essence of Nonconformist identity was to be found not in 1662 but at the foot of the cross, in the company of the faithful of all ages. Priestly worship and prophetic preaching were incomplete without each other. A new agenda had evolved—co-operation and complementarity rather than competition and antagonism.

That is why Ernest Payne was so clearly the successor of Sylvester Horne. In his review of the second volume of Michael Watts's study, W.R. Ward expressed the droll hope that Watts might 'complete his enterprise before the world of Dissent is sucked uncomplainingly into the ecumenical Hoover'.[46] The level of complaint depends, of course, on who is wielding the Hoover.

In this paper I have chosen to compare three very different twentieth-century historians of Nonconformity, partly because all works of history inevitably reflect their own times and that in itself might be helpful to a volume which is evaluating twentieth-century Nonconformity. Horne belonged to a world in which the Free Churches, in the words of Hugh Price Hughes, represented 'a majority of the Christian people at home...an immense majority in the British Empire, and an overwhelming majority in the English-speaking world'.[47] Between 1902 and 1944 the Methodists had lost 7.3% of their membership, the Baptists 8% and the Congregationalists 15%. The world of gradual denominational decline and broadening ecumenical horizons therefore came together in Ernest Payne. It remains to be seen what Michael Watts will make of the longer perspective of dramatic decline and ecumenical frustration.

They are also three very different historians because they represent three very different ways of writing church history. As we have seen, the Whig agenda lingers long, but Horne used his material quite deliberately to create a tract for the times. It was a cracking yarn, self-conscious pulpit

---

45   P.T. Forsyth, 'Congregationalism and Reunion' (London, 1919), pp. 22-24, quoted by Johnson, *Changing Shape*, p. 179.

46   Ward, review in *Journal of Ecclesiastical History* 48.1 (January, 1997), p. 187.

47   Addressing the first National Council of Evangelical Free Churches in March 1896, quoted by Kent, 'Late Nineteenth-Century Renaissance', p. 353.

rhetoric. Payne is far more the measured Oxford don, assured in his command of the secondary literature, but nonetheless conscious of his wider readership. The SCM Book Club was targeted at clergy and intelligent lay readers. This was history intended to provoke. He was an unashamed denominational historian, yet one with a true understanding of proportion—'To take merely our own branch, to extol it and exaggerate its importance, has now little or no purpose for the seeker after truth'.[48] The survival of denominational history throughout the century deserves recognition. It is one of the few meeting grounds left between amateurs and professionals, and often it is insiders whose ears are attuned to harmonies and discords that those less familiar with their worlds fail to hear. The combined journals of the denominational societies are an enviable quarry, as Michael Watts's footnotes show.

Watts writes as a professional historian for professional historians. Like Payne he is on top of his subject. But if Payne was sitting on Snowden, Watts has had to conquer Mount Everest. The subject has expanded disproportionately in the last half century. That has in part reflected the expansion of historical studies in higher education. No-one who now writes about the history of Nonconformity can do so without threading their way through the historiographical thickets of the Puritan revolution and the complex literature about nineteenth-century Nonconformity which has been produced since the publication of Owen Chadwick's *The Victorian Church* in 1966. There are few nooks and crannies of seventeenth- and nineteenth-century Nonconformity which have escaped the probing interest of historians, and the literature surrounding the Evangelical Revival and the rise of Methodism is prodigious. Michael Watts's achievement is, therefore, all the greater.

Nonconformity has been fortunate in its twentieth-century historians. Its role in British society may well have been secondary, as Daniel Jenkins famously noted, on a par with the public schools or the Liberal Party, but the quality of its historians has been exceptional. Traditions that can boast Geoffrey Nuttall, Tudur Jones and Gordon Rupp amongst their expositors, as well as Ernest Payne and Michael Watts, have been served by some of the finest historical pens of the twentieth century.

A question which nags in the back of my mind though, is why? Why have we produced such skilled historians and so few creative theologians? When I was a young research student a minister colleague asked what I was doing. When he found out he muttered, 'Another contributor to the nostalgia industry.' Is it just the English temperament, the yearning for warm beer, village cricket and chapel teas, or is it that the past is a more comfortable country than the present?

---

48   E.A. Payne 'History: Too Much or Too Little?', *Baptist Quarterly* 22.8 (October, 1968), pp 385-97, at p. 397.

CHAPTER 4

Twentieth-Century Historians of Welsh Protestant Nonconformity

D. Densil Morgan

Nonconformists in Wales have been singularly fortunate in their historians. From Joshua Thomas's elegant *Hanes y Bedyddwyr Ymhlith y Cymry* (*A History of the Baptists Among the Welsh*) in 1778 to T.M. Bassett's lucid *Welsh Baptists* in 1977, from Thomas Rees's expansive *History of Protestant Nonconformity in Wales* (1861) and his labyrinthine five volume *Hanes Eglwysi Annibynol Cymru* (*A History of the Independent Churches of Wales*) (1871–91) to R. Tudur Jones's exquisite *Hanes Annibynwyr Cymru* (*A History of the Welsh Independents*) of 1966, the history of the Dissenting cause has received ample recognition and commensurate analysis. An expansive tradition which includes Methodist historiography of both Wesleyan and Calvinist hues, it has attempted to do justice to the transcendent reality of God's mighty (and humble) acts in history while being conscious of the interplay of those social, cultural and economic forces of which human life is made. And it was in the twentieth century that this long, broad and rich tradition reached its highest point. If nineteenth century Wales was said to have been 'a nation of Nonconformists',[1] it was in the twentieth that their historians did their most sterling and lasting work.

The energy and influence which Protestant Nonconformity displayed at the turn of the twentieth century masked considerable inner tensions and weaknesses. If what the Royal Commission on religion in Wales (1906–10) described as 'the four great Nonconformist denominations' presented to the world a united Dissenting front, the divisions between the Calvinistic Methodists, Congregationalists, Baptists and Wesleyan Methodists, were still sufficiently marked for sectarianism, if not bigotry, sometimes to flourish. Despite all that chapel people held in common— puritan values, an emphasis on individual rights, Liberal politics, a zeal

---

1   Henry Richard, *Letters on the Social and Political Condition of Wales* (London: Jackson, Walford and Hodder, n.d. [1867]), p. 2.

for self-improvement and a culture of the word—the Nonconformist cause tended still to be blighted by parochialism, narrow-mindedness and not a little intellectual obscurantism. This was most readily manifested in denominational one-up-manship and an inordinate emphasis on congregational polity, or believer's baptism, or presbyterian church government, or Methodist enthusiasm, or whatever other characteristic that differentiated the traditions from one another. Despite their apparent unity, sectarian jealousies were never far beneath the surface of Victorian Nonconformity in Wales.

Yet there were other divisions which went even deeper. The fact that a Royal Commission had to be convened at all was evidence of the ongoing and still emotively bitter controversy between chapel and church on the matter of disestablishment. For more than two generations this had been the most consuming matter in Welsh politics, yet when, in August 1914, the Disestablishment Act, which cut the link bewteen the four Welsh dioceses and the state, was finally passed, only the most intransigent Nonconformists viewed it as being an unambiguous victory. For the majority of the Welsh people, disestablishment had become something of an anachronism if not an irrelevance. The world had moved on with material interests and class loyalties fast displacing religious commitment and denominational concerns. Ecclesiastical warfare was felt to be inappropriate in a world where social ills and economic necessities, to say nothing of the physical strife of the Great War, were the most pressing issues at hand.

Each of these phenomena was related to the deepening secularization of society and the Welsh mind. With compulsory secondary education for all after 1872 and the beginnings of a national university in 1883, secular values would soon enshrine a norm which would question the authority of the Bible (which, of course, had formed the basis for the Nonconformist worldview) as well as, in a more positive vein, raising intellectual standards and providing Wales with a degree of scholarly objectivity only fitfully available before. If there would be opposition between a religiously-based scheme of values and a more secular ideology of learning, those who managed to combine piety with the new system could, in fact, draw strength from the admittedly threatening situation which now prevailed. Christianity, and the study of Christian history (including Nonconformity), would persist, but its truths would have to pass through the prism of unbiased scholarship and be purged by a non-partisan spirit. In order to establish its integrity, Nonconformist learning would have to eschew sectarianism (though preserving its core historical values), appreciate all that was positive and true in what had been considered traditionally hostile viewpoints, and gain a sense of proportion in keeping with the norms of a more secularly sophisticated society. The most succesful early twentieth-century historians of Welsh Nonconformity were those who achieved such a balance.

The earlier Victorian historiography was, in the main, the product of denominational factionalism. The prime bone of contention among opposing partisans was the respective influence of the 'Methodist' versus the 'Older Dissenting' views of history. According to the former, established in 1773 with Williams Pantycelyn's celebrated elegy to the Methodist leader Howel Harris, early eighteenth-century Wales was shrouded in unremitting spiritual darkness with 'no presbyter nor priest nor bishop awake', a situation only remedied after 1735 with the startlingly effective peripatetic evangelism of Harris and his colleagues. This view became the prevailing Methodist dogma and was embellished and enshrined in such popular nineteenth-century works as John Hughes's three volume *Methodistiaeth Cymru* (*Welsh Methodism*) (1851– 56) and the even more romanticized *Y Tadau Methodistaidd* (*The Methodist Fathers*), an embarrassingly uncritical two volume work compiled by J.M. Jones and William Morgan and published in 1895–97. The reaction against such 'shameless untruth[s]' had begun even during the eighteenth century, first by such Older Dissenting worthies as the Independent minister Edmund Jones, 'the Old Prophet', of Pontypool, and had hardened into Congregational dogma in the works of Thomas Rees and others. Their anti-Methodist tirade had reached a crescendo in the radical Congregational journalist Beriah Gwynfe Evans's *Diwygwyr Cymru* (*Welsh Revivalists*) of 1900 which was contemptuous of virtually all Methodist achievements and poured scorn on the movement's leaders, Howel Harris in particular. By this time fiction had wholly taken over from fact and rank prejudice had been elevated into ultimate truth. In the words of Geraint H. Jenkins: 'No episode epitomizes more clearly the denominational bigotry which characterizes historical writing in nineteenth century Wales'.[2]

It goes without saying that neither Methodist nor Old Dissent had anything complementary to say about the established church, with whom Welsh Victorian Nonconformists of whatever stripe were currently locked in mortal combat over disestablishment, while even the different strains within Old Dissent vied with one another in order to prove which was the older and more in keeping with the pristine purity of the New Testament church. J. Spinther James's four volume *Hanes y Bedyddwyr yng Nghymru* (*A History of the Baptists in Wales*) (1896–1907) traced a fictional apostolic succession of believer's baptism throughout the Christian centuries back to the sub-apostolic church, while T. Mardy Rees's belated *A History of the Quakers in Wales* (1925), though dealing

---

2   Geraint H. Jenkins, *Protestant Dissenters in Wales, 1639–89* (Cardiff: University of Wales Press, 1992), p. 4.

with another tradition, was in the same vein. All in all these works were undisciplined, pre-critical, often intemperate, and although sometimes containing valuable local traditions and even, at times, valid insights, they served more to undermine the intellectual seriousness of Nonconformity than to establish its integrity.

With the dawn of the new century there were signs of a general dissatisfaction with historical writings such as these. The two transitional figures who did more than anyone to instil rigour and objectivity into the study of Nonconformist and Methodist beginnings in Wales were the Baptist scholar Thomas Shankland (1858–1927) and the Calvinistic Methodist historian Richard Bennett (1860–1937). Shankland had been a shoemaker, Bennett remained a farmer. Although continuing wholly committed to their respective denominations, both adopted critical methods, and their work, which reached the highest academic standards, was recognized by the University of Wales who awarded each with an honorary degree.

Thomas Shankland had left the cobbler's bench to train for the Baptist ministry first at the Llangollen Academy before transferring to the newly established university college at Bangor. He began publishing articles on Baptist history in the 1890s when a pastor in Flintshire, North Wales, yet it was his closely argued and exhaustively researched rebuttal of Beriah G. Evans's *Diwygwyr Cymru* in a series of sixteen articles in the Baptist monthly *Seren Gomer* (September 1900–January 1904) which made his scholarly reputation. Unconvinced by the 'facts' so readily marshalled by the Congregational popularizer, he perused numerous manuscript sources in such places as the Lambeth Palace Library, the British Museum and the Public Record Office and, rummaging through the records of the SPCK, ascertained for himself the true extent of the spiritual 'torpor' of pre-revival Wales and the effectiveness, or otherwise, of both Methodist and Dissenting evangelists. It was this sober and unprejudiced research *ad fontes*, and its surprisingly ready reception within Welsh Nonconformist circles, which set the scene for a new Dissenting historiography: scientific, careful, detached, fair-minded, temperate and scholarly. 'Shankland's sympathies...were catholic and comprehensive', wrote Thomas Richards, 'not in any way bound by the fences of denominationalism'. His catholicity included doing justice to the Anglican contribution to the Welsh religious past (which was almost unheard of among Welsh Nonconformists of the time), although personally he remained a staunch Liberal and convinced Free Churchman.[3] Appointed Bangor University's first keeper of its Welsh library in 1905, thereafter he gave himself wholly

---

3   Thomas Richards, 'Shankland, Thomas', in J.E. Lloyd and R.T. Jenkins (eds), *The Dictionary of Welsh Biography down to 1940* (London: The Honourable Society of Cymmrodorion, 1959), p. 909.

to bibliographical, scholarly and historical pursuits, while his editorship of, and numerous contributions to, the *Transactions* of his denomination's historical society, put early twentieth-century Baptist studies in Wales on a sure footing. Shankland broke new ground constantly and was the precursor of all subsequent Nonconformist historians in twentieth-century Wales.

Like his Baptist colleague, Richard Bennett's early education was minimal, though unlike Shankland, he would never receive a college or even a seminary training. His encyclopaedic knowledge of the beginnings of Welsh Methodism was the result of years spent perusing the vast manuscript collection at Howel Harris's home in Trefeca, Breconshire, where he spent each winter from 1905 onwards before returning to the Montgomeryshire hills during the summer months in order to tend the family farm. His *Blynyddoedd Cyntaf Methodistiaeth* (1909) (E.T. *The Early Life of Howel Harris* [1962]) was the first unbiased account of the revivalist's career placing him in a true historical context on the basis of an intimate first hand knowledge of Harris's near indecipherable manuscript diaries. His later works including the misleadingly narrowly titled *Methodistiaeth Trefaldwyn Uchaf* (*The Methodism of Upper Montgomeryshire*) (1929) and numerous scholarly contributions to the *Journal* of his denomination's historical society, put him in the forefront of early twentieth-century Welsh religious historians. Like Shankland, he refused to accept denominational mythologies, preferring rather to return to the original sources believing that the spiritual strength of the Methodist 'fathers' would be increased rather than diminished by an objective analysis of the facts. His perspective was wide, his standards exacting and his mastery of Welsh prose admirable, all of which made him, according to R.T. Jenkins, 'a researcher and historian of unusual distinction'.[4] Although lacking in all academic advantages, he was a pattern whom all subsequent scholars could emulate with immense profit.

The professionalism and academic exactitude of Shankland and Bennett was all the more extraordinary given the essentially amateur chapel culture of pre-critical Victorian Dissent. Born too early to partake fully of the scholarly renaissance of late nineteenth-century Wales, they served as the precursors of the new generation of university educated Nonconformist historians of whom two, especially, became consummate masters of their craft: they were Dr Thomas Richards, later to become *the* expert in seventeenth-century Welsh religious history, and the urbane and phenomenally learned Professor R.T. Jenkins. By the mid-twentieth century both had revolutionized the study of Wales's modern Christian

---

4   R.T. Jenkins, 'Bennett, Richard', in Lloyd and Jenkins (eds), *Dictionary of Welsh Biography*, p. 32.

past to an extent of which earlier generations could barely have imagined.

Thomas Richards (1878–1962), the loyal son of a strict Baptist family of Cardiganshire smallholders, became a pupil-teacher at local elementary schools before entering the University College of North Wales, Bangor, in 1899 to read for a degree in history. As well as playing his part in the social, cultural and political life of the university to the full, he drank deeply from the wells first opened by Sir J.E. Lloyd, Bangor's esteemed professor of history and expert on the foundations of early and medieval Wales. A career in schoolteaching beckoned, first in the pleasant seaside town of Tywyn, Merionethshire, where he was utterly miserable, then in Bootle among the vast Welsh diaspora which flourished on the banks of the Mersey, and finally in the bustling town of Maesteg in the Llynfi Valley at the hub of the South Wales coalfield. Despite his undoubted ability and popularity as a schoolmaster, Richards's consuming ambition was in the realm of scholarship, his dream being to make a serious contribution to the knowledge of Wales's past and to secure, if possible, an academic post. It was Shankland rather than his mentor, J.E. Lloyd, who convinced him that there was work to be done on the history of Welsh Puritanism, and his MA thesis, begun in 1910 and submitted four years later, became the basis for his first substantial volume, *A History of the Puritan Movement in Wales, 1639–52* (1920). Other books came in quick succession: *Religious Developments in Wales, 1654–62* (1923), *Wales Under the Penal Code, 1662–87* (1925), *Wales Under the Indulgence, 1672–75* (1928) as well as the two Welsh language volumes *Piwritaniaeth a Pholitics* (*Puritanism and Politics*) (1927) and *Cymru a'r Uchel Gomisiwn, 1633–40* (*Wales and the High Commission, 1633–40*) (1930). None of these were pamphlets; rather they were daunting, forbidding tomes, crammed full of facts, figures, tables and analysis much of which was frankly indigestible. And that was not all; he published at the same time groundbreaking articles on the Baptists in Wales after the Restoration, Henry Maurice and the Independents during the same period, and an in-depth assessment of the religious census of 1676.[5] It added up to some 1,800 pages of the most rigorous and detailed research on Welsh religious history ever to be produced which, along with earning him the degree of DLitt (only the second ever awarded to a historian by the University of Wales) secured a much desired academic position in 1926 as Librarian and Reader in Modern Welsh History at his old college at Bangor. It is astounding to

5   Thomas Richards, 'Bedyddwyr Cymru yng Nghyfnod Lewis Thomas', *Trafodion Cymdeithas Hanes y Bedyddwyr* (1916), pp. 3-45, and 'Henry Maurice: Piwritan ac Annibynwr', *Y Cofiadur* 5–6 (1928), pp. 15-67, and 'The Religious Census of 1676', *Transactions of the Honourable Society of Cymmrodorion*, Supplement (London: The Honourable Society of Cymmrodorion, 1927), pp. 1-118.

contemplate that he fulfilled the best part of this project during evenings, weekends and school vacations while earning his keep as history master at the Maesteg Intermediary School.

Just to list Richards's works does him no justice at all. The quantity increased as time progressed: he published a further three historical volumes, some 250 academic articles, seventy-seven entries in the *Dictionary of Welsh Biography*, as well as two short, shrewd and marvellously entertaining autobiographical works.[6] The quality of his academic exertions consisted of a refusal to take anything on trust, an unparalleled mastery of all possible mansucript sources in such places as the Public Records Office, the Bodleian Library, the British Museum, Dr Williams' Library, the National Library of Wales, Cardiff Central Library and Lambeth Palace to name but some, and an ability to utilize the contents of such documents as Exchequer Bills and Dispositions, Augmentation Books as well as the State Papers Domestic in a way which threw a flood of new light on a virtually unresearched period of early modern Welsh history. On the basis of information gleaned from these dry-as-dust sources, Richards conveyed, in his own way, the seventeenth-century drama of the evangelization of a poverty stricken land by such vibrant and contumacious characters as Vavasor Powell, Walter Cradoc, John Miles, Morgan Llwyd and other, lesser known Puritans, and how their labours had been sustained during the Restoration by Stephen Hughes, Lewis Thomas, Henry Maurice and others from among a no less noble generation of Dissenters, who together had laid the foundations for what would become, in time, 'Nonconformist Wales'. His recent biographer, Geraint H. Jenkins, bids us 'call to memory [Richards's] authentic scholarship, his respect for original sources, his inexhaustible energy and the talent to cut his own path as a researcher, author and lecturer'.[7]

None of this is meant to imply that Richards's work is perfect; it patently is not. His two most glaring weaknesses were an inability to pick and choose facts in a way which highlights effectively the contours and nuances of historical development, and his unremittingly turgid prose style (in English, at least). '*Ymchwilio—nid athronyddu—oedd gwaith pennaf yr hanesydd iddo ef*' ('For him it was research—not philosophizing—which consituted the historian's chief task') was the diplomatic way in which his ablest pupil, R. Tudur Jones, described Richards's historical method.[8] Obsessed, as he was, with getting the

---

6   See the biography by Geraint H. Jenkins, *'Doc Tom': Thomas Richards* (Caerdydd: Gwasg Prifysgol Cymru, 1999), *passim*.

7   Geraint H. Jenkins, *Dr Thomas Richards: Hanesydd Piwritaniaeth ac Anghydffurfiaeth Gymreig* (Abertawe: Coleg y Brifysgol, 1994), p. 21.

8   R. Tudur Jones, 'Thomas Richards—Hanesydd', *Seren Cymru*, 6 Gorffennaf 1962, p. 3.

factual minutiae of the story correct, the story itself often suffered as a result. Wider concerns, whether social, political or specifically religious, are frequently buried under a welter of facts often conveyed in an exquisitely complex literary manner: 'His works are riddled with convoluted sentences, extraordinary circumlocutions, rhetorical questions, biblical allusions and baffling digressions'.[9] On the level of phraseology and vocabulary, his biographer lists the following: 'beyond a peradventure', 'casting a nebula', 'as a wholesome corrective', 'inexpungability', 'asseverate', 'excrescences', 'irrefragable', 'inauspicious inexactitudes' and the like which blight virtually every page of his work.[10] An early reviewer, the Anglican historian John Arthur Price, described *A History of the Puritan Movement in Wales* as 'the dullest book that I ever read',[11] while fifty years later Michael R. Watts commented that 'The various studies by Thomas Richards...are a mine of information, all but buried under the author's hideous prose style'.[12] Yet for those who are willing to persevere, the work of this raconteur of a latter-day Puritan and for all his jolliness, ever the strictest of Baptists, still yields incomparable riches: 'His work, without doubt, is the foundation stone of the historiography of Welsh Nonconformity'.[13]

Although contemporaries, colleagues in the Department of History and in the Faculty of Theology at the university in Bangor, and close personal friends, Richards and R.T. Jenkins possessed hugely contrasting personalities. If Richards was a countryman at heart, Jenkins had about him the urbanity and sophistication of the city dweller. Whereas Richards produced scholarship by the pound in thick, unwieldy, heavy-spined tomes, Jenkins's forte was the scholarly essay in the style of *belles lettres*, and the slim and sleek (though never slight) volume at most. If the one had almost no gift for synthesis, the other was virtually *all* synthesis and subtlety and nuance. Richards was noisy and bold—'Shyness is not a trait one associates with Thomas Richards'[14]—who admired men of unambiguous conviction in the Vavasor Powell or John Miles mould, though Jenkins found it difficult to commit himself to any cause beyond a cultured and somewhat fastidious intellectualism. 'His books conjure up the atmosphere of a civilized parlour discourse', as R. Tudur Jones

---

9   Jenkins, *Protestant Dissenters in Wales*, p. 6.

10   Jenkins, '*Doc Tom*', p. 97.

11   Jenkins, '*Doc Tom*', p. 95.

12   Michael R. Watts, *The Dissenters: From the Reformation to the French Revolution* (Oxford: Clarendon Press, 1978), p. 513.

13   Jenkins, *Hanesydd Piwritaniaeth*, p. 21.

14   Jenkins, *Protestant Dissenters in Wales*, p. 5.

recalled.[15] And whereas Richards's prose style is ghastly, Jenkins has a lightness of touch which makes his work invariably a delight to read.

R.T. Jenkins (1881–1969) was the child of the new Welsh Victorian bourgeoisie, his father having moved from Liverpool to an administrative post in the recently founded university college at Bangor. The death of his parents marked his removal to Bala, Merionethshire, where he was brought up from the age of six by his virtually monoglot Welsh-speaking grandparents. Here he was immersed in the culture of Calvinistic Methodism at its finest which blended experiential piety and deep moral seriousness with a profound appreciation for solid theological scholarship. The spirit of Lewis Edwards, first principal at Bala's denominational seminary, still permeated the town, while even as a youth Jenkins would be mightily impressed by the theologian, exegete and patristic scholar Thomas Charles Edwards, who succeeded his father as the seminary's principal, and his supremely erudite colleague, the church historian Hugh Williams.

From Bala, where he was grounded in the classics in the local grammar school, Jenkins proceeded in 1898 to the University of Wales, Aberystwyth, and, under the tutelage of C.H. Hertford, gained an abiding fascination for the intellectual developments of the eighteenth century before graduating with first class honours in English. Further study took him to Trinity College, Cambridge, where, although reading for the English tripos, he fell under the spell of the church historian Henry Melvill Gwatkin. His intention to pursue postgraduate work in philology and linguistics on the continent was thwarted by lack of funds, though after beginning his teaching career in 1904 in the lovely rural setting of Brecon, he commenced research into the development of the feudal system during the Middle Ages. In order to gain a mastery of Roman law as part of this scheme, he enrolled for the Cambridge LlB which he passed in 1910. Nothing came of the research in terms of a higher degree, though some of his earliest scholarly articles were on late medieval and early modern history in Wales.[16] What this training had given him was an exceedingly catholic breadth of expertise in both ancient and modern history (especially the history of ideas) and an intellectual mastery of language and literature which would set him in good stead for his subsequent academic career.

Although affirming the moral tenets of Nonconformity and appreciative of the rigour of Reformed thought, Jenkins's sceptical cast of mind led him to be suspicious of dogmatism and over-definition in matters of doctrine. Yet a feeling for the numinous along with the

---

15   R. Tudur Jones, 'R.T. Jenkins: yr Hanesydd Eglwysig', *Y Traethodydd* 125 (1970), p. 92.

16   E.g., R.T. Jenkins, 'Y Chwyldroad Cymdeithasol yng Nghymru yng Nghyfnod y Tuduriaid', *Y Beirniad* 6 (1916), pp. 17-26, 88-98.

discovery, as a school-boy, of Dean Farrar's humanizing *Life of Jesus*, preserved his faith and, indeed, kept him within the Calvinistic Methodist fold. It was through a theology of experience, so characteristic of Protestant liberalism, that Jenkins discovered a key to appreciate the way in which the spiritual energies of the past had fashioned the Nonconformist culture of Wales which he would eventually elucidate with such sympathy and insight. 'The essence of religion, I suppose, is a feeling for the unseen, or rather a consciousness of that feeling', he wrote, 'while theology is the rationalization thereof'.[17] An empiricist in historical method with a fascination for the working of the religious mind, he would become a uniquely subtle interpreter of the Methodist experience in Wales, especially during the eighteenth and early nineteenth centuries.

Unlike his fellow schoolmaster, Thomas Richards, Jenkins was not apparently consumed by an ambition to contribute to his generation's knowledge of the Welsh past. Like a renaissance scholar, he was happy to follow his interests in the leisure afforded him as a teacher of classics and English in the civilized grammar school of a pleasant county town. His description of Brecon during the balmy Edwardian years is idyllic.[18] Here he learned, even more than at Cambridge, to appreciate the liturgy, life and theological breadth of the Anglican Church—the town itself was dominated by the beautiful Abbey Church of St John—and even more to read assiduously in virtually all branches of ancient and modern history. A not insignificant part of this programme of study was taken up with a voracious consumption of *cofiannau pregethwyr*, the rather stylized preachers' biographies published in their hundreds by a vibrant Welsh Nonconformity during its nineteenth-century heyday. In all he became probably the best read schoolmaster in all of Wales. An early article illustrates the scope of his interests during the Brecon years and the standards which he deemed necessary by those who would keep abreast of the study of the early church. 'Some of us will regard a sound knowledge of the history of the Church in the past a safeguard, which will enable us to keep our heads above the flood of evanescent theories so characteristic of our own days',[19] he wrote. Dispensing advice both to the denominational seminaries (of which there was one, the Congregational Memorial College, in Brecon itself) and to the nascent faculties of theology in the University of Wales, he took it for granted that study of patristic theology and early church history would demand a mastery,

---

17   R.T. Jenkins, *Yr Apêl at Hanes* (Wrecsam: Hughes a'i Fab, 1930), p. 87.

18   See 'Moreia (M.C.), Trefernard', in *Casglu Ffyrdd* (Wrecsam: Hughes a'i Fab, 1956), pp. 55-67, and the chapter in his autobiography, *Edrych Yn Ôl* (Llundain: Clwb Llyfrau Cymraeg, 1968), pp. 176-228.

19   R.T. Jenkins, 'Wales and the Study of Church History', *The Welsh Outlook* (1917), p. 149.

among students, of Greek and Latin, a grounding in the subject's foundation documents both biblical and patristic, 'a sound knowledge of Ancient History in its widest sense', and a training in the methods of historical research. 'Take an unfortunate man', he surmised, 'who had only managed to find room in his scheme for "Intermediate" Greek or Latin, imagine him settled in a country manse and wishing to read the Fathers, and then set him down in front of Clement of Alexandria or Tertullian. To put it mildly, he will receive an unpleasant shock'![20] Ministerial education and scholarly attainments among Welsh Nonconformist ordinands may have increased steeply by this time, but the discipline here presupposed was unrealistic by any standards. What it does show is that historical scholarship of the utmost integrity and rigour was now a possibility within an extension, at least, of the chapel culture of Wales.

In 1917 Jenkins moved from leisurely Brecon to the bustle of Cardiff and its distinguished High School. Here he was introduced to the company of an academic and cultural elite which revolved around W.J. Gruffydd, professor of Welsh at the University College of South Wales and Monmothshire, and one of the principal shapers of scholarly opinion in Wales during the inter-war years. Realizing Jenkins's intellectual acumen, his exceedingly wide knowledge and considerable literary talents, Gruffydd persuaded him to contribute to *Y Llenor* (*The Litterateur*), the magazine which, under Gruffydd's editorship, would become the prime focus for Welsh cultural discussion from 1922 onwards. His contributions to *Y Llenor* showed how erudite, accomplished and elegant a scholar Jenkins was, though it was his first published volume, *Hanes Cymru yn y Ddeunawfed Ganrif* (*A History of Wales in the Eighteenth Century*) (1928), which convinced Wales of his genius. It was on the basis of this, along with his a score of stylish and immensely perceptive articles in the Welsh academic press, that he was appointed, in 1930, to a lectureship in the newly created Department of Welsh History at Bangor where he would remain, latterly as professor, for the rest of his career.

Although he continued to publish on modern and even medieval European history (in, for instance, *Ffrainc a'i Phobl* (*France and her People*) (1930)), during the rest of his career he would concentrate on religious subjects, especially the Methodist and Nonconformist inheritance of Wales. Even when treating social matters, it was to the religious debate that he would return again and again. His *Hanes Cymru yn y Bedwaredd Ganrif ar Bymtheg* (*A History of Wales in the Nineteenth Century*) of 1933, a more intentionally academic study than its predecessor, treats politics and social developments in the light of religion

---

20   Jenkins, 'Wales and the Study of Church History', pp. 181-82.

and has virtually nothing at all on economics or industrialization. Thomas Richards's quip that his colleague's first book, though ostensibly on social history, was in fact a history of the Methodist Revival with a few references to spinning and weaving thrown in, encapsulated an abiding truth. Yet as time went on he would hardly even apologize for this religious bent. Subsequent volumes such as his study of the Congregational tradition in Merionethshire *Hanes Cynulleidfa Hen Gapel Llanuwchllyn* (*A History of the Congregation of the Old Chapel, Llanuwchllyn*) (1937), the minutely researched *The Moravian Brethren in North Wales* (1938), as well as the compilation of scholarship published in his final volume *Yng Nghysgod Trefeca* (*In the Shadow of Trefeca*) in 1968, are exercises in 'church history', pure and simple. Religious themes, though always presented with an envious lightness of touch, are also prevalent in a recently published memorial volume of his occassional pieces.[21] Although an unrepentant theological 'modernist' (which on occasion leads him seriously to misjudge the doctrinal integrity of such late Victorian upholders of biblical orthodoxy as Lewis Edwards of Bala), he always preserved the critical distance and detatchment of the 'objective' scholar. Neverthless, by mid-century Jenkins had become, along with Thomas Richards, the principal interpreter of the modern Welsh religious past.

As a religious historian, Jenkins's principal interest was in questions of personality or, more simply, in people. If he was suspicious of over-definition in personal faith—though he was always scrupulously fair and immensely illuminating when elucidating the doctrinal disputes of the pre-Victorian Nonconformist past—he eschewed class analysis or any interpretation of his subjects along ideological lines: 'For him the heart of the historian's work was the study of the motives and character and actions of the individual'.[22] His enthralment with individuals, the *dramatis personae* who populated both centre-stage and the more distant wings of the Nonconformist pageant, was boundless and his insights into their character were usually penetrating and judicious. In his work the hagiography and myth-making of pre-critical Dissent has wholly disappeared, replaced by the rich ambiguity of human motivation and action—even regenerate motivation—in all their complexity. 'It is good for us to remember', he claimed, 'how inexplicable man is...as we see daily the strangest combinations of opposing elements in the same personality'.[23] Ever conscious of the weaknesses of his people, their flaws of character as well as their undeniable strengths, a broad, generous humanism banishes most traces of cynicism which may have been

---

21   Emlyn Evans (ed.), *R.T. Jenkins: Cwpanaid o De a Diferion Eraill* (Dinbych: Gwasg Gee, 1997).

22   Jones, 'Yr Hanesydd Eglwysig', p. 92.

23   Jenkins, *Yr Apêl at Hanes*, p. 69.

engendered by his critique. Thus the sectarian exclusivism of the Older Dissenting Mathias Maurice, or the at times insufferable spiritual arrogance of the revivalist Howel Harris, or the ultra-Calvinist autocracy of John Elias, the nineteenth-century Methodist 'pope', are all placed in their proper context to yield a richly variagated mix of flawed but forgiven humanity through whom grace is allowed to shine: 'Whatever we want to say about heaven, in this world we are but *men*. And "a saved man" is but a *man* after all.'[24] Even the plethora of articles which he wrote for *The Dictionary of Welsh Biography*, a staggering 600 or so in all, illustrate this fascination for the personal and are a rich source not only for the factual basis of Welsh Dissent but for an understanding of its inner life as well.[25]

The different elements in Jenkins's craft—a meticulous attention to detail which rarely intrudes on the flow of his prose, a parenthetic, discursive style which included copious use of exclamation marks and much italicization, the keeping of a tight rein on the subject of discussion while roaming far and wide before returning, unerringly, to the path with the reader having learned much by the digression, as well as a deft talent for choosing the apt comparison—contributed to what Geoffrey Nuttall described as 'the genius of R.T. Jenkins'. 'His knowledge was so extensive, his curiosity so absorbing, his interests so wide, his perception of illuminating contrasts and comparisons so lively', [26] that Jenkins deserves a place not only among the foremost historians of modern Wales but as a uniquely perceptive interpreter of British Nonconformity as well. As Nuttall has said elsewhere, 'R.T. Jenkins will stand the test of time as a historian. Right to the end of his long life he was concerned to discover, establish and understand the actual facts, in all their oblivion, doubtfulness and mystery of their ramifications, detail and inter-relation'.[27] That he did so with the artistry of a master of Welsh prose will ensure that his contributions will endure for a long time to come.

By the mid-twentieth century Nonconformist historiography had long established its credentials as a scientific discipline within the theological faculties of the University of Wales. What is more, the results of research, according to its methods, were being brought to bear on the churches' self-understanding and upon how they could apply the past to the challenges of an ever more secularized present. The study of Nonconformist history even as a detatched, ecumenically sensitive discipline, still existed in order to assist the Christian witness in Wales and

---

24   R.T. Jenkins, *Yn Nghysgod Trefeca* (Caernarfon: Llyfrfa'r M.C., 1968), p. 100.

25   See G.F. Nuttall, 'R.T. Jenkins's Articles in the *Dictionary of Welsh Biography*', *Journal of the Welsh Bibliographical Society* 10 (1970), pp. 178-93.

26   G.F. Nuttall, 'The Genius of R.T. Jenkins', *Transactions of the Honourable Society of Cymmrodorion* (1977), pp. 182-83.

27   Nuttall, 'R.T. Jenkins's Articles', p. 178.

to help increase its effectiveness. In that sense it was still *committed* history and not a free or self-standing enterprise. If the discipline had come of age with such scholars as Richards and Jenkins, there were other students and researchers in each of the different traditions whose work complemented theirs. If few possessed their level of erudition or historical skills, they could at least work within the parameters which now governed the study of the Welsh Nonconformist past.

Although a contemporary of Thomas Richards and R.T. Jenkins and fellow member on the Bangor staff, the Congregational historian John Morgan Jones (1873–1946) had, in a way, more in common with an earlier generation than with the historiography of the time. A graduate of Mansfield College, Oxford, and a student of Adolf von Harnack's at Berlin, Jones held the chair of church history at the Bala–Bangor college between 1914 and his retirement in 1945. As the most pronounced theological liberal of his denomination, his interpretation of the Independent tradition as the progressive emancipation of the human soul from priestcraft and creedalism did scant justice to either the Calvinism or high ecclesiolgy of the pre-Victorian past. Despite this Jones was a scholar of distinction whose varied religious and educational interests prevented him from contributing to historical studies to the extent that he might.[28] Along with illuminating chapters in the volume celebrating the tercentenery of Welsh Independency *Hanes ac Egwyddorion Annibynwyr Cymru, 1639–1939 (The History and Principles of Welsh Congregationalism, 1639–1939)*, his principal legacy as a historian was in editing *Y Cofiadur*, the journal of his denomination's historical society, from its inception in 1923. Among the Baptists W.J. Rhys (1880–1967) combined his pastoral duties with assiduous research mostly into printed sources, to produce a useful guide entitled *Penodau yn Hanes y Bedyddwyr Cymreig (Chapters in the History of the Welsh Baptists)* in 1949 with a shorter English version, *A Brief History of the Baptists in Wales*, appearing seven years later. Through these works, a host of individual chapel histories and numerous articles in the *Transactions* of the Welsh Baptist Historical Society and other magazines as well, he became the chief link between the generation of Thomas Shankland and that of T.M. Bassett more than half a century later.

The single Calvinistic Methodist researcher who linked the work of Richard Bennett with that of R.T. Jenkins was M.H. Jones (1873–1930) whose vast and carefully mapped inventory of the manuscript collection at Howel Harris's Trefeca home surveyed in minute detail the extent of the field which Bennett, Jenkins and others, have since managed to till.

---

28   For an assessment of his theology, see Robert Pope, *Seeking God's Kingdom: The Nonconformist Social Gospel in Wales, 1906–39* (Cardiff: University of Wales Press, 1999), pp. 67-82.

His *The Itinerary of Howel Harris* published in three installations between 1923 and 1927 and his *The Trevecka Letters*, edited postumously by R.T. Jenkins in 1932, illustrate the minute and painstaking nature of his scholarship. By opening up the field, subsequent students notably John Thickens (1862–1952) in *Howel Harris yn Llundain* (*Howel Harris in London*), a study of the revivalist's interaction with the Methodism of England's capital city during the 1730s and 40s (1938), and the various transcripts made by Tom Beynon,[29] have taken the study further. What these students did for Howel Harris and the mid-eighteenth century, D.E. Jenkins (1864–1937) did for Thomas Charles, leader of the Welsh Calvinistic Methodists during the late-eighteenth and early nineteenth century. His vast, forbidding three volume biography, *Thomas Charles of Bala* (1908), is a quarry which still yields much valuable material though the reader is obliged to take along his own spade. His perceptive analysis of the Methodist fathers' ecclesiolgy *Calvinistic Methodist Holy Orders* (1911) shows that he could synthesize material as well as transcribe it, though R.T. Jenkins's wry comment is, perhaps, worth quoting: 'His style is infelicitious, and in particular he was prone to adopt an aggresive tone which led many to deem he was unkind'.[30] Neverthless he made a valuable contribution to the Welsh Calvinistic Methodists' knowledge of their heritage.

The same can be said of D.D. Williams (1862–1938) whose 1926 *Llawlyfr Hanes Cyfundeb y Methodistiaid Calfinaidd* (*A Handbook of the History of the Calvinistic Methodists*) served as a modest but surefooted guide written to coincide broadly with the constitutional changes which would transform the Welsh Calvinistic Methodist denomination into the Presbyterian Church of Wales. This was followed in 1930 by the highly thought provoking *Methodistiaeth Galfinaidd Cymru: Ymgais at Athroniaeth ei Hanes* (*Welsh Calvinistic Methodism: An Attempt at a Philosophy of its History*) and the elegant but slighter *The Calvinistic Methodism of Wales* (n.d., but c.1934), both by John Roberts (1880– 1959), the denomination's foremost ecclesiastical statesman of the inter-war years. They utilize the wealth of primary material which had by then

---

29   Tom Beynon, *Howell Harris, Reformer and Soldier* (Caernarfon: The Calvinistic Methodist Bookroom, 1958), *Howell Harris's Visits to London* (Aberystwyth: The Cambrian News Press, 1960), and the posthumously published *Howell Harris's Visits to Pembrokeshire* (Aberystwyth: The Cambrian News Press, 1966); Beynon (1886–1961) served as editor of the *Journal* of the Historical Society of the Presbyterian Church of Wales between 1933 and 1947, see E.D. Jones and B.F. Roberts (eds), *Y Bywgraffiadur Cymreig, 1951–70* (Llundain: Anrhydeddus Gymdeithas y Cymmrodorion, 1997) *s.n.* 'Beynon, Thomas', pp. 11-12.

30   R.T. Jenkins, 'Jenkins, David Erwyd', in Lloyd and Jenkins (eds), *Dictionary of Welsh Biography*, pp. 431-42.

been made available to weave a powerful and convincing theory of denominational identity.

Staying with what by the second half of the twentieth century was coming to be accepted as the Presbyterian Church of Wales, there was something romantic if not heroic about the career of its principal historian following R.T. Jenkins, namely Gomer Morgan Roberts (1904–93). One of the eleven children of a Carmarthenshire coalminer, Roberts began working at the Pencae'reithin pit in his home village of Llandybie at the age of thirteen and remained there for six years. Like many Welsh colliers, quarrymen and farm labourers of the time, by partaking in the vibrant chapel-based culture of his community, he learned the value of the word, spoken, written and in song. Membership of an evening class on Welsh literature led by John Griffiths, a local Baptist minister who was a New Testament scholar of repute, opened his eyes to the scope of his nation's cultural tradition, while attendance at a corresponding class on economics—now coming to tipify the political radicalization of the South Wales coalfield—led to his being awarded a worker's scholarship for a year's study at Fircroft College, Bournville. As it transpired, it was not to a career in politics or trades unionism that the young miner would be drawn but to the ministry of the Presbyterian Church in Wales.

In order to finance his entry to the preparatory school at Trefeca, necessary before embarking on the full theological course at Aberystwyth, a half-dozen of his fellow miners clubbed together to produce a volume of verse, the proceeds of which were intended to help him on his way. That six young colliers were proficient enough in Welsh poetry to publish a book of verse, *O Lwch y Lofa* (*From the Dust of the Mine*), with its sub-heading *A Volume of Verse by Six Carmarthenshire Miners* (1924)—was wonder enough, but that it sold immediately in its thousands throughout the anthracite field of south-west Wales, is high praise for the quality of the working-class culture engendered by the Nonconformity of the day. Gomer Roberts himself contributed sonnets and lyrics to the volume, though it was not as a poet but as a historian that his reputation would be made.

He began publishing essays on denominational history during the early 1930s with his first slim volume, *Methodistiaeth fy Mro* (*The Methodism of my Locality*), a study of the beginnings of the movement in east Carmarthenshire, appearing in 1938. A year later saw the publication, by the University of Wales Press, of a substantial and excellently crafted history of his home parish, *Hanes Plwyf Llandybie* (*A History of Llandybie Parish*). More than forty books were to follow, some 700 popular or scholaraly articles as well as 110 contributions to the *Dictionary of Welsh Biography*. All this was achieved along side a pastoral ministry first at Clydach in the Swansea Valley, then at Pontrhydyfen, Glamorganshire, and finally at St Dogmael's near

Cardigan. For a man who never claimed to be a scholar in the traditional sense, he nevertheless possessed all the abilities of the effective historian: a wide knowledge of the appropriate sources especially those of the eighteenth century, a critical eye for the transcription of texts, and a fine appreciation for poetry and literary culture which would make him a particularly good interpreter of the hymnody of Dafydd Wiliam, Morgan Rhys, Dafydd Jones of Caeo and William Williams of Pantycelyn in particular. His early work, which included a biography of Peter Williams, a younger contemporary of Howel Harris, induced the University of Wales to award him the degree of MA *honoris causa* in 1949, while further acknowledgement of his, by then, lifelong contribution to religious history occurred in 1985 with the bestowal of the senior honorary degree of DLitt.

Roberts's main scholarly contribution was in charting the factual course of the early Welsh Methodist movement, especially the development of its *seiadau* or fellowship meetings, and an assessment of the background and influence of Williams of Pantycelyn. The two volume biography of the hymnist *Y Pêr Ganiedydd (The Sweet Singer)* was published in 1949 and 1958 respectively, while full transcriptions of some of the most important manuscripts appeared in *Selected Trevecka Letters* (1956 and 1962) and thereafter in numerous supplements in the *Journal* of the Presbyterian Church of Wales. His English translation of Richard Bennett's *Blynyddoedd Cymtaf Methodistiaeth*, entitled *The Early Years of Howell Harris*, was issued in 1962 and the first volume of a much needed diplomatic edition of Williams of Pantycelyn's poetry in 1964 with his prose works following three years later. An interesting short Welsh biography of Howel Harris was forthcoming in 1969, while 1973 saw the publication, under Roberts's editorship, of *Y Deffroad Mawr (The Great Awakening)*, volume one of the denomination's official history. A second volume, covering the years 1762–1811, appeared in 1978. These, along with innumerable contributions to his church's historical *Journal* which he edited for thirty years, secured his reputation not only as a denominational historian but as an important interpreter of the history of Wales. Although he was not gifted with the academic capacity of Thomas Richards or the critical imagination of R.T. Jenkins, his energy was phenomenal and commitment to his discipline beyond reproach. A modest, self-effacing man, more conscious of his weaknesses in the realm of professional scholarship than his manifest strengths, he was, perhaps, the century's greatest single benefactor to the study and dissemination of the history of the Calvinistic Methodists in Wales.[31]

---

31 See J.E. Caerwyn Williams, 'Y Parchedig Gomer Morgan Roberts MA, DLitt', in *Cylchgrawn Hanes* 16–17 (1992–93), pp. 3-8, and Huw Walters, 'Gomer Morgan Roberts (1904–93)', *Y Traethodydd* 148 (1993), pp. 130-34.

Whereas Welsh Methodism in the eighteenth century was Calvinistic Methodism, by the nineteenth century Methodism of the Wesleyan variety began to make inroads into Wales. Its prime modern historian was A.H. Williams (1907–96) whose MA thesis, written under the supervision of R.T. Jenkins, became the basis for the movement's official history, *Welsh Wesleyan Methodism, 1800–58* (1935). Readers had to wait until 1971 in the same author's accomplished *John Wesley in Wales* to know more about the pre-1800 period, though Williams, who was a layman and professional historian, wrote much in the intervening years in *Bathafarn*, the magazine of the Wesleyan Historical Society in Wales. An equally gifted author and student was Griffith T. Roberts (1912–91), one of the ablest ministers of his generation. His succinct English biography, *Howell Harris* (1956), was a sympathetic portrait of a Calvinist revivalist by an Arminian historian. Roberts's interest in doctrinal themes was given full rein in *Dadleuon Methodistiaeth Gynnar* (*Early Methodist Controversies*) (1970), an excellent guide to the sometimes convoluted debates on election and free will were such a feature of the evangelical mind. It was Roberts, too, who was invited to contribute the chapter 'Methodism in Wales' in volume three of the standard work *A History of the Methodist Church in Great Britain* (1983) edited by Rupert Davies and Gordon Rupp.

If Methodists of both hues have reflected deeply on their heritage during the last fifty years, the same is true of other Dissenting traditions as well. T.M. Bassett's (1910–2002) *The Welsh Baptists* (1977) superceded W.J. Rhys's earlier work to earn its place as the standard denominational history to date. It is, in the view of Geraint H. Jenkins, 'a lucid work based on a thorough knowledge of primary sources and deep reflection'.[32] Among the Congregationalists John Morgan Jones's successor in the chair of church history at Bala–Bangor and later the principal of the Brecon Memorial College and of the Coleg Coffa, Swansea, following that, was the polymathic scholar W.T. Pennar Davies (1911–96). One of the most quietly charismatic Nonconformist ministers of his generation, Pennar (as he was universally known) was set for a glittering academic career in English literature when, having returned from postgraduate studies at Yale, he was converted and called to minister among the Welsh Independents. During his wartime training at Mansfield College, Oxford (he had graduated from Cardiff and Balliol in the 1930s), he married a Jewish-Christian refugee from Nazi Germany, and it was as the most internationally minded of Welsh nationalists and panoramic of Christian pacifists that he made his stand. Although a church historian by profession, he was an artist by inclination and a poet and novelist by choice. His interpretation of history was in turn romantic

---

32   Jenkins, *Protestant Dissenters in Wales*, p. 7.

and realistic, enigmatic and profound. His championing of the cause of Pelagius as a significant proto-Welsh theological figure illustrates his eccentricities as well as the depth of his patristic learning. 'Gifted, erudite, influential, beloved, not only with the Independents among whom he dwelt but throughout Wales',[33] his contribution to church history, as opposed to criticism and creative literature, was meagre: a 1951 study of church and state *Y Ddau Gleddyf* (*The Two Swords*), a 1962 pamphlet on the separatist martyr John Penry and various essays on the Christian tradition in Wales. He could, of course, write history with admirable fluency. 'His long article "Episodes in the History of Brecknockshire Dissent" is a little masterpiece', commented G.F. Nuttall. 'Its broad sweep, mastery of the subject and organization of detail, and illustrations that illuminate, make it a model among local history studies, while its insights and reflectiveness carry the reader far beyond the immediate neighbourhood. It is worth reading again and again'.[34] This attractive and frankly enigmatic figure made his contribution more as a poet and literature than as a significant researcher into the Welsh Nonconformist past.

The greatest historian of twentieth-century Congregationalism and the most substantial Welsh church historian of all was R. Tudur Jones (1921–98). He was a man who invited superlatives. For the literary critic R. M. Jones, 'He is one of our greatest historians ever'.[35] A journalist of considerable flare, a stylist of masterful elegance and an author of prodigious output, he ranked among the foremost Welsh intellectuals of the century. 'When we consider the huge sum and versatility of Tudur Jones's work, it will doubtless be concluded, in the fulness of time, that he was the principal intellectual leader of Welsh religion since Thomas Jones [of Denbigh] and Thomas Charles, and a giant of twentieth century Protestantism in Wales'.[36] If R.M. Jones's hyperbole was partly born of an inordinate theological sympathy with his subject, the words of Geraint H. Jenkins, the current doyen of Welsh social historians, are equally striking. Not only was Tudur Jones 'one of our foremost historians and a master of Welsh prose', but 'a Christian historian of import—indeed the greatest in the history of our nation'.[37]

---

33   Geoffrey F. Nuttall, 'Pennar Davies (12 November 1911–29 December 1996) Complexio oppositorum', *Journal of the United Reformed Church Historical Society* 5 (1997), p. 574.

34   Nuttall, 'Pennar Davies', p. 525; see W.T. Pennar Davies, 'Episodes in the History of Brecknockshire Dissent', in *Brycheiniog* 3 (1957), pp. 5-73.

35   R.M. Jones, 'R. Tudur Jones fel llenor a newyddiadurwr', *Cristion* 83 (1997), p. 15.

36   Jones, 'R. Tudur Jones', p. 17.

37   Geraint H. Jenkins, 'R. Tudur Jones fel ysgolhaig a hanesydd', *Cristion* 83 (1997), p. 21.

Tudur Jones' interest in church history was first kindled in the Rhyl County High School during the 1930s. His history master, A.M. Houghton, was both a fervent evangelical Protestant and a bibliophile with an encyclopaedic knowledge of the English Puritan tradition. He was encouraged by Houghton to study Spurgeon's sermons not only for spiritual edification but to appreciate plain and powerful English prose. He also received a thorough grounding in the classics by the school's headmaster, the leading Welsh Anglican layman T.I. Ellis, which was to serve him well in his subsequent career. It was in Carmel Congregational Church in Rhyl that the young Tudur Jones felt the call to Christian ministry, which took him in October 1939 to the University College of North Wales, Bangor, as a ministerial student. Despite pressure from Sir Ifor Williams, the professor of Welsh, who tried his best to persuade this obviously gifted student to read for a degree in his department, Jones chose instead to study philosophy taking a first in 1942. His specialist subjects in the BD were philosophy of religion and church history in which he gained a double distinction on the basis of the highest marks ever recorded by the University of Wales's Faculty of Theology. Both subjects were taught by the staff of the Bala–Bangor Congregational College, J.E. Daniel and John Morgan Jones. Daniel's influence was profound: it was he who provided Tudur Jones with a grounding in a biblical orthodoxy which combined the evangelical piety of his upbringing, an appreciation for the Reformed tradition from Augustine to Karl Barth and a passion for the ongoing work of the gospel in Wales. The effect of John Morgan Jones was to be quite different. Theologically they were poles apart, but it was from him that Tudur Jones learned to revere openness, liberality and the tradition of freedom which radical Nonconformity enshrined. That Morgan Jones paid more than lip service to tolerance was obvious in that it was he who urged his pupil to do research in history as Bala–Bangor would soon require a church historian on its staff. It was with that in mind that he left Bangor for Oxford in 1945 intent on doing postgraduate study in the history of the Puritan movement in Wales.

Although he was a member of Mansfield College, the board of the Faculty of Theology saw fit to appoint the eccentric and erudite Claude Jenkins, Canon of Christ Church and Professor of Ecclesiastical History, as his research supervisor. It was an excellent choice. As well as guiding his reading, Jenkins urged the young Welshman to produce a piece of writing weekly, even if he felt he had nothing new to share. This bracing discipline served the aspiring scholar well becoming one of the bases of his quite phenomenal subsequent productiveness. With characteristic assiduousness, Jones completed his DPhil, on the Puritan Vavasor Powell, in two years rather than the customary three, and spent two semesters in 1947–48 as a student in the Faculty of Protestant Theology at the

University of Strasbourg. He was ordained into the Congregational ministry by Principal Nathaniel Micklem in 1948 to serve the church of Seion, Baker Street, Aberystwyth, soon gaining a reputation in town and university alike as a powerful, popular preacher.

It was obvious from the beginning that Tudur Jones would best serve Welsh Nonconformity through his prodigious academic abilities. He was invited in 1950 to return to Bangor where he succeeded Pennar Davies as professor of church history at Bala–Bangor which formed part of the university's theological faculty. Although they were retired, both Thomas Richards and R.T. Jenkins were active during these years which meant that in the 1950s Bangor was the home of a triumvirate of Wales's most distinguished Nonconformist historians. Apart from his academic work, Jones was active in public and political life. He fought the Anglesey seat for Plaid Cymru during the general elections of 1955 and 1959 and it was during this period that his flare for popular journalism was given full reign with his editorial work on the party's newspapers *The Welsh Nation* and *Y Ddraig Goch* (*The Red Dragon*) and his highly amusing and often provocative column 'Sodlau Segur' in the literary monthly *Y Genhinen*. None of this supplanted his academic labours or his researches into church history as became obvious with the monumental *Con-gregationalism in England, 1662–1962*, published to coincide with the tercentenary of modern Nonconformity in 1962. It was, and remains, the most accomplished of all modern English denominational histories and a classic of its genre.

1966 saw the publication of *Hanes Annibynwyr Cymru* (*A History of the Welsh Independents*), the standard history of Congregationalism in Wales, a 'beautifully written book', according to Geraint H. Jenkins, which 'became an instant classic and is unlikely ever to be superseded'. In 1971 a biography of Vavasor Powell appeared while a plethora of articles, chapters and papers not only on Puritanism and the Nonconformist tradition but increasingly on Methodism and religion and society in the nineteenth century, all of which served to remind the reading public just how remarkable an author Tudur Jones was. Geraint Jenkins's comments are worth quoting in full: 'In many ways, the writings of R. Tudur Jones are akin to those of Thomas Richards insofar as they represent the fruits of meticulous research, demonic energy, and a sympathetic but critical appraisal of the subject. Where they differ is in presentation. While three generations of readers have understandably balked at Richards's hideous literary style, the writings of R. Tudur Jones bear the unmistakable stamp of a literary craftsman. He is quite simply the most prolific and important writer on religion in Stuart Wales'.[38]

---

38   Jenkins, *Protestant Dissenters in Wales*, p. 7.

Tudur Jones's skill as a historian lay in a combination of abilities rarely present in a single individual. Apart from an enormous strength of intellect, an immensely retentive memory and huge powers of concentration, he was a superb wordsmith. His command of language, expressed in the use of telling simile or apt metaphor, was unsurpassed, while his feeling for structure whether in sentences, paragraphs, chapters or whole books, was unerring. He possessed a clarity of exposition and expression which has yet to be excelled in written Welsh: 'In Tudur's hands, the Welsh language becomes an exquisite precision instrument, and it is difficult to imagine him ever fashioning an inelegant or uninteresting piece of work'.[39] Whereas other historians of Nonconformity presented facts and bid people do with them as they would, Jones chose his facts and distilled them in order to assess, analyse, describe and enlighten. Very often his opening sentences have the character of an invitation, engaging with his readers' interest immediately. 'John Thomas, minister of the Liverpool Tabernacle, alighted from the train with a spring in his step', was the memorable opening of his history of the Union of Welsh Independents, while the description of mid- to late-Victorian Wales in the first paragraph of *Ffydd ac Argyfwng Cenedl (Faith and a Nation's Crisis)*—'In 1890 Wales was a Christian country. The nation's face was set towards the dawn'—is equally arresting. Prose like this was compelling, enthralling and read like a novel. Possessed of all the skills of the consummate author, Tudur Jones used them to the full.

If style was important, it never masked lack of substance. Jones's breadth of knowledge and mastery of subject are invariably accompanied by a critical acumen of rare insight. He could measure the significance of data and draw conclusions which are generally wise, illuminating and not infrequently brilliant. His three chapters charting the course and assessing the meaning of the 1904–05 religious revival in *Ffydd ac Argyfwng Cenedl* are quite outstanding in this respect, though the same critical quality is present throughout the corpus of his work. Although indebted to his teachers, he surpassed them all. Combining John Morgan Jones's clarity of expression with J.E. Daniel's powers of advocacy and agility of mind, Thomas Richards's mastery of detail with R.T. Jenkins's understanding of people and fluency of prose, his range, depth and overall capacity put him in a class of his own. A sure conviction of God's sovereignty in the world, the outworking of his will in the dynamics of grace, and the interplay of faith and culture within the constraints of modern Welsh history, gave him a perspective which was envigorating and hopeful. It encompassed a spiritual vision which has benefitted

---

39   Jenkins, 'R. Tudur Jones', p. 22.

Nonconformity and Christian scholarship greatly and will continue to do so for the foreseeable future as well.

More and more during the 1970s Jones's interest moved towards the mid- and later nineteenth century. A remarkably compelling chapter on the Calvinistic character of Welsh culture, two magisterial essays on the history of biblical interpretation between 1860–90, a marvellous 1975 history of the Union of Welsh Independents which maps much of the social and intellectual development of Victorian and post-Victorian Wales, and other contributions besides, culminated in what will possibly be his most enduring academic legacy, the two-volume *Ffydd ac Argyfwng Cenedl: Crefydd yng Nghymru, 1890–1914* (*Faith and a Nation's Crisis: Religion in Wales, 1890–1914*) (1981–82). More than a history of Victorian and Edwardian religion, it consists of a hugely learned assessment of Welsh life in all its baffling complexity during an outwardly flourishing but inwardly anxious phase of our fairly recent past. The three chapters examining the 1904–05 religious revival comprise the most perceptive analysis of that phenomenon to have been published anywhere and will remain a key text for our understanding of revivalism generally. This work, taken as a whole, afforded the clearest understanding to date of the roots of the malaise of Welsh Nonconformity which became the defining characteristic of the social history of twentieth-century Wales. It is as much a work of prophecy as of history and its value remains inestimable.

If the chapel life of early twentieth-century Wales was ebullient and optimistic, Nonconformity at present shows signs of a sickness unto death. The denominational structures are everywhere under strain, while even the faithful have reconciled themselves to the inevitability of decline.[40] Yet despite all, Christian faith persists and there are still those who draw sustenance and inspiration from contemplating a noble past. In drawing this chapter to a close some worthy contemporary historians could well be mentioned. Eifion Evans, Goronwy P. Owen, D. Ben Rees, J.E. Wynne Davies and others still ensure that the Calvinistic Methodist contribution to the Welsh Christian past will not suffer neglect, while Geraint Tudur's recent biography of Howel Harris promises to revolutionize our understanding of both the content and context of the revivalist's life. Among the Baptists D. Hugh Matthews remains assiduous in his researches while Noel Gibbard, Dafydd Wyn Wiliam and Alun Tudur are still shedding much new light on aspects of the Independent past. If social historians of the immense calibre of Sir Glanmor Williams and Ieuan Gwynedd Jones have taken Nonconformist history with a seriousness not always afforded by a secular academe, professional

---

40   See D. Densil Morgan, *The Span of the Cross: Christian Religion and Society in Wales, 1914–2000* (Cardiff: University of Wales Press, 1999), pp. 261-79.

scholars of such distinction as Derec Llwyd Morgan, Geraint H. Jenkins and, among a younger generation, Eryn White and Robert Pope, will surely bring even more insights to bear on the glories and foibles of yesterday's Dissent. Yet whatever the new millennium has to offer, it was during the twentieth century that the historiography of Welsh Protestant Nonconformity came of age. It will always have about it something of a golden age.

CHAPTER 5

Developments in Liturgy and Worship in Twentieth-Century Protestant Nonconformity

Norman Wallwork

General Issues

Only among three Nonconformist traditions, namely the Brethren, the Scotch Baptists and the Churches of Christ has the Breaking of the Bread or the Lord's Supper been observed weekly. A key element in this narrative must therefore centre around what most Free Church congregations do at Sunday morning and evening worship when the Lord's Supper is not celebrated. Alongside this normative service we look at the observance of the two so-called gospel sacraments of the Lord's Supper and Christian initiation, at the ordinances concerning marriages, funerals, services for anointing, healing and reconciliation, and at ordination and commissioning services to various ministries. There are also one or two services generally peculiar to the Free Churches, such as the annual Methodist Covenant Service, the Watchnight, Love Feasts and various anniversaries. Does twentieth-century Free Church worship include the Whit walks and the 'Sermons' of the northern cotton and wool towns? How interesting that these were the very same communities whose merchant chapels produced their own psalm and chant books and privately bound liturgies.

General issues affecting services and service books include the observance of the Christian year, the adoption and use of lectionaries and the status of any published hymn-book, service order or agreed text, and provision for daily prayer and devotion. Liturgical history also includes the role of the laity in public worship and also the books of liturgical advice which by their nature reveal what was not happening. Constant in the twentieth-century Free Church worship debate is unfermented communion wine and individual communion glasses (from about 1875), the open table (from about the same period) and presidency at the Lord's Supper (little debated among Baptists and Congregationalists, but much discussed by pre- and post-union Methodists). A long, long debate on the ordination of women spanned fifty years, despite the fact that Constance Coltman was the first woman to be ordained as a Free Church minister by W.E. Orchard and others at the King's Weigh House, London, on 17 September 1917. The issue of inclusive language drew strong opinions from about 1975. The all-age worship practices of the 1970s were the natural successors to the 'family worship' debate of the fifties. The century's fashions in pulpit and sanctuary clerical dress began with lay or clerical frock-coats, moved for many into cassock, gown and bands, then reverted for a goodly number into cassocks only or gray suits and coloured clerical shirts. For some the current resting place is a white cassock-alb with sacramental stoles of the liturgical season. Contrasting Free Church attitudes towards Anglican, Roman and charismatic worship affect the style and approach of Nonconformist services.

Hymns in the Free Church tradition feature greatly and must be understood not as liturgical interludes to move the action on from one key moment of worship to another, but as sung texts integral to service. The words sung, the tunes adopted and the structure and content of hymn-books and the place of sacred song in worship is a primary issue. In classical Free Church worship each hymn chosen is the appropriate vehicle for that moment of praise or prayer in the movement of the service. The content of twentieth-century Free Church hymn-books and the Free Church repertoire of hymns and songs, stands alongside the content of Free Church service books and has sometimes been a better guide to the liturgy of the people than the books in the hands of their pastors and preachers.

The story of twentieth-century Free church worship includes a number of liturgical scholars, famous preachers and service book compilers who either campaigned and published alone, or worked with small pressure groups or chaired or sat on liturgical committees. The list needs to include Congregationalists such as John Hunter, P.T. Forsyth, the Micklems (Nathaniel, E.R. and Caryl), John Huxtable, James Todd, Raymond Abba and Horton Davies; Methodists such as Thomas Bowman Stephenson, J.E. Rattenbury, John Bowmer, Raymond George and Neil Dixon; Unitarians such as J.M. Lloyd Thomas and Elliott Peaston; Baptists such as F.B. Meyer, Ernest Payne, Neville Clark and Stephen Winward; English Presbyterians such as W.E. Orchard, D. Conley Eades and J. Eric Fenn; and not least the Anglican scholar of Congregationalism Bryan Spinks.

The Unitarians

The longest list of liturgical compilations belongs to the Unitarians. The studies of A. Elliott Peaston[1] and William D. Maxwell[2] have shown that following the secession of Theophilus Lindsey from the Church of England a great string of quasi-Anglican liturgies followed on from Lindsey's 1774 *Book of Common Prayer reformed according to the plan of the late Dr. Samuel Clarke.* The eighteenth and nineteenth centuries produced over ninety local or national Unitarian liturgies or service books and another thirty or more were published after 1900. Of the total Unitarian run of approximately 130 service books, over eighty are based on the *Book of Common Prayer* including over half of those published since 1900.

The most influential Unitarian liturgy at the beginning of the twentieth century was *Common Prayer for Christian Worship*, the different editions issuing from the hands of Thomas Sadler or James Martineau. Between 1861 and 1910, *Prayers for Common Worship* passed through twelve editions. The anonymous preface, commonly held by London Unitarian ministers to have been written by Sadler and Martineau themselves, contrasts free and set forms of prayer and suggests that some will always prefer 'fitness rather than newness of language'. The compilers sought 'a new Liturgical compilation, to be gathered, in a Catholic spirit, from the devotional writings of every Christian age'. This did not, of course, prevent the editors from de-trinitizing every offending formula, phrase and blessing.

Certain principles and phrases in Sadler and Martineau were to prove the test of time in successive liturgies throughout the Free Churches. In the first instance, in addition to the first orders for Anglican Morning and Evening Prayer there are another eight versions for morning or evening. This provision, in a series of services, of a variety of versicles, suffrages, psalms, canticles and collects to give the feel of the prayer book offices without invariable repetition week by week was to be a recurring Free Church service book technique. The culling of fresh canticles from scripture and original compilations was another Free Church feature, reaching its climax in Henry Allon's masterly *Salvator Mundi*, published in his 1859 *Congregationalist Psalmist*. At first this was mistakenly believed by the Anglican compilers of the *1980 Alternative Service Book* to be an ancient hymn discovered by the Free Churches, rather than themselves. Along with many subsequent Free Church liturgies Sadler

---

1   A.E. Peaston, 'The Unitarian Liturgical Tradition', *Transactions of the Unitarian Historical Society* 16.2 (October, 1976), pp. 63-81.
2   W.D. Maxwell, *The Book of Common Prayer and the Worship of the Non-Anglican Churches* (London: Friends of Dr.Williams's Library, 1950).

and Martineau kept the Christian year and its collects but, in their case with great adaptation. Epiphany and Lent are excised and the long run of Sundays after Trinity are designated as Sundays after Whit-Sunday, since there was of course, for them, no Trinity Sunday for the subsequent weeks to come after! Also to feature in subsequent Free Church service books was a compendium of newer prayers and traditional collects for a huge variety of perceived needs and occasions. In the Order for the Administration of the Lord's Supper, hidden away in one of the communion prayers, is the phrase 'we come to this table to testify not that we are righteous, but that we sincerely love our Lord Jesus Christ, and that we desire to be his true disciples'. The Congregationalist John Hunter, a few years later, in his *Devotional Services*, was to make this the basis of his much praised and much borrowed bidding to communion 'Come to this sacred table, not because you must but because you may...'

In the Baptism of Infants there is no prayer over the water and the parents' promises may be followed by baptism in the three-fold name, or in the name of Christ or there may simply be a prayer of dedication. The pre-baptismal prayer asks that the candidate may be admitted 'into the bosom of the Church, into the service of Christ, into the arms of thy mercy and into the communion of saints'.

At the beginning of the century, The Lindsey Press, the Unitarian printing house, published W. Copeland Bowie's *Seven Services for Public Worship* (1900 and 1917). This was a simplified approach to Sadler and Martineau but with whole services for Christmas and Easter and also a Children's Service. This was the first Unitarian liturgy to include pointed psalms and canticles for Anglican chanting and music for the singing of the versicles and suffrages. To keep their upwardly mobile congregations and choirs many suburban Free Churches from the 1880s went in for introits, anthems, and chanted psalms and canticles. These devices gave an Anglican feel to Free Church worship when similar sounds were being heard in the local parish church. In 1915, The Lindsey Press also published Copeland Bowie's *Handbook for Ministers* containing orders for baptism, for the dedication of infants, for the consecration of youths, for those joining the church, for communion, marriage, visitation of the sick, and for funerals. This last service must be the first Free Church funeral rite, probably via the American Unitarian Association, to include an alternative formula for the committal at a cremation. It is also in the appendix to Copeland Bowrie's *Handbook for Ministers* that we get the first anthology of non-biblical readings for use at funerals—a Unitarian trend now in full spate among both Anglican and Dissenting traditions.

Under the guidance of E. Mortimer Rowe, the British Unitarian and Free Christian Assembly published three service books to draw together the minority of Unitarian congregations who were heavily dependent on liturgical forms and the majority who, over the years, had opted for freer forms of worship. The first two books were published in 1932. *Orders of Worship for use in Unitarian and Free Christian Congregations* drew first on the work of Sadler, Martinaeu and Compton Jones' 1878 *Book of Prayer in Thirty Orders of Worship*, then on the 1901 revised edition of Hunter's Congregationalist *Devotional Services* and finally on several contemporary anthologies of traditional prayers. *A Book of Occasional Services*, a 1932 companion volume to *Orders of Worship*, was dependent on Copeland Bowie's *Handbook* and provided services for baptisms, infant dedications, church membership, communion, marriage, visitation of the sick, burial and cremation, and more non-biblical funeral readings. Horton Davies rightly judges that the communion order in particular suffers from the Free Church blight of didacticism.[3] The third modern Unitarian service book, *Prayers of Faith and Fellowship*, edited by Mortimer Rowe and Dorothy Tarrant, was basically a set of prayers for the use of lay preachers. It included an anthology of prayers by Unitarians from both sides of the Atlantic.

The Society of Free Catholics

The most dissenting of all Unitarians was J.M. Lloyd Thomas, minister of the Old Meeting House in Birmingham and founder of the Society of Free Catholics. From about 1907 to 1935 Free Catholicism flourished among a group of Free Churchmen, most notably Lloyd Thomas himself, the Congregationalist R.J. Campbell (who became an Anglo–Catholic) and W.E. Orchard the Presbyterian minister of the Congregational King's Weigh House in Mayfair, London, who finally converted to Rome. The last, but not the only fruits of the Society of Free Catholics was the 1929 *Free Church Book of Common Prayer* of which Lloyd Thomas was the 'General Editor'. In the Martineau, Hunter and Orchard tradition the book begins with ten orders of service. These orders are followed by a General Litany based on the 1662 *Prayer Book*, a Litany of Confession and a Litany of Thanksgiving. The principal communion order, 'For the Celebration of the Eucharist', is a combination of the Roman Mass and the English *Prayer Book* of 1549. There is a full and enriched version of the 1662 *Prayer Book* collects, with Epistles and Gospels, including the 1662 saints and holy days and some extras such as Mary Madgalen, The Transfiguration, Corpus Christi and Holy Cross Day. The editors obviously had access to the proposed Anglican revisions in the 1928 *Prayer Book*. There is a wealth of additional sentences, collects and

---

3   H. Davies, *Worship and Theology in England: 5. The Ecumenical Century 1900–1965* (Princeton: Princeton University Press, 1965), p. 421.

prayers, orders for baptism and confirmation, matrimony, burial and cremation, the ordering of ministers (with the laying on of hands), orders for prime and compline, a pointed psalter in the Authorized Version, and pointed canticles from the Bible and the Apocrypha. There is no evidence that members of the congregation had copies of *A Free Church Book of Common Prayer* in their hands anywhere apart from the Birmingham Old Meeting House itself. But the book had wide sales, sat in hundreds of Free Church studies, and was pillaged for years by the compilers of other Free Church liturgies and anthologies.

In 1934 there appeared one of the most fascinating of the Unitarian and Free Catholic service books which ran to only twenty-seven pages, but despite being almost the shortest Free Church service book ever, J.P. Oakden's little work had a very long title, namely *A Free Church Liturgy based on the Words of holy Scripture together with A Simplified Latin Rite and Orthodox Liturgy.* The first communion service is a simplified form of the Roman Mass, the second a much simplified version of the Liturgy of St John Chrysostom, and the third communion order, perhaps the most remarkable of the three, sets out each part of the liturgy and the whole of the eucharistic prayer entirely in verses and phrases from scripture.

The Presbyterians

In 1898, despite some opposition the English Presbyterians produced their *Directory of Public Worship* and another version in 1921. This second version contains an order of worship for the Lord's Day indicating the place of newer arrivals in the liturgy such as an address to the children, a prayer dedicating the offering and, from the Scottish tradition, a prayer of illumination before the sermon. Before the Old Testament lesson the hymn might be a metrical psalm and after it there might be the singing of a prose psalm, a canticle or an anthem. Provision is made for the major Christian festivals, for New Year and harvest and for the sacraments and ordinances of the church.

The Presbyterian Service Book of 1948, the high watermark of Presbyterian liturgy south of the border, was the first to be produced by a joint English and Welsh committee. It met under the convenership of D. Conley Eades and was the first Presbyterian service book to be issued with the authority of both General Assemblies. The work ran to over 300 pages and in its third order for Sunday worship and its third communion order reflected the non-directory tradition of the Welsh Presbyterians. An interesting feature of all the Sunday service orders was that the first three hymns in the service were to be addressed to or were about God, Father, Son and Holy Spirit respectively.

The first of the English communion services relied heavily on the first of the Scottish liturgies in the 1940 *Book of Common Order* and also from Scotland came the order for the communion of the sick in which elements already set apart 'to this holy use and mystery' at a previous communion could be given to the communicants. In addition to the other ordinances of the church, and the ordination of ministers and elders, there were orders for the setting apart and installation of church sisters and the recognition of lay preachers. There was also a much fuller provision of sentences and collects for the festivals and seasons of the calendar, a complete service for children, a dedication and consecration of teachers and youth workers, a complete service for Remembrance Sunday, an order for Compline, and a two-year morning and evening lectionary with special readings for communion Sundays. The printers pasted the Nicene and the Apostles' Creeds on to the end boards of the book.

Under the convenerships of R. Aled Davies and J. Eric Fenn a new English and Welsh *Presbyterian Service Book* was issued in 1968. The third order for Sunday worship broke out of the 'thee' and 'thou' mould and addressed God as 'you'. In its famous intercession for the church came the words, 'Come from the four winds O breath of God, and breathe upon the dry bones of those who say they are yours'. The three communion orders differed little from the 1948 service book. The third order was actually headed 'Authorized for use in the Presbyterian Church of Wales' and the 1948 prayers in the ministry of the word were reduced to headings. Also in the version of the Lord's Supper for Wales the 1948 thanksgiving for and commemoration of the saints was omitted. The 1968 *Presbyterian Service Book* was the first of the British service books to include the lectionary of the Joint Liturgical Group of which Aled Davies was a member.

It is interesting to reflect that whereas the Unitarian branch of Presbyterianism preserved a strong Anglican liturgical tradition but drifted through its writers and preachers into anti-Trinitarianism, universalism and semi-oblivion, the English Presbyterians who looked to the directory model, to Scotland and to a strong Trinitarian faith, entered the United Reformed Church in 1972 reasonably vigorous and intact.

The Congregationalists

The worship of twentieth-century English Congregationalism owed its first debt of gratitude to John Hunter's *Devotional Service*. Hunter, whose ministries from 1871 to 1911 were in York, Hull, Glasgow (twice) and London, at the King's Weigh House, was the founder in 1893 of the Congregational Church Service Society. His *Devotional Services* had first appeared as a few pages of intercessions in 1880 but had grown by 1901 to a classic seventh edition of over three-hundred pages. Hundreds of ministers who did not introduce it into either pulpit or pew carried it with them to baptisms, weddings and funerals. The 1901 edition continued with re-prints. A thousand copies were printed in 1920, 1,400 in 1924,1,025 in 1930 and again in 1935 and 1,500 in 1943. The book finally went out of print in 1943.

Hunter was influenced by his Scottish Presbyterian upbringing, by the writings of F.D. Maurice, Thomas Carlyle, John Ruskin and Charles Kingsley and by immanentism and Christian Socialism. His intercessions were full of social concerns. Much was owed, in the first instance, to Sadler and Martineau's 1861 *Common Prayer for Christian Worship* and to the Scottish divines who produced *Euchologian* in 1867. In the classic 1901 edition of *Devotional Services*, Hunter arranged the Sunday worship material in thirteen services. From 1886 Hunter had included a communion service in his book. In many ways his eucharist was heavily dependent on Martineau. One of the most significant points of his own revisions was the inclusion in the fifth edition of 'his monumental invitation' beginning 'Come to this sacred Table not because you must, but because you may...'[4]

In the sixth edition Hunter included a second eucharistic liturgy based on that of the Scottish Episcopal Church. P.T. Forsyth, who produced his own *Intercessory Services for Aid in Public Worship* when he was at Cambridge in 1896, testified that his friend John Hunter had 'helped to wear down the Nonconformist tradition against liturgical forms, and even where he did not succeed in that crusade he certainly promoted a higher standard of worshipfulness in public services'.[5]

Congregationalism's greatest twentieth-century liturgical innovations were at the King's Weigh House, Mayfair, during the ministry of W.E. Orchard from 1914 to 1932. Under Thomas Binney (1829–69) and under John Hunter (1901–04) the Weigh House had been well exposed to liturgical forms. At the age of thirty-seven, the ascending English Presbyterian Orchard arrived to stamp his name on the church as no other had done and after eighteen years it would never recover from his magnetic personality and his dramatic resignation. On his arrival Orchard accepted his inheritance of Hunter's *Devotional Services* for Sunday worship but not for communion services since Hunter's forms bore insufficient resemblance to the historic liturgies of Christendom. In October 1914, Orchard drew up what he called an order for a Reformed eucharist and by 1917 was working on his major liturgical compilation,

---

4   Bryan D. Spinks, *Freedom or Order: The Eucharistic Liturgy in English Congregationalism* (Allison Park, PA: Pickwick Publications, 1984), p. 116

5   Quoted in Spinks, *Freedom or Order*, p. 120.

Divine Service, which was published by Oxford University Press in 1919. The book was slightly, but significantly revised in 1926. Orchard had already a fine book of prayers to his credit. *The Temple: A Book of Prayers*, dating from 1913, was to run through regular editions for forty years. Its pages reveal the depth and spiritual power of Orchard's devotional prose, even more than the collections of his remarkable sermons. The offices, litanies, collects and sacramental rites in Orchard's *Divine Service* were remarkable for their grasp of the full weight of patristic and western liturgy, and showed little of the heavy and meandering liturgical prose of practically every dissenting liturgical pioneer before him. Sometime between 1920 and 1930, Orchard produced a rare but fascinating 128 page supplement to *Divine Service* under the title *The Devotional Companion*. By 1926, Orchard's already Anglo–Catholic eucharist was further revised to conform in practically every detail to the Roman Mass. Here was Orchard the pastor, the minister and the *vagans* priest (of the Bishop Herford succession) celebrating the full round of Catholic devotion in a dissenting chapel. He presided first at a high eucharist in surplice and stole and latterly at the full Mass of the western church in eucharistic vestments, beneath which it was possible to discern a pair of canonical black leather shoes adorned with the buckles which had once belonged to John Wesley!

To enter into the full round of Catholic devotion Orchard, in *The Devotional Companion*, provided aids to devotion at Holy Communion, an anthology of prayers from the saints, meditations on the life of Christ, a tabulation of moral theology as in Bishop Challoner's *Garden of the Soul*, an order for the sacrament of Penance, the Angelus, two forms of the Rosary, the traditional devotions for use at the Benediction of the Blessed Sacrament and various litanies of the saints. Orchard latterly would usually follow an evening service of hymns and sermon with Solemn Benediction including full vestments, ceremonial and incense. The *Simple Calendar of Remembrance*, in *The Devotional Companion*, included a column of the saints canonized by the western church and a second column of 'The Uncanonized' containing some sixty names. Whilst we may expect to find William Laud, Edward King, John Keble, Thomas Ken, Clement, Origen and Lancelot Andrewes, it is refreshing also to find Charles Haddon Spurgeon, John Wesley, Samuel Rutherford and David Livingstone, but it is surprising, at first, also to find B.F. Westcott, Alfred the Great, Leo Tolstoy and Keir Hardie. Orchard's *Divine Worship*, like Hunter's *Devotional Services*, did not find its way into other congregations but it undoubtedly did find its way into Free Church studies and into the devotional quiet time of hundreds of the more catholic kind of Free Church ministers in the 1930s and 40s. Orchard's *Divine Service* was still used, in part, at the King's Weigh House Church until it closed for Free Church worship in 1965.

Meanwhile, back in the real world of everyday Congregationalism in England and Wales, a committee of twelve worthies, including Bernard Snell, P.T. Forsyth and W. Charter Piggott, was busy drawing up the 1920 *Book of Congregational Worship*. The ten orders for Sunday worship provided outlines, collects and prayers for the morning and evening worship up to the sermon which always came towards the end of the service. Two of the ten orders were based on those in Hunter's *Devotional Services*, use was made of Orchard's *Divine Service*, and in a number of the services 'words to the children' could replace one of the lessons. The communion service presupposes the ministry of the word and begins with scripture sentences and penitence. The truncated eucharistic prayer is loosely based on the 1662 *Prayer Book* and the post communion section consists of a choice of three lengthy collects, the Gloria, the Johannine account of the foot-washing and the 'God of peace' blessing from the letter to the Hebrews. The book also includes a reception of church members, the baptism of children and adults with no prayer over the water, marriage, burial of adults and children, ordination in which the laying on of hands, though taking place during a fine prayer, is optional, an induction service, sentences and prayers for the Christian year, New Year and harvest, and a compendium of general prayers including a prayer that those slain in war may be at peace, offertory prayers and a lectionary for the principal Sundays of the year.

Two strange Congregational liturgical compilations also appeared about the same time. The first, in 1922, was a milder but very catholic parallel to Orchard's *Divine Service*, entitled *The Service Book containing the Liturgy for the Celebration of the Holy Eucharist and also Orders of Worship for Morning Prayer, Vespers and other Services*. It ran to 300 pages and was printed and published by the 'Service Book Revision Committee' of 3 Guildford Place, London. Its true provenance for the time being remains a mystery. The book also contained a set of pointed canticles and an extensive psalter and, like Orchard, no ordination service. The other noteworthy compilation was *The Rodborough Bede Book* of 1930 from the hand of C.E. Watson, the minister of the Rodborough Tabernacle, Stroud in Gloucestershire. Despite its eccentric lay-out with fore, mid and end bedes and its rather odd communion orders there are some very fine original collects and prayers.

In 1936, out of the Congregational Literature Committee there came *A Manual for Ministers*. This was a rather sad interlude for Congregational liturgical enterprise. All the years of eight or ten sets of services for Sunday worship had been lost and simply replaced by a list of scripture sentences, two short compendia of morning and evening prayers and a collection of benedictions and ascriptions. The first order for communion has no ministry of the word and consisted of sentences, penitence, invitation, the dominical words, a version of humble access, the words of distribution, post communion collects of intercession, the Johannine account of the foot-washing and the 'God of peace' blessing from the letter to the Hebrews. The second communion order consisted of a bidding, in which 'the solemn acts and words keep fresh in our hearts the memory of the Lord's sacrifice', the comfortable words, the collect for purity, the Lord's Prayer, the dominical words, collects of intercession, the account of the footwashing, and two benedictions, the first the Aaronic blessing and the second the standard form from Hebrews. Reception of church members came before the baptismal services and has a rubric to the effect that candidates can choose to become members either by baptism or by the right hand of fellowship. The reception of members concludes with the confirmation prayer from the 1662 *Prayer Book*. In neither the infant nor adult baptism services is there any prayer over the water nor any reference as to how baptism is to be administered. The marriage service contains a two page address to the newly married couple. In addition to the burial service there are orders for ordination, induction and dedication services, and services for Christmas, Good Friday, Easter, Whit Sunday and New Year, and for hospital, harvest, mission, church anniversary, choir and peace Sundays. There is an entire service for the Opening of a Bazaar or Sale of Work! Also included is all that a Congregational minister needed to know about legal rights into relation to marriages, burials, trust deeds, church insurance, income tax on manses, licences for dramatic performances, cinematographic exhibitions, and music and dancing.

In 1941, H.A. Hamilton began to advocate his ideas of 'Family Church' in his book *The Family Church in Principle and Practice*. A number of congregations in the main Free Churches began to reorganize themselves on 'Family Church' lines. This brought the isolated afternoon Sunday school scholars and teachers into a serious engagement with Sunday morning church worship. At first the young people were present at morning worship in greater numbers. Later the whole 'church family' would be present once a month for the whole of a shortened service. In the 1980s this grew into all-age worship and in a number of congregations there developed a serious third of each morning service being a time for the whole church to be together. In some churches this sharing together in all-age worship was transferred to the end of the service, rather than the beginning, on communion Sundays.

With the work pioneered by Hamilton of Westhill College, Selly Oak, Birmingham, and by what later became *Partners in Learning*, quality weekly material for family worship and all-age worship was provided on an annual basis and was later linked with the Sunday public lessons of the Joint Liturgical Group and the common lectionary.

In the 1940s the reaction to the liberal strand of Congregational worship came from a group of Oxford and Mansfield College ministers subsequently referred to by Horton Davies and Bryan Spinks as the neo-orthodox or high Genevan men. In theology this group included Nathaniel Micklem, J.S. Whale, C.H. Dodd and A.G. Matthews, and in churchmanship, or 'orthodox dissent' they were supported by such figures as Daniel Jenkins and the Cambridge historian Bernard Lord Manning. These Oxford 'Genevan men' used *The Presbyter* as their journal and founded the Congregational Church Order Group. These Congregational scholars drank deeply from the wells of the continental reformers and from Karl Barth and promoted a high view of the word of God creating the church and of the necessity of the full ministry of the word and sacrament, of scripture, preaching and eucharist as an indivisible unity. The classic morning worship of the Reformed church was not a choir office or a series of preludes leading up to the sermon, but the weekly preaching from a full diet of lectionary scriptures followed by a classical communion order with all the inherited ingredients of a classical western eucharistic prayer. These principles were to be enunciated in the 1936 Mansfield essays on *Christian Worship* edited by Nathaniel Micklem, by Horton Davies in his 1948 *Worship of the English Puritans* and by Raymond Abba's 1957 *Principles of Christian Worship*. Of considerable influence also were the writings of the Scottish Presbyterian liturgical scholar W.D. Maxwell in his 1931 edition of *Knox's Genevan Service Book*, his 1936 *Outline of Christian Worship* and by the 1940 Church of Scotland *Book of Common Order*.

In their 1948 *A Book of Public Worship* compiled by E.R. Micklem, J.M. Todd, John Marsh and John Huxtable a debt was acknowledge to such liturgical sources as Hunter, Orchard, Lloyd Thomas and to the Church of Scotland and the Scottish Church Service Society's *Euchologian*. The book sported a fine and lengthy introduction by John Marsh and then returned to the provision of full orders for Sunday worship. Although the services were complete in themselves they were also designed for adaptation as part one of a full communion order. In the three orders for communion clear reference is made to the foregoing word services in which the thanksgiving may be omitted in anticipation of the eucharistic prayer. The opening rubrics suggest a communion hymn during which those not staying withdraw, the minister and deacons take their places, and where there are individual cups and pieces of bread there should be a common cup on the table for raising at the due point and once piece of bread for the fraction. The first communion order begins with the dominical warrant and the comfortable words, and moves into the eucharistic prayer in which all the classical parts of the prayer are present. In the second order the eucharistic prayer is preceded by the prayer of the veil and followed by the Lord's Prayer and the dominical warrant. The third order preserves the directory model with an exhortation and a general prayer based on the Middleburg edition of the *Genevan Service Book* derived from Knox and Calvin. There follows a selection of scripture sentences, additional prayers for each stage of the ministry of the word and a set of general intercessions. The shorter order for communion is a complete service with its own readings and with the intercessions incorporated in the eucharistic prayer and is in some ways the gem of the whole book and the crowning liturgical glory of English Congregationalism. Both baptismal orders contain a prayer over the water. The other ordinances of the church follow. In the ordination of ministers the laying on of hands occurs in the ordination prayer. In 1951 one of the compliers of *A Book of Public Worship*, J.M. Todd, produced a fine companion volume, *Prayers and Services for Public Worship*. Composing his own prayers and collects and drawing from both Anglican and Reformed sources, both ancient and modern, Todd celebrates in sentences, invocation, adoration, confession, supplication, thanksgiving and intercession the fullness of the Christian year from Advent to Trinity Sunday with the inclusion of seasonal communion orders based on the fine complete shorter order in the earlier companion volume. There is also a rich provision for the days of Holy Week.

Ten years after the unofficial *A Book of Public Worship*, the Congregational Union of England and Wales published *A Book of Services and Prayers* (1959). The official committee included John Marsh and J.M. Todd from the earlier 'Genevan' group. Following the orders for morning and evening worship, and some rather long-winded baptismal rites, the communion orders are heavily dependent on the new classical Reformed models. The ordinances of the church are followed by a huge compendium of prayers for the Christian year on the Todd model and then a collection of prayers from the ancients, from the Anglican divines and the continental reformers. The book concludes with John Todd's two-year morning and evening table of lessons and the eucharistic lectionary of the Church of South India.

The last liturgical work of the Congregational Church in England and Wales was its 1970 *An Order for Public Worship*. This was a significant but sad venture. Significant, because it flowed out of the height of the liturgical movement in general and out of the membership of the Congregationalists in the Joint Liturgical Group in particular. The book consisted of one communion rite with alternative texts at each of the key points in the liturgy. Hence, after the sentences there were several versions of the prayer of approach, of the confession, of the assurances of pardon, of the intercessions, of the eucharistic prayer and of the post communion collect. The order demonstrated the best of the insights of the later stages of the liturgical movement. There were two sadnesses attached to the publication. In the first instance the book was delayed in the press from

1967 to 1970 by which time the 'you' language had overtaken it and other churches had moved on to later agreed texts. Secondly, as Bryan Spinks reveals in his study of the rite, the researches of the Congregational Liturgical Committee had revealed a back lash from the local churches. Many thought everything was becoming too Presbyterian, too Anglican and even too Roman. Many Congregationalists believed themselves to be essentially Zwinglian or Quaker and they did not need full communion orders or prescribed patterns. Alas, a general truth much feared by liturgists was being realized. The rank and file, as in all traditions, had little concern for ecumenical liturgical insights or for their own historic and liturgical origins. In the words of Spinks: 'The "Genevan" school had left many areas of Congregational life unpenetrated.'[6]

A good example of the disparity between the experts and local habit is cited by the Congregationalist Raymond Abba where he writes: 'The modern practice of the minister's being served after the people by a senior elder or deacon is the result of confusing liturgical principles with dining room etiquette'. Similarly Abba regrets the consuming of the wine together from individual cups as being too reminiscent of drinking a toast.[7] Liturgical purists longed for Free Church congregations to ensure that the communion wine was at least the fruit of the grape, but local arrangements continued to provide totally inappropriate substitutes. The return to a common loaf and a common cup was a long and slow campaign with no guarantee of success. Similarly the hope of liturgists that Free Church ministers would actually pour water over the candidate at baptism and not simply anoint them instead with a damp cross on the forehead was equally a forlorn hope.

The question of 'you' language and the desire to adapt and improvise locally was fully seen in the huge popularity of the 1967 SCM Press's *Contemporary Prayers for Public Worship* in which Caryl Micklem and his fellow Congregationalists produced a communion liturgy and other prayers and ordinances in modern speech and idiom, but with a fairly weak hold on the concepts of classical liturgical form. The book was still being published well into the 1980s.

The United Reformed Church

In 1972 the descendants of nineteenth-century Scottish settlers who made up the bulk of the Presbyterian Church of England and most of the

---

6   Spinks, *Freedom or Order*, p. 201.
7   Raymond Abba, *Principles of Christian Worship* (Oxford: Oxford University Press, 1957), p. 184.

membership of the Congregational Church came together to form the United Reformed Church. From 1973 to 1978 draft orders for ordination, initiation and communion were published. In 1975 new ground was broken by publishing the new communion order, with music, in *New Church Praise*, thus giving many English Reformed congregations the text of the communion service in their hands for the first time ever. *A Book of Services* was published in 1980. Based on the insights of the liturgical movement and the best of the Reformed tradition there is one complete order for word and sacrament with three eucharistic prayers, the third of them drawn from the work of Huub Oosterhuis. The rest of the book includes such innovations as a confirmation service, a healing service and the induction of a Provincial Moderator.

In 1985 the URC General Assembly decided their 1980 book was already in need of revision. There was now a clear need in the Free Churches for inclusive language for human beings. The debate about inclusive imagery for God was still to come. Secondly, in 1981 the Reformed Association of Churches of Christ in Great Britain and Ireland came into the URC and their liturgical traditions, including the invariability of only believers' baptism, needed to be incorporated and expressed in a new service book. A new Doctrine and Worship Committee was appointed with Colin Gunton as convener. In some Free Church circles there was, in any case, a move away from automatic assumption that strongly believing parents always desired the baptism of their infants. For them and for former members of the Churches of Christ there was to be included in the new book a service for the Dedication of Parents and the Blessing of Children. Drafters of the 1989 *Service Book* included Charles Brock who wrote the first of the eucharistic prayers, and representing the former Churches of Christ tradition, David Thompson from the Cambridge Divinity Faculty. Some of the very beautiful language in the third of the eucharistic prayers is drawn from the liturgy of the French Reformed Church. The first of the post communion prayers is from Greek Orthodoxy and the last of them from the Liturgy of Malabar. The outline for a communion order and the people's part of the eucharistic liturgy were also printed for the use of congregations as the first part of the 1991 URC hymn-book *Rejoice and Sing*. In the 1989 *Service Book* there are also services for the blessing of a civil marriage and for the renewal of baptismal promises. The confirmation service has a mandatory laying on of hands, but it is the right hand of fellowship which is given in the baptismal initiation of adults.

In 1992, under the editorship of Edmund Banyard and with the assistance of Mary Frost, Betsy King and Terry Oakley, the United Reformed Church also published *Festival Services*. This loose-leaf folder offered a full round of texts and all-age resources for Advent, Christmas, Epiphany, Lent and Holy Week, for Easter Day (but not the Easter season or Ascensiontide), Pentecost and Trinity Sunday, and for the Feast of the Transfiguration. Popular in some quarters were Alan Gaunt's 1972 *New Prayers for Worship* and his four stages of *Prayers for the Christian Year*. A number of Free church congregations came to appreciate hymns and chants from Taize and Iona.

The most thorough British treatment of the issue of inclusive language in liturgy also came out of the United Reformed tradition in Brian Wren's *What Language Shall I Borrow?* (1989). Wren was trying to move the churches on from the issue of inclusive language and behaviour towards people to our understanding of the fact that God is not ultimately male and that all language for God, including the title 'Father' is metaphorical and provisional. Wren attacked the dominant metaphor system of our preaching, liturgy and hymnody in which God is celebrated primarily as King—Almighty—Father and Protector. The Trintarian model must be re-experienced in something ultimate but still relational such as Lover, Beloved and Mutual Friend. Despite his extremism, Wren raised with many others the whole question of the gentler, alternative and feminine images for God and was right to challenge the patriarchal view of God that dominates so much of our worship. Though even Wren himself admitted you could not re-translate 'Guide me, O thou Great Jehovah, Pilgrim through this barren land' as 'Parent me, O great Sustainer, as I traverse the alienating institutions of industrial society'.[8]

The Congregational Federation

In 1992 those Congregationalists who had opted to remain outside the United Reformed Church published from their Castle Gate, Nottingham, headquarters *Patterns of Worship* under the joint names of Richard Cleaves and Michael Durber. The Foreword declared that *Patterns of Worship* was not an authorized service book. Such an approach was in keeping with the Federation's Congregational heritage and the hope was that the book would be one set of resources among many. In the Congregational tradition the most appropriate form of worship is always decided locally. Texts for the gospel canticles are printed from the English Language Liturgical Consultation internationally agreed texts and the book includes the Joint Liturgical Group's four year lectionary. The loose-leaf book has 592 pages and each service or section of the book has accompanying yellow pages with notes, suggestions and comments for the good or better ordering of the worship. The orders for

8   Brian Wren, *What Language Shall I Borrow? God-talk in Worship: A Male Response to Feminist Theology* (London: SCM Press, 1989), p. 135.

Sunday worship are based on the threefold approach of 'We speak to God', 'God speaks to us' and then 'We offer to God'. This means most of the great parts of prayer—invocation, penitence, intercession and thanksgiving—come in the first part of the worship. Scripture, preaching and even the bread and cup come in the section in which 'God speaks to us'. This leaves very little for the third section under 'We offer to God'—only announcements, collection and dedication. A similar three-fold approach is used for all-age worship. Here the model is slightly more classical: preparation for the word, presentation of the word, and response to the word. Intercession is now transferred to the third section, but thanksgiving remains in the preparatory section. The five sections of the book are laid out logically. Sunday morning and evening worship, is followed by the sacraments of the church. The life of the church includes church membership, the church meeting, commissioning and ordination services. The family and the church includes marriage, thanksgiving for the birth of a child, prayers for healing and funerals. The final section,— The world and the church—includes the traditional canticles, benedictions and blessings and lectionary material. The forms for infant and adult baptism contain no reference to water, or to the mode of baptism. There is no prayer over the water and indeed no praying at all before the baptism. There are two communion orders. In both we are reminded that the whole service of word, bread and cup constitutes the sacrament in which worshippers discern the presence of Jesus. The first order includes a 'Keynote Address' to the young people, presumably on the lectionary theme of the day. The first reading is related to the intercessions and only the second to the sermon. The invitation to the table uses the Martineau–Hunter 'Come to this sacred table' and is followed by a Trinitarian prayer of thanksgiving. In the second order the institution narrative may be either according to Paul, Matthew, Mark, Luke or, surely uniquely, a pastiche of references from John 6 and 15. The final blessing is in the dubious and defective form invoking 'the Creator, the Christ and the Holy Spirit'.

The Baptists

In 1884 Henry Bonner produced the first ever published book of Baptist services, prepared for Hamstead Road Baptist Church, Handsworth, Birmingham, and used there for at least the next forty years. In the 1900 edition acknowledgements are made to the Unitarians Crompton Jones, Sadler and Martineau. Some of the collects are from Bright's *Ancient Collects*. There were ten services for the five Sundays of the month with sung responses and the opportunity of using prose psalms, canticles, litanies and singing the Lord's Prayer. (This last custom soon to become the vogue in suburban Free Churches.) The congregation was directed to kneel for prayer. The bread and wine at communion were to be received as 'symbols' of Christ's broken body and shed blood. In 1927 F.B. Meyer published for the Free Church Federal Council a *Free Church Service Manual* for communion, marriage, dedication of infants, believers' baptism, and burial. Meyer left Elvet Lewis to provide at the back of the book a service for infant baptism. It was revised in 1940.

In 1930 a revised and larger version of Bonner's book was edited by his successor at Hamstead Road, Frederick C. Spurr, entitled *Come, Let Us Worship*. Help was given to Spurr by W.Y. Fullerton, Hugh Martin. P.T. Thompson and Carey Bonner. Included are festival services for Christmas, Easter, Whitsun and harvest. In addition to an abridgement of the Anglican litany there are litanies for the sick, for the nations, for missions and one for the use of children. Many of the responses are set to music. There are additional prayers for Advent, Palm Sunday, Good Friday and Ascensiontide. We are informed in the opening rubrics of The Order for the Administration of the Lord's Supper that the form provided is not intended as an addendum to the ordinary Morning or Evening Service but as a complete service in itself. The service begins with sentences, opening collects and confession followed by the Lord's Prayer, canticles to be sung before and after the scripture lesson. The second canticle may be replaced by some of the dominical commandments. The *Sursum Corda* and *Sanctus* stand on their own before the sermon. The communion prayer is an amalgam of the comfortable words, the dominical warrant and part of the Anglican prayer of consecration. First the bread and then the wine are shared with sentences based on the Anglican words of distribution. The service ends with part of the *Gloria in excelsis*, a prayer for the church universal, a hymn including an offering for the poor, a blessing and the *Nunc Dimittis*. The book concludes with a marriage rite and a funeral service with an option for a cremation. The book contains no baptismal rite.

Also in 1930, D. Tait Patterson published *The Call to Worship*. This was revised in 1938 and enlarged in 1940 and was still being reprinted by the press of the Baptist Union in 1956. The first half of the book contained a series of litanies with sung responses probably intended to be used as the first prayer in morning and evening worship. The last of the litanies are for Advent, Christmas, Lent, Good Friday, Easter, Ascension and Whit-Sunday. The *Prayer Book* General Confession and General Thanksgiving are followed by the *Prayer Book* canticles, the *Salvator Mundi* and a series of collects. In addition to an order for the visitation of the sick there are services for the dedication of children and the baptism of believers. The three orders for communion move towards the dominical warrant and the sharing of the bread and wine with some fine scriptural imagery and classic collect language but have no real structure.

The first service book to come into general use among Baptists was *A Manual for Free Church Ministers* edited by G.P. Gould and J.H. Shakespeare and published in 1905. In the rite for The Baptism of Believers reference is made to 'the strange deviation from primitive practice which is manifested by those who in this matter think not with us'. In 1927 Gould's and Shakespeare's service book was succeeded by *A Minister's Manual* arranged by M.E. Aubrey. The book was enlarged in 1944 and published again in 1952. It is a slim volume of seventy pages. The Dedication of Infants includes as warrant Jesus accepting the children for to such belongs the kingdom. In the bidding the church is said to have a claim on the lives of the children of Christian parents. Believer's baptism imlpies a union with Christ's death and resurrection, a renunciation of sin, a life-long commitment and the inheritance of the kingdom of God. In the order for the Lord's Supper the dominical warrant and the sharing of the bread and wine dominate the rite, but the custom may continue whereby new members are received into fellowship at the beginning of the service even though the book contains An Order for the Reception of Church Members.

In 1960 the Baptist Union reached the high watermark of its liturgical provision with *Orders and Prayers for Church Worship: A Manual for Ministers* compiled by Ernest A. Payne and Stephen Winward. The introduction to the book declares: 'Christian worship is essentially eucharistic: it is to the glory of God in Christ Jesus, incarnate, crucified, risen, exalted, coming in glory'. In many ways the book was a parallel look-a-like to the Congregational publication *A Book of Services and Prayers*. The first communion order stands in the classic high Genevan tradition as a complete rite of word and sacrament with a classic eucharistic prayer. The second order is shorter but similar. The rubrics imply that all will eat the bread and drink the wine at the same moment. The three orders for morning and evening worship have prayers drawn from Anglican, Reformed and Church of Scotland liturgies and service books or new prayers composed in the same idiom. The middle third of the book contains sentences and then prayers for general and seasonal occasions according to each of the key parts of a service of the word. In the baptismal service there is no prayer over or reference to the water prior to the baptism. The laying on of hands after baptism and the reception of church members are perceived as two separate occasions, partly because in independent congregations the second rite could be repeated for those who have arrived as transferred members from another congregation. There is an admirable section at the close of the service book headed The Ministry of Visitation. It is made of up the dedication of a new home, readings and prayers for a family, thanksgiving for childbirth, readings and prayers for the sick and the aged, the laying on of hands upon the sick, sentences and prayers for those in distress and supplication for the dying. The lectionary is John Todd's from *A Book of Services and Prayers.*

In 1977 the Baptist Union Publications Committee asked Alec Gilmore, Edward Smalley and Michael Walker to advise them on a revision or replacement for the 1960 *Orders and Prayers.* The working party resolved to work on a completely new book and published *Praise God* in 1980. They argued that for Baptists the liturgical movement as represented in the formal approach of Ernest Payne and Stephen Winward was running out of steam. The climate now was different. The formalism of the 1950s was giving way to a new wave of freedom, self-expression and informality. The 'you' mode of address to God had arrived. It was claimed by some that *Orders and Prayers* was only ever used by Baptist superintendents and college principals. There was still to be stress on Christmas, Easter and Pentecost but with less stress on Lent and Ascension. There was a hint in the introduction that the day was not far off when each minister would plan all the wedding services they conducted. There was a new hope of creating silences in the worship. The first part of the book provides scripture sentences and some fine new prayers for the Christian year from Advent to All Saints. The second part of the book provided sentences and different categories of modern prayers for each part of morning and evening worship. The shape of the one communion order and its wording were traditional in content and modern in language. The eucharistic prayer, however, stopped after the preface. Though there was a rubric referring to the mighty acts of God there was no hint of the later parts of a classical eucharistic prayer. The eucharistic acclamations were supplied as a post communion prayer. There is a rubric in the Infant Dedication order suggesting that after the blessing of the candidate, 'The children may here lift up their candles and shout hurray'. In the act of initiation there is no rubric actually mentioning the act of baptism. There were some touching pastoral phrases and insights in the funeral rite. Some years later, a very fine paperback of prayers for Christian seasons, *There's a Time and a Place*, was composed by the Baptist minister, Jamie Wallace, and published by Collins in 1982 with a fourth printing in 1987.

By 1988 the Baptist Union General Purposes and Finance Committee had commissioned another service book and under the chairmanship of Bernard Green *Patterns and Prayers for Christian Worship* was prepared and then published in 1991. The three outlines for Sunday worship were all different. The first anticipated the ministry of the word diversifying into readings, drama, discussion, sermon or craftwork in which 'the theme is explored'. The second placed the offering and the greeting in the middle of the service with the sermon near the end. The third was an open pattern but with the readings and sermon together in the middle of the service. For each of the Sundays from pre-Advent to Trinity only one prayer is provided—sometimes adoration, sometimes approach, sometimes confession, sometimes thanksgiving and so on. Clearly neither one thing nor another. The traditional parts of the eucharist are more or less present but lack any liturgical or classical coherence. In the baptism and reception into membership there is a fine baptismal prayer and a clear reference to entering the baptistery at the moment of baptism though, as usual in Baptist liturgies, the minister is not instructed to do anything. *Patterns and Prayers* was one of the few service books to include the short-lived Joint Liturgical Group four-year lectionary devised by the Methodist, Raymond George. The weakest moment in the book is a request in the Mothering Sunday prayer: 'Show us the loveliness of the baby grown pimply with puberty, the beauty of strong hands grown waxen-veined in age'!

Curiously enough, 1991 was also the year when MARC-Monarch Publications first issued Paul Beasley-Murray's paperback *Faith and Festivity: A Guide for Today's Worship Leaders.* Here was the Principal of Spurgeon's College addressing and advising a generation of Baptist pastors and Bible teachers, and their 'praise and prayer' counterparts in the other Free Churches and in the independent fellowships. He was speaking and writing to those who had been brought up on charismatic choruses and over-head projectors about how to engage with the best and the essential in the great worship tradition of the church. In the first half of the book, Beasley Murray deals with public prayer and the ministry of the word and of the Lord's Supper, with ordered worship, with infant dedication and believers' baptism and finally with worship and the outsider. The second part of *Faith and Festivity* is given over to celebrating Advent, Christmas, New Year, Lent and Holy Week, Easter and Ascension, Pentecost and Trinity, the church anniversary and harvest. The book begins with Karl Barth and ends with the Westminster Shorter Catechism!

For Beasley-Murray Christian worship must focus on the God who raised Christ from the dead. Every Sunday's praise must express praise to God for Jesus crucified and risen. Worship must include the Trafford Arms Park roar of the Book of Revelation—the sound of a great multitude like rushing waters. Worship must be offered with hearts and with voices. But if Christian worship celebration is about unrelieved happiness and joy it is also about reverence and awe. In some circles this was a required counterbalance. Some charismatics are full of froth and bubble and some devotees of liturgical niceties are as correct as a corpse in an American funeral parlour. Abba and 'Hi Dad!' are not the same thing. All the congregation must be in their places praying fifteen minutes before the service starts. That is when lift-off takes place.

Part one of public worship is preparation, then the call to worship, then an opening hymn or songs of worship, followed by praise and thanksgiving (between which Beasley-Murray does not at first distinguish), confession, the Lord's Prayer, scripture and further songs of worship. He defends this classic and natural sequence, though allowing for the Lord's Prayer to be at the end of worship as well as near the beginning. He recommends the Lord's Prayer according to the New International Version. Hymns and songs should be a balance between the deep and familiar and the dispensable paper towel variety. In strains of Isaac Watts' *Guide to Prayer*, Beasley-Murray says public prayer is not private prayer prayed through a microphone. Public prayer is not designed to impress or to inform. All prayer must be addressed to God. It includes invitation, adoration, praise, thanksgiving. Adoration and praise are centred on God himself and thanksgiving on what he has and is doing. Now is the moment to confess our sins and be assured of God's pardon. In discussing intercession, Beasley-Murray reminds us of Geoffrey Wainwright's dictum that this part of prayer is about a plea for the triumph of the divine purpose in spite of contrary expectations. In the prayer of dedication, or *oblatio*, Beasley-Murray joins the offering and dedication of both the monetary gifts and the lives of the worshippers. He lists twelve arguments for and against free and set prayers including the reminder from Bernard Manning of how he still felt as an adult the boyish horror of the long prayer which everywhere was the same. There was no chance it would ever end. You simply resigned yourself. When it was all over the congregation raised their heads like people coming out of their huts after a tornado still anxious to see if anyone was missing. This is, of course, in strong contrast to the famous 1912 laudatory description of extempore prayer by the Methodist William Russell Maltby (printed in his *Obiter Scripta* published by the Epworth Press in 1952). Beasley-Murray requires that in prayer we watch our language, watch the length and remember to whom we are speaking. Intercessory prayer must include the church, the world, the local community, the troubled and the departed.

For the ministry of the scriptures, Beasley-Murray pleads for the use of a lectionary that covers both Testaments and the Psalter but this can be used creatively alongside preaching through a book for a season. Accordingly the celebration of the Lord's Supper is central to worship. He reminds us that Calvin regarded infrequent communion as the invention of the devil. He also quotes von Allmen to the effect that the absence of the eucharist shows a contempt for grace. In this matter much Baptist and independent worship needs to be reformed. The basic minimum following scripture and sermon is (the peace), an invitation to the table, scripture and institution narrative, prayer of thanksgiving, the sharing of the bread and wine, a prayer of commitment, a hymn of triumph, and a benediction. Beasley-Murray blames the advertizers rather than the doctors for the introduction of little glasses into Free Church communions and is all for returning to the common cup. In the blessing that concludes the service there is no final argument as to whether it should be requested or pronounced.

Beasley-Murray believes that where congregations and pastors follow a more charismatic style of worship there still needs to be a threefold order of praise, proclamation and prayer. The leader must steer the excited worshippers who may be confused as to which section of the service they are in. In the so-called dedication of infants in the Baptist tradition Beasley-Murray reminds us that after giving thanks for the child, it is the parents who are dedicated and the child who is blessed. In a baptismal service there needs to be a warrant, an invocation of the Spirit, a renunciation of evil, a profession of faith in Christ and the Trinity, the use of water, a declaration of the new status of the baptizand, a sealing with the Spirit and a participation in holy communion. If an unbeliever enters public worship and is drawn to Christ this is good. However, the main purpose of Sunday worship is not evangelism and evangelistic services on Sundays should be at another or separate service. Beasley-Murray reminds us that worship is not a tool for evangelism but that true praise and genuine prayer can help visitors to our worship to ask questions about God. He believes that Baptists and independent congregations should cash in on the Christian year. Every part of it offers opportunities to engage with the visual, with folk religion and with the movement of the gospel.

The Quakers

Throughout the twentieth century the Society of Friends revised their books of Discipline and Practice. The latest revision of 1995 is entitled *Quaker Faith and Practice*. Quakers are unique among Christians in making silence the basis of their worship. Little understood by non-Quakers this is a waiting silence. Even when the silence occupies the first half of the meeting it does not imply that nothing is happening. The expectation and the intention is that the worshippers are drawing near to God and just as importantly to one another. There is, as always, the Quaker negative—no creeds, no hymns, no repeated prayers, no ceremony, no priest, and no pre-arranged service. The service begins with a period of settling down which commences as soon as the first worshipper arrives. Each worshipper is seeking in silence 'the still centre of their being'. The quietness involves body, mind and spirit. Someone in the meeting may be moved to break the silence with a contribution intended to deepen or enrich the worship. Anyone present is free to speak, or pray or read. The expectation is that those who break the silence are moved by the Spirit. Sometimes the meeting is 'full of words, but there is little ministry'—surely a point at which Quaker worship touches the weakness in other Christian traditions. The hope is that the silence is 'broken, but not interrupted'. The intention is that the reaction of worshippers to individual contributions should be constructive and positive 'looking for the Spirit behind the words'. Not all the contributions are at the same level of experience. For some the worship will be centred in the forgiving love of God in Jesus and for others the centre will be the needs of others present in the worship. The heart of Quaker worship is transcendence. Thomas Kelly believed that in the final analysis the Quakers find in their worship 'The Real Presence of God'. The close of the worship is indicated by the elders present shaking hands.

The Methodists

Apart from the Wesleyan Reform Union and the Independent Methodists, Methodism began the twentieth century more or less in three parts. In addition to the original Wesleyan body there were Primitive Methodists, both town and country, but mostly in the Midlands and the North. From 1907 three of the smaller Methodist bodies, the Bible Christians, mostly of Devon and Cornwall, and the United Methodist Free Churches and the Methodist New Connexion, the oldest of the Methodist secessionists, were to form a united third strand in the United Methodist Church. The Wesleyans, the Primitive Methodists and the United Methodists came together in the Methodist Church in 1932.

The normal Sunday morning and evening worship in most chapels of all branches of Methodism had much in common. It had begun as a preaching service with two or three hymns, a long extempore prayer, a scripture passage and a sermon, and with a short final prayer or blessing. By the mid-nineteenth century, especially in the towns, the service was beginning to be filled out with a second lesson, with two extempore prayers instead of one, and therefore with more hymns in the gaps. It would be some time before the collection was put on the communion table and even longer before it was prayed over. As town and suburban churches became upwardly mobile, many of the Wesleyans and some of the other Methodist denominations would, like their neighbours in historic Dissent, form choirs and begin singing introits and anthems and chanting psalms and the *Prayer Book* canticles. The original preaching service became a four or five hymn sandwich with the anthem and the canticles displacing some of the hymns. This was the era of the privately printed northern chapel service and chant book. Sunday evenings might be a different affair. Often with a more evangelistic flavour, the official hymn-book might be supplemented by choruses and songs from the Moody and Sankey missions. When there was a morning or evening communion, monthly or twice a quarter in the towns and more or less quarterly in the country, the Lord's Supper would be a separate service after the close of the main service.

In the Wesleyan tradition communion books or booklets would be handed out to those who stayed for 'the sacrament' and in the non-Wesleyan bodies the minister would read part of the communion service from his denomination's communion order or, as Oliver Beckerlegge made clear in his famous article in the *London Quarterly and Holborn Review*, he might make the whole communion service extempore.[9]

All the non-Wesleyan bodies that came into Methodist Union in 1932 had their own service books. The Bible Christian *Book of Services* was lasted printed in 1903, the Primitive Methodist *Order for the Administration of Baptism and Other Services* was last printed in 1880, the *Book of Services for the Use of the United Methodist Free Churches* was last printed in 1901, *A Handbook of the Methodist New Connexion* dated from 1899 and the United Methodist *Book of Services* from 1913.

No pre-union Methodist service book contained any outline for Sunday worship or the preaching service. The printed services were mostly communion, covenant, baptisms, weddings and funerals and ordinations. In 1882 the Wesleyans had published *A Book of Public Prayers and Services* to replace Wesley's 1784 revision of the *Book of Common Prayer*, namely *The Sunday Service of the Methodists*. The Wesleyan book of 1882 contained a mildly revised form of the 1662 Order of Morning Prayer, the Litany and full prose Psalter for use in a minority of Wesleyan chapels. By 1900 there were about twenty-five Morning Prayer chapels in London and about another twenty-five in the provinces.

About the turn of the century a group of Wesleyan ministers and laymen formed The Wesleyan Guild of Divine Service. Its manifesto in 1905 pleaded with Wesleyan Methodists to adopt a friendly attitude to liturgical worship. According to one of its critics, Daniel Hone, in his undated *Corrupt Methodist Worship*, the Guild wished to promote greater reverence in divine worship and a fuller and more intelligent participation of the people in prayer and praise. It advocated kneeling for prayer, standing for singing, a decent administration of the sacraments according to prescribed forms, the reading of the proper lessons, the reception of the offertory at the communion table, a fuller and more profitable observance of the church's year and greater frequency of holy communion. The Guild also hoped churches might be used only for worship, that the Lord's table be restricted to its proper use, that all

---

9   Oliver Beckerlegge, 'The Sacrament of the Lord's Supper: Dissenting Footnotes to the High Leigh Papers, July 1964', *London Quarterly and Holborn Review*, October, 1964, pp. 313-18.

entertainments on Good Friday should be thoroughly discouraged, that announcements from the pulpit should relate to the spiritual work of the church and that sensational advertisements should be excluded from all church notices. The Guild had the support of Sir Frederick Howard, the Rt. Hon. Sir H.H. Fowler (later Viscount Wolverhampton), and the committee included men like H.B. Workman, Thomas Bowman Stephenson and J.E. Rattenbury, who later became the second President of the Methodist Sacramental Fellowship after the death of A.E. Whitham in 1938. Out of the Guild of Divine Service came Thomas Bowman Stephenson's *The People's Order of Divine Service*. The book provided services with canticles and responses for each of the five Sundays of the month and then the Wesleyan orders for choral communion, marriage, baptism, the renewal of the covenant and burial. The book concluded with a select prose psalter.

When the three branches of Methodism came together in 1932 a joint committee was formed to produce a *Book of Offices* for the whole church. The four acknowledged sources were W.E. Orchard, the editor of *The Free Church Book of Common Prayer*, the United Church of Canada and the Church of England as copyright holders of the 1928 *Prayer Book*. Each of these four only contributed the odd prayer to the new book for most of it came for much more recognizable sources. Morning Prayer, the Collects, Epistles and Gospels, and the first Communion Order were Wesleyan versions of the 1662 *Prayer Book*. The 'God of peace' blessing from the Letter to the Hebrews had been added to the first communion order from the United Methodist Free Churches *Book of Services*, and the commandments of the Lord Jesus in an amended form from the 1928 *Prayer Book*. The second communion order was designed to follow a main service and to cater for the non-Wesleyan section of the united Church. The service was intended to follow on from a full morning or evening service. It consisted of sentences, offering for the poor, the Lord's Prayer, the *Prayer Book* invitation to confession, a confession from Psalm 51, the *Agnus Dei*, a form of the comfortable words, the *Sursum Corda* and *Sanctus*, the *Prayer Book* prayer of oblation, a commemoration of the departed from the 1928 *Prayer Book*, a form of humble access, the words of institution, the distribution, two verses of Charles Wesley's Easter hymn 'Love's redeeming work is done', the Gloria, the blessing from Hebrews and the Grace. In addition to ordinations for ministers and deaconesses and commissioning services, baptism, marriage and burial, there was a new version of the covenant service based on a pre-union Wesleyan revision of the work of a Wesleyan minister, G.B. Robson. This is the form of the covenant service adopted by the Church of South India. The 1936 Covenant Service order was revised, but not substantially altered, in either the 1975 *Methodist Service Book* or 1999 *Methodist Worship Book*.

In 1930 the Wesleyan Conference appointed a committee 'to consider
the best methods of giving to corporate prayer its due place in the life of
the Church'. The committee received the approval of the uniting
Conference of 1932 to provide a manual of devotional services in
addition to the new *Book of Offices* for the optional use and guidance of
those who conduct public worship. The Conference approved the manual
published as *Divine Worship* in 1935.

The book begins with an outline for morning and evening worship,
followed by ten full orders for Sunday worship, the second of them being
the Order for Morning Prayer, with hymns and sermon. Services in the
Hunter–Orchard tradition are provided for the festivals, and these are
followed by children's services and services on various themes such as
thanksgiving and intercession. The book lived with ministers and local
preachers through the 1930s and 40s and fell out of use sometime in the
1950s.

Between the 1936 *Book of Offices* and the 1975 *Methodist Service
Book* there were several movements and developments in worship trends
inside and outside Methodism. In 1935 T.S. Gregory, his cousin A.S.
Gregory, Kingsley Lloyd and A.E. Whitham among others, founded the
Methodist Sacramental Fellowship with the intention of returning
Methodism to the Nicene faith, of working for corporate re-union with
the Church of England and others, and of making holy communion
central to the life of Methodism. The Sacramental Fellowship ran regular
conferences, produced booklets and Wesley sacramental re-prints and
published its own form of daily offices. Other Free Church approaches to
a daily office included Nathaniel Micklem's *Prayers and Praises*,
published in 1941 and revised in 1954. Most popular of all, with
ministers and laity alike in the Free Churches was Leslie Weatherhead's *A
Private House of Prayer* published in 1958. Under the presidencies of
J.E. Rattenbury and Donald Soper the influence of the Sacramental
Fellowship spread slowly but surely as it gave to parts of Methodism first
a High Wesleyan spirituality, through the Wesley studies of Rattenbury
and John Bowmer, and finally gave to some Methodists a vision of full
Catholic churchmanship. A second influence was the growing liturgical
movement with Raymond George as its chief Methodist exponent. The
third influence was the work of the Methodist Renewal Group who moved
younger liturgists away from Cranmer and Wesley to the insights of the
liturgical movement.

From the mid 1960s, moves were made towards a new Methodist
service book. The most radical departure was a new communion order,
The Sunday Service, which aligned the ministry of the word with the
preaching service (approach—scriptures and sermon—response in
intercession and thanksgiving). There was to be only one eucharistic
prayer based on Hippolytus. All the new services were to be in the 'you'

form, except the re-printing of the 1662–1936 Cranmer–Wesley communion order, which survived in 1975 but was finally given up in 1999. Marriage and funeral services were new compositions and the ordination of ministers was based on the proposed Anglican–Methodist ordinal. The collects and lectionary were adopted from the work of the Joint Liturgical Group. So successful was the *Sunday Service* that by the late 1980s there was a clear desire for the Methodist Conference to ask the Faith and Order committee to draft new services especially providing a choice of eucharistic prayers.

The liturgical sub-committee met thirty times in eight years for a total of seventy-one days. Over 20,000 original drafts of various services were sent out for duplication and experimental use and over 1,000 letters were received in reply. The main areas of resistance were to the sparse use of the Prayer of Humble Access, over strong imagery in the epiclesis and a controversial reference to 'God our Mother' in one of the sixteen eucharistic prayers. Need was expressed for an alternative or revised covenant prayer avoiding the phrase 'put me to suffering'.

The approach to the 1999 *Methodist Worship Book* was to give the whole church access to every service of the church. The new book was to be a people's book as well as an essential tool for ministers and preachers. The book begins with a form of daily prayer for individuals and small groups. In no service in the book was is it necessary to turn to any other part and back again. There is a very strong emphasis on the liturgical year. There are complete communion orders for Advent, Christmas and Epiphany, Lent and Passiontide, Easter and Ascension, and Pentecost. There are a further three communion orders for the period of 'ordinary time' after Epiphany and after Pentecost. House communions, Maundy Thursday, the Renewal of the Covenant, Ordination, Marriage, and Healing and Wholeness all have their own communion material. 'God our Mother', removed by the liturgical sub-committee was put back in one of the communion orders by the Methodist Conference revision committee. This stands alongside 424 references to God our Father. There are mutual sponsors for bride and groom in marriage. A new departure is the encouragement of liturgical actions. These include the pouring of water into the font during the baptismal liturgy, the manual acts of pouring water on and signing the candidate during baptism, the use of the wreath of candles in Advent, the laying on of hands in the Service of Reconciliation, anointing in the service for Healing and Wholeness, ashing on Ash Wedesday, the blessing and distribution of crosses with procession on Palm Sunday, exaltation of the cross on Good Friday, the paschal candle in Eastertide, liturgical colours, and music in one of the communion orders. New services not in previous books include daily worship, outlines for the preaching service and communion, introductory sentences and blessings for seasons, a new set of collects, the

Revised Common Lectionary, Holy Week services, healing and wholeness, repentance and reconciliation, prayers with the dying, prayers after death, the office of commendation, committal followed by thanksgiving at a funeral, the burial of ashes, blessings and dedications and material for the preaching service. The publication of the English book was followed by a Welsh language version on parallel pages.

The Smaller Denominations with Methodist Connexions

The Independent Methodists began to revise and supplement their 1976 *Ministers' Handbook* in 1994, and in 1997 they co-operated with the Countess of Huntingdon's Connexion and the Wesleyan Reform Union to produce *Together in the Lord: A Handbook of Services*. There are twenty-eight short services in the book. Both forms of communion presuppose a first morning or evening service and contain very short eucharistic prayers. There are few responsive prayers in any part of the book and no acknowledgment of the Christian year. The Independent Methodists are in the throes of amalgamating with the Baptist Union.

The Salvation Army

The Salvation Army published *General Orders for conducting Salvation Army Ceremonies* in 1925. The book includes the Swearing-In of Soldiers, the Presentation of Colours, the Making of Holiness, War and Personal Covenants, the Dedication of Children in two forms—one for the children of Salvationists and the other for the children of non-Salvationists. (The former of course being dedicated beneath the flag.) Marriages and funerals arrangements likewise were different for Salvationists and non-Salvationists. In the 1989 revision the distinctions between Salvationists and non-Salvationists are largely done away with. For their Sunday worship the Salvation Army continues the general hymn–chorus 'sandwich' tradition and maintains the 'saints in the morning and the sinners in the evening' approach.

Conclusion

Of all the Free Churches the Unitarians were the most given to textual revision of the *Book of Common Prayer*, but their demise included their destruction of the Trinitarian theology which undergirded the Anglican tradition. However, Martineau's love of good liturgical language passed over into all the Free Churches not least into Congregationalism. The

Free Church Catholic and ritualistic revival under Lloyd Thomas and Orchard was short-lived, but the prayers in Orchard's *Divine Service* furnished other service books for over fifty years.

The movement for liturgical renewal which hit the Free Churches in the 1960s and created the Joint Liturgical Group produced some fine liturgical texts and created new service books centred on classical eucharistic texts, an increase in the frequency of communion, a shift to morning all-age celebrations, and a much greater emphasis on the Christian year. In the end, only the Methodists and the United Reformed Church would place a eucharistic rite in the hands of their congregations. In all the traditions worship leaders and preachers turned to a variety of available resources, often without the approval of any recognizable magisterium.

The memory of revival songs from the Sankey and Moody era helped to secure a place for lively and spontaneous worship revived among the Free Churches, as in Anglicanism, by a new wave of charismatic prayer and praise and the new tradition of heavy 'biblical teaching' in Sunday worship. This movement had its strongest support among the Baptists and many of the original 'Plymouth' Brethren congregations who now renamed themselves 'Evangelical Churches'. The influence of the High Genevan school of the English Reformed tradition was still seen in the liturgical texts of the United Reformed Church but much of its worship was dominated by the twin calls to inclusive all-age worship and to be relevant and engaged in issues of local and international justice. Several babies went out with the bath water.

CHAPTER 6

Strangers and Dissenters:
The Architectural Legacy of Twentieth-Century
English Nonconformity—
Context, Case Study, and Connexion

Clyde Binfield

Context

What image best captures the twentieth-century English church? Given the strong case for selecting an ecumenical image, there is almost as strong a case for arguing that the aptest image would also be the most recent and the most fleeting. It would be the Faith Zone at the Millennium Dome. Quickly dismissed by the chattering and praying classes alike, it was designed for the century's, indeed the millennium's, end-turn by a Czech-born humanist, Eva Jiricna. 'Like a large tent where travellers meet, Faith is a stopping point on a journey through the faith landscape of the UK'. That is the official guide's introduction to what turned out to be a surprisingly successful synthesis of structure and concept. By all accounts the Faith Zone grew from sharp engagements sparked by a committee-bound culture. It is a salutary reminder that committees, those engines of ecumenism, can create as well as kill. It is also the only construction described in this chapter that was designed by a woman.[1]

Large images come naturally to mind. From the turn of the 1980s, and moving from ecumenism in the broadest sense to Christian ecumenism, there is the Church of Christ the Cornerstone (see p. 170), pandenominational at Milton Keynes, commanding, focal, domed and artful, more post-modish than post-modern, its architects not so much a name as a code. It could be a law courts or a state capitol or—were such places still built in the 1990s—a public library.[2]

---

1   R. McCrum (ed.), *Millennium Experience* (London: The New Millennium Experiences Company, 1999). For Eva Jiricna CBE (b. 1939) see *Who's Who*.

2   T. Hunter, *Church of Christ the Cornerstone, Milton Keynes* (Milton Keynes: Publication Committee, The Church of Christ the Cornerstone, 1992). The architects

Christ the Cornerstone is a church. Cathedrals are more likely to command attention. Liverpool's span the century in double vision. Liverpool's Anglican Cathedral, by the Catholic Giles Gilbert Scott, is one of the greatest of gothic cathedrals although only contemporary building techniques can account for it. It is, nonetheless, traditional in all the ways that one expects and probably wants a cathedral to be. Liverpool's Catholic Cathedral, by the Methodist-born Frederic Gibberd, is by contrast a great tent, a latter-day metropolitan tabernacle, squatting on the footings of what might have been. It is a monument to an imperial church's failure of nerve. Had it been built as designed by Edwin Lutyens and as intended by Archbishop Downey the cathedral would have been one of the world's as well as the century's great churches, quite as traditional in its way as Scott's, a breathtakingly complex and boldly toned arcuated geometry. An earlier century could have conceived it but only the twentieth century might have built it. As it is, Paddy's Wigwam has its own charm. Its Catholicism, shaped in the wake of Vatican II, is more corybantic than mysterious. The imperialism remains, but it is a populist Christian imperialism rather than that of the Viceroy's House for God which might now be standing there.[3]

Or should we stay with the cathedrals of the 1960s, opting for Basil Spence's Coventry? This too is a traditional cathedral however well disguised as nothing of the sort. Like the two Liverpools it houses a nation's best consecrated art, it has made itself accessible to a well-tried liturgy of common prayer, and it has one unique feature: it enshrines a particular historical moment, perhaps the nation's defining twentieth-century moment.[4]

These buildings are large in size and comprehensive in scope. What if one scales down the size and narrows the scope? What of the Nonconformist church building, apparently great only in its largely nineteenth-century variety? It is easy to think that the twentieth century was not a chapel-building age. It furnishes little to rival let alone beat the

---

were PDD Architects. The turf was cut 31 May 1990, and the building was dedicated Friday 13 March 1992. Between April 1981 and January 1992 the congregation had in fact worshipped in the new County Library. Hunter, *Church of Christ the Cornerstone*, pp. 2 and 8.

3   The Anglican Cathedral's foundation stone was laid 19 July 1904 and its completion stone was unveiled 25 October 1978. The Catholic Cathedral's foundation stone was laid 5 June 1933. Work stopped in 1941; Lutyens's crypt was formally opened in 1958. In 1959 a competition was announced for a new design, to be built on the crypt, and Frederick Gibberd's cathedral was completed in 1967.

4   Coventry Cathedral was destroyed 14 November 1940. Basil Spence won the competition for its reconstruction which began in June 1954. The new cathedral was consecrated 25 May 1962. For the architect's own account, see B. Spence, *Phoenix at Coventry: The Building of a Cathedral* (London: Geoffrey Bles, 1962).

Victorian chapel or the Georgian meeting in the general imagination. Yet that cannot possibly be so, as any random selection might demonstrate.

To start at Nonconformity's cathedral end and the twentieth-century's explosive beginning: Wesleyan Methodism struck unerringly at the Edwardian heart of imperial Westminster with Lanchester and Rickards's *Beaux-Arts* vision of what a Central Hall should be, a monumental fusion of Hapsburg Vienna, Hohenzollern Berlin, and the commercial purple of a nation of shopkeepers. It was in more senses that one a memorial to 'Imperial Perks'.[5] Central Hall, Westminster, has more qualities than that of mere size but although it would be hard to find a more Edwardian building it is not a typical chapel. Nonetheless it alerts us to the surprises Nonconformist architecture could spring in a century which saw the Baptist Church House fronting Kingsway as to the manner born and when even the Religious Society of Friends succumbed to its own restrained version of gigantism.[6] That element of Nonconformist surprise can be illustrated by three far smaller examples, one Unitarian, one Congregational, and one Methodist, taken from between 1928 and 1934, with a fourth added from 1971 to suggest an apparently wilful contrast.

The Unitarian example is a church in Cambridge by Ronald Potter Jones, a Liverpool architect who managed to be related to both Beatrix and Beatrice Potter. It is a modest Wrenaissance essay discreetly situated on a busy road behind Emmanuel College. Here the fun begins since its exterior echoes that of Wren's Pembroke College Chapel rather than his Emmanuel College Chapel. Its interior sustains the modesty but in size rather than impact for that, though duly proportioned, is decidedly opulent, carefully reminding Cambridge's enlightened inquirers where rational religion might yet be found and suitably enjoyed.[7]

At Oxted, in the southern foothills of Surrey's white highlands, is set the Church of the Peace of God (see p. 171). It is a cruciform building designed in an almost style-free Romanesque by Frederic Lawrence, a midland Methodist of psychic sensitivity who had found a home among south-coast Congregationalists. It was for refined Congregationalists, suburban refugees who might equally be stockbrokers or Fabians, that he recreated the spirit of St Francis in rose red, blue, and amber. Lawrence's Peace of God is as artful a use of colour, mass, and texture, as clever a combination of Christian tradition, congregational need, and artistic

---

5   It was opened in October 1912. Sir Robert Perks (1849–1934), its great protagonist and a leading Liberal Imperialist, was nicknamed 'Imperial Perks' by Beatrice Webb.

6   Baptist Church House, by Arthur Keen (1861–1938), was opened in 1903. Friends House, Euston Road, by Hubert Lidbetter (1885–1966), was built 1925–27. Its large meeting house held 1500.

7   Built 1928, although its meeting hall was built in 1922, by R.P. Jones (1875–1965), author of *Nonconformist Church Architecture* (London: Lindsey Press, 1914).

idiosyncracy, as one might hope to see. Here A.G. Matthews completed *Calamy Revised*.[8]

In Sheffield, in the southern foothills of the Pennines, where the city's Edwardian surge had paused for breath before rushing on in its version of Metroland, is Banner Cross Methodist Church. Its architect, W.J. Hale, was a locally well-connected Wesleyan. His clients were United Methodists. Banner Cross must have been one of the last United Methodist churches built before the twentieth century's second and more significant essay in Methodist union. Here too is an artful combination of tradition and texture, this time for self-consciously no-nonsense northern suburbia. It is less gently streamlined than the church at Oxted but then its materials are much harder. There is more than a touch of Scotland about this staging post to the Peak. Celtic motifs are juxtaposed with an almost abstract gothic tracery. Hale's earlier work was liable to flower into a roseate Tudoresque. Banner Cross's accent is more romanesque, the Roman element explaining the classical proportions. The tower's cenotaph air is not accidental, for it was also a war memorial.[9]

Trinity, Hunter's Bar, (see p. 172) lies downhill from Banner Cross and is forty years younger. This too is a landmark building, one of the last Congregational churches to be formed and built before most of them joined with the Presbyterian Church of England to become the United Reformed Church. As its name might suggest, Trinity was a union of three Congregational churches, one of them itself a union of two, whose history charts the flow and ebb of Sheffield's west-side Congregationalism. Its building is uncompromising, a concrete blockhouse for God, repelling the invader more obviously than it welcomes the inquirer, unconsciously reflecting the business interests and technical expertise of its leading member, inevitably announcing the socialist city which had pioneered Lewis Womersley's council-flat 'streets in the sky', but also suggesting the elegant brutalism of Denys Lasdun. Trinity, Hunter's Bar, is neither Sheffield's answer to the National Theatre nor to the Royal College of Physicians, but like them it is a striking symbol with much to tell the determined visitor who refuses to be repelled.

Trinity's architect, J.M.M. Jenkinson, was as locally well-connected a Congregationalist as W.J. Hale had been a Wesleyan Methodist, but his had been the more vigorous professional training of a later generation,

---

8   For Oxted (1935) and Lawrence (1882–1948) see C. Binfield, 'Art and Spirituality in Chapel Architecture: F.W. Lawrence (1882–1948) and his Churches', in D. Loades (ed.), *The End of Strife* (Edinburgh: T. & T. Clark, 1984), pp. 200-226.

9   For Banner Cross (1929) and Hale (1862–1929) see N.D. Wilson, '"Sane if Unheroic": The Work of William John Hale (1862–1929), Wesleyan Methodist and Architect', *Miscellany* 1 (London: The Chapels Society, 1998), pp. 51-73.

hence the whiff of Womersley, the strong external dash of Lasdun and, less expectedly, the internal touch of Frank Lloyd Wright.

Jenkinson was faced with a limited budget and a difficult site. His church stood against the sharp outcrop which explained the name of its district, Endcliffe. It looked across a busy road to a municipal park, ideal for weekend fêtes and visiting fairs. Or rather, if the preacher were to be heard above the traffic and seen as more than a pulpit silhouette, the one thing Jenkinson's church could not do was look across the road to the park, hence the blank façade of textured concrete, mass in miniature rather than creeper-friendly brick. This church was to be a rock of faith, an end cliff of Christianity.[10]

Inside (p. 173), the symbolism is less severe. The rock has become a meeting. There, at the foot of the cross designed by the Sheffield silversmith, David Mellor, and placed where light from the windows in the roof can catch it each mid-morning to best advantage, the church gathers round the table on which the Bible lies open and behind which stands the plain stone pulpit whence the Word is expounded.[11] Inside and out there are reassuring continuities. Stone roundels from one of the constituent churches are set in the cliff of concrete. There is Victorian stained glass from the same church and stripped country Chippendale chairs from one of the others. The organ came from the recently closed and since demolished institute of an east-end Congregational church, but it had begun life much nearer to hand as a chamber organ in an Anglican steel manufacturer's mansion.[12] Thus has the blockhouse been domesticated into a meeting house and the Puritan tradition affirmed. John Jenkinson's Trinity, Hunter's Bar, is quite as artful as William Hale's Banner Cross, Frederic Lawrence's Peace of God, and Ronald Jones's Memorial Church, Cambridge. Like theirs its art is rooted in tradition.

This should come as no surprise. However worldly ('relevant' might be a kinder word), churches are embassies of eternity and eternity encompasses the accumulated past as much as it embraces an endlessly extending future. Churches express continuity as powerfully as they witness to discontinuity. If it sometimes seems that twentieth-century churches were more determined to signal discontinuity with their past than with the world, that too is understandable. They were built when any age of faith had long since been overtaken by successive crises of faith.

10   Information about Trinity, Hunter's Bar (1971) and John Jenkinson (1917–78) is drawn from personal knowledge and C. Binfield, 'Trinity 1971 or When Three Churches Came Together' (unpublished typescript, 1992).

11   The Cross was commissioned by John Jenkinson in memory of his aunt, Grace Jenkinson. [D. Mellor to C. Binfield, 6 July 1999]. For Mellor (b. 1930), see *David Mellor: Master Metalworker* (Sheffield: Sheffield Galleries and Museums Trust, 1998).

12   A. Wortley, 'The Story of the "Weetwood" Chamber Organ in Trinity United Reformed Church, Hunter's Bar Sheffield' (unpublished typescript, 1983).

Their architecture was crisis architecture, useful sheds where spires once soared. If, however, it is recalled that 'crisis' is less 'point of disaster' than 'point of decision' or 'turning point' a dimension unfolds which tells of decisions taken about theology, liturgy, mission, people, money, and politics, as well as about site, style, and architect. Tradition has its place in such decision making. It is not necessarily an escape from the present or a capitulation to congregational conservatism.

Tradition, moreover, had been as powerful a spring board for twentieth-century architecture as it had been for the nineteenth century. Many, perhaps most, of the formative twentieth-century English architects had been trained in the Arts and Crafts tradition. Throughout their youth the complicated legacy of Pugin, Ruskin, and William Morris was still working its way tenaciously through the English cultural psyche. The moral, communal, and artistic imperatives of the Arts and Crafts Movement still held sway. That phrase, 'Arts and Crafts', was coined in 1888 when a talented group of artists and craftsmen set up the Arts and Crafts Exhibition Society with a widely reported exhibition as its annual focus. The true English Arts-and-Craftsman was a doctrinaire before he was a showman. Honesty of purpose, sense of place, joy in craftsmanship, sensitivity to colour, texture, and material encouraged in him a horrified reaction to what technology might exploit. Technology opened the door to whim. It fostered an uninformed taste regardless of place or need. The English Arts and Crafts pioneers had international standing, but the Europeans and Americans whom they influenced were seldom so doctrinaire, or not in the same way, and neither in fact were most English practitioners. They could not afford to be. They had practices to keep afloat, families to raise, a position to maintain. They were professional men, women too as the century wore on. They liked to think that they were artists, but they were also businessmen, not always very far removed from tradesmen. J.M.M. Jenkinson's grandfather had been a Sheffield estate agent in the days when estate agency usually meant rent-collecting. W.J. Hale married into an estate agency. Such men learned instinctively to make ends meet. They were pragmatic. The spirit of their training, which in the early days could still be summarized as 'in the round, on the ground', taught them honesty, propriety, and proportion. The congenital eclecticism of the Victorians was educated, some might say tamed, by their best successes into a seemly flexibility. That was the essence of the true gothic spirit for public buildings and of its domestic variant, the Queen Anne Revival: the porch here, the bay there, the gable, the warm yet humble brick, the white wood and apple-green stain, the local stone where sensible, the touch of class on a demanding site with a slender budget, all of it exercised by people increasingly alert to the social implications of their work. These latest heirs to the moralism of Ruskin and Morris were out to improve society, perhaps transform it. They were interested in legislation, attracted by social engineering, and a significant proportion of them saw an extension of their formative ideals, even their fulfilment, in the modernism which was evolving in the 1920s and 1930s. The Arts and Craftsman's moral imperatives could be worked into a sane modernism, with architecture as an increasingly well-tuned vehicle for society's transformation. Here, anchored in civic responsibility, was the continuity which linked the modern and the traditional, Trinity Hunter's Bar, Peace of God Oxted, Coventry Cathedral and Liverpool's too.

It is also the continuity connecting a significant group of Free Churches built in the 1950s. Like Coventry Cathedral these new buildings were in fact rebuildings of churches severely damaged or totally destroyed in the Second World War. Today they are period pieces, now past their point of lowest esteem but increasingly vulnerable to the ravages of contemporary relevance, demography, the economy, and the uneven new techniques of their time. They reflect the needs and taste of their age, the more so because they had been forced to restart with a clean state, but they had not in fact started with a clean slate because they were shaped by a factor unique to this period, the constraints of the War Damage Commission.

They include some historic names. That great Baptist tent of meeting, Spurgeon's Metropolitan Tabernacle, was rebuilt between 1957 and 1959 by a Surrey Congregationalist, J. Mountford Pigott.[13] He managed to retain the grand façade originally designed by the Wesleyan W.W. Pocock. Joseph Parker's City Temple, Congregationalism's answer to Spurgeon and St Paul's alike, was rebuilt for the Methodist crowd puller, Leslie Weatherhead, in 1958. It too retained its façade designed, Wrenaissance before its time, by the northern partnership of Mawson and Lockwood, but behind it, on a far from smooth site, the gold carat firm of Seely and Paget, which had been sensibly selected after the sudden death of Frederic Lawrence, constructed a smooth St Odeon's.[14] West of Southwark and the City a famous Presbyterian church reopened in 1955. This time nothing survived of the original structure. Instead Edward Maufe, whose family were the Muffs of Brown, Muff, once the Harrods of Bradford, created in the neighbourhood of the real Harrods an uncannily apt embassy church. It fits uneasily here, for St Columba's, Pont Street, is Church of Scotland. It is therefore Reformed but not Free,

---

13   Mountford Pigott, a member of Sutton Congregational Church and architect of Congregational churches at Mitcham and Morden, had been consulted by the City Temple after its destruction in May 1940. For his rebuilding of the Metropolitan Tabernacle, see *Baptist Handbook* (London: Carey Kingsgate Press, 1959), 'Architectural Supplement', p. xi.

14   For the rebuilding of the City Temple, see C. Binfield, 'Victims of Success: Twentieth-Century Free Church Architecture', iin Jane Shaw and A. Kreider (eds), *Culture and the Nonconformist Tradition* (Cardiff: University of Wales Press, 1999) pp. 144-60.

but its inclusion is appropriate because it introduces the consciously Reformed ecclesiological element, pithily encapsulated as 'New Genevan', which now influenced Free Church architecture. In this grey-white Scots Kirk, set amidst the red Pont Street Dutch, Maufe exerted all the restrained, expensive charm of which he was master, fey because it was Celtic and clean-limbed because it was Presbyterian. St Columba's could not be more Sloane Square (or Pont Street) when the grouse are not in season. Maufe is a master who deserves reappraisal.[15]

Poplar lies east of Southwark and the City. Today its Trinity Church is Methodist, but up to 1976 it had been Congregational, latterly United Reformed. The date of its rebuilding, 1951, indicates its architectural significance (see p. 174).

The cause dated from the 1840s. It had been a shipowner's church, a heavily dignified classical structure fronting East India Dock road, built at the sole expense of the Green family of Stepney Meeting. Successive Greens were prominent in City and shipping circles until Lloyds exploded in the 1980s. Their direct interest in Trinity remained significant early in the twentieth century and their house flag was still flown at the church on high days in the 1950s. In the 1920s and 1930s, however, Trinity caught the attention of a wider public as an East End beacon of hope under 'Dick of Poplar', William Dick, the Congregational counterpart of Methodism's 'Lax of Poplar', William Lax. It almost survived the War, buoyed by great plans for its future on settlement lines, but a flying bomb destroyed it in 1944.[16]

Trinity's relatively swift rebuilding is attributable to its role in that last achievement of the Attlee years, the 1951 Festival of Britain, as part of its 'Live Architecture' section. It was a beacon relit, the Festival's Faith Zone on location. Here was the communitarian and purposeful London of Herbert Morrison distilled into Lansbury, reborn in the heart of Poplar. Trinity's architects, Handisyde and Stark, were in their early forties. Cecil Handisyde is regarded as the prime mover. He was at once theorist and technician. D. Rogers Stark, however, had been brought up

---

15   For Maufe (1883–1974) and Pont Street, see [J.H. McIndoe] *St. Columba's Pont Street London. Its Building and History: A Brief Guide* (London: St Columba's, 1992).

16   For Trinity, Poplar, see *Trinity Church, Poplar (Congregational): Deeds 1842–1942 and Dreams 1942—and Celebrations May 9–24, 1942* (London: Trinity Hall, Augusta Street, Poplar, 1942); and *Trinity Church Poplar* (London: Westminster Press, 1952). For William Lax (1868–1937), at the Poplar (Methodist) Mission from 1902, see W. Lax, *Lax of Poplar* (London: Epworth Press, 1927). For William Dick (1877–1945), at Trinity from 1924, see *Congregational Year Book* (London: Congregational Union of England and Wales, 1946), p. 440.

in the church and he was well placed in London County Council. He knew the ropes.[17]

All Nonconformist churches needed vestries, meeting rooms and halls. Their Edwardian Institutes and Central Missions and their Victorian Sunday Schools had been crucibles for architectural experiment. So Handisyde and Stark were doing nothing new at Trinity, Poplar, save that its spirit seemed quite new. It was streamlined, spacious, efficient, and natural, at once aspiring and to human scale, what a later generation would call 'user friendly'. Here was church-as-social-complex, at one with the new society. It had offices, consulting rooms, playrooms, storage rooms, canteens, and courtyards. It liberated space for spiritual and social growth in the East End as it was at last to be.

Its church space reflected this. It was lofty, its table end demonstrating the tall simplicity characteristic of contemporary churches, but it was not as large as it seemed. It seated 400 in cinematic efficiency. The structure was artfully up-to-date: reinforced concrete frame, yellow stock bricks, copper-covered sloping side walls, sensibly self-coloured materials wherever possible, save for the nave's blue ceiling. It was no less artfully conscious of its tradition. The George Green Memorial Hall is self-explanatory. The tower held the bell salvaged from the bombed Trinity. As the rebuilding brochure put it:

> THE SIGN KEPT AT TRINITY
> surmounting the tower, on the gable ends of the sanctuary, on pulpit, Communion Table and organ-screen, is the sign of the Cross.
> THE BUILDINGS ARE THEMSELVES A SIGN—
> inviting your judgment on contemporary architecture; claiming that the Christian Church (to which we owe the glories of Notre Dame and Salisbury Cathedral, the Jordans Meeting House and St. Paul's) is integral to the newest 'Neighbourhood Unit'; asking again, as the one question of abiding moment, 'What think ye of Christ?'[18]

Thus a Neighbourhood Unit is set full in the grand continuity. Yet an affirmative answer to the question posed in its brochure implies a commitment to discontinuity. Trinity is a true embassy of eternity.[19]

---

17   For Handisyde (b. 1908) and Stark (b. 1908) see N. Bingham *et. al.*, *The Twentieth Century Church* (London: RIBA Heinz Gallery and Twentieth Century Society, 1997), p. 26.

18   *Trinity Church Poplar*, unpaginated.

19   When Trinity passed from United Reformed to Methodist hands, it was adapted by the Methodist architect, Edward D. Mills (b. 1915), author of the influential *The Modern Church* (London: The Architectural Press, 1956), in which Trinity is illustrated, pp. 94-95.

War damage was restricted neither to London nor the great industrial cities. Punshon Memorial Methodist Church, Bournemouth, was dedicated in mid-December 1958, replacing on a new site a totally destroyed example of spired Wesleyan Gothic. Its architect, Ronald Sims, had come straight from architectural school to take over Frederic Lawrence's practice: the two men shared residual Methodism and a love for Umbria. Sims, therefore, was the young man whom the City Temple felt would be too risky to take on when Lawrence died in mid-commission. Punshon Memorial both made and marred him. Its evolving form aroused intense controversy which Sims's combative mix of ability, temperament, and forensic skill kept on the boil. He retained the support of Punshon's local trustees, pitted against the united experience of the local authority and the Methodist Department for Chapel Affairs, up in Manchester. Sims won, although he soon exchanged Bournemouth for Canada.[20]

And his Church (see p. 175)? Punshon Memorial remains uncompromisingly modern, a great church redeemed by its careful use of brick and its enjoyment of exotic woods and lighting, its muhuhu and idigbo building up to the table end's high dignity. It is a fine church for a car-owning society and it greatly interested Sims's old teacher, the influential R. Furneaux Jordan, who found in Sims one of that select band of young architects who refused to be enslaved by new technology. They were entirely competent to handle that technology, but they 'admired Wright more than Mies'; they were organic. Jordan's reference to the contemporary architectural world's two American-based heavyweights was not accidental. Both Frank Lloyd Wright and Mies van der Rohe had recently designed widely publicized churches.[21]

Bournemouth's Punshon Memorial, dedicated in December 1958, and Stowmarket's Congregational Church, dedicated in March 1955, have little in common beyond prosperity yet they are comparable.

It must have been a vexation to local Anglicans that Stowmarket's old Congregational Church was so prominent. Well placed and better attended, it was a joyously guildhallish structure in fidgety gothic. Its twin survives in Ipswich as Christ Church, Tacket Street. Fison's fertilisers, Prentice's gun-cotton, Webb's leathergoods, had worshipped there under energetic ministers. At noon on 31 January 1941, a suggestive date for Anglicans and Dissenters alike, the church secretary, a solicitor whose local ancestry dissented almost to 1800 and whose East Anglian ancestry dissented beyond 1662, was walking by in his capacity as Chief A.R.P.

20   For Sims and Punshon Memorial see Binfield, 'Victims of Success', pp. 160-73.

21   Binfield, 'Victims of Success', pp. 171-72. The two churches were Mies's Chapel for the Illinois Institute of Technology, Chicago (referred to in Mills, *The Modern Church*, p. 17) and Wright's Unitarian Meeting House, Madison, Wisconsin, also designed for a university congregation (1947–51).

Warden. He heard the approach of a stray German aeroplane. He took appropriate cover. When he emerged his church had vanished.[22]

For nine years its people worshipped in the Regal Cinema. Perhaps they felt they still were when they returned to the old site. Their new building put its architect, Alan Cooke, on the Free Church map. In the next decade he designed Congregational churches for East Ham, Wembley Park, and Stepney. The local newspaper wrote cheerfully: 'When...its sheer lines in the contemporary style, unadorned as they are by any form of traditional embellishments first became apparent, it was heralded by varying opinion as resembling an ultra-modern cinema, a town hall, and a community centre. Even Stowmarket Urban District Council, in the preliminary stages, withheld their blessing.'[23]

One can see why. It is not an endearing building. It has not mellowed. It takes some ingenuity to appreciate that the rhythm of its entrance front echoes that of its predecessor, or even that it is in fact adorned by traditional embellishments, for it has a tower and a cross. Yet it has wholly justified its usefulness. It was built for enlargement and enlarged it has been. It has wide corridors, ample lavatories, generous cupboardage. Circulation flows. The prime test, of course, comes in the church itself. When it is empty the cinema air is inescapable, but it was not designed to be empty and on Sundays, high days and holidays it seldom was. And if what the preacher sees is a cinema, what the worshipper sees is altogether nobler (see p. 176). Once more the dominant note is a lofty enjoyment of wood—wood for pulpit and table, wood curtain to enfold Word and Sacrament, wood for chairs. There is also a notable sense of church order. At the point of their rebuilding these Free Churches took their liturgy seriously. There was more to it than a holy club sandwich of hymns, prayers, and readings dignified by the Nonconformist crouch of popular mythology. At Stowmarket this was not achieved without tension. The old church's last minister had been cast in an extrovert mould. He was a vigorous Liberal, an exciting preacher, a young man's man. The

---

22   For information about Stowmarket United Reformed Church I am indebted to Mr Norman Baker, the Revd Edmund Banyard, Mr Martin Prentice and the late Mrs Elizabeth Prentice, the Revd John Pugh, and Ms Judith Tydeman (Public Service Archivist, Ipswich Record Office). See also, N.B. Frost and J.P.M. Prentice, *Stowmarket Congregational Church 1861–1941* (Stowmarket: Stowmarket Congregational Church, 1955) and E. Banyard, *The First 300 Years: The Unfinished Story of Stowmarket Congregational Church* (Stowmarket: Stowmarket Congregational Church, 1970). The architect of the original building was Frederick Barnes (1813–98).

23   *East Anglian Daily Times* 4 March 1955, quoted in Banyard, *First 300 Years*, pp. 45-46. For Congregational churches by Alan D. Cooke 1953–67, see Elain Harwood and A. Foster, 'Places of Christian Worship 1914–1990: A Selection', in Roland Jeffery *et al* (eds), *The Twentieth Century Church, Twentieth Century Architecture 3, Journal of the Twentieth Century Society* (London: The Twentieth Century Society, 1998), p. 109.

new church's first minister was quite different. He became an Anglican.[24] An equilibrium was nonetheless achieved.The new building passed its test. It worked.

Case Study

The context has been set for a more extended case study. All the elements so far outlined are to be found in that prime Dissenting heartland, Norwich. That fine city's buildings for Congregationalists, Quakers, and Unitarians proclaim an established tradition, an educated ministry, and an influential lay infrastructure. It was also a heartland for strangers, Dutch, Flemish, and French, Geldart, De Carle, and Martineau. Three of its most instructive twentieth-century Dissenting churches might be described as strangers' churches.

The smallest, now Greek Orthodox, was built in the 1930s for the Christian Scientists. They were an American sect responsible for some distinguished buildings. Their Norwich church in Recorder Road, however, was designed by Herbert Ibberson, a Fenland Baptist settled in Hunstanton and married to a Leicester Congregationalist, for a locally entrenched congregation. Ibberson's solution was churchier than Christian Scientists were used to. It is an artful little masterpiece of textured streamlining punctuated with apt vernacular touches (see p. 177).[25]

The largest of the three, Norwich's Roman Catholic Cathedral, is a contrast in every way (see p. 178). Begun by George Gilbert Scott in 1882 and completed by his brother John Oldrid Scott in 1910, it is not really a twentieth-century church at all.[26] It makes no concession to contemporary taste. It sets no pace even in its traditionalism. Here is no Westminster Cathedral. Yet its quality as townscape is undeniable. And it is undeniably a strangers' church, the more so for owing its presence in Norwich to the fifteenth Duke of Norfolk. As its historian, Anthony Rossi, has reminded us, this is how it struck Percy Lubbock driving as a boy into Norwich with his grandmother from Earlham:

---

24   Frost and Prentice, *Stowmarket Congregational Church 1861–1941*, pp. 7-11, 12; Banyard, *First 300 Years*, pp. 42, 45-47.

25   For Ibberson (1866–1935) and Recorder Road, see C. Binfield, 'An Excursion into Architectural Cousinhood: The East Anglian Connexion', in Norma Virgoe and Tom Williamson (eds), *Religious Dissent in East Anglia: Historical Perspectives* (Norwich: The Centre of East Anglia Studies, University of East Anglia, 1993), pp. 92-98, 113-29.

26   A. Rossi, 'Norwich Roman Catholic Cathedral: A Building History', *Miscellany* 1 (London: The Chapels Society, 1998), pp. 1-34.

a large and splendid church, scrupulously Gothic...not an ordinary church, it was a Roman Catholic Cathedral; and I looked at it, I well remember, with a shade of mute and mournful regret, puzzled and interested, wondering at so vast a monument of perversity and yet compelled to admire its insolence. But we scarcely spoke of it, the exotic upstart—we looked and passed; it could by no manner of means be regarded as part of our Norwich, and on the whole we ignored its intrusion.[27]

The careful observer will find another intrusion sheltered under its wing. This, too, is a strangers' church.

The Presbyterian Church of England was formed in 1876 from two largely nineteenth-century branches of Presbyterianism. Although links could be established, especially in the north east, with seventeenth-century Presbyterianism, these Presbyterians, firmly trinitarian of course, owed their strength and their accent to incomers from Ireland, Scotland, and Wales. The Scottish element predominated but there was always a certain distance from the Church of Scotland because these Presbyterians tended to come from secessions from the Kirk. Given the steady emigration from Ireland, Scotland, and Wales in the nineteenth and earlier twentieth centuries (Scottish emigration was on a notably large scale in the 1920s and 1930s), the presence of distinctive Presbyterian congregations in English towns becomes natural. It was not just Irish Catholics who flooded out.

Nonetheless, East Anglia was not natural Presbyterian territory, which was perhaps why it was in the Presbytery of London North. There was a congregation in Ipswich, with a building in respectable Dissenting Gothic from the 1870s. There was another in Cambridge from 1891, its building the image of Auchtermuchty, thanks to the influence of Sir George Barclay Bruce and the design of J. McVicar Anderson. From the turn of the century their theological college was also in Cambridge, a superior essay in Arts and Crafts by Hare, the architect of Oxford Town Hall.[28] That was all, Norwich apart.

The Norwich congregation began in 1867, largely formed by the families of Scottish credit drapers. They had a good town-centre church in Theatre Street from 1884, Lombardic with a tower and a slight spire, and only one of their ministers, other than an American, has so far had an English name.[29] The credit drapers were soon supplemented by those

27 Rossi, 'Norwich Roman Catholic Cathedral', pp. 29-30, quoting P. Lubbock, *Earlham* (London: Jonathan Cape, 1922, re-issued 1963), pp. 209-10.

28 The Ipswich church, in Portman Road, was by Frederick Barnes. For Henry Thomas Hare (1861–1921) and Westminster College, see R. Buick Knox, *Westminster College Cambridge: Its Background and History* (Cambridge: Westminster College, n.d. [1979]).

29 The American was Simeon S. Jewkes, minister 1936–40. 'History Notes of Trinity United Reformed Church, Norwich' (unpublished typescript, [c. 1996]).

professionals who always seem to be Scottish and by a group of farming families who came to Norfolk between the wars. It was, therefore, a scattered congregation. Membership grew from seventy-four in 1867 to a peak of 272 in 1907, and then it declined steadily to 147 in 1947.[30] So when the church was reduced to a shell in June 1942 and its people retreated to the hall behind it, their future might reasonably seem to be in doubt.

Yet fourteen years later they had moved to a new site with a new building which might be regarded as warp and woof of Norwich while yet expressing what Presbyterian worship and polity should be. It stands as one of the best representative buildings of its period, a model of the 'evolutionary' dimension of contemporary architecture, the issue of opportunity, people, process, and structure. These are the determinants which explain a building.[31]

The opportunity was a disaster. It destroyed the church, although not its hall or its caretaker's house. The realistic solution was closure. The congregation was small and scattered. There were few growth points in a town with a flourishing Congregational tradition. In many places Congregationalism, which had its own distinctive urban presence in Scotland, provided a satisfactory home for the Scottish diaspora. The alternative was to rebuild. The twist of opportunity came with the question of site.

The people, of course, are crucial. The congregation was welded together first by the frustration of adversity, then by their shared enterprise in funding and planning the new building under the leadership of a small, admirably balanced group of men, each a distinctive personality in his own right. What happened under them was not particularly democratic, but it was truly representative, the work of a trio or so of deacons with the minister and architect apparently kept at arm's length, on the whole to their mutual convenience. These men were in the best sense responsible. They got on well with each other. They played meticulously by the rules but they could see how rules might be turned to best advantage and they understood the bureaucratic mind. Since they had to deal with three bureaucracies, each of which could have tripped them up at innumerable points and none of which did (although there were some near misses), their understanding was of inestimable value. The Presbyterian authorities in London were the least of their worries. They were far-distant and overstretched, cruelly so after a bomb destroyed their London headquarters in February 1945. They offered what help they could, and Norwich appears dutifully in Presbyterian

30   'Notes on Trinity Presbyterian Church' (unpublished typescript [1956]) p. 17.

31   In what follows on Trinity Church, I have been particularly indebted to Mrs Margo Benns, Sir Bernard Feilden, Messrs Feilden and Mawson, Mr Alex. Grant and the late Revd D. Howell Jones.

minutes.[32] More immediate were the War Damage Commission, with their regional offices in Cambridge. They were inundated with requests and competing need. On the doorstep was the City Council. It is easy to forget the clout and expertise which local authorities could muster before the late 1970s. In the 1940s war-time destruction coincided with and in some cases followed plans for urban regeneration. Norwich had such plans and Theatre Street was in the heart of them.

Theatre Street's five key rebuilders need to be introduced at this point. Despite his name, Kenneth Christie was a local man who had married into the congregation. He worked for the City Council, moving in this period from the Waterworks Department to become Lord Mayor's Secretary. He knew everybody and how each should be approached. Blunt, calm, clear, with a genius for writing a good letter, he was the perfect Clerk of Works. J.R. Crawford was the stage Scotsman, President of the Burns Federation in 1952, a prominent local businessman, on the sales and publicity side of Caley Mackintosh. Archibald Clark was just as Scottish but he was a partner in a leading county firm of quantity surveyors, and the architect found his professional knowledge and contacts invaluable. Crawford knew what he did not want, Clark knew what could be done.

These three were deacons. The minister, W.R. Cameron Joyce, arrived late on the scene, in 1946. He had been an army chaplain, mentioned in despatches and under him the congregation not just revived but grew. He is remembered as an ideal minister in those last years before television up-ended community life. He was the man who made the new building work. As, of course, was the architect.

The church's architects at the point of rebuilding (1954–56) were Edward Boardman and Son, Old Bank of England Court, Queen Street. There were two partners. Frank Swindells, whose background was north Cheshire Methodist, was the senior partner, by then in his late sixties. He had kept the firm afloat through depression and war. Humphrey Colman Boardman, the junior partner, was a third generation architect. His background was Prince's Street Congregational Church, for the Boardmans were part of the fabric of Norwich and Norfolk life. Humphrey's father, the 'Son' of Boardman and Son, had married a Colman daughter. There were few major streets in later Victorian or Edwardian Norwich without a Boardman building. Thus the firm had designed the Lombardic Presbyterian chapel in Theatre Street and the Decorated Gothic Chapel on Unthank Road to which the Presbyterians were now to move.

---

32   I am indebted for confirmation of references in Presbytery Minutes, 1942–46 and 1949–56, to Mrs Margaret Thompson (Westminster College, Cambridge). What follows is drawn from the file of correspondence, memoranda, and related material, meticulously compiled by the late K.S. Christie and now in possession of Trinity United Reformed Church, Norwich (hereafter TF).

After the War the firm's work picked up. Swindells specialized in hospital and bank work, which in Norwich meant Barclay's, and in industrial projects; Boardman did council housing. In 1950 they had been joined by a young man, just turned thirty, fresh from a brief but suggestive spell in a London office, newly married (his wife's family knew the Boardmans), and newly qualified (he had been a contemporary of Ronald Sims's at the Architectural Association). He was Bernard Melchior Feilden and he quickly became involved in Swindells's bank and hospital work: the tricky reinvention of Barclay's St Stephen's Branch; pathology laboratories and operating theatres for the Norfolk and Norwich Hospital and then, just at the point at which he handed in his notice, because the firm could not yet return to the old complement of three partners and Swindells was not yet minded to retire, there came the commission for Trinity Presbyterian Church. This was to be Feilden's project and although he left Boardman and Son in June 1954, to set up in Pull's Ferry, the firm allowed him to finish Trinity. That makes it at once another Boardman church and the first Feilden one.

So to the process which these men mastered. Kenneth Christie's file survives, an informative correspondence from 1942 to 1956 in which professional etiquette, congregational concern and mutual respect tied strong characters into productive relationships, giving the measure of the men involved, conveying the authentic Presbyterian accent, leading the reader through the twists and turns of the new bureaucracy. The elements of the story could be replicated nationwide. In Norwich, as in Coventry, Canterbury, or Bristol, it was a city which was taking shape and not just a building or the community shaped by that building. This case study, therefore, is at once representative and particular.

On 18 February 1941 the church in Theatre Street was damaged. Just over a year later, 29 April 1942, there was further damage, and on 27 June 1942 the church was totally destroyed, and its small hall was rendered 'incapable of repair'. The main hall and caretaker's house survived with slight damage although the latter was by now an unappealing residence, roomy enough (kitchen, two living rooms and four bedrooms) but Dickensian; it had a washhouse but no bathroom, lots of damp and bulging walls in perished brick and flint. Already Kenneth Christie was coordinating the defence.

An appeal was issued in August 1944: 'When hostilities cease, the question will arise of the rebuilding of the Church and Halls...but the details of the new buildings will depend on the decision of the Government and Presbytery'. Nonetheless they had a special fund of £3,000 in view. 'DO PLEASE REPLY'. And an architect had been approached: Frank Swindells of Boardman and Son, which at that point still had three partners.

Until they knew where they stood over war damage nothing could be done. A circular from the denomination's General Secretary, Drummond Harcus, set out the situation in July 1945, the first summer of peace: the amount allocated for church repair by the Ministry of Works was very small in relation to the demand, so there must be rationing. Applications for licenses for repair had first to be approved by the Area Reconstruction Committee. In due course congregations with destroyed or seriously damaged buildings would fall under one of three categories: Plain Repair, Plain Substitute Building, or Doubtful. As will be seen, Trinity's future hinged on that classification.

By now rumours were circulating. Ever since the 1944 Town Planning Act it had been all sections go in the town halls of war-battered Britain. Late in July 1945 Trinity's minister-in-charge, W.H. Macallan, a retired man whose father had been the congregation's first full time minister nearly eighty years earlier, wrote to Sydney Myers, minister of Princes Street Congregational Church: 'To judge by the published "City Plan", the site of this church is obliterated, and in its place appears a "Parking Place"... It appears now that we are to be dispossessed...' Myers spoke to the bishop, Percy Herbert, who could say little except that things took time, did not happen without due notice, and would not happen without due compensation. At the same time Christie wrote to Drummond Harcus in London, who promptly lost the letter although we know what was in it because Christie kept a copy on file: 'The Norwich Council has just had published a very ambitious "Plan of Norwich" setting out the Norwich of 50 years hence. In this Plan the Church site is included in that of the Civic Centre and no mention is made of the Presbyterian Church...' Two months later the City Engineer confirmed that this was indeed so: 'In these circumstances I myself feel that it is unlikely the Town Planning Committee would approve the permanent rebuilding of your church on this site'.

There were now two separate yet interlocking challenges: the rebuilding of the church and its resiting. The former depended on what war damage would allow and the latter depended on the City Plan.

At this point the War Damage Commission's Regional Manager intervened from his office in Cambridge's County Bowling Club. The church had been scheduled as 'Plain Substitute Building'. His inspector felt it should be rescheduled as 'Plain Repair'. He suggested a site inspection to resolve the matter. His reasoning, following an unprompted visit, was that since the church, halls, and caretaker's house had been interconnecting, they should be viewed as one unit. A substitute, that is to say a separate building, for the church alone, was insufficient. The complex should be treated as a totality. That, logically, put it into the 'Plain Repair' category. Consequently any negotiation with the council would have to deal with the complete site and not just that of the church.

This was an immensely helpful suggestion since it was bound to affect any compensation should the rumours about the City Plan prove justified and the church find itself faced with an alternative site for an entirely new building. To press this point home, Kenneth Christie wrote feelingly to the City Engineer: 'This Church is the only Presbyterian Church in Norfolk and having conducted its services there for the last 80 years, is therefore very jealous of its freehold site in the heart of this city'.

By December 1945 it was thus clear that any rebuilding would be on a new site. 1946 saw the serving of compulsory purchase orders. And then—standstill. Only in late May 1949 did Christie write again to the City Engineer, with a formal application to rebuild. His timing, however, was impeccable. Any detailed city development plan needed the approval of the Minister for Town and Country Planning. What the *Eastern Daily News* described as a 'desperate shortage of skilled staff' was holding back the submission of such plans, hence the strategy of asking the Council to designate thirteen areas for comprehensive development, ranked in order of priority and timed accordingly; 250 acres of central Norwich were thus covered. It was clear that Theatre Street would be in one of the most urgent schemes.[33] It was time to alert the architect although as Christie wrote to Swindells, 'this is only a very rough draft of what we may need'.

The next stage began a year and a half later, marked by a minute of the City's General Purposes Committee, 17 April 1951. This approved in principle the exchange of Trinity's Theatre Street site for that of a disused Baptist chapel on Unthank Road. It was to be an exchange of freeholds, but in addition the Corporation would demolish the Baptist chapel, repair its hall, and incorporate a caretaker's flat. That was an excellent deal for Trinity and a good deal for Norwich, since if the Presbyterians had stood their ground, the council would have been forced to complete the procedures for compulsory purchase and those could have involved heavy compensation.

The new site was not ideal. It was narrow, and the redundant chapel's baptistery proved surprisingly awkward to fill, but it was accessible, almost central, and the best of the four so far proposed; and it had a history to which its new users were sensitive. The old church had played a vigorous part in Baptist and civic life on various locations since 1788 but, since its latest site was leasehold and it could afford neither to buy the freehold nor to pay the annual rent, it had surrendered its claim in May 1941.[34] For some years the chapel was used as a store by Mackintosh's.

---

33   'Taking Shape', *Eastern Daily Press* 1 July 1949 (TF).

34   For Unthank Road Baptist Church and its prehistory, see C.B. Jewson, *The Baptists in Norfolk* (London: Carey Kingsgate Press, 1957), *passim*. On the eve of closure the church had 123 members (*Baptist Handbook* [London: Baptist Union Publication Department, 1940], p. 118).

Jack Crawford knew it well; indeed he and Archibald Clark lived on Unthank Road. There survives a dignified exchange of letters between Kenneth Christie and a descendant of Unthank Road's formative Victorian minister about the dispersal of various memorials, two disrupted traditions acknowledging each other.

All was by no means over. There remained long and never wholly predictable negotiations with the War Damage Commission which now introduced the concept of 'redundancy' on the reasonable ground that if a congregation were leaving a 600 seater like Theatre Street for a 250 seater as proposed for Unthank Road, there was probably taxpayers' money to be saved in the compensation. In the event a sum of £26,000 was agreed as a base line and preparations for rebuilding began in earnest. By December 1951 Bernard Feilden was in the picture. By April 1952 it looked as if his scheme would reach £33,000 and in July 1952 there came a tiresomely inevitable letter. It was from the Deputy Regional Licensing Officer, Ministry of Works, Cambridge:

> The present demands on the restricted licensing allocation for this Ministry are so great that this allocation is already committed for a considerable time ahead... If however you will renew the application in January next it will again be considered in the light of conditions then prevailing.

There had also been ruffled proprieties in Trinity's Building Sub-Committee. On 6 March Crawford wrote at length to his minister, Cameron Joyce. It was a Presbyterian letter. No Baptist or Congregationalist could have written it, and probably no Methodist. It merits full quotation:

> I have had a call this afternoon from Mr. Christie and Mr. Clark and the latter informs me that he is tending his resignation as a member of the Building Sub-Committee. He explains that he does so as a matter of principle and I can only agree with his decision.
>
> I understand from Mr. Clark that you spoke to him on Wednesday night and in the course of the questions you put to him with regard to the stage we are now at with the architect and the War Damage Claim, you informed him that you personally must see these plans again to finally agree with them before they were lodged with the War Damage Commission.
>
> With the very greatest respect, I must point out that the Sub-Committee, composed of Mr. Christie, Mr. Clark and myself, were given full powers to finalise the plans to a stage necessary for submission to the War Damage Commission. At the Deacons' Court meeting I made it perfectly plain that we must have that authority before we could accept our brief and we have not exceeded that brief. I personally realise that as a matter of courtesy we might have invited you to join us at the meeting with Mr. Feilden, but having been given the full authority from the

Deacons Court, I must take full responsibility for having urged my colleagues on the Committee to give Mr. Feilden full authority there and then to proceed and I confirmed that authority in writing. On learning from Mr. Clark that you intended to call on Mr. Feilden, I had perforce to advise Mr. Feilden that although you might possibly not agree with our decision, our directive must stand as it is absolutely essential that the architect must know from whom he takes his instruction.

Let me assure you that we are not disrespecting your authority as Minister of the Church; we realise only too well your value to the Norwich congregation and your anxiety to see not only a new Church built, but a Church which will meet with the approval of all members of your congregation, but I do put it to you most respectfully that you should leave this matter in the hands of the Sub-Committee who were duly authorized at the Deacons Court under your Chairmanship.

I am not au fait with the Presbyterian Church Law and it may be that the Minister is ex officio on all Committees and if that is so, then of course we have erred, but I would assure you again that our interests are mutual and we were anxious to get ahead. If we hold up the architect now, we may hold up the claim for weeks and it should be appreciated that there will be an opportunity of making any little adjustments at a later date.

While it will be a great loss to the Sub-Committee, I know that Mr. Clark will still give his professional services and his advice as a member of the Deacons Court.

Kind regards...[35]

The minister's response is not on file but the incident was turned to best account since it seems to have resulted in that rare ideal, a building sub-committee of two, with Mr Clark loyally freewheeling in a way which accorded perfectly wth his meticulous sense of professional propriety. He wrote about it to Kenneth Christie on 24 March:

Following my 'withdrawal' from the [Building Sub-Committee]...I have acquainted Messrs Boardman (Mr. Fielden [sic]) of my altered status and discussed the regularizing of our future relationship on the project...

I have proposed that my liaison with Messrs Boardman shall be of a purely professional basis as Quantity Surveyor acting on behalf of and with full authority for my firm, Philip Pank & Partners...

Whereas this leaves the Architects and myself free to collaborate on purely routine professional aspects, it now produces a much improved state of affairs whereby in cases where you wish my advice, you can approach me, the matter in question can be discussed, and you can indicate whether I have to regard this as confidential pro tem, as far as any discussion in the Deacons Court is concerned. Whatever your direction, I will readily follow same and as professional ethics indicate, no

---

35   J.R. Crawford to Revd W.R.C. Joyce, 6 March 1952 (TF).

information whatsoever will be given by me at any time to any unauthorized individuals outside the Deacons Courts Meetings.

Wishing the project every success and it does appear to be moving along favourable lines at the moment and thanking you for your generous supporting attitude on Friday evening last.[36]

After July 1952 the project resumed its favourable lines. In May 1953 Kenneth Christie reported to Presbytery that the congregation, the session (that is, the elders' meeting), the diaconate, the Town Planning Committee and the Chief Fire Officer had all approved their scheme. Better yet, 'we are informed that the present time is opportune both from a building licence and financial angle'. The hurdles were almost over. An uncharacteristic last straw came from the Cambridge Regional Manager when he suggested that the congregation might now like to consider the adaptation rather than the demolition of the existing Baptist chapel, but perhaps he made it from a sense of duty rather than cussedness or even precocious conservationism; and on 17 June 1953 this letter came from Cambridge: 'I am now able to inform you that this Department is in a position to sponsor the work under the special arrangements for the reconstruction of war damaged central areas'. Two days later Bernard Feilden wrote to Kenneth Christie: 'we confirm your instructions to prepare working drawings'. A month later the licence had arrived, 'with the proviso that work must not commence before the 1st January 1954'. And Feilden reported: 'We have surveyed and taken levels on the site'.

The correspondence now changes key. It is about bricks, and suppliers, and engineering consultants to design the roof structure, and an organ 'finances permitting'. There is a formal report on all that had happened since 1945, drawn up and signed by Christie and Crawford and ending: 'We would like to place on record our appreciation of the helpful cooperation and advice received from the Council's officials throughout these negotiations'.[37] The issue of tendering and builders interweaves with that of the size, design, and disposition of communion table and chairs, of pulpit and choir stalls and pews; of the position and wording of the foundation stones; of the question of gravel as opposed to paving stones and flint cobbles in the forecourt; of the colour scheme (there was talk of cream with 'a very slight pinky hue'). A furnishing committee is mentioned, with the first reference in the file to a woman (Mrs Crawford) but with apologies from another woman. Then, 6 September 1954, the

---

36   A. Clark to K.S. Christie, 24 March 1952 (TF).

37   'Report of the Negotiations with the Norwich City Council and the War Damage Commission regarding the exchange of the site of the Church at Theatre Street for the site of the Baptist Chapel, Unthank Road, Norwich', 21 April 1954 (TF).

architect wrote to accept the lowest tender, from T. Gill and Son. It was for £34,405.15.10.

It was now time to despatch a carefully graded trio of appeal letters: A, B, and C. Letter 'A' set out the case for all 'members and adherents of the Church'. It outlined the 'old story' of a dozen years work 'in the limited confines of one hall'. It wrote of how 'Protracted negotiations...have gone on and on', but now 'a final settlement has been reached. Plans have been completed, the builders are on the new site...at long last we can visualize the new edifice which will arise' on a site 'as well situated and more commodious' than the old: 'the future of Presbyterianism in Norfolk is assured'. But they needed money. War damage would cover the rebuilding but not the refurnishing. Insurance would cover 'a small part of that' and there was £3,000 in the kitty. Another £3,000 was needed 'if we are to have a Church worthy of our Minister and a very active and enthusiastic congregation, a Church comfortably and adequately furnished and including a suitable pipe or electronic organ'. The Scottish cadences are inescapable. 'Will you give as your heart dictates; it is a great opportunity'.

Letter 'B' narrowed the target. This letter was 'sent to specially selected members of the Church by the member of the Committee best known to the recipient'. Its gist was simple. A congregation of 150 suggested an average gift of £20, but averages cover less than average giving, 'so we must rely on those more fortunately placed to give more liberally'. It urges the use of covenants, that gleam of light for every church treasurer for the next forty years. 'If 20 members could, and would, do that the total sum required would be assured'.

Letter 'C' might be called the 'Strangers' Letter'. It was addressed 'to members of the Norfolk Caledonian Society and the Scots Society of St Andrew who are not members of the Church':

as a Scot you will, we feel sure, be interested to know that the rebuilding of the Church on the new site at Unthank Road has commenced and in twelve months from now this Church, so akin to the Church of our forbears, will once more play its part in the Church life of Norwich and Norfolk.

Our forefathers fought for the Presbyterian form of Church government and we are fortunate indeed that here in Norwich we have the opportunity to worship as our fathers did in the form for which they gave so much. So great a sacrifice is not now called for, but the opportunity to do something worth while for the cause is still at hand...

We like to feel that all Scots in Norfolk whether or not members and adherents, should have a part in the building of this Church and have a claim on it.[38]

---

38   Was a copy sent to Sandringham?

The stone was laid by the Senior Elder on 23 October 1954 in the presence of the Lord Mayor, the Sheriff, the Dean (Norman Hook), and their wives, Bernard Feilden (now in his own practice) and Frank Swindells, and a representative of the disbanded Baptist church. The press gave generous coverage and had clearly been well briefed, helped by a model of the proposed building, since what it described had yet to be built. Nonetheless all the essentials were outlined—the narrow site, the dominating neighbourhood of the great Catholic church, the marriage of modern and traditional to provide 'a truly contemporary church, modest and simple in character with none of the exaggerated features found in some modern structures designed for worship'. The *Eastern Evening News* was especially careful to note both continuities and practicalities. As to the former, the architect had

> gone to the past for his inspiration just as the Presbyterians have gone back to the early Christian form of Church government.
>
> It is noticeable, too, that the building, while not square, as are old meeting houses, tends that way and obviously has the spoken word and preaching rather than organ music as the decisive factor in its shape. Running through the design, even to the forecourt, is a triangular motif suggested by the symbol for the Trinity.

As for the latter:

> Worshippers will enter the church by the lobby, which is not very brightly lit, into the vestibule lit by cross lights, and then into the bright light above the stairs leading to the church. The staircase brings the worshipper to the back of the church where he can be received by an elder and directed either way past a deacon who has a store for hymn books.

Meanwhile the minister could proceed to his vestry on the ground floor and thence by his own staircase 'near to the position in which he conducts the service'. With minister and people ready now for worship:

> As much space as possible has been allowed in the plan around the communion table and the font is moveable. The pulpit is in a wide apse and deeply-recessed windows are arranged down each side of the church to give diffused light forward without distracting the congregation. Space has been allowed for an organ in the west wall with a remote console which enables the organist to be near the choir and lead the singing as well as play.[39]

Revisiting the site nearly thirty-two years after the model had turned into reality the *Eastern Evening News* was whimsically affectionate about what it called 'Norwich's look back to the 1951 Festival of Britain'. It

---

39   *Eastern Evening News* 21 and 25 October 1954 (TF).

found Trinity 'curiously dated like the extensive chrome fittings on an aging motor car'.[40]

Over fifteen years on from that reassessment we can be more confident in admiring a period piece, although we need to be reminded of its defining facts. An urban congregation with a weather eye to all those Scottish farmers needed car-parking space: hence the practical as well as the spatial significance of the forecourt; hence, too, the carriageway through the tower to the courtyard and hall behind. That tower perplexed local reporters as, at first, it had perplexed Messrs Crawford, Christie, and Clark. The *Eastern Daily Press* felt that it 'really had little practical purpose', beyond a possible use as a store, although it added 'considerably to the dignity of the building' and the use of its base as a carriageway was surely a nod at 'a local inspiration of the medieval master masons' reflected in the towers of two famous Norwich churches, St Peter Mancroft and St John Maddermarket.[41]

If Trinity's need for a tower was more aesthetic than practical, there could be no doubt as to its need for gathering, cloakroom, and coffee space, or for its minister's vestry, or for rooms for the Deacons' Court and Elders' Session. Such space, however, was defined by the existing footprint of the old Baptist chapel, hence the two-storey solution with room for a lift should it ever be needed, could it ever be afforded.

Trinity posed three challenges for an architect. It had to work for Presbyterians, it had to work visually, given its setting under the wingspan of Rome, and it had to work technically. When Frank Swindells saw the model which was later illustrated in the *Daily Press* and *Evening News* he professed to be mystified. He did not understand what Feilden was doing, or so he said. Feilden, however, knew exactly what he was doing:

> I had proposed an entrance screen and detached tower, which initially had lukewarm support of the Church Building Committee. One member [it was Crawford], when he saw the stone cross on the green Westmoreland gable, said 'Scrub it off'. Appreciation of the design increased, however, the tower, screen and cross were all reinstated. These were necessary in order to establish the semi-detached forecourt to give visual protection for my little church from the large Roman Catholic Cathedral close by.

That tower was a tease as well as a perplexity. Perhaps St Peter Mancroft and St John Maddermarket did play their part in its genesis. One art historian, surely influenced by the City Hall, discerned Swedish influences in its design. Feilden, however, had turned neither to Norwich nor Stockholm but to Ravenna: 'I was alluding to the early Christian

40 *Eastern Evening News* 27 September 1986.
41 *Eastern Daily Press* 22 October 1954 (TF).

Church of St. Appolinari in Nuovo near Ravenna, which I had seen during the war'.[42]

Feilden's chief technical challenge lay in his roof. The *Eastern Evening News* had noted the 'absolutely clean roof line' save for the complicating gable which gave the effect of a large cross (there was to be no escape from symbolism for this congregation's less reconstructed Presbyterians). Its construction had necessitated the advice of a London firm. There was a space frame of steel, with a reinforced concrete ring beam. True to that generation's love affair with wood, the spaces were to have been filled with timber, but in the event a deep plywood panel called Trofdeck (obtained from Newsum's the well-known Lincoln firm, whose founders had been active Congregationalists) was used in the rectangular spaces. The roof was insulated by strawboard and covered in copper: 'I hesitate to think what would happen if the copper roof leaked persistently, causing [the] strawboard to rot'.[43]

The architect's particular care, however, lay in his details (see p. 179): the texture of his forecourt; his brick—grey with buff designs in different bonds and with black pointing for emphasis. Trinity may be a church in miniature, but it is also spacious. Why else would there be such care with a gateway, or with sign and symbol and continuity? Thus the foundation stones which were transferred from both Theatre Street and the old Baptist church in Unthank Road. Thus the cross, its Portland stone set in river green Westmoreland slate, standing as the universal symbol of the church above the particular symbols of Presbyterianism—the burning bush and the open Bible framed in palm leaves, representing the trials of faith and faith's victory, the Word's victory. Thus the visitor's short walk through the sequenced entrance into the vestibule. This too is an exercise in tone and texture and space: quarry-tiled floor, sand-coloured brick walls, concrete columns, hard surfaces contrasting with smooth, pale blue ceiling, doorways in rhythm. It is friendly, gathering, unassuming and yet processional, a reassuring breathing space when wedding parties arrive, a homecoming for funerals. Stairs sweep up from it as much as is proper. They too are carefully toned and textured, Portland stone treads, blue and brown York stone slabs, black and green marble insets, lifting one's steps to the church, lighting the spirit with a touch of surprise—the effect of the window—and of expectation for what might be in store, once one is past the elder's handshake and the deacon's hymn book.

And what is in store is satisfying (see p. 180). From the door one is struck by roof, apse, pews, and floor, in that order. From the pulpit or the choir it is the rhythm of the pews and the west wall which catches the

---

42   Sir Bernard Feilden to C. Binfield, 14 November 1998.

43   Sir Bernard Feilden to C. Binfield, 14 November 1998. The Newsums had had active links with both Doncaster Road Congregational Church, Rotherham, and Newland Congregational Church, Lincoln.

attention. Those are the three impacts, tone, texture, and rhythm. There is a fourth impact: totality. This church has been altered since its opening but its development has never been haphazard. Its integrity has been respected.

The roof makes the most impact. One may not see the steel space frame or the Stransit strawboard insulation, but one does see the African mahogany fitted over the frame, the triangular panels, three layers thick of rough boarding, and the rectangular panels of Trofdeck finished in mahogany.

The apse is where the minister had his say. Cameron Joyce wrote at some length about it to Kenneth Christie in November 1951. None could deny that this was minister's business, although perhaps it opened the way for that little flurry of professional dignity by Crawford and Clark the following March. It too merits full quotation:

I have been thinking, as no doubt we all have about the suggestions made at our building sub committee for the sketch plan for the new church...in particular I have been thinking about the placing of the *choir*.

A suggestion put forward by one member at the meeting was that this might be at the front and the side of the church. It seems clear to me now that this might be the best solution of the matter for us. Perhaps it would be simpler if I just list the reasons why I feel this...

1. The most important reason is the liturgical one, that is to say the one connected with the church's worship. Our worship centres in the Word and Sacraments. I think we were right therefore in deciding for the central pulpit with the font visible to one side of the communion table (A reading desk, tho' not essential would be useful and might balance the font on the other side). To place the choir then up near the table will I think be confusing to the worshipper making too many things in the centre to look at (All worshippers may not be as aware of this as some, but I think it is true).

2. From the point of view of appearance, in a more general way, I think it will be job enough to fit in pulpit, table and font without putting something else as well before the immediate gaze of the worshipper. I have not, of course, consulted Mr. Fielden [sic] about this, but I imagine that he would at once say that his work would be simplified by this suggestion.

3. The function of the choir in our church is primarily to lead and help the congregation's praise. For that reason its best position is at the back of the church and this is not practicable for us for several reasons. But in a small church, such as we envisage, the choir should be able to lead the singing as effectively together from one side as divided in the centre...

4. On merely practical grounds it's worth consideration. Seats for choir on right hand side could be balanced by a corresponding block of seats on the left hand side,

by the font. These seats could be used for christening parties at Baptisms, by Girl Guides when parading, by the Sunday School at Christmas and, for special occasions might seat an augmanted [sic] choir.

5.   Another practical reason: The consideration given to the size of the congregation applies also to the choir. If the average congregation were say 70 and choir 8 (a fairly optimistic guess) then the 8 would be as well, probably better placed and heard together at the side than divided in the centre.[44]

That letter, carefully targeted in the best Presbyterian way—liturgy, aesthetics, and a double dose of practicality—gives a triple snapshot. Here are the minister, his congregation responding to his third year of ministry among them, and a foretaste of how things turned out. Three and a half years later Bernard Feilden designed the apse's accoutrements: communion table, chairs, pulpit, font, reader's desk, and hymn board, all in Australian black bean and Yugoslavian oak. He took great care over their size and proportion, and on the whole his work is what we now see. There have, of course, been additions and alterations. Four of today's chairs are by another hand. The minister's chair is Victorian, with the stain removed. More questionable, though wholly understandable, are the rails placed on the platform steps to help ageing elders and deacons maintain their balance. These are carefully designed and positioned but they still distract the eye. And above the pulpit looms a cross, back-and-side-lit, and powerful. It is hard not to sympathize with that authentic voice of an older Presbyterianism which commented on its first appearance: 'looks like a fairground'.

What of the main body of the church? The floor is cork-tiled, for quietness as well as texture. The walls are in natural lime plaster to help the acoustics. The seven tall windows are in 'pink clouded glass' to give natural light. Most period of all there are the central duodecagon with its cluster of lights, the spotlights for table, font, and lectern, and the fluorescent tubes ringing the perimeter in light. But best of all are the pews.

Feilden worked hard on his pews. He provided a specimen for testing. Kenneth Christie wrote to him about it at the beginning of September 1954:

Regarding the pew, my Committee were pleased to learn that you propose to experiment on two sections of the existing specimen pew and they would like you to visit St. Thomas' Church, Earlham Road, to see the finish of the pews in that Church and wondered whether the colour employed there would fit in with your own ideas... It was considered that an economy might be effected by removing the resting rail for the hymn books, lowering the supporting rail and using the base of the rail for the communion glasses for the dual purpose. Would you test the

44   Revd W.R.C. Joyce to K.S. Christie, 15 November 1951 (TF).

specimen pew and see if, in your opinion, you think it would be more comfortable if the top rail on the end were made level with the end of the pew as it was found that the rail cut into the shoulder. There is no strong feeling on this point if it will upset the architectural lines of your proposals.[45]

Christie wrote again, a month later:

Regarding the specimen pew you kindly had made, my Committee agreed that the original position was the most comfortable, but that the whole pew should be raised another inch from the ground. There was a suggestion that the point of contact with the back was possibly too pronounced. Will you kindly look into this and see if, in your opinion, this point could be rounded off more without upsetting the balance.[46]

The committee may not have abated their concern for detail one jot, but by Autumn 1954 they clearly had complete faith in their architect's aesthetic judgment. Indeed, Feilden's pews make the church. They draw it together. Members of the congregation had gone pew crawling and here, to repay their efforts, were carefully shaped pews (scientifically so, for they derived from a design by Lord Zuckerman),[47] pews for sitting in, not kneeling from, with a good rest for the feet, the back supported at the best angle, the aisle edge cut away so that one did not bang a leg or snag a coat, grouped into the rhythm and warmth and atmosphere of meeting-house box pews. They were not box pews and this was not quite a meeting house, but tone, texture, and totality deftly conveyed that message.

Two further points should be made. The church contains a piano. It is German, from Bielefeld. In many churches a piano is an embarrassing gift, out of tune and out of place. This piano was indeed a gift, but it is marvellously apt in grain, colour, and position. Then there is the west wall. In too many Free Churches these are the least satisfactory walls of all. Here dissatisfaction is kept at bay by the detailing of the doors and by the organ case. The former provides a vernacular, local, flint touch, almost but not quite precious. The latter almost proved a bridge too far. The money took long to find. Indeed, a lift came first, installed in 1970 and duly dedicated by the Moderator of Assembly; the pipe organ was

---

45   K.S. Christie to B.M. Feilden, 1 September 1954 (TF). St Thomas, Earlham Road, a church of the 1880s by Ewan Christian, was severely damaged in 1943 and restored in 1954. I am indebted to the Revd R. Bocking and Mr T. Nash for this information.

46   K.S. Christie to B.M. Feilden, 6 October 1954 (TF).

47   Sir Bernard Feilden to C. Binfield, 9 January 2000. Solly Zuckerman (b. 1904), scientist, environmentalist, and strategist was an immensely influential adviser to successive governments: CB (1946), Knighted (1956) and OM (1968), he was a Norfolk man by adoption and took the title, Baron Zuckerman of Burnham Thorpe, in 1971.

installed only in 1987, not indeed from St Peter Mancroft or St John Maddermarket but from St Michael Coslany. It might have been there from the first.

The intervening thirty or so years had justified the care. The 147 members of 1947 rose to 380 twenty years later. By 1967 the elders were younger, and four of them were women; the congregation also was younger, though over half of them were still Scottish.[48] By 1967, too, the architect had made his way in his profession as practitioner, author, and specialist in conservation. He was architect to Norwich Cathedral and surveyor to York Minster, and was shortly to add St Paul's Cathedral to his portfolio as well as the University of East Anglia.[49]

He returned in the 1990s to talk to Trinity's congregation, relieved to find them at ease still in their Zion. 'They...asked me whether I could have done better. I replied without hesitation that I had learned a lot about glass, especially white glass, and would have given them better glazing'.[50]

That might still be remedied, but he should be allowed the last word. Reflecting on the aesthetics of architectural conservation, Sir Bernard Feilden remarks that 'Architectural values are related to the participants' movement through spaces, to...sensations which are not purely visual in these spaces.' And what are 'architectural values'? They are what Vitruvius listed as commodity, firmness, and delight: delight in the relation of building to site, in its massing, its silhouette, its propriety; firmness in structure—that beauty, perhaps, inherent in great engineering; and commodity? That is simple utility. 'It is by walking through an architectural ensemble that one senses its quality, using eyes, nose, ears and touch'. What is now Trinity United Reformed Church, Norwich, invites suggestive and satisfying perambulation on those terms.[51]

Connexion

There remains the question of connexions. An essay-length study of a century's Nonconformist architecture is bound to be selective and no brief selection could claim to be representative. This selection has been anglocentric and confined to the Dissenting mainstream. Worse yet, its twentieth century seems to have stopped in the 1970s, thus evading Nonconformity's version of the downsizing, rationalization, and value-

---

48   Trinity Presbyterian Church Norwich: One Hundred Years 1867–1967 (Norwich: Trinity Presbyterian Church, [c. 1967]), pp. 14, 16, 17.

49   For Sir Bernard Feilden (b. 1919) see *Who's Who*.

50   Sir Bernard Feilden to C. Binfield, 14 November 1998.

51   B. Feilden, 'The Aesthetics of Architectural Conservation', *Annals for Aesthetics* 36 (1996), pp. 13-17.

for-money efficiencies which seized British society in the last quarter of the century. Nonconformity changed course. As its constituency shrank numerically and its public confidence wilted so the nation's streetscapes were diminished as chapels tumbled or were transformed. Now their spires and gablets housed night clubs, discount stores, apartments for loft-living young professionals or sheltered accommodation for their grandparents. Sometimes a worship centre and heritage room could be squeezed in, with just enough room for tasteful stacking chairs and a flexibility which was seldom put to the test. For anybody with a sense of place the process was distressing, but for anybody with a sense of history it was neither surprising nor entirely dispiriting. Sentiment, obstinacy, the communal pressures exerted by secular amenity societies and the inescapable tentacles of planning law confronted the Free Churches with the responsibility of shaping a philosophy, even a theology, of conservation.[52] Four walls and a roof were still useful containers for such worship as remained, and the nature of the space liberated by what the walls and roof enclosed would never cease to challenge the worship enabled—and constrained—by its creators: it is not size that is at issue, but space. Twenty-first-century critics will find much to engage them in the way late-twentieth-century Nonconformity shaped its space.

This chapter's selectivity in fact focuses on two determinants of Nonconformity's response. The first is its localism. Nonconformist history is a local counterpoint to national history. Its witness is a constant critique of what is accepted as normal because it has been successful. Nonconformity is at once proof of failure and evidence of aspiration; and its persistence suggests the exercise of some political skills, not least those of accommodation. Yet it never ceases to offer an alternative. It finds its credibility in the locality or on the periphery, most notably among what the Methodist Herbert Butterfield identified in eighteenth-century terms as the educated underworld. All this can be seen in Nonconformist buildings and traced through their creators from the seventeenth century to the present day. The second determinant, however, entered a distinctive phase in the twentieth century: it is external regulation. Trinity Presbyterian (now United Reformed) Church, Norwich, illustrates this admirably: locality, periphery, personality, professional artistry, and regulation all come representatively into play, forced on one particular constituency by wholly external circumstances. The representativeness, however, might be tested by a thread of connexion.

---

52   To give a Methodist example: the District Property Secretaries' Conference, Loughborough 5-6 January 1989, included two lectures, Revd Dr Henry McKeating, Principal of Wesley College, Bristol, on 'The Theology of Conservation', and John Newman, a Commissioner of English Heritage, on 'The Practicalities of Conservation'. I am indebted to the late A.N. Cass for drawing my attention to these lectures.

Trinity was not the only ecclesiastical casualty of wartime Norwich. The case of St Mary's Baptist Church was more powerfully dramatic. There was little peripheral about St Mary's. That Baptist church was as significant a force in Norwich and Norfolk Free Church life as it was in national Free Church life. It had occupied its present site since 1744. Since its rebuilding in 1812 it had been Norwich's 'fashionable watering place', 'one of the handsomest Baptist meeting-houses in the Kingdom', distinguished outside by its 'handsome iron palisades and gates; its imposing front of white bricks, with Grecian portico and an ample flight of stone steps', and inside by the groined vault of its plaster ceiling. In the words of one of its leading supporters it was 'free...from all Popery and Popish adornments of Gothic within and Gothic without, as well as from all vestiges of the Popish canonicals' (see p. 181).[53]

That freedom was moderated in 1886 when the all but inevitable Edward Boardman updated St Mary's for its masterful new minister, J.H. Shakespeare (see p. 182). Fifty years later Charles Jewson, the church's twentieth-century lay statesman and Edward Boardman's grandson, reflected loyally on that updating. As a Congregational deacon Boardman 'well understood the requirements of a Nonconformist sanctuary'. Consequently,

> While his designs were not always admired by the taste of the twentieth century, his work at St Mary's was the best of its kind. The panelled screen behind the pulpit was an object on which the eye rested with pleasure. The pulpit itself, a curious translation into woodwork of a design based on the marble pulpits of Italy, had mahogany panels carved with birds and flowers by the famous Norwich wood-carver, Mr. Minns.[54]

Thus were the the worlds of Ruskin and Morris infiltrated into the fashionable Regency watering place just as the Arts and Crafts movement took root. They vanished, however, twice over.

At lunch time on Sunday 10 September 1939 the caretaker heard wood crackling in the organ gallery. Soon smoke was billowing from the roof as the proverbial wild-fire spread through the beams above the wooden laths of the celebrated ceiling's groined vault. 'Unaware of the fire many members of the congregation stood aghast upon their arrival at

---

53   C.B. Jewson, 'Rebuilding St. Mary's Norwich. A Long Tradition of Baptist Building', *Baptist Times* 15 June 1944. See also *St. Mary's Norwich: The Church Fellowship 1669–1961* (Norwich: St Mary's Baptist Church, n.d., unpaginated); *St. Mary's in Four Centuries 1669–1969* (Norwich: St Mary's Baptist Church, 1969). For information about St Mary's I am particularly grateful to Mr K. Hipper, the church archivist.

54   Jewson, 'Rebuilding St. Mary's Norwich', *Baptist Times* 15 June 1944.

the church last evening when a baptismal service was to have been held'.[55]

These were the months of phoney war. What the minister, Gilbert Laws, called a denominational calamity, was swiftly made good. A year and twelve days later an 'improved copy of the old' was reopened. The groined ceiling was replicated. The pulpit was reconstructed, incorporating Mr Minns's famous carved panels, for those had survived. The organ was back in position, the new pews were still pitch pine, the gallery still had fluted columns with 'delicately modelled caps', the entrance was as it had been since 1812.[56]

Twenty-one months later the church was again destroyed, this time by enemy action, this time with no hope of reconstruction within its existing walls. This time the reconstruction took ten years.

The rebuilding of St Mary's, like that of Trinity, depended chiefly on external factors from the interpretation of war damage regulations to the powers open to licensing authorities and the priorities of the City Plan. To these, however, had to be added the loyalty of a large membership, the strategic sense and personal chemistry of the church's leadership as it balanced personal preference, local tradition, and missionary need, and the ability of an architect to shape what resulted.

The membership's loyalty was marked. There were 657 members in 1939, and 517 in 1952.[57] The leadership was represented by a father and son, the timber importers Percy and Charles Jewson. The former was senior deacon, the latter was church secretary. Both were natural Liberals. Percy excelled in music, tennis, and Sunday school work, Charles was an instinctive historian. Percy had just been returned unopposed as Liberal National MP for Great Yarmouth and had been Norwich's Lord Mayor in 1934–35; Charles would be Norwich's Lord Mayor in 1965–66.[58] Charles's temper is reflected by what he wrote for the *Baptist Times* in June 1944:

> Love of the sanctuary is a characteristic of Baptists... All that concerns the House of Prayer is sacred to us—the great central pulpit whence the Word of God is proclaimed; the baptistery in whose waters we once pledged our vows to Christ and the Church; the Table where we have come face to face with the crucified Lord; the

---

55   *Eastern Evening News* 11 September 1939.

56   *St Mary's Baptist Church Norwich Magazine* (October, 1940).

57   *Baptist Handbook* (London: Baptist Union Publication Department, 1940), p.118; *Baptist Handbook* (London: Carey Kingsgate Press, 1952), p. 138.

58   For Percy William Jewson (1881–1962), MP Great Yarmouth 1941–45, see C.B.Jewson, *P.W. Jewson: Verses and a Biographical Note* (Norwich: privately published, 1964). For Charles Boardman Jewson (1909–81), see 'Mr C.B. Jewson', *Baptist Quarterly* 29.4 (October, 1981), p. 152, and 'Charles Jewson: In Memoriam', *Baptist Quarterly* 29.5 (January, 1982), pp. 144-47.

organ which led our praises; the very pews where we were wont to worship God in company. Separation and loss have made us realise how dear these things were. Many churches are homeless. God has preserved our fellowship 'yet so as by fire'... It is a sign of the turning tide that we are directing our thoughts to post-war planning.[59]

Percy's temper is reflected by his outburst four years later at an anniversary tea meeting, with Trinity's Cameron Joyce among his hearers. His frustration overboiled at all the post-war planning procedures:

> To me it is a distressing thing—to use no stronger adjective—that a nominally Christian country refuses to allow the rebuilding of the House of God and the premises essential for the work of the church. No wonder that our juvenile courts are hard-worked and our prisons crowded to overflowing. I cannot help thinking that if we had with us today J.H. Shakespeare or Dr. Clifford they would by now have carried the fiery cross through the country to arouse the Christian community to indignant protest. Perhaps the hour may yet bring the man.[60]

Did the hour eventually bring forth the building (see p. 183)? The new St Mary's was quite unlike the old, though it reflected its essentials. It was to be built in three stages, although it is unlikely that there will now ever be a third stage. The first stage was completed in 1950. It was for multi-purpose hall and rooms. The hall's central block had a meeting-house feel to it, perhaps early Georgian in inspiration, although its flanking wings were quite simply utilitarian. Utility was the keynote: cycle space for forty, careful circulation, and a pulpit, organ, and baptistery in a hall which on weekdays hosted 'badminton, plays, and lunches'. The roofs were flat, not from choice but 'to comply with the timber and steel restriction in force'. The architect did his best to turn his constraints to advantage:

> consideration has been given to minimum upkeep costs. Externally a good facing brick will be the most important feature with a sparing use of reconstructed Clipsham stone for entrances and copings. Metal windows fixed in the surrounds. The finish of walls internally will be plaster and if funds will allow, a 4-ft. high tiled dado will be provided throughout, care being taken as to colour.[61]

A local journalist, affecting a modest anonymity as 'Whiffler', approved of the result. He found 'a light, spacious building far in advance of the rather sombre halls in which the social life of a church was

---

59   Jewson, 'Rebuilding St. Mary's Norwich', *Baptist Times* 15 June 1944.
60   *Eastern Daily Press* 28 April 1948.
61   S.J. Wearing, 'Notes on the Rebuilding Scheme', *Rebuilding Souvenir of St. Mary's Baptist Church* (Norwich: St Mary's Baptist Church, June 1950).

carried on in years gone by'. Its interior walls were coffee-tiled to waist height and coloured cream above that. The intention was 'to facilitate cleaning and, perhaps because of the soft colouring, the usual chilly effect is not produced'. And he was 'particularly impressed by the deacons' vestry with its comfortable chairs and carpet'.[62]

Stage Two, the church, was completed two years later. 'Whiffler' continued to approve. Here was a Baptist church 'abreast of new ideas', which managed, 'above all', to be 'simple without being austere', and which seemed to be efficient: 'There is even a switch to indicate to the organist the arrival of a bride'. He noted how four thermostats controlled the heat, how 'The death-watch beetle will certainly not affect the steel roof', how 'Shadowless and partly concealed lights will make it impossible for a shadow to fall on a hymn book during the evening service', and how 'Except for the narrow steel frame of the windows there is practically no paintwork and there is an almost complete absence of ledges to collect dust. The floors can be cleaned and polished in big level stretches'. He also noted the desire to retain a central pulpit without being dominated by it (a desire which later led to its removal to the side) and, 'Something not particularly common in Baptist churches as far as I am aware', 'the symbol of the Cross on the top of the organ screen and repeated in a cloth adorning the lectern'.[63]

Another local journalist enlarged on this next day. He encountered a building in rustic brick, with a high pitched roof, its gable pierced by three tall, narrow windows, 'whose decoration consists in their brick surrounds'. He entered under a shallow portico 'upheld by plain, slender stone pillars' (catching the essence of the pre-war entrance), into a generous vestibule 'large, because of the sociable Nonconformist habit of standing about for a gossip after service'. The church itself was wide, lofty, and light, 'for the steel roof is a single span, with no pillars. A daring expedient of the architect's was to line this steel-pitched roof with a barrel-shaped plaster ceiling'. Thus the old groined vault had become a barrel vault, and the result was not as acoustically perilous as might have been feared.[64]

The Jewsons' church had a timber-free fabric although its organ case and furnishings, like the pews which preceded Edward Boardman's pitch-pine refurbishment, were of oak 'and are fine examples of modern joinery'. Since 'Whiffler' had earlier noticed in the hall 'a beautifully inlaid desk under the pulpit made by a local craftsman to the architect's design, with matching chairs', it was apparent that the spirit of James

---

62 Whiffler, 'St. Mary's Baptists', *Eastern Evening News*, cutting 1950, by courtesy of Mr K. Hipper. A whiffle is a trifle; a whiffler could be an 'insignificant person'.

63 Whiffler, *Eastern Evening News* 24 September 1952.

64 *Eastern Daily Press* 25 September 1952.

Minns lived on. That was not a chance touch, for there were others. The old, war-shattered memorial tablets had been replaced by new 'beautifully lettered' tablets, and the gable end's three tall windows contained three coats of arms, one for the Wilkin family, whose St Mary's prime spanned the eighteenth century, one for the Colmans, whose attendance spanned seven nineteenth-century decades, and one for the Jewsons, 'leaders in the present reconstruction'. All in all, St Mary's was 'an interesting example of modern church building. The architect has sought to relate it to the history and surroundings of the site, but the design has grown out of the economical use of modern materials, and the ornament of the building has developed from its function'.[65]

Neither Percy nor Charles Jewson was architecturally illiterate. Percy Jewson's Boardman father-in-law, brother-in-law, and nephew were Norwich's leading hereditary architects. His cousin, Herbert Ibberson of Hunstanton, was an architect of unusual quality with a widely spread if choice practice. His brother, Norman Jewson, was a central figure in the Cotswold Arts and Crafts revival.[66] The St Mary's architect, Stanley Wearing, was no relation, indeed he was an incomer to Norwich, but he was in every other way a kindred spirit. His is the thread of connexion.[67]

The Wearings were Baptists and Stanley's father was a bank manager who could afford to send his sons away to school. These were the three determinants of Stanley's professional career. They explain the west-country childhood (Swindon, Faringdon, Penarth, Cirencester), the Nonconformist boarding schools (Taunton and Bishops Stortford), the decision to become an architect and the eventual decision to settle in Norwich. At school young Wearing excelled only in drawing, so his father asked the headmaster for names of Old Boy architects, hence the articles to Coales and Johnson of Market Harborough: 'In fact it couldn't have been a better choice... Johnson had talent and he kept one's nose to the grindstone'.[68] Wearing's architectural formation was thus the normal one for his generation, a practical training in a succession of provincial practices, varied by sketching tours, spiced by competition, garnished academically with classes at the local Art School. It could be

---

65   *Eastern Daily Press* 25 September 1952.

66   For Norman Jewson (1883–1975), see his autobiography, a minor classic, *By Chance I Did Rove* (n.p.: privately published, 1973).

67   For information about Stanley Wearing (1880–1960) I am much indebted to his daughter, Mrs Janet Matthew, who made available to me a privately compiled and printed memoir, S.J. Wearing, *Memories: Recorded Experiences from Birth to the Present Day made at 4 Eaton Road, Norwich in the Spring of 1957* (Norwich, privately published, [c. 1994]). I am also grateful to Mr T.W. Norton (Wearing, Hastings and Norton); Mr Nigel Nichols and Ms Jane Oldfield (RIBA Library and Information Unit), and to the late C.B. Jewson, who first alerted me to Norman Jewson and Stanley Wearing in the early 1970s.

68   Wearing, *Memories*, p. 17.

hit and miss but given a good practice, an inquisitive and competitive spirit, an eye for the vernacular, and helpful contacts, it could also be a perfect preparation for the instinctive good manners of the Arts and Crafts free style at its best. Stanley Wearing's architectural formation was lengthy (1897–1910). It included brief spells in Bradford and Gloucester, but it was spent chiefly in Market Harborough and Leicester. Like many important provincial towns Leicester had a thriving and adventurous architectural profession and an excellent School of Art. Wearing's firm, Everard and Pick, was highly regarded.[69]

Leicester was also grateful ground for Baptists and Congregationalists. Professionally Wearing responded to the competitive edge of its younger architects and socially he responded to the busy activities of Victoria Road Baptist Church. There he met the daughter, sister, and briefly the fiancée, of Baptist ministers and eventually married her;[70] and when at the age of thirty he set up on his own, it was in answer to an advertisement in *The Builder* which offered an architectural practice for 100 guineas. He took it against an accountant's advice because it was in Norwich, where his fiancée's brother was a Baptist minister. Thus began Wearing's fifty-years practice in Norwich and his thirty-year association with that minister's church, Unthank Road Baptist Church, where he became deacon, Sunday-school superintendent, and treasurer. When war precipitated Unthank Road's closure he transferred his membership to St Mary's.[71]

The Baptist connexion was significant but it could not be sufficient in Boardman country. Wearing made his own mark with the variety of his specialisms, their style, and the range of his sociability. He was a freemason, a golfer, and a pillar of the Science Gossip Club and the Norfolk and Norwich Archaeological Society, and held office in each. His years of designing everything under the sun for the competitions regularly promoted by the *Building News* Designing Club bore fruit. Between 1910 and 1960 his work included a hospital, a factory, a YMCA, Memorial Cottage Homes, shops, dairies and an abattoir for the Co-op,

---

69   Leicester's lively Victorian and Edwardian churchscape is explored in *Earthly Kingdoms: A Report on Leicester Churches both Past and Present* (n.p.: The Victorian Society: Leicester Group, n.d. [c.1994]). The contribution of J.B. Everard (d. 1923) and S.P. Pick (d. 1919) included St Michael and All Angels, Knighton 1897–98 and St Philip, Evington Road, 1904–10.

70   Charlotte Elsie George was the daughter of Elias George, who had been the Wearings' minister at Faringdon 1878–85, and had been a Bible Society District Secretary since 1888; her brother, Alfred Robert George, moved to Unthank Road, his second pastorate, in 1908. At that point Unthank Road had 196 members, St Mary's had 624 (*Baptist Handbook* [London: Baptist Union Publication Department, 1910], pp. 112, 333).

71   I am grateful to Mr K. Hipper for confirming this.

school extensions, a masonic building, a museum, a surgery, bungalows, and large local authority housing schemes. Something of their style is indicated by the *nom-de-plume* which he used for his competition entries, 'Corinium', the Roman name for Cirencester.

For this Norwich architect was also a Cotswold man. Thanks to his father's presence at a London Cirencester dinner at which Lord Bathurst had declared that houses were no longer built in the Cotswolds as they had been 300 years back, Stanley secured a series of commissions to do just that for Bathurst's Cirencester estate. He thus contributed signally to later stages of the Cotswold vernacular revival, and it was that vernacular touch which distinguished his Norfolk work. This was the Stanley Wearing who in seven years visited every one of Norfolk's 650 churches and in the 1940s worked tirelessly as the Norfolk representative of the National Buildings Record. There was, however, another but related aspect to the Wearing style, reflected in his premiated design of 1911 for the RIBA's headquarters in Conduit Street. *The Builder* praised this as 'a good example of traditional classic treatment...simple and dignified...the details worked out with knowledge and refinement'.[72] This was the Stanley Wearing who brought the Georgian revival to Norfolk, alerting his adopted county to its eighteenth-century heritage. Both Wearings are to be seen at St Mary's Baptist Church. Together they represent not just the surprisingly resilient twentieth-century vernacular tradition but also the paradoxically nationwide strength of a locally focused profession.

To illustrate this we need to return to Leicester, where the young Cotswold architect met his future wife, both of them Baptists. It had been in Leicester that the young Baptist Fenland architect, Herbert Ibberson, met his Congregational wife, and it was to be in Leicester that the young Sheffield Congregational architect, Mansell Jenkinson, met his Baptist wife. The Melbourne Hall and Victoria Road Baptist churches and Clarendon Park Congregational Church provided the meeting points for these matches and Leicester's growing professional and commercial opportunities did most of the rest. Mrs Mansell Jenkinson came from the Baptist side of the Unitarian and secularist Gimson family. The Jenkinsons were very conscious of those Gimsons's craft and architectural links and of their contributions to the multi-rooted Cotswold renaissance. Mansell Jenkinson was a near contemporary of Stanley Wearing and his place among Sheffield's Congregationalists and architects was very similar to Wearing's among Norwich's Baptists and architects.[73] His local vernacular passions were the Council for the Preservation of Rural England and the Peak National Park. Those

---

72   *The Builder* 25 December 1911, quoted in Wearing, *Memories*, Appendix.

73   For John Mansell Jenkinson (1883–1965), see J.C.G. Binfield, '"A Climate for Art's Encouragement": A Provincial Architect and his Contacts: John Mansell Jenkinson (1883–1965)', *Sheffield Art Review* (1992), pp. 2-11.

passions were inherited by his son, John Jenkinson, the architect of Trinity, Hunter's Bar, a near contemporary of Bernard Feilden, the architect of Trinity, Norwich. Theirs was a markedly different professional formation but it still allowed room for a sense of place. Trinity, Norwich, and Trinity, Sheffield, are small buildings, each already a period piece. Sheffield's Trinity is apparently the more uncompromising of the two, but the careful observer will find in it the curiously interlocking worlds of Frank Lloyd Wright, Le Corbusier, and Denys Lasdun grafted on to genuinely provincial practice, a local counterpoint to national, indeed international history, reflecting generations of community threaded nationwide, seldom heroic but always suggestive to those who are prepared to look and to read. Such buildings capture the twentieth century.

The Church of Christ the Cornerstone, Milton Keynes (PDD Architects 1990-02).
Pandenominational, commanding, focal, domed and artful, more post-modish than post-modern, it could be a law courts, or a state capitol, even a public library. (All photographs by C. Binfield.)

The Church of the Peace of God, Oxted, Surrey (F.W. Lawrence, 1935).
The spirit of St Francis recreated in rose red, blue, and amber for refined Congregationalists who might equally be stockbrokers or Fabians.

Trinity Congregational (now United Reformed) Church, Hunter's Bar,
Sheffield (J.M.M. Jenkinson, 1971). Exterior.
An uncompromising blockhouse for God, conceived as a rock of faith,
a cliff's end of Christianity confronting Sheffield's Endcliffe Park.

Trinity, Hunter's Bar. Interior.
The blockhouse has been domesticated into a meeting house; the
Puritan tradition has been affirmed.

Trinity Congregational (now Methodist) Church, Poplar (Handisyde
and Stark, 1951).
Church as a social complex, at one with the new society, liberating
space for spiritual and social growth in the East End as it was at last to be.

Punshon Memorial Methodist Church, Bournemouth (Ronald Sims, 1958).
A fine example for a car-owning society, enlivened by its careful use of brick and its enjoyment of exotic woods and lighting.

Stowmarket Congregational (now United Reformed) Church, Suffolk
(Alan D. Cooke, 1955).
Its dominant notes are a lofty enjoyment of wood and a careful sense
of church order.

The First Church of Christ, Scientist (now Greek Orthodox), Recorder
Road, Norwich (H.G. Ibberson, 1935).
An artful little masterpiece of textured streamlining punctuated with
apt vernacular touches.

St John's Roman Catholic Church (now Cathedral), Norwich (G.G. and
J.O. Scott, 1882-1910).
Scrupulously gothic, yet setting no pace even in its traditionalism and
making no concession to contemporary taste, its quality as townscape is
undeniable.

Trinity Presbyterian (now United Reformed) Church, Unthank Road,
Norwich (Bernard Feilden, 1954-56). Exterior.
A church in minature, yet spacious, meticulously detailed, and
carefully packed with Presbyterian symbolism.

Trinity Church, Norwich. Interior.
An exercise in tone, texture, and space: from the door one is struck by
roof, apse, pews, and floor, in that order.

St Mary's Baptist Church, Norwich. Interior as it was in the mid-
nineteenth century.
Austerely dignified and already conscious of a distinguished past.

St Mary's Baptist Church, Norwich.
Interior as it was between 1886 and 1939, updated by Edward
Boardman for J.H. Shakespeare.

St Mary's Baptist Church, Norwich (Stanley Wearing, 1950-52).
'[T]he design has grown out of the economical use of modern
materials'; it had also been shaped by an unusual alertness to an
established but still lively sense of tradition.

CHAPTER 7

Evangelism and Spirituality in Twentieth-Century Protestant Nonconformity

David Bebbington

At the opening of the twentieth century, in January and February 1901, the Free Church Councils of England and Wales organized a grand Simultaneous Mission. 'What results do you expect?', asked a leaflet about the mission issued by three London churches. 'We dare not expect small results', was the answer. 'That would not be God's way. He is waiting to give us large things. Christians will be revived, led into larger truth, raised into holier experience. Backsliders will be brought back. The cold and indifferent will be warmed into interest. *Sinners will be saved.*'[1] Here was an expression of the confident, almost ebullient, spirituality of the times that generated the mission. There were elaborate preparations: prayer meetings, house-to-house visitation, the distribution of literature. The enterprise opened with a meeting in the London Guildhall chaired by the veteran Congregational minister of the City Temple, Joseph Parker, on 28 January. Only six days before, Queen Victoria had died; but that event probably quickened rather than dampened enthusiasm for a venture offering answers to ultimate problems. For ten days eminent preachers delivered gospel addresses in large buildings throughout the capital. Missioners then fanned out to large cities in the provinces, and there were also visits to some smaller places in order to achieve an approximation to nationwide coverage.[2] 'Is not this mission *something new*?', asked the London leaflet. 'Yes', ran the answer, 'never before in all their history have the Free Churches joined before in this manner.'[3] The claim was slightly exaggerated: there had been joint missions in the past on a local basis; and the unity of the Free Churches was not total.

---

1   Charles Booth, *Life and Labour of the People in England: Third Series: Religious Influences* (7 vols; London: Macmillan, 1902), VII, p. 239. These volumes constitute a treasury of source material for the opening of the century.

2   E.K.H. Jordan, *Free Church Unity: History of the Free Church Council Movement, 1896–1941* (London: Lutterworth Press, 1956), pp. 66-72.

3   Booth, *Life and Labour*, VII, p. 239.

Unitarians were excluded on doctrinal grounds and the Salvation Army on sacramental grounds, while the Quakers often, though not consistently, avoided the clamour of evangelistic campaigns. Yet the Simultaneous Mission was one of the most striking accomplishments of the Free Church Council movement that during the 1890s had covered much of England and Wales with organizations for interdenominational co-operation. It bore witness to the shared spiritual tone and united evangelistic purpose of the bulk of Protestant Nonconformists at the start of the new century.

The common ethos of the Free Churches at the time was essentially Evangelical. The centuries-old disputes between Calvinists and Arminians had been largely healed. In 1899 the Free Church Council had been able to issue a common catechism representing the shared convictions of all its constituent bodies, the attitudes inherited from the Evangelical Revival of the eighteenth century. There was an expectation that the Christian life must open with conversion: 'before you can even begin to serve God', according to a Baptist chapel leaflet, 'you have to be *born anew*'.[4] Although there was an acceptance, especially in the more liberal circles, that the process might be scarcely distinguishable from nurturing in a Christian home, there was still a belief that there must be a sense of having entered on a religious commitment. In almost all branches of Nonconformity there was also a stress on the atonement. A sermon at a hall of the Wesleyan West London Mission, for example, made 'a strong emotional appeal on the love of the Cross'.[5] The Bible was accorded enormous respect. An investigator was astonished to discover a south-east London Primitive Methodist minister telling an audience of unchurched men that they ought 'so to know our Bibles that whatever might be read, we could say at once in what book and in what chapter it was to be found'.[6] A detailed appreciation of the scriptures clearly came as second nature to the speaker. And activism was equally a feature of the common temper of the Free Churches. 'He preaches a gospel of active effort', reported a Congregational minister, 'and finds great encouragement in the way in which young men take up the work and persevere in what they undertake.'[7] A programme of conversionism, crucicentrism, biblicism, and activism marked Evangelical Nonconformity. It is true that there were denominational differences: in general Methodists were less shy of emotion, Baptists more certain of doctrine and Congregationalists more appreciative of progressive thought than the others. Yet, particularly in the pews, there was a remarkable extent of common ground. There was a continuing debt to the American revivalists Dwight L. Moody and Ira D.

---

4   Booth, *Life and Labour*, VII, p. 187.
5   Booth, *Life and Labour*, II, p. 217.
6   Booth, *Life and Labour*, IV, p. 178.
7   Booth, *Life and Labour*, I, p. 84.

Sankey who had made a great impact on the British Isles in the 1870s. The message of Moody, evangelistic but loving, and the hymnody of Sankey, sentimental but pointed, represented the persisting atmosphere of the Free Churches. A current of popular Evangelicalism still flowed through the chapels.

The century that followed can usefully be divided into periods for analysis of the intertwined themes of evangelism and spirituality. During the first period, from the opening of the century down to the Second World War, the buoyant spirit of the Simultaneous Mission evaporated. The year 1906 marked the high point of the membership of the major Free Churches before the long-term collapse that was the most salient feature of their experience during the twentieth century.[8] The decay had actually set in earlier: relative to population, membership had declined since the 1880s. But it was only after absolute numbers started to fall that the malaise began to be widely noticed. By 1912, for example, the Wesleyans were despairing over the sixth annual decrease in their numbers.[9] The downward trend in attendances, though we have fewer reliable figures, was even more alarming. Between 1902 and 1927, Nonconformist attendances in an unnamed suburban area of London surveyed by the *British Weekly* fell absolutely by 44 per cent, and in a working-class district by as much as 75 per cent.[10] Although the number of worshippers probably declined less rapidly elsewhere, the direction was uniformly downward. Church activity, remarked a Wesleyan minister in 1919, was becoming a treadmill, 'and the world is not responding'.[11] The nation did not seem to want the gospel the chapels were proclaiming. Why was evangelism proving less effective?

A number of social challenges faced Nonconformity in the period from 1901 to 1939. There was, in the first place, a growing segregation of classes. Suburbanization, accelerating from the 1870s, was extracting the middle classes from the inner-city areas. Churchgoing levels, as Hugh McLeod has shown, correlated closely with class, so that, in general, the higher the social level the larger the church attendance.[12] The poorer working classes in particular had decreasing opportunities of social contact with the increasingly middle-class chapelgoers. Amongst the working classes a distinctive culture, as Sarah Williams has shown, had

---

8   Robert Currie *et al.* (eds), *Churches and Churchgoers: Patterns of Church Growth in the British Isles since 1700* (Oxford: Clarendon Press, 1977), p. 34.

9   *Methodist Recorder* [hereafter *MR*], 18 April 1912, pp. 5, 6, 12.

10   Jeffrey Cox, *The English Churches in a Secular Society: Lambeth, 1870–1830* (New York: Oxford University Press, 1982), p. 305.

11   J. Arundel Chapman, *Our Methodist Heritage* (n.p., [1919]), p. 13.

12   Hugh McLeod, *Class and Religion in the Late Victorian City* (London: Croom Helm, 1974).

emerged in the inner cities.[13] It was partly shaped, especially among the women, by Christian values, but churchgoing was not *de rigueur* and the men generally preferred their clubs and pubs, their drinking and betting. Leisure opportunities had hugely expanded, and cinema and radio became potent counter-attractions during these years. Traditionally the churches had maintained contact with potential converts through district visitors, who often brought practical benefits such as food tickets. As Jeffrey Cox has argued, however, the growth of welfare facilities, especially after the Liberal reforms from 1906 laid the foundations of the welfare state, rendered the philanthropy of the churches largely superfluous.[14] So the main religious bodies, Anglican as well as Nonconformist, suffered from new and increasing disadvantages in their appeal to the mass of the people. It was not that the First World War, as has often been supposed, dealt a fatal blow to earlier evangelistic methods. Already before the war the chapels were losing contact with the bulk of the working classes. Even the Twentieth Century Simultaneous Mission failed in this respect. It did reach young people already associated with the Free Churches, but, as a committed participant admitted, 'We have scarcely touched the "outsiders"'.[15] There was a serious problem of working-class alienation from the churches.

Nonconformity made sustained efforts to come to terms with these difficulties. In response to growing class segregation, suburban middle-class congregations often established missions in deprived areas. Lyndhurst Road Congregational Church, Hampstead, under the inspiration of its minister R.F. Horton, created a flourishing example of such a mission in Kentish Town. At the turn of the century it was staffed by 130 volunteer workers and ran services of worship, an adult school, Sunday schools, a Band of Hope, senior and junior classes and institutes, a Boys' Brigade, a Girls' Parlour, a Girls' Club, a Girls' Brigade, a Mothers' union, sick and benefit societies, provident clubs and a savings bank, district visiting, a women's workroom, educational classes, a lending library and Saturday concerts.[16] The Wesleyans planted similarly elaborate organizations in the heart of the cities, the central missions. The most celebrated was the West London Mission under Hugh Price Hughes, but connexional policy was the creation of a central hall as a preaching centre with a plethora of associated institutions in every major town of the land. Outside the denominational agencies were hosts of mission halls, large and small. The aim of virtually all these bodies was the spread of the gospel. Recognizing that the poor were reluctant to enter ordinary

---

13   S.C. Williams, *Religious Belief and Popular Culture in Southwark, c. 1880–1939* (Oxford: Oxford University Press, 1999).

14   Cox, *English Churches*, pp. 198-201.

15   Booth, *Life and Labour*, VII, p. 240.

16   Booth, *Life and Labour*, I, p. 178.

churches, their promoters adapted to the needs of those they were trying
to reach. The problem, however, was that when the enterprise succeeded
in establishing a working-class congregation, it normally remained
dependent on middle-class staffing from outside. Only rarely, as at
branches of the Metropolitan Tabernacle, formerly the church of the
Baptist preacher C.H. Spurgeon, was responsibility entrusted to working
people themselves.[17] Most of the missions therefore failed to encourage,
according to the genius of Nonconformity, their own lay leadership and
so to put down deep roots in their neighbourhoods. They did not provide
a long-lasting solution to the complex difficulties of evangelistic
outreach.

The challenge of a resistant working-class culture was also confronted
in other ways. The problem was diagnosed as essentially one created by
strong drink. Alcohol, it was supposed by many Nonconformists, was the
cause not only of poverty but also of refusal to heed the claims of the
gospel. By 1904 five out of six Congregational ministers were teetotallers
and it was natural for such men to believe that the abstinence pledge
should go hand in hand with evangelism.[18] George White, a Baptist shoe
manufacturer from Norwich, proposed that the Twentieth Century
Simultaneous Mission should be followed by a Million Pledges
Crusade.[19] Although the idea did not come to fruition, its serious
consideration was an indication that to many Free Churchmen of the time
the propagation of total abstinence was as important as the
communication of the gospel. Bands of Hope, as at the Lyndhurst Road
mission, taught children the virtues of temperance at most urban and
many rural chapels, often securing mass attendance. At the turn of the
century the movement claimed over three million members.[20] Another
obstacle to hearing the gospel was Sunday recreation. Chapel leaders set
their faces against the desecration of the day of rest as much because it
competed with worship activities as because of sabbatarian principle. It is
noticeable that protests over the abuse of Sunday multiplied after the
downturn in membership statistics in 1906. Three years later, for instance,
when Barrow Free Church Council organized a series of conferences on
practical evils affecting church work, the topic of the first was 'Sabbath
Observance'.[21] Later there was sympathy for the inter-war campaigns
spearheaded by the Lord's Day Observance Society against Sunday

---

17   Booth, *Life and Labour*, IV, p. 192.
18   D.W. Bebbington, *The Nonconformist Conscience: Chapel and Politics, 1870–
1914* (London: Allen & Unwin, 1982), p. 46.
19   *British Weekly* [hereafter *BW*], 25 April 1901, p. 30.
20   L.L. Shiman, *Crusade against Drink in Victorian England* (London: Macmillan,
1988), p. 154.
21   *Christian World* [hereafter *CW*], 25 November 1909, p. 7.

cinema.[22] These efforts to combat alcohol and Sunday recreation were intended as a reinforcement of missionary outreach, the demolition of the barriers that prevented the people from embracing the message of the chapels. But there can be little doubt that they were counter-productive. 'Religious folk are a queer sort', remarked a man encountered by a London City missionary at the end of the First World War. 'No beer, no "pictures", not even a pantomime.'[23] The image of being spoilsports had the effect of hampering Nonconformist growth.

An alternative strategy, however, was the provision of leisure facilities by the chapels themselves with the aim of retaining the allegiance of the masses. Football, cricket, cycling and tennis became standard outdoor sports associated with places of worship. The technique could work. At Brighouse in Yorkshire in 1920 there were mission services in the United Methodist circuit that yielded a number of converts from the congregations' football teams.[24] But there were problems too. Among indoor recreations billiards was thought the most acceptable. 'We don't expect to make Christians by billiards', declared J.H. Jowett, minister of Carr's Lane Congregational Church, Birmingham, in 1908, 'but we do intend to teach men that they can play a clean game of billiards.'[25] In that comment, however, lurked a lowering of sights. The activity was being provided as a good thing in itself rather than as an evangelistic tool. To that extent leisure facilities constituted a secularizing factor in church life. That became the complaint of the traditionalists associated, for example, with the Wesley Bible Union. A disgusted member of this Fundamentalist organization protested in 1915 about the entertainments at a Methodist mission. 'When the platform held by the preacher on a Sunday has been occupied the previous evening by a conjurer or ventriloquist as well as Popular Pantomime Pictures being given to edify our young life, surely it is time to obey the commandment, "Come out from among them".'[26] Fun and games, such people lamented, were supplanting the prayer and class meetings. The prayer meeting, it seems, had become rather routinized. Prayers were usually long, conventionally phrased and offered by individuals summoned to the task from the front.[27] So it is perhaps not surprising that it commonly disappeared during the interwar years.[28] Likewise the class meeting in Methodism fell into decay. Already it had ceased to be the basis of Methodist

---

22   *Christian* [hereafter *C*], 7 April 1932, p. 9.
23   *London City Mission Magazine*, February 1919, p. 18.
24   *BW*, 11 March 1920, p. 535.
25   *CW*, 23 January 1908, p. 4.
26   *Journal of the Wesley Bible Union*, January 1916, pp. 21-22.
27   E.g. Booth, *Life and Labour*, I, pp. 235-36.
28   *Bible Call*, December 1925, p. 169. *MR*, 10 March 1932, p. 20. *Fundamentalist* [hereafter *F*], August 1934, p. 183.

membership. Now the class meeting often changed from a warm context
for the interchange of spiritual experience to a straightforward discussion
group or else to a Wesley Guild, which ran a programme combining
informative lectures with less probing devotional sessions.[29] The efforts to
maintain contact with the community through leisure activities were
therefore highly ambiguous. Although they drew in some, they tended to
replace the more distinctly religious activities and so to dilute the
spirituality of the chapels.

Perhaps the best known attempt of the early twentieth century to bridge
the growing gulf between the chapels and the bulk of the working classes
was the social gospel. It had already emerged in the 1880s under the
leadership of Hugh Price Hughes and the Baptist John Clifford as a
campaign to apply Christian principles to the organization of society.[30]
The social gospel questioned competition as an economic method and so
had affinities with the emerging socialist movement. Clifford, in fact,
wrote Fabian tracts, and Samuel Keeble, the founder of the Wesleyan
Methodist Union for Social Service, had come to terms with Marx.[31] The
Wesleyan minister of the Kingsway Hall, J.E. Rattenbury, packed his
building to the roof in 1907 with 'rough youths and frivolous-looking
young women' by preaching on 'The Socialism of Jesus'.[32] Much of the
alleged socialism was, in fact, merely an expression of the rising tide of
collectivism, a reaction against *laissez-faire* social policies that at the same
period undergirded the New Liberalism. Yet it was theologically
grounded. Clifford, for instance, expounded a typical theme of the era by
identifying the coming just social order with the Kingdom of God.[33] In
retrospect, the social gospel commonly seemed an alternative to the
gospel for the individual, and so a diversion from evangelism. A few at
the time did see it in those terms. At the Baptist Union assembly of 1908,
for example, there was a lively debate after a paper on 'The Social
System compared with the Principles and Ideals of the Kingdom of
God'. G.W. Macalpine, the owner of an Accrington building firm,
declared that it was wrong to assert that the first duty of the church was to
follow up the moral implications of Christianity; its first duty, on the

---

29   G.S. Wakefield, *Methodist Devotion: The Spiritual Life in the Methodist
Tradition* (London: Epworth Press, 1966), pp. 20-21.

30   P. d'A. Jones, *The Christian Socialist Revival, 1877–1914: Religion, Class
and Social Conscience in Late Victorian England* (Princeton, NJ: Princeton University
Press, 1968), chs 8 and 9.

31   Maldwyn Edwards, *S.E. Keeble: Pioneer and Prophet* (London: Epworth Press,
1949), p. 34.

32   *CW*, 28 November 1907, p. 3.

33   John Clifford, 'The Sphere of the Church in the Coming Social *Régime*', in C.
Ensor Walters (ed.), *The Social Mission of the Church* (London: National Council of the
Evangelical Free Churches, 1906), p. 44.

contrary, was to preach the gospel.[34] It was far more frequent, however, to root attention to social questions in Evangelical faith, as was done at the Congregational Union autumn assembly in 1902 by A.E. Garvie, who rose to become the leading Free Church specialist in the field. The gospel, he argued, was the basis of all love to man, and ministers, standing in the prophetic succession, must proclaim all it entailed.[35] F.B. Meyer, a prominent Baptist devotional writer, was initially suspicious of the social gospel, but in 1907 turned into its outspoken advocate. Clifford rejoiced to announce 'the conversion of Mr. Meyer'.[36] A version of social Christianity was entirely compatible with evangelistic zeal. Yet, like entertainments, it could elbow aside the aim of changing the lives of individuals. Methodist sermons, commented a minister grimly in 1913, often contained 'a social gospel, without a saving Christ'.[37] Again, therefore, there was an ambiguity about the Nonconformist approach to the needs of the age. The social gospel may well have retained the allegiance of many working men for the chapels; but equally it blunted the distinctly religious appeal of their message. All these oblique strategies for mass evangelisation, in fact, turned into secularizing influences over Free Church life. The chapels rose to the social challenge of the times, but their response contributed to their decline.

At the same period Nonconformity faced an intellectual challenge. The popular Evangelical spirituality was sustained by regular worship and especially by the hymnody that was so powerful a tradition in the chapels. The hymns of Charles Wesley and Isaac Watts in particular taught salvation through the work of Christ in powerfully memorable terms.[38] Yet the theology that framed this piety was being modified by milder currents of thought associated with the spreading Romantic taste of the times. The general trend was in a liberalizing direction. The Almighty was increasingly regarded not as Supreme Governor of the universe but as Father. Any theological position perceived as inconsistent with the Fatherhood of God tended to recede into the background or else to disappear entirely. 'If the all-embracing doctrine of the Fatherhood', announced F.W. Norwood at the opening of his ministry at the City Temple in 1920, 'is not in harmony with any expressions in the creeds, then...so much the worse for the creeds.'[39] Hell in particular seemed incompatible with the paternal kindness. The Congregational leader J.D. Jones spoke during the First World War in favour of probation after

---

34   *CW*, 7 May 1908, p. 21.

35   *CW*, 2 October 1902, p. 21.

36   *BW*, 19 December 1907, p. 317.

37   *MR*, 9 October 1913, p. 29 (T.J. Price).

38   B.L. Manning, *The Hymns of Wesley and Watts: Five Informal Papers* (London: Epworth Press, 1942).

39   *BW*, 25 March 1920, p. 569.

death; and the young Wesleyan Leslie Weatherhead could accept a concept of hell only if it was relative, temporary and subjective.[40] Michael Watts has placed great weight on the decline of hell as an explanation of the decay of churchgoing in the twentieth century.[41] Even if we estimate the fear of damnation as a less powerful motive for conversion in earlier years than does Watts, the erosion of belief in eternal punishment must have played a part in the weakening of religious attachment. Faith was less likely to be treated as a possession of ultimate importance.

Perhaps more serious, however, was the undermining of the convictions at the core of Evangelical belief. As Kenneth Brown has pointed out, in the first decade of the twentieth century not even candidates for the ministry could necessarily identify a conversion experience.[42] The Romantic preference was to look for gradual growth into the Christian life, the model being a flower emerging from its bud. The cross, furthermore, was fading from some Nonconformist preaching. The newer emphasis in society at large, as Boyd Hilton has suggested, was on the incarnation, the human Jesus, rather than on his atoning work.[43] By the Edwardian years the fresh approach was beginning to make significant inroads into Nonconformity. R.J. Campbell at the City Temple pushed the new understanding to its limits, preaching a form of philosophical idealism.[44] He was powerfully answered by P.T. Forsyth, a champion of crucicentric theology, but the trend towards neglecting the atonement continued. Methodists began around 1920 to notice the virtual disappearance of the subject of the cross from their pulpits.[45] And the Bible, the bedrock of Evangelical piety, was being reinterpreted by higher criticism in a way that seemed to challenge inherited modes of understanding. Nearly all the Nonconformist colleges and leaders of opinion, as W.B. Glover has demonstrated, had embraced the principles of biblical criticism from Germany before the end of the nineteenth

---

40   *Witness*, March 1920, p. 233. Kingsley Weatherhead, *Leslie Weatherhead: A Personal Portrait* (London: Hodder & Stoughton, 1975), p. 76.

41   M.R. Watts, *Why Did the English Stop Going to Church?* (London: Dr Williams's Trust, 1995).

42   K.D. Brown, *A Social History of the Nonconformist Ministry in England and Wales, 1800–1930* (Oxford: Clarendon Press, 1988), pp. 52-53.

43   Boyd Hilton, *The Age of Atonement: The Influence of Evangelicalism on Social and Economic Thought, 1785–1865* (Oxford: Clarendon Press, 1988), chs 7 and 8.

44   K.W. Clements, *Lovers of Discord: Twentieth-Century Theological Controversies in England* (London: SPCK, 1988), ch. 2.

45   Chapman, *Methodist Heritage*, p. 14. George Jackson, 'Has the Preaching of the Cross Ceased?' [1920], in his *Reasonable Religion* (London: James Clarke, 1922), p. 29.

century.[46] Although generally accepted by the younger generation in the pulpits by the eve of the First World War, higher criticism had not yet percolated down to many in the pews. In 1913 Wesleyanism was shaken by a Fundamentalist controversy over the appointment to a theological chair of George Jackson, a known though moderate advocate of biblical criticism.[47] Jackson was confirmed in office, but the disturbance was an indication that deeply cherished convictions seemed under threat. The theological framework of Evangelical spirituality was under reconstruction.

Those who welcomed the changes wholeheartedly formed a significant proportion of the ministry, especially among the Congregationalists and Methodists. Many Congregationalists were sympathetic to 'A Re-statement of Christian Thought' issued in 1933.[48] It was modernist in tone and was to lead eventually to the creation of a Modern Free Churchmen's Union in imitation of the Modern Churchmen's Union in the Church of England. Some in its circle, such as T. Rhondda Williams, chairman of the Congregational Union in 1929, were willing to repudiate the Evangelical tradition altogether.[49] Even in Rhondda Williams's native Wales, this advanced liberal theology held a firm place in his denomination during the inter-war years.[50] In Methodism the same liberal impulse was recast in a Wesleyan mould, so becoming more a matter of the heart. The Evangelical inheritance was reinterpreted rather than repudiated. Three Wesleyan ministers profoundly dissatisfied with their Christian experience started meeting in a small fellowship group to renew their spiritual lives, a process they came to call a quest. Soon they felt confident enough of their message to launch local missions, each of which they called a crusade. Quest, crusade and fellowship became the watchwords of the Fellowship of the Kingdom that was established in 1919 and gathered force during the inter-war years.[51] Its members unequivocally accepted scholarly developments, but they reasserted the Methodist priorities of seeking assurance of faith and proclaiming it to

---

46   W.B. Glover, *Evangelical Nonconformists and Higher Criticism in the Nineteenth Century* (London: Independent Press, 1954).

47   D.W. Bebbington, 'The Persecution of George Jackson: A British Fundamentalist Controversy', in W.J. Sheils (ed.), *Persecution and Toleration* (Studies in Church History, 21; Oxford: Basil Blackwell, 1984), pp. 421-33.

48   *CW*, 9 February 1933, p. 7.

49   T. Rhondda Williams, *How I Found My Faith: A Religious Pilgrimage* (London: Cassell, 1938).

50   D. Densil Morgan, *The Span of the Cross: Christian Religion and Society in Wales, 1914–2000* (Cardiff: University of Wales Press, 1999), pp. 130-33.

51   I.M. Randall, *Evangelical Experiences: A Study in the Spirituality of English Evangelicalism, 1918–1939* (Studies in Evangelical History and Thought; Carlisle: Paternoster, 1999), ch. 5.

others. The key text was *The Meaning of the Cross* (1920) by Russell Maltby, warden of the Wesley Deaconess Institute, a book which rejected the traditional Evangelical doctrine of penal substitution yet drew inspiration from the sacrifice of Christ. The members of the Fellowship nourished a devotional life that was at once profoundly Methodist and deeply tinctured by the sub-Romantic feeling of the era: the very terminology of quest and crusade was redolent of knightly enterprise at the court of King Arthur. Spirituality was adapting to the age.

The prevailing direction of change was not only towards a broader theology but also towards a higher churchmanship. Adrian Hastings has proposed that a central theme of twentieth-century English church history was a drift in the direction of the Catholic, and there is evidence from the Free Churches to support his case.[52] W.E. Orchard, the Congregational minister of the King's Weigh House, pressed his liturgical practice so high that by 1925 he was planning for Holy Week 'The Stations of the Cross', the 'Tenebrae' and, on Good Friday, a 'Mass of the Pre-Sanctified'.[53] He was eventually to go over to Rome in 1932.[54] Orchard was by no means alone: A.J. Stanton, the minister of West Cliff Baptist Church, Bournemouth, had become a Roman Catholic in 1921; and the Wesleyan T.S. Gregory took the same path in 1935.[55] It was far more common, however, to remain within the Free Churches and adopt aspects of Roman Catholic devotion. A.E. Whitham, a loyal Wesleyan, cultivated a piety with deep Catholic roots, recommending 'the adoration of Christ in His sacrament'.[56] Whitham was one of the founders, in 1935, of the Methodist Sacramental Fellowship, a body that initially evoked strong protests in the connexion but went on to promote successfully the more frequent observance of communion in Methodism.[57] Among Congregationalists the equivalent development, perhaps oddly, was the so-called Genevan Movement led by Nathaniel Micklem, principal of Mansfield College, Oxford. The movement was at once a rebuttal of theological liberalism and an assertion of the vitality of the Reformed tradition of thought and worship. Yet it was less a revival of Calvinism as such than a retrieval of a portion of the heritage of Catholic Christendom.

---

52   Adrian Hastings, *A History of English Christianity, 1920–1985* (London: Collins, 1986), p. 668.

53   *The Life of Faith* [hereafter *LF*], 27 May 1925, p. 596.

54   Elaine Kaye and Ross Mackenzie, *W.E. Orchard: A Study in Christian Exploration* (Oxford: Christian Education, 1990), p. 100.

55   *BW*, 14 July 1921, p. 275. G.S. Wakefield, *Methodist Spirituality* (London: Epworth Press, 1999), p. 72.

56   A.E. Whitham, *The Discipline and Culture of the Spiritual Life* (London: Hodder & Stoughton, 1938), p. 248.

57   G.T. Brake, *Policy and Politics in British Methodism, 1932–1982* (London: Edsall, 1984), pp. 365-67.

B.L. Manning, the Cambridge historian who wrote the most enduring memorial of the Genevan tendency in his *Essays in Orthodox Dissent* (1939), contended for the essential identity of the Evangelical experience with mediaeval piety.[58] The Genevans were part of the Catholic drift.

The mood of the times also fostered distinctly conservative trends in spirituality. Belief in a premillennial second advent, that is the imminent personal return of Christ to the earth, had gathered support in the Victorian years. By the end of the First World War the advent hope was just beginning to make headway in Wales. One of its more bizarre symptoms was the erection by a 'zealous lady' at Carmarthen of a watch tower to look out for the second coming.[59] The belief was much more common among Evangelical Anglicans than among mainstream Nonconformists. In 1925 J.D. Jones protested against such an antique view of prophecy and a decade later it was suggested that the second advent in any form was fading from Methodist thinking altogether.[60] Baptists were most likely to embrace premillennialism, and it was one of their number, F.B. Meyer, who in 1917 launched the Advent Testimony Movement to bear witness to the teaching.[61] The doctrine was also, however, the prized possession of one of the most vigorous smaller Christian bodies of the period, the (so-called Plymouth) Brethren. 'The coming of the Lord' occupied fully one eighth of the standard doctrinal handbook of the movement in the period.[62] Often associated with adventism on the sectarian fringe of Nonconformity was Keswick teaching. Named after the location of its annual convention in the Lake District, the Keswick movement taught that holiness could be attained by the exercise of faith alone.[63] Although the movement's strength was once more among Evangelicals in the Church of England, F.B. Meyer was again a distinguished Nonconformist exponent. In 1906 Meyer actually organized a Free Church Keswick-style convention at Harrogate, but it encountered criticism from Thomas Phillips, the respected minister of Bloomsbury Baptist Church, London, and the experiment was not repeated.[64] Twenty years later George Jackson dismissed Keswick piety as 'sorry, syrupy stuff'.[65] Like the advent hope, Keswick teaching made a

---

58   Randall, *Evangelical Experiences*, pp. 196-98.

59   *C*, 6 March 1919, p. 19.

60   *LF*, 20 May 1925, p. 573. *MR*, 9 January 1936, p. 18.

61   D.W. Bebbington, 'The Advent Hope in British Evangelicalism since 1800', *Scottish Journal of Religious Studies* 9 (1988), pp. 103-14.

62   Henry Pickering, *The Believer's Blue Book* (London: Pickering & Inglis, n.d.), sect. 8.

63   Charles Price and Ian Randall, *Transforming Keswick* (Carlisle: Paternoster, 2000), pp. 14-15.

64   *BaptistTimes* [hereafter *BT*], 21 August 1906.

65   George Jackson, *A Parson's Log* (London: Epworth Press, 1927), p. 143.

measure of headway only among the Baptists and some of the smaller sects.

The related holiness teaching stemming from John Wesley nevertheless retained some endorsement in Methodism. It was the conviction that in a moment the believer could be freed from all known sin. This idea of entire sanctification had gradually faded during the nineteenth century, but from the 1870s it had enjoyed renewed popularity as a holiness movement within Methodism.[66] During the twentieth century its bastions were the annual Southport Convention and Cliff College in Derbyshire, a training centre for evangelists. At Southport the message was conveyed in fresh language—in 1914, one of the young speakers expressed a desire to be 'rippingly good'—but Samuel Chadwick, the principal of Cliff, had to admit that by the interwar years testimony to the blessing had become 'exceedingly rare'.[67] Nevertheless small separate denominations were established to sustain and propagate the experience: the International Holiness Mission (1906) and the Calvary Holiness Church (1934).[68] It was the holiness impulse that lay behind another group of small but dynamic bodies founded in these years, the Pentecostalists. The second blessing that they identified with the baptism of the Holy Spirit was a modification of the teaching of the holiness denominations. Pentecostalists were distinctive, however, in urging that speaking in tongues was to be expected of the true believer. Indeed for the Assemblies of God, the largest of the Pentecostal denominations, glossolalia were the essential sign of the baptism of the Spirit. The movement, and particularly the evangelist of the Elim Church, George Jeffreys, also came to notice through public healing services, often associated with missionary campaigns.[69] The whole phenomenon, however, was rejected by the more traditional Free Churches. Even the weekly newspaper connected with Keswick, which might have been expected to sympathize more than most strands of Nonconformity, in 1922 dismissed Pentecostal activities as 'corybantic exhibitions'.[70] Second blessings, of whatever kind, were generally viewed with suspicion in this period.

The enterprising outreach of the Pentecostalists, however, was by no means alone among Nonconformists. Notwithstanding the downward

---

66   D.W. Bebbington, *Holiness in Nineteenth-Century England* (Carlisle: Paternoster, 2000), ch. 3.

67   *MR*, 2 July 1914, p. 7. Samuel Chadwick, *The Call to Christian Perfection* (London: Epworth Press, 1936), p. 27.

68   Jack Ford, *In the Steps of John Wesley: The Church of the Nazarene in Britain* (Kansas City, MO: Nazarene Publishing House, 1968).

69   B.R. Wilson, *Sects and Society: A Sociological Study of Three Religious Groups in Britain* (London: Heinemann, 1961), pp. 38-39.

70   *LF*, 14 June 1922, p. 732.

trend of the statistics, the gathering in of the unconverted remained a central feature of the chapel world. Spontaneous revivals still took place, with free prayer, extended meetings and cries for mercy. The greatest by far was the Welsh Revival of 1904–05.[71] Its otherworldly leader, Evan Roberts, appeared to reflect the exuberance of the thronged chapels. 'The spiritual atmosphere', it was said, 'pervading the worship of the people so thrilled him when he came that his countenance seemed to be luminous.'[72] East Anglia enjoyed a similar awakening in 1921 and a definitely revivalistic atmosphere survived in the 'fire and urgency of soul' of Cornish Methodism.[73] Prayer for revival became a hallmark of conservative Evangelicals in the 1930s, leading, for instance, in 1938 to the creation of the Baptist Revival Fellowship.[74] Yet organized methods were more normal in evangelism. Strict and Particular Baptists, it is true, repudiated them altogether. They had no mothers' meetings, other agencies or tract distribution, said one pastor: 'If the Lord wishes to save the people He will bring them in.'[75] Likewise Presbyterians could sometimes express the opinion that 'the stated ordinances of the Lord's house' were to be preferred to special efforts.[76] But these were exceptional views. Chapels organized visitations, mission bands and open-air meetings; Gospel Mission Cars, Pilgrim Preachers and Methodist Trekkers fanned out across the land;[77] and there were strivings after novelty with female evangelists, picture shows and a Kinema Mission Movement.[78] And in these years the Salvation Army, often officered by women, led the way in evangelistic ventures. 'Its officers and soldiers preach in-doors and out', it was noticed, 'they march through the streets in all weathers, they gesticulate and shout, and the noise of their trumpets penetrates everywhere.'[79] Vigorous methods still made an impact on the unchurched.

---

71   Eifion Evans, *The Welsh Revival of 1904* (London: Evangelical Press, 1969).

72   B.P. Jones, *An Instrument of Revival: The Complete Life of Evan Roberts (1878–1951)* (South Plainfield, NJ: Bridge Publishing, 1995), p. 73. N.G. Dunning, *Samuel Chadwick* (London: Hodder & Stoughton, 1933), p. 235.

73   S.C. Griffin, *A Forgotten Revival: East Anglia and NE Scotland—1921* (Bromley, Kent: Day One Publications, 1992). Thomas Shaw, *A History of Cornish Methodism* (Truro, Cornwall: D. Bradford Barton, 1967), p. 131.

74   *F*, February 1939, p. 47.

75   Booth, *Life and Labour*, I, p. 236.

76   Booth, *Life and Labour*, VII, p. 227.

77   H.T. Smart, *The Life of Thomas Cook* (London: Charles H. Kelly, 1913), ch. 9. P.W. Petter, *The Story of the Pilgrim Preachers and their Message* (London: Marshall Brothers, n.d.). N.G. Dunning, *Samuel Chadwick* (London: Hodder & Stoughton, 1933), p. 235.

78   *LF*, 7 February 1923, p. 149. Wilson, *Sects and Society*, pp. 92, 102. *MR*, 7 November 1912, p. 8. *BC*, July 1923, p. 3.

79   Booth, *Life and Labour*, I, p. 43.

Perhaps the chief explanation of the continuing degree of success enjoyed in evangelism was the extent to which young people were prepared to hear the message. Despite the traditional protest of many Nonconformists against state involvement in education, the publicly provided schools ensured that the population at large imbibed a basic understanding of Christianity. A dispassionate observer commented of the board schools at the opening of the century that 'their Bible teaching, though undogmatic, is very thorough'.[80] To the day schools' religious education, the chapels added instruction in their own Sunday schools. Although their techniques were often inefficient, they did raise expectations of religious commitment. They were also extraordinarily popular. A single Congregational church in London at the turn of the century ran a Sunday school with 284 teachers and more than 2,600 children.[81] It was guessed in 1919 that 70 per cent of Londoners had passed through a Sunday school. Nor were the chapels' efforts for the young confined to Sunday school. They ran organizations such as the Free Church Girls' Guild and the Boys' Life Brigade, usually preferred by Nonconformists to the Boys' Brigade because it avoided using guns for drill.[82] Scouting existed in certain chapels, but was suspect in other quarters. 'The Scout movement', one critic suggested, 'would appear to savour of Nimrod and Esau. Do not wolves bark and howl, not to mention the name "wolf-cub" suggest[s] the wolf in sheep's clothing?'[83] Training for youth was supplemented by adult education. The Quakers specialized in adult schools[84] and the Unitarians made some notable efforts to encourage bookishness. Their Highgate Hill church, for example, had a reading room with 7,000 volumes from which 1,500 families borrowed—but only eleven Unitarians used the library themselves, because, it was explained, 'our people' have books in their homes.[85] So religious knowledge was widely diffused. There was a latent body of Christian understanding waiting to be quickened into life in the population.

A strikingly novel approach to stirring up new life emerged during the 1930s in the form of the Oxford Group. Organized by Frank Buchman, an American Lutheran minister, the movement concentrated on students in the 1920s, but during the following decade made a major impact on religious life in Britain. Its members arranged groups where there was open confession of failings and where 'life-changing', that is conversion,

---

80   Booth, *Life and Labour*, I, p. 29.

81   Booth, *Life and Labour*, I, p. 123.

82   John Springhall, *Sure and Stedfast: A History of the Boys' Brigade, 1883 to 1983* (London: Collins, 1983), pp. 70-71.

83   *LF*, 21 March 1923, p. 322.

84   Booth, *Life and Labour*, VII, pp. 231-33.

85   Booth, *Life and Labour*, I, p. 125.

was encouraged. The message and method held great appeal for educated young people, and both Congregationalism and Methodism were significantly affected. The Congregational moderators commended Groupism in 1932[86] and Methodists organized their own version of the movement, sometimes called Cambridge Groups. By 1935 the Methodist Conference had set aside six ministers to co-ordinate the work of these bodies.[87] Many subsequent Methodist leaders were touched by the movement. Gordon Rupp, later Professor of Ecclesiastical History at Cambridge, was a secretary of the Methodist Groups; Bill Gowland was stimulated into wartime evangelism by an Oxford Grouper; and W.E. Sangster's thinking was transformed by Group techniques.[88] There was nothing stuffy about the Groups, whether Oxford or Cambridge. Their members used first names only; they were prepared to confess openly to sexual sins; and they took an interest in psychology. The barriers between the sacred and the secular were demolished. Religion, claimed the predominantly Methodist journal *Groups*, was not 'a separate compartment of life' but rather 'a way of life'.[89] There were no inhibitions, therefore, about attending the theatre or using Sunday for recreation. In this ethos were the first signs of the impact on the Free Churches of the new cultural mood of the twentieth century that was just beginning to supplant Romantic taste among the *avant-garde*.[90] The cultural currents flowed from the Modernist revolution in literature and the arts in the early years of the twentieth century, perhaps supremely in association with depth psychology. Already before the Second World War a few in the Free Churches were starting to look inside themselves to discern how spirituality impinged on the subconscious.

The years from the outbreak of the Second World War to the early 1960s represent a coda to the earlier period. There was a great deal of continuity with what went before. The Salvation Army still ran its open airs. In 1957 its Marylebone corps continued to hold four each Sunday.[91] Donald Soper, by the 1950s a significant figure in the Labour movement, maintained the speaking on Tower Hill that he had begun in the 1920s.[92] Mission bands were re-formed after the Second World War,

---

86   *The Times*, 19 March 1932, p. 15.

87   *Groups* [hereafter *G*], October 1935, p. 92.

88   *G*, August 1934, p. 108. David Gowland and Stuart Roebuck, *Never Call Retreat: A Biography of Bill Gowland* (London: Chester House, 1990), p. 43. W.E. Sangster, *Methodism can be Born Again* (London: Hodder & Stoughton, 1938), ch. 5.

89   *G*, April 1934, pp. 545-46.

90   D.W. Bebbington, *Evangelicalism in Modern Britain: A History from the 1730s to the 1980s* (London: Unwin Hyman, 1989), ch. 7.

91   *BW*, 9 May 1957, p. 7.

92   William Purcell, *Odd Man Out: A Biography of Lord Soper of Kingsway* (London: Mowbray, 1983), ch. 7.

as at Wesley Church, Oldbury, and the Methodist superintendent of the
Wye Valley Mission reported seeing 'a gracious revival'.[93] There were
the same obstacles to mission. Elsie Chamberlain, Congregational
minister and the first female commissioned chaplain, feared (she said in
1946) that 'women were apt to lose a sense of responsibility for souls
over their tea cups and knitting'.[94] There were self-imposed handicaps by
would-be evangelistic bodies. 'If an unsaved girl', asked a correspondent
of the Brethren *Believer's Magazine* in 1948, 'should come into the
Gospel Meeting without a hat, should she be approached and told, or
turned away at the door?'[95] More constructively, Newton Flew, principal
of Wesley House, Cambridge, declared two years earlier as president of
Conference that the best form of evangelism came through 'the
fellowship of a local church'.[96] Churches surrounded themselves with
auxiliaries, which, though slightly different from those at the start of the
century, were in recognizable continuity with them. In 1957, for example,
Emmanuel Congregational Church, West Wickham, had a flourishing
Sunday school of 360 (though now called 'Church of Youth'), a youth
fellowship of fifty, a young wives' club specifically designed as an
evangelistic contact, a ladies' sewing and social party for older women, a
winter programme of visiting lecturers and a summer sequence of Bible
studies, which were less popular.[97] There was a measure of novelty in the
evangelistic films that Lord Rank produced and Methodists showed, but
the revolution in evangelism that marked the United States in these years
passed Britain by: there was very little adoption of radio and the
emergent television for gospel purposes. Although an interdenominational 'Radio Mission' was broadcast in 1954, there was
reluctance on the part of the churches to enter the field as well as fear of
charges of propagandism in the BBC.[98] Elsie Chamberlain, as producer
of 'Lift up your Hearts', was able to make an effective Free Church
contribution to religious broadcasting,[99] but, because of the BBC
monopoly, the medium was generally closed for evangelism. So in many
respects the 1940s and 1950s had a very similar feel to the previous era.

Yet the trauma of the Second World War jolted the churches into new
ventures. It was partly a matter of the imperative to reconstruction
following the loss of physical plant in air raids. Already by the summer

---

93   *BW*, 4 April 1946, p. 8.

94   *BW*, 18 April 1946, p. 8.

95   *Believer's Magazine*, October 1948, p. 237. I owe this reference to Roger Shuff.

96   *BW*, 18 July 1946, p. 218.

97   *BW*, 16 May 1957, p. 7.

98   K.M. Wolfe, *The Churches and the British Broadcasting Corporation, 1922–
1956* (London: SCM Press, 1984), pp. 461-67.

99   Janette Williams, *First Lady of the Pulpit: A Biography of Elsie Chamberlain*
(Lewes, Sussex: Book Guild, 1993), pp. 61-66.

of 1941, of the 118 centres of the West London Methodist Mission, fully 108 had suffered war damage.[100] There was consequently an incentive to contrivance and innovation. During the war about twenty Presbyterian causes were begun in converted shops, school halls and huts, a basis in each case for future church growth.[101] It was partly, too, the sense that the struggle against Nazism was ideological, so that the principles of Christian civilisation needed to be propounded anew. It is significant that prayer meetings revived in wartime.[102] There was a fresh awareness of the priority of the spiritual, reinforced among a few by the spread of Neo-orthodox theology. And there was a sense that, in the flux of critical times, the population, and especially the armed forces, were looking for fixed values. 'The time had come', declared J.H. Winn Haswell in chaplain's uniform at the 1946 Free Church Congress, 'when men were no longer indifferent to religion, and the Church had not had such an opportunity for years.'[103] As the emergency came to a close, there were calls by Welsh Independents for a 'New Advance' in Wales;[104] there were interdenominational missions co-ordinated by Tom Rees, an evangelist of Brethren background;[105] and, above all, the Methodists developed their Commando Campaigns. Operating under the slogan 'New Men for a New World', from 1942 to 1947 teams of commandos descended on particular towns, entering schools, colleges and specially factories with a down-to-earth evangelistic message. The mastermind was Colin Roberts of the Methodist Home Mission Department, and the most famous missioner Bill Gowland, who was later to develop work on the gospel in modern society through the Luton Industrial College.[106] Gowland, like many others at the time, put his emphasis on work with youth. The rising generation, including the young people who had fought the war, seemed the most promising mission field. Thus in 1946 Crook Methodist circuit in County Durham organized a youth week; Bramall Lane Wesleyan Reform Union chapel in Sheffield started a young peoples' fellowship, specially for those returning from the forces; and the American organization Youth for Christ sent over its twenty-seven-year-old field

---

100 Brake, *Policy and Politics*, p. 398.
101 *BW*, 16 May 1946, p. 91.
102 Wakefield, *Methodist Devotion*, p. 21.
103 *BW*, 4 April 1946, p. 9.
104 *BW*, 4 April 1946, p. 8.
105 Jean Rees, *His Name was Tom: A Biography of Tom Rees* (London: Hodder & Stoughton, 1971), ch. 10.
106 Gowland and Roebuck, *Never Call Retreat*, ch. 3.

director Billy Graham to undertake a six-month tour in an Evangelical version of Marshall Aid.[107] The war gave a fresh stimulus to evangelism.

The legacy remained powerful down to the beginning of the 1960s. In Methodism other emphases, sacramental and social, were turned in an evangelistic direction. The Order of Christian Witness, founded in 1946 by Donald Soper, ran local missions culminating in a eucharistic service; and a 1952 report declared that a shift of London Mission resources from social work to evangelism was 'imperative'.[108] W.E. Sangster, the most eminent Free Churchman of his generation, called as President of Conference in 1950 for a fresh stress on evangelism and as secretary of the Home Mission Department from 1955 to 1957 made schools for evangelism its principal policy.[109] The message on Sangster's lips was firmly grounded in profound personal consecration. 'The purpose of God for man', he wrote at the start of his study of Christian sanctity, *The Pure in Heart* (1954), 'is to make him holy.'[110] The quality of Sangster's devotion as well as the power of his preaching at the Westminster Central Hall helped inspire Methodists in their worldwide year of evangelism in 1953, the coronation year when Everest was also conquered and all things seemed possible. During the 1950s the Elim Pentecostal Church was organizing six pioneer thrusts of church planting each year, and when Baptists decided at the end of the decade to celebrate the ter-jubilee of their Union, a year was allocated to evangelistic activity.[111] F.P. Copeland Symons told the General Assembly of the Presbyterian Church as its moderator in 1959 that evangelism, as much as ecumenism, had been the theme of the decade.[112] It was this mood that Billy Graham was able to catch in his celebrated Harringay mission of 1954. Night after night thousands streamed in to hear the rousing oratory of Graham and the massed choirs under Cliff Barrows. A high proportion of the participants, it is true, were already church attenders, but a year after the crusade the number of previously unchurched converts still attending worship was variously estimated between 4,000 and 11,000.[113] Probably the greatest impact was the boost to the confidence of the Evangelical section of the Church of England, but the venture also stirred many in the Free Churches. If Soper condemned, Weatherhead as

---

107 *BW*, 9 May 1946, p. 80. I.M. Randall, 'Conservative Constructionist: The Early Influence of Billy Graham in Britain', *Evangelical Quarterly* 67 (1995), pp. 310, 313.

108 Thompson, *Soper*, pp. 102-109. Brake, *Policy and Politics*, p. 402.

109 Paul Sangster, *Doctor Sangster* (London: Epworth Press, 1952), pp. 208, 225.

110 W.E. Sangster, *The Pure in Heart: A Study in Christian Sanctity* (London: Epworth Press, 1954), p. xi.

111 *BW*, 4 June 1959, p. 7; 7 May 1959, p. 3.

112 *BW*, 7 May 1959, p. 6.

113 *BW*, 10 February 1955, p. 1.

president of the Methodist Conference defended the mission; and if Leslie Cooke, the secretary of the Congregational Union, criticized, Norman Goodall as chairman supported it.[114] In 1960, five of the fifty candidates offering for the Methodist ministry were Harringay converts.[115] Billy Graham embodied the vogue for outreach that still gripped much of Nonconformity down to the early 1960s.

In the 1960s, however, came the great change. Social trends impinged sharply on church work in that decade and continued to have a drastic impact thereafter. Much of the transformation could be attributed to growing affluence. In the quarter-century after 1951 the real income of the average male manual worker went up by more than two thirds.[116] Consumer goods mushroomed in number and sophistication. Two of them were crucial for the churches. First, car ownership, largely a middle-class preserve until the 1950s, became general. Greater mobility meant a willingness to leave the home district, specially on Sunday. Secondly, television became almost universal. So nearly every home possessed its own potent counter-attraction to church. Affluence, furthermore, particularly affected the young. By the 1960s there was a consumerist youth culture of pop and boutiques that seemed alien to most churches and so created a fresh barrier to mission. The sexual revolution starting in the 1960s also played its part, fostering a set of values different from those sustained in the Free Churches. With the end of Victorianism, as Arthur Marwick has put it, there was a decline of family solidarity and a growth of solitariness.[117] Family attendance, still a chapel strength in the 1950s, came under threat. Inner-city decay and rural depopulation meant that buildings were even more frequently in the wrong places. The social challenge to the churches was vast and growing.

The impact was most serious on the Sunday schools. In 1960 24 per cent of the relevant age cohort in the United Kingdom still attended some Sunday school. By 1980 the proportion had collapsed to 9 per cent; and by 2000 it was estimated to have plunged further to 4 per cent.[118] The afternoon Sunday school, which had been more popular than the morning session during the first half of the century, ceased to attract

---

114 Purcell, *Odd Man Out*, p. 103. Weatherhead, *Weatherhead*, p. 199. R. Tudur Jones, *Congregationalism in England, 1662–1962* (London: Independent Press), p. 461. C.T. Cook, *London Hears Billy Graham: The Greater London Crusade* (London: Marshall, Morgan & Scott, 1954), p. 100.

115 Randall, 'Conservative Constructionist', p. 330.

116 Sue Toland, 'Change in Living Standards since the 1950s', *Social Trends* 10 (1980), p. 15.

117 Arthur Marwick, *British Society since 1945* (Harmondsworth, Middlesex: Penguin, 1982), ch. 9.

118 Peter Brierley (ed.), *UK Christian Handbook Religious Trends No. 2* (London: Christian Research, 1999), p. 2.15.

attenders and normally had to be abandoned. Church policy was sometimes responsible, because it was increasingly felt that children should be included in worship for part of the morning service.[119] The effect, whatever the cause, was that Sunday school attenders became almost exclusively the children of worshippers and the mass function of the Sunday school came to an end. With it, the annual Sunday school anniversary, often a key time for evangelism with extra meetings and a visiting preacher, fell into decay. The anniversary was still surviving in the north and midlands, it was noted in 1959, but it was already becoming less special and less folksy.[120] The eclipse of the Sunday school meant the closing of the chief recruiting agency for the chapels and so posed a serious threat to their future. At the same time state education underwent a transformation. Down to the 1960s local authority syllabuses were designed to inculcate Christian knowledge, especially of the Bible. From that decade, however, the curriculum increasingly tried to cover all major religions and so fostered the belief that none could plausibly claim a monopoly of truth.[121] Education, the greatest aid to evangelism in the earlier part of the century, turned into a factor that actually tended to subvert it.

Previous evangelistic methods commonly ceased to be fruitful in the circumstances created by these changes. There were bright spots: the Methodist Association of Youth Clubs, started in 1945, continued to flourish down to the end of the century; and baptisms among Baptists reached almost as high a peak in 1984, the year of Mission England conducted by Billy Graham, as during the evangelist's Harringay campaign thirty years before.[122] Nevertheless the general pattern was of dwindling effectiveness. The tradition of evening gospel services, deeply rooted among the more theologically conservative, disintegrated in the 1960s under the twin pressures of car and television. Open airs ceased to draw crowds, so that even Bill Gowland, a great exponent of the technique, abandoned them in 1970,[123] though Soper persisted with them into the 1990s. The great Methodist city-centre missions fell into debt and faced closure, the ones that survived usually turning into ordinary neighbourhood congregations.[124] The traditional short mission events run by visiting ministers that enlivened Methodist circuits, still operating in the mid-1960s, no longer attracted outsiders. The Methodist Home

---

119 D.M. Thompson, 'The Older Free Churches', in Rupert Davies (ed.), *The Testing of the Churches, 1932–1982: A Symposium* (London: Epworth Press, 1982), p. 94.

120 *BW*, 21 May 1959, p. 6.

121 Grace Davie, *Religion in Britain since 1945: Believing without Belonging* (Oxford: Blackwell, 1984), p. 133.

122 Brake, *Policy and Politics*, pp. 612-16. Brierley (ed.), *Religious Trends*, p. 9.4.

123 Gowland and Roebuck, *Never Call Retreat*, p. 127.

124 Brake, *Policy and Politics*, pp. 388-90.

Mission Department asked in 1968 what results were visible three or four years after such missions. Most local officials reported that an initial wave of interest had subsided. One church, though submitting a glowing report at the time of the mission, now declared 'that it had been a waste of time and money which could have been better spent'. The Department concluded that such missions were no longer useful because the people were 'so far from us'.[125] The verdict was reflected in the statistics. By 1985 in Wales there were more Roman Catholics than members of the four historic Nonconformist denominations put together.[126] The Methodist Church, by far the largest of the Nonconformist bodies, saw its total British membership plummet from 729,000 in 1960 to an estimate of 335,000 in 2000.[127] It was less than half its former size. As president of conference in 1980, Gowland summed up the woeful result of his observations: 'We are not making Christians.'[128]

At the same time there was a falling away of inherited forms of piety. Expectation of a premillennial second advent faded from those conservative Evangelical circles where it had flourished. The Advent Preparation Movement had shrunk to a tiny rump by the 1950s. Even among the Brethren, for whom it was received teaching, premillennialism ceased to be the norm after the 1960s.[129] The version of holiness upheld by the Keswick Convention, often associated with premillennial doctrine, continued to play a part on the conservative edge of Free Church life down to the 1960s. There were actually more Nonconformist speakers at Keswick in the post-war period than before: they included, for example, Arthur Skevington Wood, a principal of Cliff College.[130] Yet, even at Keswick itself, confidence in the message was sapped. The Convention ceased to proclaim holiness by faith and became a general Bible teaching gathering. By 1996 it was treating its earlier teaching as just one view of holiness among many.[131] The Wesleyan version of sanctification continued to invigorate the holiness churches, especially the Church of the Nazarene, but in Methodism it decayed further. Cliff College no longer stood exclusively for Wesleyan holiness after the retirement of Skevington Wood in 1983, and the Southport Convention was attracting

---

125 Leslie Davison (ed.), *Evangelism Today* (London: Methodist Church Home Mission Department, 1969), pp. 23, 13.

126 Morgan, *Span of the Cross*, pp. 264-65.

127 Brierley (ed.), *Religious Trends*, p. 9.10.

128 Gowland and Roebuck, *Never Call Retreat*, p. 216.

129 Bebbington, *Evangelicalism in Modern Britain*, p. 264.

130 Paul Taylor and Howard Mellor, *Travelling Man: A Tribute to the Life and Ministry of the Reverend Dr Arthur Skevington Wood* (Calver, Sheffield: Cliff College Publishing, 1994), p. 34.

131 Personal observation.

fewer than 200 people to its celebration events by 1995.[132] Some of the earlier spiritual traditions were fading from Nonconformist life.

Equally striking, however, was the range of new approaches to evangelism and spirituality of the period from the 1960s to the end of the century. Fresh ways of thinking were impinging on generations that had passed in larger numbers through higher education. A study of evangelism by Leslie Davison, head of the Methodist Home Mission Department, called *Sender and Sent* (1969), referred knowledgeably to Marx, Freud, and (among theologians) Paul Tillich, Harvey Cox, Thomas Altizer and Teilhard de Chardin. Such influences, diffusing in the wake of John Robinson's *Honest to God* (1963), encouraged drastic reformulations of mission. Radical theology and sociological method led, for instance, to the strategy of the Barking Methodist Team Ministry led by Howard Booth in the late 1960s. There mission consisted of educational workshops inside the church and community development outside.[133] The Urban Theology Unit at Sheffield under John Vincent issued a booklet in association with the Methodist Home Mission Department in 1981 entitled *Two Nations—One Gospel*. Reacting against the early rhetoric of Margaret Thatcher's government, it declared its purpose to be: 'To expose the divisions of society today. To arouse the Christian conscience about poverty and deprivation. To study the Gospel as good news to the poor'.[134] The gospel is translated into wholly this-worldly terms and any notion of trying to make new Christians is tacitly dropped. A similar approach was taken up in sections of the United Reformed Church, formed by the merger of the Congregationalists and Presbyterians in 1972. A United Reformed Church member of the Salford Urban Mission Team explained in 1985 that he was 'searching for places where Christ was already to be found'.[135] The discovery was to be by the missioner, not the missioned. Methodism and the United Reformed Church were much more affected by such radical methods than other denominations. They did not exclude traditional evangelism from their programmes, but official policy tended to marginalize it. In 1994 the Methodist Home Mission Division, once Sangster's base for the conversion of England, defined mission as involving 'evangelisation, social caring, the struggle for justice and care for the well-being of the planet'.[136] Evangelism, that is to say, had been relegated to roughly one

---

132 *MR*, 10 August 1995, p. 17.

133 Davison (ed.), *Evangelism Today*, pp. 31-45.

134 Brake, *Policy and Politics*, p. 412.

135 Edmund Banyard, *Straws in the Wind* (London: United Reformed Church, 1992), p. 50.

136 *The Methodist Church: The Minutes of the Annual Conference* (London: Methodist Church, 1994), p. 3.

quarter of the aim of home mission. Radical theology encouraged a drastic rethinking of priorities.

Ecumenical contacts were also potentially revolutionary. Down to the 1960s, apart from Free Church Council initiatives and mass crusades, most evangelism was denominational. From that decade, however, Councils of Churches brought the Free Churches into regular contact with Christians of other traditions. Local Ecumenical Projects (LEPs) proliferated, especially in new housing developments. At Shaw, on the western edge of Swindon, for instance, a LEP was started on a new estate in 1985 with a minister and manse provided by the United Reformed Church. By 1990 it had forty-five members, many of them new Christians, though only five were United Reformed. Outreach was essentially a matter of building community through house groups, coffee mornings, banner making, beetle drives, summer picnics, a parent and toddler group and a playgroup.[137] The United Reformed and Methodist Churches officially encouraged maximum ecumenical activity.[138] It could lead to large-scale ventures such as the Nationwide Initiative in Evangelism, spearheaded by Donald English, who launched it as Methodist president at Lambeth Palace in 1979.[139] More commonly it led to mergers at local level. By 1992 there were as many as 200 combined Methodist/United Reformed congregations.[140] Perhaps the most significant result of ecumenical co-operation, however, was the rapprochement with the Roman Catholics, who down to the 1960s had figured more in Nonconformist demonology than as Christian partners. By the end of the century it was common even for Baptists, who had been strongly marked by anti-Catholicism, to co-operate with Roman Catholics in local evangelistic ventures.[141] The Catholic pull now meant, furthermore, that aspects of Roman practice were imitated in Nonconformist devotion. In 1974 a Methodist Commission on Spirituality under Gordon Wakefield recommended to church members the voluntary acceptance of a rule of life and the formation of religious communities.[142] In the United Reformed Church a Silence and Retreat Network emerged in 1987–88.[143] Most surprisingly, the Baptists produced a nunnery. Margaret Jarman, an ex-president of the Baptist Union, established in 1999 a Community of the Prince of Peace at Riddings in Derbyshire, with

---

137 Banyard, *Straws in the Wind*, p. 12. *The United Reformed Church Year Book, 1990/91*, p. 78.

138 *Minutes of the Annual Conference*, 1993, p. 3.

139 Donald English, *From Wesley's Chair: Presidential Addresses* (London: Epworth Press, 1979), ch. 12.

140 Banyard, *Straws in the Wind*, p. 110.

141 E.g. *BT*, 16 March 2000, p. 13.

142 Wakefield, *Methodist Spirituality*, p. 84.

143 Banyard, *Straws in the Wind*, p. 91.

its first three members pledged to a three-year period of prayer and meditation before making a lifelong commitment. One withdrew at an early stage, but the project continued.[144] Novelty inspired by the ecumenical movement could hardly go further.

Another fresh development sprang from immigration into Britain from the New Commonwealth. Even before the arrival of the first vessel bearing mass immigrants from the Caribbean, the *Empire Windrush* in 1947, a Methodist minister, formerly of Jamaica, had been appointed to serve 'the coloured people' of Cardiff.[145] Ten years later, when Ghana became independent, there was already a congregation of Ghanaians from all over London meeting for worship on Sunday afternoons in King's Cross Methodist Mission.[146] Soon black congregations, often affiliated to Caribbean denominations of the Pentecostal or holiness traditions, were proliferating in areas of migrant settlement. These bodies were often highly motivated towards outreach. The New Testament Church of God, for example, declared that its vision was 'to see every member fully matured in Christ and actively involved in *evangelism* as a lifestyle'.[147] Growth was the inevitable result. In 1960 there were some 1,400 members in black-led churches; by 2000 there were estimated to be 48,600. In an English church survey of 1998 they formed as many as 7.2 per cent of church attenders in England.[148] Other black Christians, however, joined existing Free Churches. The Methodist congregation at Harlesdon, an inner London suburb, for example, was overwhelmingly Caribbean and African by 2000.[149] Whole black congregations affiliated to the Baptist Union. A remarkable case was the Calvary-Charismatic Baptist Church led by Francis Sarpong at Plaistow in east London. Started in 1994, it attracted about 800 to join it in only six years. Members were encouraged to draw up a 'ten most wanted list'. They would pray for friends on the list for a month, then do their utmost to witness to them and bring them to church. The formula worked, leading to a baptismal service on 31 December 1999 when seventy-nine were immersed.[150] The black-led sector of English Christianity was not swept along by the tide of decline.

A further new impulse was associated with the student world. The Student Christian Movement had long provided a forum for the training of future Christian leaders, and its work in universities had been

---

144 *BT*, 24 February 2000, p. 12.

145 *BW*, 4 April 1946, p. 8.

146 *BW*, 30 May 1957, p.7.

147 *Black Christians: Black Church Traditions in Britain* (Birmingham: Centre for Black and White Christian Partnership, 1995), p. 18.

148 Brierley (ed.), *Religious Trends*, pp. 9.16, 12.3.

149 *MR*, 27 January 2000, p. 9.

150 *BT*, 16 March 2000, p. 8.

supplemented by denominational societies. During the 1960s, however, the Inter-Varsity Fellowship (IVF) of Christian Unions, conservative Evangelical in theology and evangelistic in practice, overhauled them in most British universities and colleges. In 1958 there were some 190 Christian Unions with ten supporting 'travelling secretaries'; twenty years later there were some 540 Christian Unions with forty-one travelling secretaries.[151] As higher education expanded, catering for a total of 665,000 students by 1978, the churches increasingly felt the presence of graduates who had been through Christian Unions. The movement's leaders rejected Fundamentalism. Its members, according to the eminent Brethren New Testament scholar F.F. Bruce, wanted others to be 'rationally convinced that Evangelical Christianity has nothing to do with a pseudo-conservatism that fears to face the facts of Biblical or any other science'.[152] Some turned to the Princeton theology of Charles Hodge and B.B. Warfield in order to replace 'hypothetical and subjective scholarship'.[153] The doughty minister of Westminster Chapel, Martyn Lloyd-Jones, promoted the revival of Calvinist theology, holding annual Puritan conferences and backing the Banner of Truth Trust as a publishing agency. Others such as the Congregationalist J.S. Whale had encouraged an interest in Calvinism in earlier years,[154] but now its advocacy became a passion with some of the young. To students on the IVF staff in the 1960s Reformed doctrine was a striking novelty, 'intoxicating to some, unnerving to many'.[155] It persuaded Leith Samuel, the minister of Above Bar Church, Southampton, to change the emphasis of his ministry from human responsibility to the sovereignty of God.[156] Samuel was one of those who, following their mentor Lloyd-Jones, carried their churches into the uniformly conservative Fellowship of Independent Evangelical Churches. Its members nurtured a piety that was commonly highly cerebral and believed strongly in pulpit proclamation. Their numbers grew from roughly 14,000 in 1960 to some 33,200 in

---

151 Douglas Johnson, *Contending for the Faith: A History of the Evangelical Movement in the Universities and Colleges* (Leicester: Inter-Varsity Press, 1979), p. 338.

152 F.F. Bruce, 'The Tyndale Fellowship for Biblical Research', *Evangelical Quarterly* 19 (1947), p. 60.

153 Johnson, *Contending for the Faith*, p. 243.

154 J.S. Whale, *The Protestant Tradition: An Essay in Interpretation* (Cambridge: Cambridge University Press, 1955), part II.

155 Robert Horn, 'His Place in Evangelicalism', in Christopher Catherwood (ed.), *Martyn Lloyd-Jones: Chosen by God* (Crowborough, East Sussex: Highland Books, 1986), p. 16.

156 Leith Samuel, *A Man under Authority: The Autobiography of Leith Samuel* (Fearn, Ross-shire: Christian Focus, 1993), p. 167.

2000.[157] The broader influence of the IVF and the narrower influence of the Calvinist revival in its circles both gave new backbone to the more conservative Free Churches.

There was also novelty in the techniques for sustaining and spreading the faith. House groups became a standard feature of church life from the 1960s and 1970s, partly through the advocacy of the Methodist Michael Skinner.[158] They met for discussion, Bible study, prayer and sometimes evangelism too. The Methodist Conference formally commended them for these purposes in 1992.[159] Larger gatherings also achieved popularity. Probably the most significant was the annual Spring Harvest, organized from 1979 as an intensive round of meetings at holiday camps by the enterprising general secretary of the Evangelical Alliance, Clive Calver.[160] A Methodist equivalent was Easter People, a week-long gathering that attracted some 13,000 each year by the end of the century.[161] Although they appealed almost exclusively to self-professed Evangelicals, these semi-holiday events were vibrant affairs that caught the imagination of the young. Music was part of their programme, and in this period there was a tentative rapprochement between some Christian youth and the pop scene. In the 1960s the pioneers were the Venturers, a pop group based on the Baptist Spurgeon's College, and the Joystrings, a Salvation Army ensemble.[162] Cliff Richard, a converted pop singer who at first became a Baptist, was the star attraction at a variety of Christian entertainments over the years such as, in 1983 and 1984, the Banquet, a weekend of gospel events in Wembley Arena.[163] There were forays into broadcasting as the century wore on, usually on an undenominational and broadly Evangelical basis. Premier Radio became a permanent Christian radio station for London and by 2000 was sponsoring a host of local stations with temporary licences for a month around Pentecost.[164] Satellite television, introduced steadily from the mid-1980s, gave fresh opportunities for Christian programming that a few seized. Religious videos became common, fulfilling the prophecy of Lord Rank in the 1960s that the 'modern marvel of Electronic Video Recording' could transform evangelism.[165] In spring 2000 there was a

---

157 Brierley (ed.), *Religious Trends*, p. 9.8.

158 Michael Skinner, *House Groups* (London: Epworth Press, 1969).

159 *Minutes of the Annual Conference*, 1992, p. 3.

160 Clive Calver, *He Brings us Together: Joining Hands where Truth and Justice Meet* (London: Hodder & Stoughton, 1987), pp. 66-67.

161 *MR*, 27 April 2000, p. 24.

162 *BT*, 16 March 2000, p. 6. A.J. Gilliard, *Joy and the Joystrings: The Salvation Army's 'Pop Group'* (London: Lutterworth Press, 1967).

163 Gerald Coates, *An Intelligent Fire* (Eastbourne: Kingsway, 1991), p. 110.

164 *BT*, 17 February 2000, p. 2.

165 Davison (ed.), *Evangelism Today*, p. 49.

concerted project to distribute Jesus videos from house to house and subsequently enquire about the impression they made.[166] Most potentially drastic was experimentation with seeker services specifically targeting the unchurched on the model of the Willow Creek church in the Chicago suburbs. At Skipton in Yorkshire, for example, the Baptist church developed a professional newspaper, humorous presentations and preaching on contemporary issues.[167] Especially in the more Evangelical congregations of the various denominations, there was less reserve over innovation than there had been earlier in the century.

A large part of the explanation for the new flexibility lies in the side-effects of charismatic renewal, which exercised a powerful influence far beyond the ranks of its committed adherents. Renewal was a movement laying emphasis on the work of the Holy Spirit that gathered force from the 1960s. Initially, like Pentecostalism, it was distinguished chiefly by speaking in tongues, but increasingly it generated healing ministries, community life and the transformation of worship. 'My vision of the Contemporary Church', declared the keen charismatic Clifford Hill to the annual assembly of the Congregational Federation in 1973, 'is a church reborn, born again of the Holy Spirit and filled with Pentecostal power.'[168] The movement encouraged such practices as hand raising and sacred dance, unstructured expressions of devotion shaped by a postmodern age. There were stern critics from within the Free Churches: Paul Fiddes, a Baptist at Regent's Park College, Oxford, portrayed the movement's theology as shallow; Donald English charged that renewal could lead to 'narrowness of an unhelpful kind'; and Victor Budgen, from a conservative Calvinist standpoint, condemned it because 'modernists and Roman Catholics are drawn in and do not cease to be modernists and Roman Catholics'.[169] Nevertheless the movement made headway in traditional Nonconformity, partly as a result of the patient work of the Fountain Trust, set up in 1964 to propagate charismatic experience in the existing churches.[170] Two years after the creation of the United Reformed Church, in 1974, there was established a Group for Evangelism and Renewal (GEAR), without formal membership but

---

166 *BT*, 24 February 2000, p. 16.

167 Martin Robinson, *A World Apart: Creating a Church for the Unchurched* (Tunbridge Wells: Monarch, 1992), pp. 190-91.

168 R.W. Cleaves, *The Story of the Federation* (Swansea: John Penry Press, 1977), p. 104.

169 P.S. Fiddes, 'The Theology of the Charismatic Movement', in David Martin and Peter Mullen (eds), *Strange Gifts? A Guide to Charismatic Renewal* (Oxford: Basil Blackwell, 1984). English, *From Wesley's Chair*, p. 100. Victor Budgen, *The Charismatics and the Word of God: A Biblical and Historical Perspective on the Charismatic Movement* (Welwyn, Hertfordshire: Evangelical Press, 1985), pp. 206-207.

170 Edward England, *The Spirit of Renewal* (Eastbourne: Kingsway, 1982), p. 62.

supported by individuals who were mostly charismatic.[171] In Methodism, the first charismatic conference was held in 1973, by which time Leslie Davison, the general secretary of the Home Mission Division, was fully identified with the movement.[172] Two years later there were about 250 Methodist ministers on the circulation list of the denominational renewal magazine, *Dunamis*.[173] The Baptists, however, were more affected than any other Free Church denomination, especially in the south of England. At Durrington Free Church (Baptist) in Sussex, for example, the minister started clapping, hand raising and dancing at a Bible Week he attended in 1973. A small group in his church enjoyed pursuing life in the Spirit in private until, two years later, the minister, prophet-like, announced his vision for the renewal of the church. Nineteen members left and another dozen did not identify with the change, but another eight years on the church had grown to over 500 members.[174] There were parallel disruptions and similar growth in many a congregation. Charismatic renewal was sufficiently potent a brew to burst the old wineskins.

It also induced the fashioning of fresh wineskins, the so-called 'New Churches'. From the 1950s a few individuals had received the gift of speaking in tongues from Pentecostalists and had started small 'house churches' of their own. Several leaders began to meet regularly from 1967, but the great leap forward came after 1976, when there commenced a series of annual Dales Bible Weeks to disseminate renewal teaching. The leaders, recognized by others as 'apostles', bound themselves to each other by 'covenantal relationships'. Five of the seven apostles were from Brethren backgrounds and so imparted their separatist spirit to the growing movement.[175] Like the Brethren, it soon splintered. The largest fragment initially was the network led by Bryn Jones and based at Bradford, subsequently called Harvestime and Covenant Ministries. Its increasingly institutional structures, however, alienated many in the south-east, where the movement was strongest. There New Frontiers under Terry Virgo, begun as a separate body in 1980, steadily gathered strength until by 2000 it possessed the largest membership of the New Churches, some 25,000.[176] Most salient, perhaps, was Gerald Coates, the leader of the Pioneer churches, who specialized in 'words of

171 Banyard, *Straws in the Wind*, pp. 92-93.

172 Leslie Davison, *Pathway to Power: The Charismatic Movement in Historical Perspective* (London: Fountain Trust, 1971).

173 Ross Peart and W.R. Davies, *What about the Charismatic Movement?* (London: Epworth Press, 1980), p. 1.

174 Andrew Kane, *Let There be Life* (Basingstoke: Marshalls, 1983), pp. 36, 71-72, 76.

175 Andrew Walker, *Restoring the Kingdom* (London: Hodder & Stoughton, 1985), p. 73.

176 Brierley (ed.), *Religious Trends*, p. 9.13.

knowledge'. He found he could identify unknown people by name, and, as a result, many came to faith.[177] By unexpected methods such as this the movement spread until by the end of the century it claimed 137,000 members.[178] Measured by the proportion who attended once a week or more, they were the most committed of any Christian grouping: 79 per cent did so, some 5 per cent ahead of the next sector, the Baptists and the heterogeneous independents.[179] Here was a powerful new force on the Christian scene.

The charismatic world that encompassed those outside and those inside the historic denominations went through periodic spiritual fashions over the years. One arose under the influence of John Wimber, the American founder of Vineyard Ministries, who visited Britain several times from 1982 onwards. He advocated evangelism by means of signs and wonders such as healing, exorcism and other patently supernatural events, what he called 'power encounters, the clashing of the kingdom of God and the kingdom of Satan'.[180] Believing in a fusion of charismatics and traditional Evangelicals, he gathered enormous support among Baptists before losing the confidence of most of them.[181] His institutional legacy was a network of Vineyard churches which possessed some 8,000 members by 2000.[182] Another vogue was the March for Jesus movement, which lasted from 1987 to 2000. Drawing inspiration from Gerald Coates and the charismatic hymn-writer Graham Kendrick, the marches briefly gathered thousands from a variety of Christian backgrounds to demonstrate their faith by parading through city centres.[183] Then in the mid-1990s there was the impact of the Toronto Blessing. At the Vineyard church at Toronto Airport, people had started falling over when receiving prayer counselling and uttering animal cries to express their exuberance. There was general charismatic satisfaction with the former, 'being slain in the Spirit', but acute division over the latter, which to some savoured of the demonic.[184] Finally, stemming from Holy Trinity, Brompton, the epicentre of the Toronto Blessing in Britain, sprang the Alpha movement, a method of evangelism through meals and conversation about the basics

---

177 Coates, *Intelligent Fire*, p. 125.

178 Brierley (ed.), *Religious Trends*, p. 9.12.

179 Brierley (ed.), *Religious Trends*, p. 12.3.

180 John Wimber, *Power Evangelism: Signs and Wonders Today* (London: Hodder & Stoughton, 1985), p. 29.

181 Douglas McBain, *Fire over the Waters: Renewal among Baptists and Others from the 1960s to the 1990s* (London: Darton, Longman and Todd, 1997), pp. 91-107.

182 Brierley (ed.), *Religious Trends*, p. 9.12.

183 Graham Kendrick, *Shine Jesus Shine* (Milton Keynes: Word Publishing, 1993). *BT*, 15 June 2000, p.3.

184 Guy Chevreau, *Catch the Fire: The Toronto Blessing* (London: Marshall Pickering, 1994).

of the Christian faith. Again this development extended far beyond renewal circles to be adopted even in many Roman Catholic parishes, and proved popular in the Free Churches. Altogether over 7,000 congregations were said to have tried it by 2000. More seemed to be converted by this low-key method than by any other in the closing years of the century.[185] Charismatic spirituality, with all its vim and gusto, brought new life to individuals and churches as the new millennium approached.

What, then, may be concluded overall about evangelism and spirituality in Nonconformity during the twentieth century? First, there is the question of effectiveness. The Free Churches at the end of the century were part of a declining Christian presence in the land. United Kingdom church membership, which had included roughly 33 per cent of the population in 1900, was down to a mere 12 per cent by 2000.[186] Much of the evidence assembled here has been of decreasing appeal by the Free Churches, and their collapse has often been recognized as contributing substantially to the decay of twentieth-century religion. Yet it must also be appreciated that by the end of the century their achievement compared favourably with that of the other two main divisions of English Christianity. In an analysis of attendance extrapolated from questionnaires completed by one third of the English churches in 1998, the figures were as follows: the Church of England had 980,600 worshippers; the Roman Catholics 1,230,100; and the Free Churches 1,478,800.[187] The Free Church total comes from including not just historic Nonconformity but also bodies classified as Independent, New, Pentecostal and Other—all expressions of the Protestant faith outside the Anglican fold. On that basis, the Free Churches formed the largest sector of modern English Christianity. Thus a relative assessment shows that Nonconformity's record of evangelistic effectiveness was better than is usually supposed.

Secondly, that result flowed from a transformation in the Christian scene from the 1960s. Down to that decade there was a predominant pattern of continuity, in which problems of an urban industrial society seemed well-nigh insuperable. Despite an evangelistic upsurge following the Second World War, the traditional forms of piety were retreating before secularizing forces, not least within the chapels. From the 1960s, however, older tastes and techniques were superseded. Radical theology probably contributed more to decline than to advance; and the ecumenical movement was more often associated with consolidation than with growth. But black-led churches, the Christian Unions, the Reformed

---

185   E.g. *BT*, 2 March 2000, p. 8; 9 March 2000, p. 3.
186   Brierley (ed.), *Religious Trends*, p. 8.17.
187   Brierley (ed.), *Religious Trends*, p. 12.3.

movement and a greater willingness to innovate did produce an increase in numbers. Supremely charismatic renewal, a new spirituality for a new age, brought about rejuvenating change. There was an associated resurgence of confidence. Among a host of symptoms was a marked increase in belief in the physical resurrection of Jesus in the ranks of the Free Churches, by contrast with a decline in the Anglican and Roman Catholic Churches, between 1984 and 1996.[188] Nonconformist piety was gaining in dogmatic content. The decade of the 1960s therefore represents a turning point in the trajectory of the Free Churches, the emergence of a new Nonconformity.

Consequently, and thirdly, by 2000 the situation was totally different from in 1901. At the start of the century a common body of popular Evangelicalism united most of the chapels, which willingly co-operated in the Free Church Council movement. At its end there was, by contrast, astonishing diversity, with smaller bodies such as 'The Jesus Fellowship Church and Multiply Network' and the 'Shiloh United Church of Christ Apostolic World Wide' alongside the rumps of Methodism, the United Reformed Church and the Baptist Union. It was symbolic that in the last year of the century, after successive budget shortfalls, it was proposed to close down the Free Churches' Council altogether, transferring its functions to other interdenominational organizations.[189] The popular Evangelical unity it had once represented had disappeared. The institutional divisions of the later twentieth century were mirrored in an immense variety of expressions of the faith, ranging from words of knowledge to a nunnery. During the last third of the century the evangelism and spirituality of Protestant Nonconformity were partly reinvigorated but also enormously diversified.

188 Brierley (ed.), *Religious Trends*, p. 5.6.
189 *BT*, 16 March 2000, p. 2.

CHAPTER 8

Protestant Nonconformists
and the Peace Question

Keith Robbins

It would certainly be misleading to characterize the twentieth century as 'the century of peace', but it may also be too glib to describe it as pre-eminently 'the century of violence'. The wars that have taken place within it have been vastly different in scope and scale. Political theorists, philosophers, theologians and historians, amongst others, have continued, as they have done for centuries, to ask themselves why wars occur and have sought to devise structures and procedures designed to make them less likely or even impossible. Some of the century's peace treaties, however, seem in retrospect to be mere holding operations between conflicts and indeed to have themselves been the basis of new conflicts.[1] Despite the fact that there have been very considerable changes in European attitudes towards war in the twentieth century it remains the case, in the words of one prominent writer on the subject, that 'there is still a long way to go before the entire planet becomes "de-bellicized"'.[2] A detailed enquiry into why this should be so is beyond the scope of this article but any consideration of the attitudes and aspirations of Nonconformists on the question of 'peace' needs to show an awareness of this total context. They were themselves British subjects and their attitudes to 'peace' cannot properly be abstracted from a whole range of other matters—their attitudes towards nationality and nationalism and towards the role and purpose of the state in particular—even though these other matters cannot be systematically explored here. They were inescapably living in the world and shared many of the preconceptions and assumptions of their contemporaries who did not share either their theology or their views on church-state relations.

---

1   Keith Robbins, 'The Treaty of Versailles, "Never Again" and Appeasement', in Michael Dockrill and John Fisher (eds), *The Paris Peace Conference, 1919: Peace without Victory?* (Basingstoke: Palgrave, 2001), pp. 103-14.

2   Kalevi J. Hosti, *Peace and War: Armed Conflicts and International Order 1648–1989* (Cambridge: Cambridge University Press, 1991), p. 328.

It would be unwise, however, to believe that Nonconformists were so conditioned by the external environment in which they lived that their attitudes and activities in relation to peace merely reflect a broader national pattern. They played some part in shaping it. Here, what happened in the nineteenth century is of formative importance. In his recent books, Martin Ceadel has paid great attention to the emerging British Peace Movement in the years from 1730 and 1854. He has identified the factors—Enlightenment thinking, evangelicalism and changes in the international system—which gave rise in Britain to a peace-or-war debate in which, as he puts it, 'a pacific theory of international relations became more deeply entrenched than in any other country'. He sees this unusual receptiveness to peace thinking as the product of a political culture which possessed the right degree of liberalism and a strategic situation which provided the right degree of security. This combination gave British thinking about peace and war its distinctive flavour.[3] And, within the 'evangelicalism' he has identified, Protestant Nonconformity had a prominent and, in certain respects, a distinctive place.

Ceadel concludes his assessment of the British moral and intellectual climate by referring to *The League of Nations*, a book written by H.N. Brailsford in 1917 in which this rebel son of a Methodist manse ruminated on British attitudes. The British, Brailsford believed, had a horror of using force or of writing or talking in terms of force. The contrast with continental peoples was striking.[4] It was no accident, in his view, that in adopting conscription in the war which still raged, the British government had chosen to respect the scruples of the uncompromising pacifist in a way in which no other government was doing. The explanation did not rest in any innate racial peculiarity but rather in the relative antiquity of the British Constitution, the relative remoteness, in

---

3   Martin Ceadel, *The Origins of War Prevention: The British Peace Movement and International Relations, 1730–1854* (Oxford: Oxford University Press, 1996), p. 517, and *Semi-detached Idealists: The British Peace Movement and International Relations, 1854–1945* (Oxford: Oxford University Press, 2000). Ceadel's earlier *Thinking about Peace and War* (Oxford: Oxford University Press, 1987) and his *Pacifism in Britain 1914–1945: The Defining of a Faith* (Oxford: Oxford University Press, 1980) are both invaluable in establishing conceptual clarity. In a survey of the kind being attempted here, however, it is not possible to elaborate in detail the complexities attaching to the word 'pacifism' as understood amongst Nonconformists. Nineteenth-century Baptist peacemakers, as Paul Dekar points out, manifested a variety of paradigms: objection to specific wars or to all wars; advocacy of human rights and racial justice; protest against military expenditure; civil disobedience: 'Baptist Peacemakers in Nineteenth-Century Peace Societies', *Baptist Quarterly* 34.1 (January, 1991), pp. 3-12.

4   Keith Robbins, 'The British Experience of Conscientious Objection', in Hugh Cecil and Peter Liddle (eds), *Facing Armageddon: The First World War Experienced* (London: Leo Cooper, 1996) pp.691-708.

time, of Britain's last civil war and in the island's long immunity from invasion. A nation with a vast empire and little army ended by disliking force. It lapsed easily into a comfortable habit 'of regarding international policy as a reasonable exchange of views' which was by no means governed by the concept of force. Even more important was that Britain was a satisfied power which had latterly grown up without the hungers and appetites which dictated the views of other nations towards the use of force for political or other purposes. Britons had not experienced the need to liberate kinsmen under a foreign yoke or avenge some earlier military defeat. It was easy for Britain to condemn force, Brailsford wrote, 'for we possessed all that force can win'.[5] Brailsford's thesis, which has been echoed subsequently by many other writers, can no doubt appear too sweeping in particulars but it still seems basically sound. A mindset had evolved in these islands, arising out of a peculiar set of circumstances, which pervaded British attitudes, even when those circumstances changed substantially as the world order itself changed through the twentieth century. Of course, one must be careful not to exaggerate British peculiarity or ignore a certain element of national hypocrisy—which foreign observers were on occasion not slow to detect.

So, while it is indeed the case that in the major world wars of the first half of the twentieth century, and in occasional conflicts since, British governments have been able to take the country to war with remarkably high levels of consent and support, it has been largely because they have appeared to be 'just' and 'inevitable'. It would be difficult, in the case of either world war, to argue that British involvement stemmed from a pervasive national enthusiasm and eagerness for war. In 1914 Britain went to war under the guidance of a Foreign Secretary who loathed war and 'militarism'.[6] In 1939, it was only when another attempt at 'a reasonable exchange of views' had at length conspicuously failed that war came to seem unavoidable to the majority of the British public. In other words, we may risk the generalization—to which there are inevitably some exceptions—that in its stance on peace and war Nonconformists were not invariably and inevitably battling against the tide. In this respect, their circumstances have been different from those of religious Dissenters in other countries in which 'bellicist' values have been dominant.[7] And, if we take the second half of the twentieth century as a whole, what is remarkable about it, when viewed in a long historical

---

5   H.N. Brailsford, *The League of Nations* (London: Headley Bros, 1917), pp. 5-8.

6   Keith Robbins, *Sir Edward Grey* (London: Cassell, 1971), pp. 288-89: 'Britain in the Summer of 1914', in Keith Robbins, *Politicians, Diplomacy and War in Modern British History* (London: Hambledon Press, 1994), pp. 175-88.

7   For comparison see the essays in Peter Brock and Thomas P. Socknat (eds), *Challenge to Mars: Essays on Pacifism from 1918 to 1945* (Toronto/London: University of Toronto Press, 1999).

perspective, is how little the British have been involved in war and hence how few have been the specific occasions, therefore, when Nonconformity might have found itself at variance on issues of peace with the wider society.[8] Admittedly, the peace that has been enjoyed since 1945 has not been a perfect peace, and it has been lived under the shadow of potential nuclear conflict, but it has nevertheless meant that for the generation which came to maturity after 1945, and subsequent generations, there has been nothing like 1914–18 or 1939–45 to dominate and to an extent define their lives in a way to which those major conflicts did for those who took part or lived through them as adults.

These factors, summarily considered though they have been, are important in any consideration of Nonconformity and the 'peace question' in the twentieth century. Attitudes to peace and war do not exist in a vacuum but respond to and interact with the domestic political context on the one hand and global developments on the other. There is, however, difficulty in speaking simply of 'Nonconformity' as if it were a single coherent force. It obviously was not. It is equally misleading to suppose, in the twentieth century, even before the advent of devolution, that 'England and Wales' forms a uniform polity. Although the mindset did not disappear, and although new terminology proved virtually impossible to devise, the fact remains that since the implementation of disestablishment in Wales after the First World War Nonconformity has ceased to exist. So, to an extent, what Nonconformists have felt in the twentieth century about the 'peace question' has in considerable measure reflected what they felt about themselves and the society in which they lived—and that has not been the same in England and Wales even though some denominations have organisationally continued to straddle the Anglo–Welsh border.[9] And that process of reflection must include what they considered their heritage to be.

Ceadel sees Nonconformity as a significant element in that 'confident, moralistic, versatile and highly influential force' which he takes nineteenth-century Liberalism in Britain to be.[10] Nonconformity itself, however, is seen by Michael Watts as uneasily poised at this juncture between 'Dissidence' and 'Respectability'. Its increasing national social presence is illustrated by the fact that the number of Nonconformist MPs rose from thirty-three to sixty-two as a result of the 1868 general

---

8   Keith Robbins, *Appeasement* (Oxford: Blackwell, 1997)

9   See Goronwy J. Jones, *Wales and the Quest for Peace* (Cardiff: University of Wales Press, 1969), and the essay by Kenneth O. Morgan on 'Peace Movements in Wales, 1899–1945', in his *Modern Wales: Politics, Places and People* (Cardiff: University of Wales Press, 1995), pp. 84-116.

10   Ceadel, *Origins of War Prevention*, p. 129.

election.[11] John Bright became the first Dissenter to sit in a British cabinet in that same year when he became President of the Board of Trade.[12] Watts sees the growing confidence of English and Welsh Dissent exemplified in the way they celebrated the two hundredth anniversary of the 1662 ejection. Arguably, half the churchgoers were Dissenters and their numbers were increasing. In the face of legislation which progressively removed discriminations from which they had suffered, the sense that Nonconformists constituted a separate society—a people apart—was weakening, though it had not yet waned. Certain injustices, or perceived injustices, still smarted, but they were ceasing to cement a tradition. In the latter decades of the century, in short, acute observers recognized that the dissolution of Dissent was imminent, if it had not already arrived.[13] 'Nonconformity' sounded negative. Charles Berry, one of the inspirations behind the Free Church Federation movement, was one of those who taught that 'we must no longer be satisfied with such title as Protestant, Nonconformist, Dissenter, but that we must transmute them into their positive equivalents'.[14] John Bright's uncomfortable occupancy of high political office perhaps exemplifies, in part at least, the disagreeable dilemmas confronting those whose careers had been forged in Dissent when they were confronted by the exercise of at least a modicum of power. It remained the case, however, that some Nonconformists still spoke the language of prophetic outsiders.[15] They confidently asserted that the 'war system' had its basis in 'society', though acquaintance with at least some real live diplomats prompted the possibility that they were not all by definition cunning liars. There still remained a pervasive assumption in Dissenting quarters that peace depended upon the bringing together of the peoples of the world, as distinguished from their rulers.[16] Governments, as a matter of principle, were not to be trusted. Somehow or other, they could be by-passed. So,

---

11   Michael Watts, *The Dissenters: Volume II. The Expansion of Evangelical Nonconformity 1791–1859* (Oxford: Clarendon Press, 1995), p. 591.

12   Keith Robbins, *John Bright* (London: Routledge & Kegan Paul, 1979), pp. 204-206.

13   'The political aggression of the Nonconformists during the last half of the century represents the final Nonconformist assault against the remnants of a privileged society, but it was also a manifestation of their attempts to retain a sense of purpose and distinct identity under the pressure of rapid social and political change'. Mark D. Johnson, *The Dissolution of Dissent, 1850–1918* (New York and London: Garland Publishing, 1987), p. 297.

14   J.S. Drummond, *Charles A. Berry, D.D.* (London: Cassell, 1899), p. 120.

15   See 'On Prophecy and Politics: Some Pragmatic Reflexions', in Keith Robbins, *History, Religion and Identity in Modern Britain*, pp. 105-18.

16   J.P. Parry, *Democracy and Religion* (Cambridge: Cambridge University Press, 1989), p. 208.

there was a deep and unresolved, perhaps unresolvable, tension between an 'oppositional' or 'prophetic' stance characteristic of 'outsiders' and one which was fully participatory but which necessarily also exposed participants to all the ambiguities of power and working compromises of the political process—in a society which trembled on the verge of fully-enfranchised democracy.

The outbreak of the South African War in October 1899 brought some of these tensions to the fore. There had been colonial 'small wars' over previous decades as part of the process of imperial consolidation, especially in Africa. It can be plausibly argued that, on balance, Nonconformity had come to accept the legitimacy of empire and was increasingly persuaded of the benefits that British rule could convey to conquered peoples, amongst them being conversion to Christianity.[17] There were signs, many believed, of an ordained special British mission and responsibility, perhaps a pan-Protestant 'Anglo–Saxon' one, in the era of the Spanish–American war of 1898. In southern Europe, it was the Cretan rebellion against Ottoman control which reinforced longstanding anti-Turkish feelings. Robertson Nicoll of the *British Weekly* urged his readers to prevent the Peace Society from using chapel premises because its members resisted the calls for support and intervention. Pride in the Royal Navy was frequently expressed. David Bebbington goes so far as to suggest that before the outbreak of war in South Africa Nonconformists had ceased to regard armaments spending as a dangerous waste. They shared, he suggests, a racially-based nationalism, widespread at the time, which ensured that any residual reluctance to use force for imperial purposes largely disappeared.[18] This is, of course, a generalization and it is only right to mention that exceptions can be found both amongst the older and younger generation of ministers. It is also well-known that attitudes varied between as well as within the various denominations.[19] It is always problematic what weight should be attached to the views of particular organs or individuals and the extent to which they were truly 'representative'. Even so, with all necessary caveats having been made, Nonconformity did not as a whole stand out for the belief that war was

---

17   Brian Stanley, *The Bible and the Flag* (Leicester: Apollos, 1990), shows, however, that the relationship between missionary activity and imperial development is rather more complicated than this statement suggests. See also Andrew Porter, 'Religion, Missionary Enthusiasm, and Empire', in Andrew Porter (ed.), *The Oxford History of the British Empire: The Nineteenth Century* (Oxford: Oxford University Press, 1999), pp. 222-46.

18   David Bebbington, *The Nonconformist Conscience: Chapel and Politics 1870–1914* (London: George Allen & Unwin, 1982), pp. 120-21.

19   Stephen Koss, 'Wesleyanism and Empire', *Historical Journal* 18 (1975), pp. 105-18: C. Oldstone-Moore, *Hugh Price Hughes: Founder of a New Methodism, Conscience of a New Nonconformity* (Cardiff: University of Wales Press, 1999).

always wrong. Indeed, when they believed that a particular war was 'just' Nonconformists were likely to support it with exceptional conviction.

Was the Boer War 'just'? It was the first war which the British people had engaged in against fellow-Christians since the Crimean War. Nonconformists might be said to have much in common with Afrikaner Calvinists and therefore have reservations about fighting a 'Bible-loving people'. Some certainly did, but the view substantially prevailed that the British ideal for South Africa was nobler than that of the Boers. Those who continued to have reservations, or were strongly hostile, included John Clifford, Silas Hocking and Joshua Rowntree. They and others were excoriated as 'pro-Boers'. R.J. Campbell, a coming man, was enthusiastic for the imperial cause and went to South Africa to express it. England occupied a position in the world 'from which she cannot recede if she would. Millions of swarthy subjects receive, or ought to receive, at her hands peace and good government'.[20] The divisions amongst Nonconformists mirrored those in the Liberal Party and Nonconformists were to be found in all of its factions. Some who gave general support for the war nevertheless were upset by what Sir Henry Campbell-Bannerman famously referred to as 'methods of barbarism' in its conduct. From time to time, during the war, there were attempts to find a basis on which all Nonconformists could agree that the war should end. It transpired, however, that large numbers of ministerial signatories could only be gathered around a formula of transparent uselessness. Specific resolutions still revealed sharp differences.

It could hardly be said, therefore, as the war came to an end, that Nonconformity as a whole had displayed any effective 'witness'. It had become evident, for example, from the use of smokeless rifles and of 'concentration camps' that war in the twentieth century was an increasingly inhumane affair but, beyond that obvious conclusion, there was little consensus as to how it might be avoided in future. The picture in Europe itself looked threatening. Just what did peace mean?[21] The conclusion of the 1904 Anglo–French agreement was sometimes taken to indicate that Europe was dividing into two opposing camps. The entente with France, of course, had been concluded by a Conservative government. A problem before the incoming Liberal government in December 1905 was the extent to which Great Britain should be drawn ever deeper into the European alliance system. The January 1906 Liberal election triumph brought a major increase in Nonconformist strength in

---

20   Cited in Keith Robbins, 'The Spiritual Pilgrimage of R.J. Campbell', in *History, Religion and Identity in Modern Britain* (London: Hambledon Press, 1993), pp. 139-40.

21   Keith Robbins, 'L'ambiguité du mot "Paix" au royaume-uni avant 1914', in J. Vandenrath, *1914: Les Psychoses de Guerre* (Rouen: Publications de l'Université Rouen, 1984), pp. 59-73.

the House of Commons and also, generously defined, in the cabinet itself. It was another matter, however, whether that increased Nonconformist presence constituted a coherent body of opinion capable of advocating a common policy. Certainly, in the country at large, denominational meetings at local and national level passed resolutions deploring the developing arms race and urging the merits of arbitration agreements as a method of resolving international disputes, but to what effect?[22] There was alarm that it was with Germany, 'home of the Reformation', that tension seemed to be becoming most acute. A clash 'between the two great Teutonic peoples' would be a disaster—it was assumed, apparently, that all the inhabitants of Britain were Teutons. Nonconformists accordingly took part in schemes which were arranged from 1907 onwards to try to bring about 'friendly relations' between the two peoples. J. Allen Baker, the Quaker Liberal MP, was prominent in these activities. A journal, *The Peacemaker*, was founded. Its issue of June 1914 concluded that it was 'almost difficult to realize that there were still unresolved problems' between Britain and Germany.[23]

It was sometimes argued that Britain should try to mediate between France and Germany and avoid commitment to either power. That would be the best way to secure peace. When the 1911 Agadir crisis broke the *British Weekly* warned that the British people would not go to war for the sake of France. It was, however, Lloyd George who famously declared at the time that Britain was not to be treated as of no account in the Cabinet of Nations. Peace at that price would be a humiliation intolerable for a great country. That difference of emphasis can be taken to encapsulate the general dilemma in which Nonconformists frequently found themselves. The Liberal governments after 1905 were 'their' governments to a degree without previous (or, as it happens, subsequent) precedent. Even Asquith, the Prime Minister after 1908, could still be thought to have an element of ancestral Nonconformity about him.[24]

---

22   It was the 'scale of the land arms race between the blocs that took off after 1910' which concerned Nonconformists rather the existence of armies as such. We may now believe that the armaments race was a necessary precondition for the outbreak of hostilities but still doubt whether considered in isolation armaments offer a sufficient or all-embracing explanation of the destruction of peace. David Stevenson, *Armaments and the Coming of War: Europe 1904–1914* (Oxford: Oxford University Press, 1996), p. 421.

23   Keith Robbins, 'Public Opinion, the Press and Pressure Groups', in F.H. Hinsley (ed.), *British Foreign Policy under Sir Edward Grey* (Cambridge: Cambridge University Press, 1977), pp. 82-83.

24   While there may have been satisfaction with the apparent strength of Nonconformity in the House of Commons, there was also increasing concern, sometimes publicly aired, about the appeal of Nonconformity, and indeed of Christianity, in the country as a whole: see Keith Robbins, 'The Churches in Edwardian Society', in Robbins, *History, Religion and Identity in Modern Britain*, pp. 119-32.

When the domestic agenda of those governments is also remembered, it was inconceivable that Nonconformists should seek to destroy 'their own' because of an element of concern over foreign policy. They shared now, to some degree, in the responsibility of power. Therefore, while there were some who joined in the criticisms of Grey which occasionally surfaced after 1911, it cannot be said there was any sustained Nonconformist critique of the government's foreign policy as a whole. Some were, however, influenced by the arguments advanced by Norman Angell in his best-selling *The Great Illusion* which suggested that in the modern world war never 'paid'. They saw 'Angellism' as a reinforcement of an opposition to war which rested on ethical grounds. The 'peace question' therefore to an extent took on a new dimension.[25]

In November 1914, therefore, when Lloyd George came to address a huge gathering in the City Temple and told his audience, amongst other things, that Britain had entered the war three months earlier 'from motives of purest chivalry to defend the weak', he did not need to do much persuading. The militancy of Nonconformity had already made itself apparent.[26] Latter-day Cromwells should rediscover their fighting qualities against Charles I *redivivus* in the person of Kaiser Wilhelm. The veteran John Clifford, who had laboured long for international peace, told his Baptist congregation at Westbourne Park, London, that what was taking place was a struggle between the forces of freedom and those of slavery. It was a theme, with many variations, which could be found in many places. The progress of humanity depended upon the outcome. In this mood, Nonconformity was anxious to emphasize its position at the heart of the nation. If it did not play its part in the war, Robertson Nicoll wrote in 1915, Nonconformity would have lost its place in English life. One symbol of this concern to be fully accepted in the national effort was the successful campaign to secure the appointment of Free Church chaplains in the armed services. Other preachers, while lamenting the slaughter and destruction which the war was bringing, nevertheless drew some consolation from the supposition that out of evil good would come. Every nation would be made so sick by the experience of this war as to renounce it for ever. There can be little doubt that these views prevailed, at least initially, in pulpits throughout England and Wales, though it would be wrong to suppose that even some of the more blatant statements

---

25   J.D.B. Miller, *Norman Angell and the Futility of War* (London: Macmillan, 1986). Angell himself, however, argued as he did partly because experience seemed to suggest that arguments that wars were 'wrong' were ineffective if countries continued to believe that they could benefit by conquest. Paul Laity, *The British Peace Movement 1870–1914* (Oxford: Clarendon Press, 2001), provides the most recent scholarly study of the Edwardian peace movement.

26   Alan Wilkinson, *Dissent or Conform? War, Peace and the English Churches 1900–1945* (London: SCM Press, 1986), 'Dissent and the First World War', pp. 21-53.

of 'obsolete patriotism', as they may now appear, were reached without heart-searching and inner qualms. As the years passed, Nonconformists were neither immune from, nor indifferent to, the deeper questions which the war posed for all Christians as they contemplated its carnage.[27]

Nonconformist men of military age, however, if they declined to volunteer to fight, were certainly subject to social pressure to do so but they were not yet in direct conflict with the British state. There was no conscription for military service, a fact which made Britain distinctive amongst the belligerents. Despite vigorous campaigning, headed by Lord Roberts, pressure for 'National Service' had not been successful in the pre-war years. Arnold Rowntree, the Liberal MP for York and a Quaker, was one of those who had spoken in the Commons on the matter when he had declared that there were 'large numbers of people in this country' who had a profound regard for the sanctity of human life. Parliament had no right to force men against their will to train to kill one another.[28] Even so, as the war continued, so did the demand for the introduction of conscription. The first two years of the war had already demonstrated that there were not in fact the 'large numbers' of men hopefully referred to by Rowntree. It was not even the case that there was unanimity within the Society of Friends as to the appropriate course of action. Debate and discussion among Friends over the preceding couple of decades had led to increased emphasis upon that peace testimony with which the Society was most associated in the public mind. Even so, approximately a third of Quakers of military age responded to the call to arms. It should not be thought that this was only a response on the part of birthright Friends whose involvement in Quaker affairs was nominal. The result was a certain tension in some meetings, though that lessened as the majority who opposed any participation in the war strengthened with the disappearance, to fight, of their opponents.[29]

Even though, as it appeared, the convictions which Dissenters held on the subject of peace were not widely shared, nevertheless groups did emerge who distanced themselves from the prevailing sentiment. The Union of Democratic Control was formed in the early months of the war

---

27   The literature on this subject is enormous. See, for example, Gerhard Besier, *Die protestantischen Kirchen Europas im Ersten Weltkrieg* (Göttingen: Vandenhoeck & Ruprecht, 1983); Keith Robbins, *The First World War* (Oxford: Oxford University Press, 1984); R.N. Stromberg, *Redemption by War: The Intellectuals and 1914* (Lawrence: Kansas University Press, 1982); W.J. Reader, *'At Duty's Call': A Study in Obsolete Patriotism* (Manchester: Manchester University Press, 1988).

28   Cited in T.C. Kennedy, *The Hound of Conscience: A History of the No-Conscription Fellowship, 1914–1919* (Fayetteville: University of Arkansas Press, 1981), p. 27.

29   Thomas C. Kennedy, *British Quakerism 1860–1920: The Transformation of a Religious Community* (Oxford: Oxford University Press, 2001), provides a full account.

committed to what it believed were necessary measures to avoid future conflict. Immediately, however, there was some uncertainty about its stance. Some members regarded the union as the successor to the pre-war peace movement and believed that the objective should be to secure peace at the earliest possible moment. Others took note of the view of the historian G.M. Trevelyan whose brother Charles was a UDC founder. Fresh from his biography of John Bright, George argued that Charles and his friends would be 'more effective for peace' when the time came if they showed themselves to be patriotic and refrained from making themselves wildly unpopular.[30] Advice of this kind was no doubt also offered to Nonconformists who might have been attracted to the long-term programme, and they were not prominent in the UDC's leadership and activity.

Nonconformist presence, unsurprisingly, is much more evident in another new body, the Fellowship of Reconciliation, whose basis was explicitly Christian. In its founding declaration it stated that its members held the view that Christians were forbidden to wage war and that they were instead called to a life of service and the enthronement of love in personal, social, commercial and national life. Peace was given a positive quality—'shalom' rather than 'pax'.[31] Amongst those instrumental in creating the fellowship were Henry Hodgkin, Richard Roberts, Alan Knott, Leyton Richards and W.E. Orchard. At the time Richards was minister of Bowdon Downs Congregational Church outside Manchester and took a vigorous anti-war stance from the start.[32] The Fellowship of Reconciliation, of which Richards went on to be General Secretary, claimed a membership of 2,000 by July 1915, with Nonconformists from the main denominations preponderating in its ranks.

The existence of the UDC and the FoR, and other even smaller bodies, testified to the fact that criticism of the war had not altogether disappeared. Indeed, the existence of such groups gave fresh substance to terms like Nonconformity and Dissent. Critics were clearly swimming 'against the stream' and encountered, on occasion, ostracism and hostility. Such treatment in turn frequently served to promote solidarity and stiffen resistance amongst those involved. There remained, however, underlying and unresolved questions. Was a refusal to fight simply a

---

30   Keith Robbins, *The Abolition of War: The 'Peace Movement' in Britain, 1914–1919* (Cardiff: University of Wales Press, 1976), pp. 38-39.

31   J. Wallis, *Valiant for Peace: A History of the Fellowship of Reconciliation 1914 to 1989* (London: Fellowship of Reconciliation, 1991), pp. 6-8.

32   E.R. Richards, *Private View of a Public Man: The Life of Leyton Richards* (London: Allen & Unwin, 1950), pp. 57-67. See also Clyde Binfield, *So Down to Prayers: Studies in English Nonconformity 1780–1920* (London: J.M. Dent & Sons, 1977), pp. 232-48, for an illuminating study of the tensions within the Bowdon Downs congregation during the war.

personal matter or did it entail a commitment, above and beyond any other considerations, actively to try to bring about peace? Should peace be sought even if it could only be obtained at the price of national surrender? Did the 'struggle for peace' also require a far-reaching commitment to economic and social transformation, even revolution, without which, some said, the conditions that led to war would be perpetuated? These and other cognate questions formed the staple of debate and discussion amongst Nonconformist pacifists, particularly amongst Quakers, for whom pacifism was emphatically not passivism.

The introduction of compulsory military service by the Asquith coalition government in 1916 put some of these matters to the test.[33] It had sometimes been supposed that such a measure would still arouse substantial opposition, but in the event that proved not to be the case. What the new act did, however, was inevitably to identify those who still resisted conscription and to focus attention on the complex and not always compatible reasons why they did so. The fact that the act made provision for exemption brought further complexity into the picture, particularly since it was not altogether clear whether there could be absolute exemption or only from a requirement to fight. Objectors came to be divided into 'absolutists' (the minority) and 'alternativists' (the majority)—categories which themselves hide various shades of opinion. The local tribunals set up across the country tried, not always very sympathetically, to test the 'genuine' character of those who claimed 'conscientious objection'.

On the one hand, any reference to conscience reawakened memories of Nonconformist persecution and suspicion of state power. It stirred some sympathy for conscientious objectors amongst many fellow-Nonconformists who continued to disagree with them on the attitude to be adopted towards the war itself. One such was F.B. Meyer whose pamphlet *The Majesty of Conscience* (1917) was a significant contribution to the cause of the conscientious objectors. On the other hand, December 1916 saw the advent to power of Lloyd George and there was some satisfaction expressed that he was the first Nonconformist in actual membership of a Free Church to become Prime Minister. There were some hopes that he would exercise patronage and promote the interests on Nonconformity. It was also indisputable, however, that Lloyd George was determined to win the war, cost what it might. Was it necessary, therefore, temporarily to put aside reservations and qualms, as it was supposed that Lloyd George himself must have done, in the pursuit of this outcome? If Lloyd George, the supposed erstwhile pacifist, now

---

33   John Rae, *Conscience and Politics: The British Government and the Conscientious Objector to Military Service 1916–1919* (Oxford: Oxford University Press, 1970), remains the standard account.

saw no alternative but to fight on for victory to ensure the success of the cause of liberty and justice, for which the allies stood, was it not necessary for Nonconformity as a whole also to do so? In this situation, inviduals and congregations vacillated uneasily seeking a 'middle ground' which doubtfully existed and laying themselves open to criticism from one side or the other. R.F. Horton, in his autobiography, captures the atmosphere of a period when 'everything has become unnatural, feverish, aguish, through the anxieties which pressed upon the public mind'. He found that pacifists deserted him because they charged him with 'supporting the war' and chauvinists turned away because he wanted peace.[34]

It is not surprising, in these polarized circumstances, that as the war and disagreement continued, the focus began to shift to envisaging the world after its conclusion, whenever that should turn out to be. The majority of Nonconformists who resisted the claims of some of their colleagues that there was an honourable peace which could be obtained by negotiation became ever more emphatic that this war, once won, would have indeed to be the war to end war. Nothing less than a new era of world peace could justify the price that was being paid. It soon became clear, however, that while such a goal was indeed highly desirable it was far from clear how it could be achieved. It would surely not be enough to rely on revulsion from the horrors of war as disclosed in the existing conflict, though such revulsion could no doubt be effectively harnessed in favour of perpetual peace. To go beyond such a reaction, however, involved asking questions to which Nonconformists could not give unanimous answers. Was the war of 1914 the inescapable outcome of a flawed international system which had rested upon the false god of 'the balance of power'? Was it the result of a pervasive militarism, a militarism which perhaps found its most obnoxious expression in Germany, but which was not confined to that country? Was the European state-system as it existed in 1914 so inadequate that only its wholesale replacement would be acceptable?

It was in relation to such questions that the idea of a 'League of Nations' emerged and gained ground during the latter stages of the war. The idea was discussed in various quarters in different countries and at varying levels of influence. It became an element in Anglo–American political discourse and engaged minds eager to find a way out of the impasse disclosed by the coming of war in 1914. Yet adherence to the general idea was by no means accompanied by unanimity as to detail. Pushed to an ultimate conclusion, the notion of 'collective security' could challenge the right of any state to maintain forces simply for its own defence. It was far from clear that any state would abandon such a primeval responsibility. Some critics already perceived what they believed to be a flaw in the notion that peace would be maintained in the future by

---

34   R.F. Horton, *An Autobiography* (London: Allen & Unwin, 1917), p. 342.

the willingness and capacity of a majority of states to take action against an aggressor state. They argued that this was an over-simple scenario. States would continue to be governed by their perception of self-interest and neither their governments nor their populations would embark on a war to defend something as remote and abstruse as the integrity of world-order if their own interests did not seem to be directly involved. There were two further issues to be faced. The first was whether a new League of Nations should be an immediate agency of reconciliation by admitting Germany and other enemy states into membership from the start or should the Germans 'work their passage' back to international polite society? The second was whether it was necessary or sensible to think at all of this League of Nations as being endowed with military force through its member states (the idea of the League having its own forces was scarcely a viable proposition) or was that merely to continue to sup with the devil? Was not the radical solution to insist upon comprehensive disarmament with any 'aggression' being responded to by the implementation of a programme of economic sanctions, sanctions which, it was argued, would be efficacious in calling a halt to such action?[35]

It is scarcely surprising that there were many different emphases on these matters and that they showed themselves as much amongst Nonconformists as amongst public opinion at large. By the end of hostilities, however, the pressure for some kind of League had become irresistible, though the form it came to have was probably the only structure possible in the circumstances. There was a Nonconformist consensus that the League of Nations represented a great leap forward in international relations. What seemed important was to get the idea embedded in the public mind rather than to argue over what were considered details in relation to the implementation of sanctions. In any case, it was hoped that the League would gain such prestige that it would never be actually operationally tested. It was pointless, in these circumstances, for opponents of any kind of military sanction to argue with supporters of such action. It seemed that a certain fuzziness on these matters caused no harm and allowed the generation of a substantial wave of enthusiasm. It was also clear, however, that while there was certainly substantial demobilization in the post-war world it could not be claimed that there was an all-pervasive disarmament. If it was accepted, as it widely was, that the maintenance of armed forces had contributed to, if not caused, the war of 1914 then there was still much to be worked for. The

---

35   Henry R. Winkler, *The League of Nations Movement in Great Britain: 1914–1919* (New Brunswick, NJ: Rutgers University Press, 1952); G.W. Egerton, *Great Britain and the Creation of the League of Nations: Strategy, Politics and International Organization, 1914–1919* (Chapel Hill, NC: University of North Carolina Press, 1978); Keith Robbins, 'Lord Bryce and the First World War', in *Politicians, Diplomacy and War in Modern British History* (London: Hambledon, 1994), pp. 189-214.

twin objectives—supporting the League of Nations and urging disarmament—seemed entirely compatible.

There were, however, some uncomfortable issues to be faced if there was to be substance in a Nonconformist contribution to these objectives. Perhaps the most difficult was the nature of Nonconformity itself in post-war circumstances. Was the era of fragmentation and division coming to an end? Was it not time to seek Nonconformist unity, perhaps even the creation of a single Free Church? That was certain an objective set out by J.H. Shakespeare. The cross-roads had been reached and it was time to move on. No one could forecast the future for religion in Britain after the war. Nothing would be taken for granted. The most sacred and venerable institutions would have to justify themselves.[36] The war had shown the emptiness of European ecclesiastical structures. Protestantism was not a sufficient guarantee for liberty or righteousness. The hatred of the Russian masses for the Orthodox Church had now come into the open. If the church was ever to be effective in preventing or restraining war it would have to be 'a very different Church from anything the world has ever seen'. Ministers of Christianity of all denominations and in all countries would have 'to enforce as a commonplace, not only that War is inconsistent with Christianity, but that Nationalism is inconsistent with Christianity'.[37] While he advocated a United Free Church, that was not as an end in itself but rather a prelude to a greater ecumenism. Viewed simply as an element in British public life, Nonconformity would never, could never be effective on its own. The Lambeth Conference of 1920, reflecting some similar impressions, seemed to open up some new possibilities.

It also appeared to be the case that Nonconformity was in numerical decline, though its scale was still obscure in the initial post-war decade. By the 1930s, it could not be ignored.[38] Whilst decline might seem to be an aspect of a more general indifference towards or alienation from religion in post-war Britain, it seemed that Nonconformity was hit particularly hard. Moreover, the political landscape was changing dramatically. The Liberal Party was in deep difficulty. In its divided and

---

36   J.H. Shakespeare, *The Churches at the Cross-Roads* (London: Williams & Norgate, 1918), pp. 208-209; M. Townsend, 'John Howard Shakespeare: Prophet of Ecumenism', *Baptist Quarterly* 37.6 (April, 1998), pp. 298-312.

37   Shakespeare, *Cross-Roads*, pp. 38-39. The most detailed study of Shakespeare is Peter Shepherd, *The Making of a Modern Denomination: John Howard Shakespeare and the English Baptists 1898–1924* (Studies in Baptist History and Thought, 4; Carlisle: Paternoster, 2001). On Shakespeare's views on unity, see especially pp. 93-138 and 182-85.

38   See, for example, the discussion by Michael Goodman, 'Numerical Decline amongst English Baptists 1930–1939', *Baptist Quarterly* 36.5 (January, 1996), pp.241-51.

declining condition it could no longer be (in so far as it ever was) Nonconformity at prayer. Confronted by the advance of Labour, Nonconformist ministers, voters and politicians moved in a variety of directions and the party-political expression of the Nonconformist conscience became blurred and contentious. Fear of socialism pointed erstwhile Liberal Nonconformists in a Conservative direction, particularly after 1931, although the Labour Party itself of course contained prominent Nonconformists in its ranks, perhaps most notably the Wesleyan, Arthur Henderson, a staunch advocate of the League of Nations. What was cause and what was effect in the disintegrating Nonconformist/Liberal symbiosis may be speculated upon but is not particularly pertinent here. The fact remains that the fate of the peace witness of Nonconformity had become bound up with the fate of Nonconformity itself. In this respect we may regard the two decades after 1918 as a period of uncomfortable and unsuccessful adjustment.[39]

On the one hand, old landmarks and alignments still seemed in place. It was, for example, still obviously the case that the League of Nations Union, the inter-party body set up to support the League, had greater success with 'chapel' than 'church'. The view of the Free Church Federal Council that in the League of Nations lay the only hope for world peace found a clear expression in the enrolment of Free Church congregations in the League of Nations Union. In the early thirties, their membership outnumbered Anglican congregations by some five to one.[40] Yet the controversy surrounding the infant Council of Action for Peace and Reconstruction showed how impossible it was to 'rally' old Nonconformity around the tarnished but still engaging figure of Lloyd George. M.E. Aubrey resigned from the Free Church Council Executive in 1935 because he objected 'most strongly to the Free Churches in a day like this being made to appear to play a game that is contrary both to the National Government on the one hand and the Labour Party on the other. There are great and good Christian men in both and they are doing their best'. Since this was indeed the case, it is not surprising that the council fizzled out in failure.[41] In addition to this reluctance or inability to forge party political alignments, there were spiritual and theological tendencies which engaged the time and energy of leading

---

39   I have explored some of these issues in more detail in 'Free Churchmen and the Twenty Years' Crisis', republished in Robbins, *History, Religion and Identity*, pp. 149-60.

40   D.S. Birn, *The League of Nations Union 1918–1945* (Oxford: Oxford University Press, 1981), pp. 136-37.

41   W.M.S. West, 'The Reverend Secretary Aubrey: Part 1', *Baptist Quarterly* 34.5 (January, 1992), p. 210.

Nonconformist figures, movements which pointed away from politics altogether.[42]

In addition, it was also the case that experience of the war had radically changed the attitude of a number of Anglican clergy who now began to be identified with 'pacifism'. 'Peace' was no longer a Nonconformist preserve in 'issue politics'. Charles Raven and H.R.L. Sheppard, both Anglican clergymen, became, by the early 1930s, amongst the most well-known 'pacifist' names in the country: 'pacifism' could no longer be said to be the particular, even the defining characteristic of Nonconformity. Raven became Chairman of the Fellowship of Reconciliation in 1932 and the latter founded the Peace Pledge Union in 1934. Names such as Leyton Richards, G.H.C. Macgregor, C.J. Cadoux, Stuart Morris, Charles Raven, Donald Soper and George Macleod who featured amongst the PPU's original sponsors testified to the extent to which the base of the 'peace movement' had broadened beyond English Nonconformity. Fifty thousand people signed, a figure which had more than doubled by 1939. Peace pledgers declared, on a postcard, as follows: 'We renounce war, and never again, directly or indirectly, will we support or sanction another'. The language is significant. What was being made was a personal pledge, an act of commitment and faith which would be valid irrespective of circumstances. It was a kind of pacifism which did not depend for its validity upon its conceivable success as a means of preventing future war.

The timing of the foundation of the PPU is also significant—October 1934. Events over the previous few years—most notably the Japanese invasion of Manchuria in September 1931 and Hitler's accession to power in January 1933—made it increasingly difficult to sustain a broad-based pacifism of the kind that had largely existed in the 1920s when no immediate threat to peace had presented itself. Hope could still be placed in the League of Nations. In 1928 in his *Christianity and the League of Nations*, the Methodist scholar A.W. Harrison considered the next few years to be critical for the League. At last, he believed, what he called the 'vague and tremulous will to peace is coming to self-realization'.[43] A year later, a fellow-Methodist, Arthur Henderson, was Foreign Secretary and his devotion to the League was well-known, and to the cause of disarmament, even if his Prime Minister did not altogether share his

---

42   I.M. Randall, '"Arresting People for Christ': Baptists and the Oxford Group in the 1930s', *Baptist Quarterly* 38.1 (January 1999) pp. 3-18; D.W. Bebbington, 'Baptists and Fundamentalism in Inter-War Britain', in Keith Robbins (ed.), *Protestant Evangelicalism: Britain, Ireland, Germany and America, c.1750–c.1950, Essays in Honour of W.R. Ward* (Studies in Church History, 7; Oxford: Basil Blackwell, 1990), pp. 297-325.

43   A.W. Harrison, *Christianity and the League of Nations* (London: Sharp, 1928), p. 171.

enthusiasm.[44] By 1931, however, the Labour Government had fallen, Henderson's career was in ruins, the Disarmament Conference appeared to be going nowhere and the world in general appeared much more dangerous. It was time to wake up to the gravity of the position into which the world appeared to be drifting. It was a concern 'to make new efforts to bring the message and action of Christian pacifism to bear on the critical situation in the world that led in 1936 to the attempt to send 'Embassies of Reconciliation' worldwide in the persons of Percy Bartlett, Alfred Salter and Henry Carter, and spurred on Muriel Lister in her work as international ambassador for the Fellowship of Reconciliation.[45]

These were individual and group responses to crisis, working on the edge of mainstream political processes. Others, however, felt that it was still not too late to prevent the drift to war by working through established structures. The view was increasingly expressed that the League of Nations had never been given a proper chance to succeed because it had been too closely linked with the Treaty of Versailles and the other post-war settlements. Criticism of the treaty became ever more vocal the further it receded into the past. It had been harshly punitive and unimaginative. Whatever many Nonconformists might have felt in 1919 about the peace treaty, for the most part they now felt ashamed. Surely it was obvious that the way to build lasting peace was to seek reconciliation and a fresh start? It had been short-sighted to seek to 'make Germany pay'. Even that Nonconformist who had most connection with the treaty now felt obliged to distance himself. Lloyd George told a Free Church gathering in Sheffield in 1933 that the Germans had carried out their treaty obligations in the letter and the spirit—until those who had enforced the treaty broke it.[46] It was a remark which appealed to those who still regretted the fact that it was with Germany, the home of the Reformation, that Britain had gone to war.[47] A spiteful peace had produced Hitler, but it was not too late to repair the damage. There was a widespread belief amongst Nonconformists that the path to peace led through a prudent policy of appeasement, a word which had yet to gain

---

44   Keith Robbins, 'Arthur Henderson—die Welt braucht Abrüstung', in *Der Friedens-Nobelpreis von 1933 bis 1945* (Munich: Edition Pacis, 1990), pp. 44-51; 'Labour Foreign Policy and International Socialism: MacDonald and the League of Nations', in Robbins, *Politicians, Diplomacy and War*, pp. 239-72.

45   J. Wallis, *Mother of World Peace: The Life of Muriel Lister* (Enfield Lock: Hisarlik Press, 1993), p. 154

46   Stephen Koss, *Nonconformity in Modern British Politics* (London: B.T. Batsford, 1975), pp. 189-90.

47   Keith Robbins, *Present and Past: British Images of Germany in the First Half of the Twentieth Century and their Historical Legacy* (Göttingen: Wallstein Verlag, 1999).

its predominantly pejorative connotation. It would be wrong, however, to see such views as specifically or exclusively Nonconformist.[48]

The argument looked simple. It was the task of intelligent statesmanship to recognize that Germany had certain legitimate grievances (though opinion differed as to what they precisely were) and it only made sense to attempt to remedy them by diplomacy and negotiation. The challenge was to bring about 'peaceful change'. The stark alternative was to believe that at some point Germany would inevitably begin a new war. There was, therefore, a widespread yearning to 'get on better terms with Germany diplomatically' as the only realistic option. In detail, 'appeasement' meant different things to different people, but stated in these bold terms the propositions met with general agreement, at least until after the Munich agreement of September 1938.[49] Two prominent Nonconformist members of the government, the Methodist Kingsley Wood as Air Secretary and the Baptist Ernest Brown as Minister of Labour, agreed with this analysis. Indeed, A.L. Rowse took the view that leading figures in the government—Neville Chamberlain, John Simon, Samuel Hoare, Kingsley Wood, Walter Runciman and Ernest Brown—all had in common a Nonconformist origin and shared 'its characteristic self-righteousness'. The fact that their political judgment was in his view 'palpably wrong' could similarly be laid at the door of their ignorance of continental realities.[50]

Whether or not there is substance in that general contention—and 'appeasement' has its own massive historiography—there were few Nonconformists who supposed that Hitler himself was a man of pure benevolence (though, conceivably the 'practical Christianity' he apparently offered might be preferable to Soviet Communism—a point of view not without Nonconformist adherents). The plight of Christians in Germany at the hands of the Nazi regime was a matter of increasing concern but it seemed to some that there was a tension between taking up their cause with the German government and 'getting on better terms with Germany diplomatically'. 'It is rather difficult', wrote the Baptist M.E. Aubrey in March 1937, 'to persuade Germans that as individuals we cherish friendly sentiments towards their nation while at the same time we are critical of the actions of rulers for whom they have a regard that is almost akin to admiration'. He did not want to do anything which would stir up passion. In addition, there was a problem for English Nonconformists—their German brethren and sisters. Methodist minister Kingsley Lloyd lamented what he called the 'baneful reaction' which the

---

48   C.A. Cline, 'Ecumenism and Appeasement: The Bishops of the Church of England and the Treaty of Versailles', *Journal of Modern History* 61.4 (December, 1989), pp. 683-703.

49   Keith Robbins, *Munich 1938* (London: Cassell, 1968), and *Appeasement*.

50   A.L. Rowse, *All Souls and Appeasement* (London: Macmillan, 1961), p. 19.

'compromising attitude of the Free Churches in Germany' caused in Britain. He was constantly being told that German Baptists and Methodists were free to carry on their work. He feared that this was only too true but it did not reflect much credit on their conception of their work.[51] Free Churchmen who were moved by the stand of the Confessing Church wondered whether, if international peace prevailed, there would ever be any amelioration in its position. On the other hand, it was scarcely feasible or desirable to think of going to war to bring about domestic change in Germany. In the immediate pre-war years (as it turned out) individuals and congregations found it difficult to balance their underlying commitment to peace with these other considerations. It began to look as though the very survival of Britain was at stake. The view put forward in May 1939 in an editorial in the FoR monthly *Reconciliation* that 'those who are holding on to empire by force must share the blame with those who are taking empire by the same method' did not seem to most Free Church people to be a pertinent comparison. Despite all its faults, and however imperfectly embodied, Britain (and its empire) still stood as a bastion of 'Christian Civilization' and, as such, should be defended.[52]

In these circumstances, it is difficult to identify a distinctively Nonconformist 'peace stance' during the Second World War. After 1940, it could not be said that Churchill instinctively drew Nonconformists about him in his war cabinet. If war was ever just, it seemed so in these years and there was accordingly no widespread Free Church interest in a peace by negotiation. Hitler had to be defeated. Yet pacifism did not completely disappear and at a local level clear evidence of a continuing correlation between Nonconformity and conscientious objection existed. It is generally agreed that tribunals went about their work of assessment with greater sensitivity than had been the case with their predecessors in the First World War. In the South West of England tribunal, for example, Methodist, Baptist, Congregationalist and Quaker objectors outnumbered Anglicans by more than two to one. At a national level, however, Anglican pacifists were as prominent as Nonconformists—and perhaps only Donald Soper gained substantial public stature, though that was not thanks to the BBC.[53] Even though it might be thought that defeating

---

51   I discuss these matters in more detail in two articles, 'Martin Niemöller, the German Church Struggle and English Opinion', and 'Church and Politics: Dorothy Buxton and the German Church Struggle', reprinted in Robbins, *History, Religion and Identity*, pp. 161-94. For a recent discussion of the German Free Churches themselves in this period, see Nicholas M. Railton, 'German Free Churches and the Nazi Regime', *Journal of Ecclesiastical History* 49.1 (January, 1998), pp. 85-139.

52   Keith Robbins, 'Britain, 1940 and "Christian Civilization"', reprinted in *History, Religion and Identity*, pp. 195-213.

53   Wilkinson, *Dissent or Conform?*, pp. 290-92.

Hitler was more self-evidently necessary than defeating the Kaiser had been, pacifists seem in general to have been treated more sympathetically both by their fellow-Christians and by society at large than had been the case in the First World War.[54]

The latter stages of the Second World War had naturally seen a good deal of speculation about the basis of a post-war international order. On the analogy of 1919 and the Treaty of Versailles, it was widely supposed that the actual nature of peacemaking would play a major part in determining whether or not there would be a lasting peace. Sermons spoke out against an excessively punitive peace settlement which, it was argued, would only create a desire for subsequent revenge. In practice, however, the pattern of events rather precluded the application of 'lessons' from 1919. Germany was not only defeated, it was occupied and reshaped according to the wishes of the victors. It was hard to argue against 'de-Nazification'. It was indeed a 'victor's peace' but was there any other feasible or desirable alternative? Most Free Church people did not think so.

It was soon apparent, however, that the mere defeat of Nazi Germany did not in itself usher in a new era of peace. On the contrary, as the Cold War became colder in the immediate post-1945 years awkward realities had to be confronted.[55] Was peace again being threatened and, if so, how might it effectively be preserved? The role of the Soviet Union in the defeat of Hitler could not be denied, but it could hardly be said that Stalinism sat readily with the ethos of the British Free Churches. No Free Churchman matched, or sought to match, the prominence gained by Dr Hewlett Johnson, the 'Red Dean' of Canterbury, in praising what were thought to be the achievements of Soviet society. No British Free Churchman received a Stalin Peace Prize, as he did.[56] British Baptists, in particular, had some knowledge of the circumstances in which the substantial community of Russian Baptists found themselves. In these circumstances, whether or not the majority of Free Church people believed in a Soviet intention to over-run Western Europe, there was little opposition to the formation of NATO in 1949 and the steady consolidation of a Western defence community. The participation of the

---

54   General accounts can be found in the following: Denis Hayes, *Challenge of Conscience: The Story of the Conscientious Objectors of 1939–45* (London: Allen & Unwin, 1949), and Rachel Barker, *Conscience, Government and War: Conscientious Objection in Great Britain 1939–1945* (London: Routledge, 1982); Richard Rempel explores 'The Dilemmas of British Pacifists during World War II', in *Journal of Modern History* 19 (1978), pp. 1-9.

55   I have summarized these developments in Keith Robbins, *The World since 1945: A Concise History* (Oxford: Oxford University Press, 1998), pp. 5-60.

56   Robert Hughes, *The Red Dean: The Life and Riddle of Dr Hewlett Johnson* (Worthing: Churchman, 1987), pp. 116-71.

United States in the Second World War had strengthened Pan-Protestant English-speaking sentiment. Billy Graham, who was to crusade in Britain, was a Baptist brother. Financial factors were at work too. Leslie Weatherhead, seeking American financial help for the rebuilding of the City Temple in London, was not the only minister who visited the United States with a begging bowl.[57] Of course, there were elements of the post-war 'Americanization' of Britain which caused Free Church people much anxiety but, in the polarization of the post-war world, there was little doubt on which 'side' they stood.

The politics of the Cold War largely crushed, or at least restrained the hopes that had been placed at the end of the war in a new organization which would succeed where the League of Nations had failed: the United Nations Organization. The United Kingdom was to be a permanent member of its Security Council. Yet, in some quarters, that very word 'Security' raised again the debates which had taken place a quarter of a century earlier about the possible use of force to uphold international order in the face of aggression. Was it feasible or desirable that a new world body should seek to 'maintain peace'? It was an issue which came to the fore in Korea where, somewhat fortuitously, the 'United Nations' was in a position to intervene. Whether the United Nations, as originally conceived, would be able to operate in comparable contexts elsewhere in the world on subsequent occasions was another matter. What moral authority did it possess and how far could it in practice operate as any kind of arbiter in the Cold War world? In this increasingly ambiguous situation, while individual Free Church people associated themselves with the work of the United Nations Association, the United Nations Organization never succeeded in engendering the idealistic commitment which had once been evident in the early supporters of the League of Nations.

One factor in this situation may be what was happening to Britain itself in the post-war world. For decades, Free Church people had sought what they conceived to be an 'ethical foreign policy' in a context in which what policy Britain did follow actually mattered. The decades after 1945 witnessed a steady erosion of British power to act independently in the world. The Suez Crisis of 1956 brought that aspect home vividly. In that particular instance, many Free Church people, otherwise accustomed to voting Conservative, were deeply disturbed by British action (the more historically-minded may even have recalled that John Bright had resigned from the Liberal Government in 1882 in protest against the bombardment of Alexandria and felt a certain kinship with him). It was

---

57   See the chapter 'Rebuilding: Thanks to Rockerfeller', in John Travell, *Doctor of Souls: Leslie D. Weatherhead 1893–1976* (Cambridge: Lutterworth Press, 1999), pp. 196-208. More generally, see David Reynolds, *Rich Relations: The American Occupation of Britain 1942–1945* (London: Harper Collins, 1995).

appalling that a British government had perpetrated an act of aggression. In a sense, there was consolation to be drawn from the fact that the Suez expedition failed. Yet, taken in the context of accelerating British decolonization across the globe, it was also accompanied by some dismay at the extent to which it inevitably entailed a loss of global influence. There had always been Free Church critics of the British Empire but probably a majority of Free Church people felt that as empires go the British was one of the best. It was evident, however, that the transition to independence should not be resisted. If, in Central and Southern Africa, the claims of justice competed with the claims of enforced peace, then justice should prevail. 'Peaceful change', however, should in general be the watchword. There was optimism that the Commonwealth of Nations should emerge as an agency of inter-racial harmony. The activities of Free Church missionary societies in different parts of the empire had given Free Church people an exceptional awareness of some of the issues involved and at both local and national level enabled them to play a part in accommodating the British people to the loss of empire.

Yet, as their own memberships continued to decline in the post-war decades so there was a melancholic awareness that their capacity to influence either national or world policy in matters of peace and war had diminished and indeed, as a distinctively identifiable element, might be said to be extinct. The decline of Nonconformity and the decline of Britain as a world power might even be thought to go in tandem. The Christian democracy of post-war Western Europe, in so far as it contributed to the reconciliation of national animosities and the search for European unity did not engage the Free Churches as such.[58] The further development of an ecumenical spirit, while it might have disappointed those who believed that it had to find expression in formal unity, had nevertheless increasingly resulted, through the British Council of Churches and other bodies, in the formulation of Christian approaches to issues of war and peace which transcended any particular ecclesiastical location. Not that the reaching of a common mind on these matters proved any easier than it had ever been. This was even true of the other overshadowing issue which distinctively characterized discussion of peace in the post-war world: the possibility of nuclear war. The destruction of Hiroshima and Nagasaki was a sobering and alarming precedent. Did it mean that a turning point had been reached? Did the advent of the new weapons, and the further developments that were possible, invalidate all previous arguments about war and peace? Confronted by the possibility of nuclear annihilation was nuclear disarmament the only conceivable

---

58   It is sometimes suggested that fear of the power of the papacy present in the vestigial Nonconformity of some members of the post-war Labour government was an element in the reluctance to engage deeply in post-war 'European unity'.

option for the Nonconformist conscience? There were Free Church people prominent in the ranks of the Campaign for Nuclear Disarmament but it was the Anglican clergyman Canon L. John Collins who stood out as its leading Christian figure. There was a whiff of 'old Dissent' in the persons of the Quaker-educated historian A.J.P. Taylor or the politician and Methodist scion Michael Foot, both now men without religion, but it cannot be said that as a whole the Free Churches were solidly and unambiguously in favour of unilateral nuclear disarmament by Britain. While, for some, the question was simple and straightforward, for others it remained a matter of a choice of evils.[59] To the discussion of these issues the Methodist historian Herbert Butterfield brought an exceptional range of knowledge and capacity for reflection.[60]

For some, the failure of the Free Churches in this matter was a final indication of their ethical bankruptcy and ecclesiastical futility. For others, it was indication of their maturity in forswearing empty gestures and their recognition of the inescapable complexity of all consideration of peace and war in the contemporary world. There was a conceivable moment after 1918 when a United Free Church, if achieved, might have still maintained a politically significant stance on issues of peace and war but, if so, that moment passed. Put this way, the debates over nuclear disarmament only sharpened and exacerbated that debate which in one way or another had preoccupied Nonconformists, in all their vicissitudes (though of course not them alone), throughout the greater part of the twentieth century. What is the relation between power and the pursuit of peace and how far, if at all, can they be reasonably and religiously reconciled? In the twentieth century, individually and collectively, Nonconformists had wrestled with these dilemmas and had still given British debates on these issues a somewhat distinctive moral character, but they had not found 'solutions'. It should not come as a surprise that at the beginning of a new century these age-old problems are still with us.

---

59   These issues can be followed in more detail in Christopher Driver, *The Disarmers: A Study in Protest* (London: Hodder & Stoughton, 1964); R.K. Taylor and Colin Pritchard, *The Protest Makers: The British Nuclear Disarmament Movement of 1958–1965: Twenty Years On* (Oxford: Oxford University Press, 1985); Paul Byrne, *The Campaign for Nuclear Disarmament* (London: Croom Helm, 1988); Richard K. Taylor, *Against the Bomb: The British Peace Movement 1958–1965* (Oxford:Oxford University Press, 1988).

60   Alberto R. Coll, *The Wisdom of Statecraft: Sir Herbert Butterfield and the Philosophy of International Politics* (Durham, NC:University of North Carolina Press, 1985). For a recent critical assessment, see Ian Hall, 'History, Christianity and Diplomacy: Sir Herbert Butterfield and International Relations', *Review of International Studies* 28.4 (October, 2002), pp. 719-36.

CHAPTER 9

Protestant Nonconformist Attitudes towards the First World War

Alan Ruston

> War has had its apologians ever since history began, but if you ask me to name the best sir, head and shoulders above the rest stands the war of 14–18, stands the war of 14–18...
>
> There have been many wars in history, but none of them have made the same impression as the war of 14–18... Every war has its own attractions, but if you'll pardon my effrontery, give me the war of 14–18, give me the war of 14–18.

These words are taken from a satirical song, sung with gusto by Michael Flanders in 1967 whose theme is the dreadful nature of wars both ancient and modern.[1] This article could be said to be based around the statement that none have made the same impression as the war of 14–18 as far as its impact on Nonconformity is concerned. The Great, or First World War, saw the Nonconformist churches become more a part of the establishment than they had ever been before, particularly in attitude. They became an integral element within the political machine in almost the same terms as the established church. But flying into the sun in this way burnt their wings and like Icarus they fell to the sea. They did not drown like Icarus but the weakness engendered by the war remained with them for the rest of the century.

Entry into War

Long expected and long feared, the European War has come at last, and this country, to its great surprise and grief of most people, finds itself at war with Germany. We

---

1   'The Bestiary of Flanders and Swan', CD, track 25, 1967, reissued 1991. Words by Brassen.

have no quarrel with the German people, neither have they with us, but the action of the German Government has made war inevitable.[2]

These words from the editorial, 'The Dogs of War', in the *Christian World* of 6 August 1914 signalled the onset of the Great War that was to affect Nonconformity in England as nothing else had done, before or since. The decline in chapel attendance and much else was clear by 1914. In the previous month (July 1914) the President of the United Methodists at their conference at Redruth, had talked about the 'present decline in the habit of public worship', and the Secretary of the Wesleyan Sunday School Department at their conference at Leeds reported a decrease in the numbers attending Sunday school for the eighth successive year.[3]

This was, of course, just the precursor of what was to come, with the drop in numbers in both members and attendance for most churches accelerating as the war went on, plus the dreadful loss of life amongst the brightest and best of the young men of Nonconformity. The War knocked the stuffing out of them, and none were ever able to regain the social, economic or political position they held before 1914. Many of the liberal Christian suppositions, so clear in Edwardian times, virtually disappeared in the trenches of the Great War. For example, the aphorism 'mankind onward and upward for ever' was rarely heard after the early days of the war.

In this paper I argue that this 'War to end all Wars' was the cathartic event of the twentieth century for Nonconformity, and its impact is still being worked through at the beginning of the twenty-first century. The Second World War had nowhere near the same impact. The cherished and long established positions which Nonconformity held in the early years of the century, like voluntarism, were swept away by the actions of the government, and the churches had no option but to follow with their support. The conclusion of the Executive Committee of the British and Foreign Unitarian Association in October 1916 applied to all the churches: 'The War overshadows everyone and everything; and churches and religious societies find themselves faced by problems of life and death for which there is no ready made solution.'[4]

Plotting the Changes

One of the best sources to chart the changes in viewpoints, attitudes and affirmations over the period 1914–18 and the defeat of much that was

---

2   *Christian World* (*CW*), 6 August 1914, p. 8.
3   *CW*, 16 July 1914, p. 5; 23 July 1914, p. 4.
4   *Minute Book*, Executive Committee, British & Foreign Unitarian Association, 25 October 1916 (Dr Williams's Library).

previously held sacred amongst Nonconformists, is the denominational press. Researchers in the field include include Keith Clements who used the *Baptist Times* to assess the changes in Baptist attitudes at the outbreak of the war in an important article in the *Baptist Quarterly*, and I took the columns of the *Inquirer* to chart the evolution of Unitarian attitudes in the same period in articles in the *Transactions of the Unitarian Historical Society*.[5] It is possible to repeat this process across the denominations. Perhaps the best source across the denominations can be found in the columns of the *Christian World*, though others have found the *British Weekly* equally valuable. The *Christian World* was a remarkable production that each week gathered the most detailed news from any source which could be described as Nonconformist. It appeared between 1857 and 1961, and many of my illustrations and examples expressing Free Church views on the war come from this source.

The Position at the Start

The *Christian World* in the hot summer of 1914 reflected the calm of the churches. The Wesleyan Conference at Leeds was exercised that the government had done little about stopping rifle practice by the territorial forces on the Lord's Day, and was to send a deputation to the Secretary of State for War.[6] The *Christian World* was notable in that it had a regular column on German issues, contributed by its Berlin correspondent. In June 1914 it was asking questions like 'Is Germany Isolated? What England should do', and evaluating the prospects for war: 'There is probably no immediate danger, for the nation as a whole loves peace, and its destinies are guided by a man who during the 25 years of his reign has given ample proof that he is always to be found on the side of justice and righteousness; but we are clearly witnesses of the excitability of public opinion, and the placid stream of today may be the raging stream of tomorrow.'[7]

---

5   K.W. Clements, 'Baptists and the Outbreak of the First World War', *Baptist Quarterly* 26.2 (April, 1975), pp. 74-91: A. Ruston, 'Killed Fighting for their Country—Two Unitarian Ministers', *Transactions of the Unitarian Historical Society* (*TUHS*) 20.3 (April, 1993), pp. 51-160, and 'Unitarian Attitudes towards World War 1', *TUHS* 21.4 (April, 1998), pp. 269-84. S. Koss used the *British Weekly* and *CW* for chapter 6 of his *Nonconformity in Modern British Politics* (London: B.T. Batsford, 1975), and P. Ackers the *Bible Advocate* for the attitude of the Churches of Christ to conscientious objection in, 'Who Speaks for Christians?', *Journal of the United Reformed Church History Society* 5.3 (October, 1993), pp. 153-67.

6   *CW*, 23 July 1914, p. 4.

7   *CW*, 18 June 1914, p. 11.

There were the international peace councils to reflect opinion, and J. Allen Baker, Member of Parliament for East Finsbury, later known as 'the fighting Quaker', stated that he knew from conversations with both King George and the German Emperor, how warmly they both sympathized with the work of the councils.[8] David Bebbington has pointed out that the Free Churches became more devoted to peace in the few months before the war than they had been for twenty years. The Free Church Council organizing committee urged the government to reduce its armaments and the *British Weekly* ran a series of articles on 'War and Christianity' in which several writers called on Christians to be pacifists.[9] The admiration for German biblical scholarship was of long standing. Adolf Harnack's book, *The Origins of the New Testament* (1914), had recently been published in English, and the *Christian World* concluded that it was a 'notable addition to the...wonderful collection of writings on the history and literature of the Bible etc. which Dr. Harnack has created in the course of 25 years'.[10]

All seemed set fair and Dr John Clifford led the British delegation to Constance to set up the World Alliance for Promoting International Friendship through the Churches due to meet on 1 August. The conference broke up without a conclusion and the journey back to England was far from easy because war was declared a few days later.

These were among the factors which made church leaders and the denominational press hesitate to fix their attitude towards the war during the first few days of August. However, the German invasion of Belgium was universally presented as a moral issue to which Nonconformity reacted positively and quickly. Within a few weeks the attitude of the *Christian World* changed entirely: 'We are sure that the British people will cherish no bitterness against the German people, who will have the most cause to rue this last result of War Lordism, but the nations opposed to Prussian War Lordism, must in the interest of the World, and for the safeguarding of the future, end War Lordism, and what War Lordism stands for, for ever.'[11]

A month later the German state was labelled as the enemy, and the phrase the 'Anti-Christ' was applied to it in the *Christian World*: 'In the present conflict it is clear that we are not fighting against the scientific acumen, the philosophical or theological learning of Germany, nor, indeed, against the German people as such, but against the manifestation

---

8   *CW*, 14 May 1914, p. 5; Koss, *Nonconformity in Modern British Politics*, pp. 63, 104.

9   D.W. Bebbington, *The Nonconformist Conscience: Chapel and Politics 1870–1914* (London: George Allen & Unwin, 1982), p. 125. Bebbington also used the *CW* extensively in his researches for this book.

10   *CW*, 30 July 1914, p. 6.

11   *CW*, 13 August 1914, p. 8.

of the Anti-Christ which expresses itself in the masterful, the imperious, and the power-loving Zeitgeist.'[12]

The irony here is obvious, denigrating the German state and using a German word to do it. J.H. Rushbrooke, the Baptist leader, was in the British delegation and travelled back through Germany to meet his family. He was put under arrest and only got out in October. The content of his letter sent from Germany, via America, to his congregation at the Hampstead Garden Suburb Free Church showed the shock suffered by a devoted internationalist and no doubt inflamed feeling at home. 'Perhaps the shock of this war has fallen on few as heavily as upon me... My personal faith has almost reeled in the presence of the awful fact.'[13]

Adolf Harnack and his fellow scholar Professor Rudolf Eucken had expressed support for Germany in its war effort, and almost overnight they became the personification of the enemy. A letter to Harnack in protest at his strictures on the actions of Britain was sent by a group of theologians of all hues.[14] Professor Eucken at Jena, the proponent of a spiritual philosophy of life, was seen as even worse. The *Christian World* reported a letter sent by Professor Eucken to Dr Wendte, a Unitarian minister in America: 'His ignorance of the actual facts and the English point of view seems appalling. He speaks of extreme bitterness of England as "hereafter always" to be reckoned Germany's worst enemy, and regards any type of intellectual co-operation as ended "for an incalculable time."'[15]

There were protests at the stridency of these views. Both the *Christian World* and the *Inquirer* reported that Dr Tudor Jones, the Unitarian minister in Islington and a leading member of the peace councils, had recently returned from Germany from seeing Dr Eucken and deplored the fact that war could be possible between Christians. Dr Stanley Mellor, minister of Hope Street Unitarian Chapel, Liverpool protested: 'It is not possible to charge the whole German nation and its literature as without redemption. I will not participate in your boasted intolerance, I will not forget the debt I owe to German thought, the joy I have received from German learning and culture.'[16]

This protest came as a result of anti-German feelings expressed by the editor of the *Inquirer*, W.H. Drummond, who became more bellicose as the war progressed. The *Christian World* presented no alternative to the strictures against the German theologians. Not only were Harnack and Eucken being personally rejected but also it seems the worth and validity

---

12   *CW*, 10 September 1914, 'Second Editorial', p. 8.
13   *CW*, 10 September 1914, p. 12; Koss, *Nonconformity in Modern British Politics*, p. 126.
14   *CW*, 3 September 1914, p. 4.
15   *CW*, 8 October 1914, p. 1.
16   *Inquirer*, 12 September 1914, p. 568.

of their thought as well, so strong was the depth of feeling that the onset of war created.

The switch from admiration of Germany and things German to demonic status came in just a few months, perhaps the most extreme change ever to spread through the Free Churches. The editorial 'Outlaws of the Modern World' in the *Christian World*, expressed the majority view across Nonconformity stirred up no doubt by the popular press, and in particular the *Daily Mail*. The message was now not just against the Kaiser but Germany as a whole: 'Germany wages war in a manner that would have disgraced the barbarians who over-ran the Roman Empire... Germany is a criminal among the nations, a criminal first in the breaking of the peace, a criminal in her method of waging war.'[17]

The Moral Position

The war dragged on and the problems which it posed for Nonconformity seemed to increase in number and their impact was more and more severe. There was always a small minority in the churches, much reviled, who opposed the war, but the majority more than sanctioned it and were dragged along unforeseen paths. Dr John Clifford, 'our Grand Old Man', who strongly opposed the Boer War, 'appeared (at a big Nonconformist meeting in November 1914) as a Cromwellian Ironside, taunting the shirkers and urging that the War should be pursued with our whole force and brought to an end as soon as possible.'[18]

However, the responses were often contradictory especially when it came to the question of conscription. The war must be won at almost any cost but not by conscription which had long been totally rejected by the churches as adopting the methods of the enemy and a complete denial of the voluntary principle. As early as 12 November 1914 the *Christian World* stated: 'In the end, conscription means a military dictatorship. There can be no real democracy where conscription reigns, and if, as a result of the war, conscription were forced upon this country, we should have imposed on ourselves the very thing against which we are fighting.'[19]

In order to avoid conscription Nonconformist ministers urged the members of their congregations and Sunday schools to enlist in the forces. Denominational newspapers included accounts of whole families of sons who had volunteered for war service, but rarely reported the pain and bitterness when they were killed. Many ministers often led the way

17   *CW*, 15 October 1914, p. 10.
18   W.R. Nicholl to J. Strachey, 11 November 1914, Strachey Papers, quoted in Koss, *Nonconformity in Modern British Politics*, pp. 131 and 255.
19   *CW*, 12 November 1914, p. 10.

by encouraging their own sons to go, and in consequence needed to justify this great sacrifice morally to themselves at least.

J.H. Shakespeare, the Baptist leader, was a loud and vociferous supporter of the war effort, as was W. Robertson Nicoll who wrote regularly in the *British Weekly*. As early as September 1914 he concluded in its columns that the Prussian military system was the most flagrant iniquity on earth. Another enthusiast was L.P. Jacks, editor of the *Hibbert Journal* since its inception, and from 1915 Principal of Manchester College, Oxford. Like Principal Garvie at New College, London, he soon emptied his college of ministerial students, believing that their place was at the front as soldiers. Jacks came from the Unitarian tradition but in his journey to becoming a well known and popular writer and lecturer in the inter-war period he found he did not sit easily in any denomination. His intelligent and perceptive justification of the war both led and reflected Nonconformist thinking and gave him a wider audience than the readership of the oft-quoted but highly intellectual *Hibbert Journal* could ever do. Jacks was amongst those Nonconformists who saw the war as both a challenge and an opportunity. His three sons went into the forces, and while two were badly injured, they all returned.

The Vision of L.P. Jacks

Lawrence Pearsall Jacks (1860–1955) nailed his colours to the mast in the early days of the war. His article in the *Inquirer* 15 August, was headed 'Our Duty to the State' in which he threw voluntaryism, and seemingly most other principles long cherished by Nonconformity, out of the window in a couple of paragraphs:

> From one point of view this is the wickedest war in the history of the human race. From another point of view it is the most righteous. It is the wickedest on the side of those who have forced it on the world. It is the most righteous on the side of those upon whom it has been forced. So far as England is concerned it is a war against war... Under the circumstances one thought alone should dominate us—the thought of our Duty to the State. All other duties, to God, to humanity, and to ourselves are summed up in that.

> Let us concentrate our minds upon it and let no nightmare horrors weaken our service...now that (war) has come, let us economise our emotion and indulge neither in speech nor in feeling, save so far as it strengthens us for suffering and action. All our moral forces are needed for our duty. Let our hatred of war be a strength and not a weakness—as it was with Cromwell... Would that Reason had prevailed! But the Powers which have engineered this thing have shown themselves deaf to Reason—to Humanity, to Religion. All peaceable proposals have only rendered them the more obdurate, the more contemptuous of Right. They have

forced upon the world the task of chastising the wicked with their own weapons. It is hideous necessity, but shrinking from it will only increase its hideousness.[20]

The words are stark and were subsequently quoted by Nonconformists who took a very different attitude towards the war.[21] The lauding of the duty to the state was a startling development and few went as far as Jacks in this direction. However, the invocation of Cromwell in support of the war effort became a common occurrence among leading Nonconformists, which was a new slant as hitherto he had hardly been seen as a supporter of the voluntary principle.

It is difficult to determine exactly which of Cromwell's attributes and activities were considered as role models by those who cited him in time of war. Was it Cromwell's militaristic defence of liberty, or his expansion of the role of the state? I argue that Cromwell and the government of 1914-1918 in following similar courses should be seen in the same light. Under both, militariarism grew within the country, claimed as being in defence of a wider liberty. Both brought the dissenting denominations within the national picture in a new way, but the longer term results in the seventeenth and twentieth centuries led to persecution in the first instance and decline in the other.

A few weeks later Jacks was arguing against the contemplative spirit and for the God of war:

> You do not propose that the Liberal Churches should raise a regiment and send it to the front... Since the thing is impossible it is futile to enlarge upon the matter; but I cannot refrain from expressing my feeling that it would do us more good than a century of organisation and propaganda... One of those rare moments in the history of nations has arrived, which reveal the truth hidden in the old saying, 'The Lord is a man of war'... The merely contemplative spirit will either break down in despair or end in affectation unless it is reinforced by the resolution to resist unto death. There is no other way of dealing with a moral ultimatum...it is the appeal for a complete self-surrender to the good cause.[22]

It was, however, in the *Hibbert Journal*, which was amongst the most influential religious journals of its time, that Jacks made his most impassioned plea. He had been its founding editor in 1902 and his name was thereafter closely associated with it. In 1916 his leading article was entitled 'An Interim Religion'.[23] It is vividly and simply written, qualities

---

20   *Inquirer* 15 August 1914, p. 519.

21   Quoted in Basil Martin, *An Impossible Parson* (London: George Allen and Unwin, 1935), pp. 142-43.

22   *Inquirer*, 12 September 1914, pp. 566-67. The possibility of a Nonconformist regiment was raised from time to time.

23   L.P. Jacks, 'An Interim Religion', *Hibbert Journal* 14.3 (1916), pp. 465-79.

always associated with Jacks' writing, but his tone is strong and unyielding.

Jacks argues that to see religion as solely concerned with the possession and enjoyment of peace is wrong as it does not reflect the facts of the world nor the nature of the soul. Just as bad is the view that the Lord is a war lord. Both are one-sided and corrupting. The fruit of the first was Britain as she was before the war, full of idle dreams and discontent, while the fruit of the second is Germany as she was then and is now.

Religion, according to Jacks, alternates between the preaching of peace and the preaching of war, which is expressed in the Bible. 'A pacifist Psalter would do no less violence to the spirit of Hebrew religion than would an anthology of the fighting Psalms so dear to the Ironsides... In the New Testament, also, peace and war are interdependent. The "non-resistance" sayings of Christ, torn out of the context of a life which reviled evil to the uttermost, would be meaningless... The movement between peace and war is the "diastole and systole" of the religious heart.'[24]

Jacks concluded that the religion of peace had to transform itself into the religion of strife. The action of Britain's opponents had raised the conflict to the highest level as they had 'identified their cause with naked evil, thereby giving the war such a character that all who oppose them become defenders of the Right'. Through the action of the enemy Britain had become the champion of the Good. 'Once that be fully realised our strength will be doubled; our power to endure until the end will become a certainty. For the prosecution of the war will be thenceforward a religious act.'[25]

The British had acquired sufficient decency to render themselves unprepared for the wickedness that Germany was carrying out. 'We ought to have known that the final objective of their ambitions was to overthrow the Empire and to seize the spoils...behind the attack on the British Empire lay a deeper design, which was nothing less than the overthrow of the moral foundation on which Western civilisation has been built up...for this nobody was prepared.'[26]

Jacks believed that in Belgium there was 'an orgy of treachery, cruelty, and bestiality such as the modern world has ever seen'.[27] The sinking of the Lusitania and the killing of Nurse Cavell proved the key to Germany's policy of crushing the weak. 'This put the final seal to our conviction that the work we have to resist, and overthrow is, from first to last, the devil's... If there is a being who, on receiving the challenge of evil, refuses to fight, that being has forgotten his nature... By the

---

24   Jacks, 'An Interim Religion', pp. 466-67.
25   Jacks, 'An Interim Religion', p. 468.
26   Jacks, 'An Interim Religion', pp. 469-70.
27   Jacks, 'An Interim Religion', p. 472.

innermost definition of his nature he is a fighter against evil. I say a fighter, and mean it literally. With naked evil there is no other way.'[28]

Jacks saw virtually all Germany performing evil, a word he constantly uses as well as 'orgy' and 'treachery'. Like a good Nonconformist Jacks cities Bunyan, and the encounter that the Pilgrim has with Apollyon in the Vale of Humiliation. If Christian had mused on the point, 'Apollyon would have hewn him to pieces. And he would have deserved his fate.'[29] Nothing now matters but to finish the war. No sacrifice can be too great: 'Our response to this commanding duty is the resurrection of the national soul—long asleep. I write with deliberation when I say that we are fighting hell.'[30]

The religion of a calmer time, the religion of love and peace, is not endangered and will return again when evil has been put down. 'The only people who will have a right in the coming years to preach the gospel of love and peace will be those who can give a good answer when the question is asked: "What were you doing in the Great Day?"'[31]

Before the war, Britain was 'growing unworthy of our mighty Empire, whose profound significance we had so long ignored.'[32] He ended his article with the clarion call:

> Welcome the hour which tests the manhood of this nation to the uttermost! Welcome the call to show ourselves worthy of the great inheritance our fathers have bequeathed to us! Welcome the opportunity of proving the words we have so often uttered, that there are things dearer than life! Welcome the summons which brings us face to face with the business for which men were created![33]

The article is amongst the most remarkable statements to appear in a leading British religious journal. Its extremes match the outpourings of the most rabid of Anglican bishops, but parts echoed other Nonconformist leaders particularly on the Empire. Jacks' views had support amongst Nonconformists in many denominations, but he expressed what others did not dare utter. His views were strongly opposed by many Unitarians, but not by W.H. Drummond who was the editor for much of the war of the *Inquirer* and who sometimes went to similar extremes.

Jacks' falling out with the Unitarian movement can be seen as dating from his forthright and extreme statements on the moral and religious implications of the war. Some never forgave him, and he like others went

---

28   Jacks, 'An Interim Religion', pp. 472-73.
29   Jacks, 'An Interim Religion', p. 476.
30   Jacks, 'An Interim Religion', pp. 476-77.
31   Jacks, 'An Interim Religion', pp. 477-78.
32   Jacks, 'An Interim Religion', p. 478.
33   Jacks, 'An Interim Religion', p. 478.

silent after 1917 no doubt affected by war weariness. Reports of his sermons and talks of this time show a more temperate approach. Jacks lived to a great age and wrote two autobiographies, and in neither does he refer to the First World War. He was not the type of man to admit that he had gone too far.

Many years later others put it in different terms. E.G. Lee had served in the trenches, was Jacks' student in the 1920s, and later a well read author on both popular and religious topics as well as editor of the *Inquirer*. In his autobiography, *The Minute Particular*, Lee tells of Charles Hargrove, a Roman Catholic priest turned Unitarian minister, and Jacks' attitude to the Great War:

> These two men were devoted to the ministry, and to religious and philosophical speculation. They were tender and sensitive in their personal relationships. They were able to judge passing historical events in terms of realism as most other men, yet they shared in a most passionate manner the conventional ideas of the 1914 War. Here is what Dr Jacks says about his friend, as the friend approached his end:

> 'Alas! he was not to live to see the end of the Great War, which he regarded as holy on our side, ever maintaining with perfervid conviction that we must fight on until the evil thing had been utterly and finally overthrown.'

> That is how the First World War appeared to a couple of the best of Englishmen. That is not as it appears fifty years later. They were, with all their wisdom and moral sensitivities, living in an historic illusion as seen from the present... When two deeply religious men, in the best possible sense, describe the First World War as holy, something has gone wrong—and some of the noblest men of the period thought of it in that sense, and a heart-breaking generation of youth and courage gave their lives because they believed it.[34]

Support for the War Effort

Nonconformists in general quickly became avid supporters of the war effort and the few voices raised in opposition were brushed aside. Stephen Koss sees Nonconformity at this time as being split between 'hard' and 'soft' components, between the majority who sanctioned the war and a small minority who utterly opposed the war effort.[35]

There was a unity of feeling, hitherto unknown within Nonconformity, described by Stanley Mews as falling into well defined stages. 'At first

---

34   E.G. Lee, *The Minute Particular* (London: SCM Press, 1966), pp. 130-31. The quote from L.P. Jacks is from his book *From Authority to Freedom: The Spiritual Pilgrimage of Charles Hargrove* (London: Williams and Norgate, 1920), p. 359.

35   Koss, *Nonconformity in Modern British Politics*, p. 129.

there was a period of high morale, of flag waving, patriotic songs and high emotion. There was a tendency for clergymen to identify the Christian community with the nation in arms... The gap between church and state which had been widening throughout the nineteenth century was easily overcome, and the Christian community was extended to cover the whole nation. The barriers went down. The whole nation was shrouded in a thin veil of Christian sentiment.'[36]

This thin veil persisted though there were developments which disturbed but did not destroy the strong Nonconformist support for the war. The biggest issue was conscription which came early in 1916. The churches opposed its introduction at every stage, but by 1918 even they were meekly accepting its extension to yet other categories. In 1915 conscription was on the horizon. The *Christian World* remained clear on the issue: 'In England we understand the volunteer, we do not understand the conscript, and we must get through the war without that compulsion which is so hateful to the British mind and genius.'[37]

In January 1916 when the Military Service Bill was before the House of Commons, the *Christian World* went near to opposing the government on a key issue: 'The passing of a Compulsion Bill in this country will be a victory for Germany in one of the things for which Germany went to war... We are not in the least weakening in our support of the causes for which we are at war, but we do think it is time for us to ask what is our part in the war? The Government has one and a half million men, and yet they are asking for compulsion in order to get more.'[38]

The Conscription Bill went through Parliament early in 1916 becoming the Military Service Act. Its scope was limited and its coverage was later expanded. Conscription, once at the forefront of Nonconformist attention, became an accepted fact. 'What was unthinkable in 1913 was not even thought about in 1939 with the arrival of the Second World War.'[39] Voluntaryism as a guiding principle was dead.

Another issue which strained the support of Nonconformists was the pressure, moral and otherwise, to get younger ministers to enlist and leave their congregations. This seemed to many like an attack on the maintenance of the faith, and was strongly felt in 1915. The ministerial training colleges 'did their bit' in virtually suspending their work and sending ministerial students to the front, but the moral imperative on younger ministers to enlist became strong. How could they stay at home when men in the congregations were being exhorted by them to enlist?

---

36   S. Mews, 'Spiritual Mobilization in the First World War', *Theology* 74 (June, 1971), pp. 259-60.

37   *CW*, 3 June 1915, p. 8.

38   *CW*, 6 January 1916, p. 10.

39   C. Binfield, *So Down to Prayers: Studies in English Noncoformity 1780–1920* (London: J.M. Dent, 1977), p. 247.

As recognized ministers they were exempted from conscription but were encouraged to enlist by the government. Many took a halfway house position and served as welfare and spiritual guides at the YMCA huts in France but some did enlist as combatants and a few were killed.[40]

The pressure struck a discordant chord in Nonconformity. The editorial in the *Christian World* in November 1915 voiced the exasperation: 'The Church is not a religious club which for national purposes could be suppressed like a newspaper, and its servants commandeered...from a utilitarian point of view, the ministry is not one of the industries society can most readily dispense with, nor can its apprenticeship safely cease.'[41]

Most denominations sat on the fence. For example, the Council of the Baptist Union in November 1915, while it rejoiced in the patriotism displayed by so many of its members in joining the forces, could not 'accept responsibility for giving directions as to what younger ministers and students should do'.[42] The Unitarians took a similar stand.[43] Dr Campbell Morgan of Westminster Chapel summed up the Nonconformist position when he pointed out that the attempt on the part of the government to invade the sphere of human conscience was a direct challenge to every religious teacher and preacher.[44]

The churches played a role in obtaining the right of conscientious objection to military service by individuals, but the pressure denominations exerted on the government to ensure that it was fairly enforced was patchy. There were protests in church assemblies but these were muted and carefully worded not to upset government ministers. A group of leading Manchester churchmen sent a memorandum to the Prime Minister in May 1916 stating that 300 Englishmen were in prison for conscience sake. 'No community can trample with impunity upon its most precious spiritual possession.'[45] The veteran Dr John Clifford pointed out in August 1916, about passive resistors, that if they are subject to any authority outside themselves, 'you make an end of the resistor as such, and you will go far towards making an end to the State as

---

40   *Congregational Year Book (CYB)* (1917–1919) shows nine Congregational ministers as being killed or having died in the war, either as combatants or chaplains. The obituaries in the *Baptist Handbook* are more difficult to interpret: five chaplains are shown as having died during 1918 in the 1919 edition. Two Unitarian ministers were killed as combatants, see Ruston, 'Killed Fighting for their Country', pp. 151-60.
41   *CW*, 18 November 1915, p. 5.
42   *CW*, 18 November 1915, p. 18.
43   *Inquirer*, 10 July 1915, p. 343; 18 December 1915, p. 633.
44   *CW*, 13 January 1916, p. 6.
45   *CW*, 25 May 1916, p. 10.

well. For you destroy that fidelity to conviction, which is the nerve of human progress and the source of the well-being of nations.'[46]

Protests about the treatment of conscientious objectors were rarely made by the churches themselves. It was left to individuals to express their strong convictions, often led by statements made by radical MPs in the House of Commons. For example, H.G. Chancellor (1863–1945), Member of Parliament for Haggerston, a lifelong and active Unitarian, maintained a strong witness for civil and religious liberty. He refused to be silenced, despite protests from his fellow religionists and the national newspapers. His exchange with the Home Secretary reveals much about the attitude of all involved:

> On 31 July 1917 H.G. Chancellor asked the Home Secretary in the House of Commons whether any complaints had been received about the conduct of the Chaplain at Winchester Prison; whether he was aware that he sneers at the beliefs of conscientious objectors (COs) and of Nonconformists in particular; whether he is aware that he told a CO that Christ would spit at him, and that he refers to COs as vermin and lice, and if he would make enquiries as to this person's conduct from COs to whose spiritual needs he has ministered?
>
> Sir G. Cave: I have received no complaints against the Chaplain at Winchester, and I am satisfied that the allegations made in the question grossly misrepresent the language used by the reverend gentleman.
>
> Mr Chancellor: Has the Rt. Hon gentleman enquired of any of the prisoners to whom this Christian gentleman addressed himself, or of the Nonconformist Chaplain?
>
> Sir G. Cave: I have made no enquiries.
>
> Mr Chancellor: Made no enquiries, and yet you deny the statements![47]

Protests like this aside, and the *Christian World* made few references to the treatment of COs, Nonconformity accepted conscription without disturbing the *modus vivendi* with the government, but at a cost. David M. Thompson sees the fact of conscription as dramatic proof of the inadequacy of the old style voluntaryist assumptions about church, state and society.[48]

---

46   *CW*, 24 August 1916, p. 4.

47   J.W. Graham, *Conscription and Conscience, A History 1916–1919* (London: George Allen and Unwin, 1922), p. 14, quoting Hansard.

48   D.M. Thompson, 'Book Review: C. Binfield, *So Down to Prayers*', *Social History* 5.3 (1980), p. 470.

The Moral Dimension

Historians have long disputed whether the 'Nonconformist Conscience' ever existed as an identifiable political force; what is clear is that, if it ever did, any vestige of its influence on government had gone by 1918. Not that questions of conscience were muted by the war, as moral issues remained key concerns for Nonconformists. Moral dilemmas came thick and fast, and more often than not they proved uncomfortable to deal with.

Not unexpectedly, the attitude of Nonconformists was the most consistent on the consumption of alcohol issue, one of the deepest concerns of all the churches in 1914. During the war they got near to supporting the total prohibition movement in order, at least in part, to help the war effort. The drink question, as it was known, was regularly debated at the annual meetings of the denominations throughout the war. Lloyd George was respected all the more when he said to a representative Nonconformist gathering in 1915, 'We are fighting Germany, Austria and Drink, and the greatest of these deadly foes is Drink', the *Christian World* adding that 'the lure of the drink is even imperilling our success in the war'.[49] The churches' position changed little during the four years, the issue remaining at the top of their agendas.

The need for redemption is always high on the list of Nonconformist concerns, and the war gave them considerable opportunity to apply the need for it to themselves. In the main they saw themselves, both on an individual and corporate level, as being 'soft' in 1914, and as Jacks had pointed out, change was essential. Many appeared to wallow in their moral turpitude, not only of themselves but of society in general. R.J. Campbell, prior to his departure to the Church of England, touched a raw nerve when he considered the condition of England of only a year before at the spring assembly of the Congregational Union in May 1915: 'Drunkenness, gambling, debauchery, greed, a general materialistic outlook on life, a decline of idealism and of the religious sense was widely observable... They were being purged of much of this in the fiery trial through which they were passing, but not for a moment did this justify war...be thankful for the outpouring of self-sacrificial service that the war has called forth.'[50]

In May 1917, B.J. Snell, as Chairman of the Congregational Union, put the position of past and present in vivid terms, an amazing statement coming from a church leader.

---

49   *CW*, 1 April 1915, p. 8.
50   *CW*, 13 May 1915, p. 22.

The churches are still the abode of intolerance and contempt. The Churches of Christ as at present constituted in this realm are an apparatus for keeping the people of England apart... One would have thought that in the greatest war of all time ecclesiastical differences would have been buried out of sight for shame's sake... We are standing at the watershed of history, we are standing at the crisis of the fate of all things human, and—let our successors marvel at it—while this stable earth rocks, the religious papers report discussions on liturgies, apostolic succession etc.[51]

The President of the Baptist Union, J.E. Roberts at the spring assembly in April 1918, was equally forthright in pointing out that the churches had attempted to rebuild civilization on a pagan basis, a civilization in which the pursuit of riches had been far more eager than the pursuit of righteousness. He saw any definition of religion as inadequate and misleading which claimed people as religious because they went to church.[52]

Another shift in Nonconformist attitudes was towards the Empire which was increasingly seen as a moral force. The preservation of the ideals that were claimed to lie behind the Empire was presented as being amongst the chief moral justifications for the war. This area of national life was generally ignored by Nonconformists before 1914, but in wartime it was different. Suddenly everyone was affirming the worth of Empire and the main concern was to prevent Germany taking possession of it from Britain.

The Chairman of the Congregational Union in October 1915 claimed that perhaps the most impressive example of freedom that has ever been witnessed was the case of the British Empire. 'Freedom and self government have made the Empire.'[53] Dr A. Alexander, Moderator of the Presbyterian Church of England, stated in May 1917 that the British race and Empire occupies the place of ethical leadership in the world, to whom support is being given by men of goodwill as well as the nations that dare to possess a soul.[54]

Leading out of the concern that Nonconformity had hitherto got it all wrong came in 1917, when increased attention and support was given to the Brotherhood movement. It was argued that as the churches had created and fostered division, they now had the chance to make amends and build for the future. The war had given this opportunity and the men in the trenches had created a new brotherhood which would sweep so

---

51 *CYB* (1918), p. 23. Chairman of the Congregational Union, B.J. Snell, 'Address', 7 May 1917.

52 *CW*, 25 April 1918, p. 3.

53 *CYB* (1916), p. 63. Chairman of the Congregational Union, Sir A. Haworth, 'Address', 4 October 1915.

54 *CW*, 10 May 1917, p. 5.

much away and create a brave new world when the war was over. Dr Monro Gordon, President of the Presbyterian Church of England, at the Synod of May 1916 envisaged that the comradeship of the trenches, carried into the fields of capital and labour, could promise a golden age.[55]

Indeed the Brotherhood movement was enthusiastically taken up by many individual churches. For example, at Doddridge Congregational Church, Northampton, at a special service in February 1915, were 300 members from the Brotherhood movement in khaki present out of 1,000, and the singing was led by a band from the Worcestershire Regiment.[56] The President of the Wesleyan Conference in July 1916 asked the question: 'might it not be that if Christianity had been more social, Socialism might have been more Christian'.[57] The war had created a new social vision which did not last into the peace.

Can the moral agenda of Nonconformity in war time be summarized? The National Free Church Council effectively did this early in 1915. In setting the programme for its meetings at Manchester in March, and arranging speakers to cover each aspect, the council listed the moral agenda for Nonconformity under the title, 'The Problem of the War from a Christian Standpoint'. These were:

To render such service to the nation as the war demands
To maintain the Christian attitude in the national life
To combat the tendency to militarism
    — the basis for a lasting peace
    — the new opportunity offered by the war for Christian work in our own country
    — the elevation of national ideals
The effect of the war on
    — the rest day
    — Temperance
    — Women's work
The call to the Christian Church created by the rally of the Empire (the joining of Christian forces for common work)
    — To the Colonies
    — Continent of Europe
    — To the World (Is the comity of Christian missions possible?)
The essential unity of the Church of God.[58]

---

55   *CW*, 4 May 1916, p. 6.
56   *CW*, 18 Feb. 1915, p. 4.
57   *CW*, 27 July 1916, p. 4.
58   *CW*, 28 January 1915, p. 5.

The list appears in this order in the *Christian World*, but it is not clear if the elements were set out in order of importance. The first was undoubtedly seen as being the primary requirement, and it was the most novel—in essence giving to the state what it wants. On this aspect alone the war had created within Nonconformity an overarching new moral and religious imperative in just a few months, which appeared to take precedence even above its religious affirmations. A new and strange Nonconformist morality indeed.

The Ability to Choose

Revd Dr Nigel Collinson, Secretary of the Methodist Conference, speaking at the Unitarian General Assembly meetings in London on 14 April 2000 stated that the most profound change that has happened to the churches in the twentieth century was the availability of choice. For the first time people could choose to ignore the church in all its forms and go their own way. The poorest sections of community had always done so, but this was an entirely new departure for the more affluent. Other forms of entertainment now hold sway.

Most would see the creation of the entertainment society commencing somewhere between the 1930s and the 1950s. However, I argue that it was created out of the First World War as far as the churches are concerned. The church was ignored after 1918 and was no longer a focus for social living and entertainment in the way it had been prior to 1914. Although not necessarily in terms of membership (some denominations showed an increase in the 1920s[59]), after 1918 it was downhill all the way as far as political and social influence was concerned. Churches and ministers were knocked off their pedestals by the war and one of the reasons for this was their almost abject support for the state.

The subject of this chapter may appear narrow in comparison with others in this volume which cover broad issues of theology and social practice over a century. However, the Great War (can we call it anything else?) was the key event of the century for Nonconformity whose effects still linger. It drained the confidence of most Nonconformist churches and this affected the outlook in the pew. The removal of the cream of a whole male generation meant that their leadership was substantially weakened in the 1930s.

---

59   James Munson, *The Nonconformists: In Search of a Lost Culture* (London: SPCK, 1991), p. 294: 'between 1901 there was an increase in the membership of all four major denominations, in some cases by over seven per cent despite war losses'. See also p. 348 n. 7. The *Baptist Handbook* (1916), p. 196, shows membership as 411,949 and the *Baptist Handbook* (1927), p. 174, as 416,665.

Aspects of Nonconformist thinking had been dented almost beyond repair. Clyde Binfield puts it crisply: 'Within five years the inadequacies of their theologies and the naivities of their social responses were cruelly revealed.'[60] For example, the Liberal Christians had their confidence in a liberal theology of Jesus, the nature of humanity and of perfectibility of society severely shaken, which led the way to a different trend in theology in the 1920s and 1930s—a direct reflection of the experience of the first of the modern total wars.

Part of the State Machine

While the war lasted, Nonconformity took a greater part in government than it had ever aspired to before, becoming effectively part of the establishment. This gave comfort and indirect power to its leaders. They were very pleased when one of their own, David Lloyd George, became Prime Minister in 1916. Koss puts it very bluntly: 'As if to atone for their earlier pacifism and to compensate for centuries of outsidedness, leading Free Churchmen made a comparable *volte-face*. Apostles of peace, they were transformed into holy warriors, who often asserted their patriotism with calculated truculence.'[61]

This identification with the establishment had its dangers. With the ending of hostilities the Nonconformist churches lost their distinct role as supporters of the war effort. Even Lloyd George did not see the need to listen to Nonconformist leaders more than was strictly necessary after 1920 and the easy access they had enjoyed to many leading statesmen had gone. As G.I.T. Machin has pointed out, the bitter Liberal divisions deprived Nonconformists of their traditional strong party means of expression.[62]

Perhaps the high spot in the Nonconformist connection with power and social influence came on 21 November 1918 with the Free Church Thanksgiving Service held in the Albert Hall in the presence of the King and Queen. Nonconformists could be excused for believing that they had arrived, and possibly gain a status similar to that held by the Church of England. J.H. Jowett in his address gave them every hope of the good times to come: 'We would hallow a larger, richer, nobler patriotism. We would consecrate our national unity in the presence of our beloved King and Queen; and in the name of God who has given us this victory...we

---

60   Binfield, *So Down to Prayers*, p. 234: M. Watts, 'Why did the English Stop Going to Church?', Dr Williams's Library Lecture (London, 1995), p. 11.

61   Koss, *Nonconformity in Modern British Politics*, p. 127.

62   G.I.T. Machin, *Politics and the Churches in Great Britain 1869–1921* (Oxford: Oxford University Press, 1987), pp. 310-13.

pledge ourselves to use the strength and fruits of victory in the service of right and in the ministry of truth and freedom.'[63]

But it was not to be. The proposals for unity between the churches, discussed long and ardently with high hopes during the darkest days of the war, came apart before its end and were ditched with the peace.

Coming Together?

Most of the old rivalries were gone never to return. This piece of optimism on the part of the President of the United Methodist Conference at Leeds in July 1918 was hardly true even at the time it was spoken.[64] However, at a superficial level he was right; the old bitterness between the denominations that was so part of the religious scene disappeared with the war and did not return. There were signs of rapprochement well before 1914, and the maelstrom of world war showed how ridiculous much of the old inter-denominational bombast had been. This may have arisen from war weariness which rendered the old assertions untenable. Despite the dissidence of Dissent, improved relations amongst the mainstream Nonconformist denominations arose at least in part from enforced co-operation during the war.

The Great War, and that is truly its proper title as far as Nonconformity is concerned, produced a success story and a failure in the long continuing saga of the relationships between Nonconformists and their attitudes towards each other.

The Chaplains

The success was the Nonconformists denominations agreeing with the government to appoint their ministers as employees of the state. This was a unique development, though not for the Wesleyan Methodists who had been appointing chaplains to the forces since the 1880s. Before 1914 the Congregationalists and the Baptists had an informal arrangement with the Admiralty and the War Office whereby their union secretaries jointly nominated chaplains and officiating clergymen to minister to sailors and troops of the two denominations.[65] With the arrival of war the War Office were approached by these two unions, led by Richard Wells and J.H. Shakespeare respectively, to obtain adequate arrangements to record the religious registration of recruits and the appointment of more

---

63   *CW*, 21 November 1918, p. 5.
64   *CW*, 11 July 1918, p. 3.
65   *CYB* (1916), pp. 10-11.

Nonconformist chaplains and officiating ministers to the forces, 'for just now they must regard the Baptist and Congregational bodies as one'.[66] Their aim was achieve parity with the Church of England in this area at least, and to a large extent they succeeded. A critic might say it was a rather small return for the unwavering support which Nonconformists had given to the government. It is claimed that it only happened because Lloyd George insisted on it in discussions with Lord Kitchener.[67]

A United Army and Navy Board was set up to supply chaplains to the forces which was soon joined by the Primitive and United Methodists, the Welsh Baptists and Independents, and others as the war progressed. The Board was run by Wells and Shakespeare, who were acting as direct agents of the government in their capacity as denominational secretaries. The *Congregational Year Book* for 1917 reports that by late 1916 there were 120 full-time Nonconformist chaplains and more than 500 officiating ministers.

Registration of the religious affiliation of solders and sailors was working satisfactorarily, although many Nonconformists felt that the Church of England was claiming too many adherents amongst the troops. Up until 1917 it appeared as if there was competition between denominations on which could supply the most recruits. The churches seemed to be vying with each other to claim who was sending ever more young men to fight. Part of this bombast was to justify the voluntaryist principle and avoid conscription. In consequence, after 1916, the numbers game took a back seat.

Exultation was very much present. Revd D.B. Hooke, Chairman of the Congregational Union, stated in May 1916: 'The Free churches have provided 400,000 men, and men with a conscience; men against whom no conscripted army can wage war on equal terms. When the war began the authorities said there was no hope of a Baptist or Congregationalist being appointed a chaplain to the Expeditionary Force. Today there are a hundred such men.'[68]

The figure of 400,000 was widely quoted, and the Congregationalists claimed that they had 70,000 of this number, the Primitive Methodists 30,000 and the Welsh Independents 10,500.[69] This was Nonconformist triumphalism the like of which had not been seen before or since.

---

66   J.H. Shakespeare, *CW*, 12 November 1914, p. 5. On Shakespeare's involvement, see Peter Shepherd, *The Making of a Modern Denomination: John Howard Shakespeare and the English Baptists 1898–1924* (Studies in Baptist History and Thought, 4; Carlisle: Paternoster Press, 2001), pp. 96-103.

67   Machin, *Politics and the Churches*, p. 312.

68   *CYB* (1917), p. 53. Chairman of the Congregational Union, Dr D.B. Hooke, 'Address', 8 May 1916.

69   *CYB* (1917), Report of Representative Council 1915–16.

A Failed Initiative

By 1916 many Nonconformist leaders recognized that a coming together of the denominations was needed. J.H. Shakespeare was a leader again in this effort. As Chairman of the Free Church Council in 1916 he affirmed: 'We have reached a stage in the religious life of this country, when if we are simply denominations and not a united church, we are doomed.'[70] A key address at the Baptist Union Board in May 1917 included the statement: 'In the past God had saved his church by division; now it was by union.'[71] Proposals were put forward in 1917 by the churches for organic union in a United Free Church. Even the relationship with the Church of England was earnestly discussed and the extent to which the established church might be part of this initiative.

But it came to nothing and even before the war was over support for the United Free Church idea had fallen away. The war had lowered the boundaries but as the summer of 1918 progressed, with the prospect of peace, enthusiasm for union based on the proposals on the table evaporated. Revd B.J. Snell, Chairman of the Congregational Union in October 1917, affirmed that the opportunity lay squarely with each church when the war was over:

Religion has lost hold of the masses of the people: the sense of truth and reality in religion is largely lost. But men cannot do without religion. Then it must be presented to them in form expressive of the highest religious needs and their satisfaction. Let us be ready cost what it may... Here is our opportunity: there is nothing in Independency to hinder, there is much to inspire... Let us make our churches, churches of the open way, churches of the free spirit.[72]

Each denomination apparently thought similarly. The prospect of success for their version of the Christian Gospel rendered a wider unity unattractive.

An Attitude Shift

It is impossible to summarize the viewpoint of Nonconformity to the war over the four year period. It is an area worthy of more research, and so

---

70   Quoted in R. Hayden, 'Still at the Crossroads? J.H. Shakespeare and Ecumenism', in K.W. Clements (ed.), *Baptists in the Twentieth Century* (London: Baptist Historical Society, 1983), p. 45. On Shakespeare's contribution to ecumenism, see Shepherd, *Making of a Modern Denomination*, pp. 93-138 and 182-85.

71   *CW*, 12 April 1917, 8. J.H. Shakespeare, speech to the Baptist Board.

72   *CYB* (1918), pp. 36-37. Chairman of the Congregational Union, B.J. Snell, 'Address', 3 October 1917.

far the surface has just been scratched. The voice against the extremes of
war was never lost in Nonconformity: some were willing to speak out. It
cost many of them dearly in personal terms, as people would attack them
for lack of supposed patriotism. Revd R.F. Horton of Hampstead Free
Church was one of those not afraid. In July 1917, on speaking about the
need for reprisals against Germany for their air raids on British cities, he
said: 'It would be better to be defeated, retaining honour, chivalry and
humanity, than to obtain a victory by methods which have brought on
Germany universal execration.'[73] Perhaps this was a view more in
keeping with the traditions of Nonconformity than most of the
preachments of the time by the leaders of Dissent.

Training courses in business and administration adopt methods to
evaluate the success of their efforts. These courses aim at achieving
changes in attitude so attempts are made to measure attitude shift. What
was the view of the participant before the course, and how had it changed
after the event? I want to attempt something similar by taking
Nonconformist attitudes (or the lack of them) towards an event of 1917
and compare that with the likely approach to a similar happening if it had
taken place in 1914.

Revd Dr Stanley A. Mellor (1881–1926) is considered to have been
amongst the most significant Unitarian ministers of the twentieth century,
though his importance was limited by his early death. During the war he
was minister of Hope Street Church, Liverpool, and a recognized leader
of Nonconformity in the city. He was a fine preacher, and he was firm in
his view that the war had led Nonconformists into strange paths, and a
witness for another viewpoint was needed.

Many saw him as a pacifist, and his voice was a signal one. One
example will suffice. At the British and Foreign Unitarian Association
meetings in May 1915, Mellor delivered a speech 'which emphasised a
totally different point of view and revealed a wide cleavage of opinion in
the audience, some of which uttered words of protest from time to time...
He would ask them to bear with him...for the attitude he was bound to
take, although it had exposed him to violent criticism... It had been said
that this crisis had deepened the religious feeling in this country; the
same thing was said in Germany. It was not for him to express an opinion
as to that, but he felt that there was something wrong with their ideas of
religion when they contemplated the spectacle of the great belligerent
nations each praying to the same God for the defeat of the enemy'.[74]

That gives the flavour of his views, and now to the event, reported in
the *Christian Life*, a weekly Unitarian journal: 'Dr Stanley A Mellor of
Hope Street Church was invited to deliver the opening sermon at the

73   *CW*, 5 July 1917, p. 10.
74   *Inquirer*, 29 May 1915, p. 266.

biennial sessions of the General Unitarian Conference of the USA and Canada to be held at Montreal next week... The British Government has, however, refused to grant him the necessary passports—presumably on account of his activities as a pacifist.'[75]

This action by the British government was attacked in the New York press, but in Britain there is nothing apart from the reference in the *Christian Life*. There is no mention in the other Unitarian journal, the *Inquirer*, nor have I been able to find anything in the rest of the Nonconformist or general British press. Nonconformists were willing to be mute about what amounts to the state suppression of someone who wanted to travel and might, with the emphasis on might, be critical of its position.[76]

Passports to visit Montreal, then part of the British Empire, were not needed in 1914 and the circumstances were entirely different, but would Nonconformists have been as silent in 1914 towards a similar act by the British government? No, the *Christian World* and the Nonconformist press would have protested strongly at this infringement of religious liberty. But in 1917 it was accepted without comment, the shift in attitude had been so great.

Michael Watts in his seminal work, *The Dissenters*, states that a consistent thread links the Tudor Anabaptist with the twentieth-century Free Churchman—a refusal to accept the dictates of the state in matters of conscience. The refusal to render to Caesar the things that are God's is the very essence of Dissent.[77] Between 1914 and 1918 Nonconformity chose to forget this vital principle in following the seemingly overwhelming desire, almost an imperative, to support the war effort in every way possible. The result was the loss of Nonconformist influence in national affairs which it was never to recover.

75   *Christian Life*, 22 September 1917, p. 297.
76   For background, see the 'Introduction' by J. Middleton Murray to S.A. Mellor, *Liberation* (London: Constable, 1929).
77   M.J. Watts, *The Dissenters: From the Reformation to the French Revolution* (Oxford: Clarendon Press, 1978), p. 3.

CHAPTER 10

Twentieth-Century Protestant Nonconformists in the World of Business

David J. Jeremy

Introduction: Nonconformity and Business

Nonconformist stances towards business in the twentieth century have been ambivalent. On the one hand, the norm of missionary-minded preaching from Nonconformist pulpits, coupled with the disreputable aspects of commerce, suggested that business was an inferior calling to the full-time ministry. Joseph Rowntree Gillett, partner in Gillett Bros., bill brokers, Lombard Street, London, decided near the end of the First World War that, as a Quaker and a pacifist, he must leave the banking business 'to do God's work as he should be guided'.[1] In 1923, as a minister in the Society of Friends, Gillett asked readers of the *Friends' Intelligencer*, 'The Christian view of business is that it is a method of rendering essential service for the community. But is it not in actual fact a method of exploiting the needs of the community for private gain?'[2]

On the other hand, Nonconformity's Puritan legacy justified business as a Christian calling. So, Angus Watson, fish processor of 'Skipper' sardines fame, took as the subject for his chairman's address to the Congregational Union in 1935, 'The sense of stewardship'. '"You don't mean to say to me that you would mix business with religion and spoil both," said an American Church member to me once', Watson reported. 'And that', he went on, 'is still the attitude of some well-meaning business men. They simply do not recognise that a business life divorced from religious faith is a hollow mockery; either Christ must have the whole man—body, mind and spirit—or he is none of His.'[3] Sir Harold Bellman, building society chairman and active Methodist layman,

---

1   George M.L. Davies, *Joseph Rowntree Gillett: A Memoir* (London: George Allen & Unwin, 1942), p. 23.

2   *Friends Intelligencer* 27 January 1923, reprinted in Davies, *Gillett*, p. 126.

3   Angus Watson, *The Faith of a Business Man* (London: Ivor Nicholson & Watson, 1936), p. 31.

published a similar credo in 1947: 'the true Christian view...sees life clearly and sees it whole, portraying no false distinction by which a man's business activity is regarded as selfish while only his church and social work is considered religious and consecrated'.[4]

Attitudes are one thing, activity and action are another. What impact have Nonconformists had on business in Britain in the twentieth century? Conversely, what influence have business people had on the Nonconformist churches? Answers to these two questions can be sought at both quantitative and qualitative levels.

The Quantitative Picture of Nonconformists in Business 1900–1990s

If we look in the business history literature there is relatively little awareness of the church connections of business people, apart from the Quakers.[5] Where there is some awareness, most attention has been directed at the heroes of big business. Small business, in villages and market towns, is probably where Nonconformist networks and values had their greatest impact. Examining a random five per cent sample of the 21,100 names listed in *The Methodist Local Preachers' Who's Who, 1934*, Clive Field found that, proportionately, business-related occupations were two or three times more numerous among local preachers than among the male population at large.[6] The majority of these local preachers in business would have been in small and medium sized businesses.

However, we lack in-depth historical studies of small businesses. Regional and local studies of business elites would provide profiles, but few if any of these spanning the twentieth century have looked specifically for religious affiliations. This obliges me to return to my

---

4   Harold Bellman, *Cornish Cockney: Reminiscences and Reflections* (London: Hutchinson, 1947), pp. 251-52.

5   See James Walvin, *The Quakers: Money and Morals* (London: John Murray, 1997), for a recent synthesis.

6   Clive D. Field, 'The Methodist Local Preacher: An Occupational Analysis', in Geoffrey Milburn and Margaret Batty (eds), *Workaday Preachers: The Story of Methodist Local Preaching* (London: Methodist Publishing House, 1995), p. 240. His 'intermediate' occupations were, relatively, twice and his professional occupations three times the size of the male population of England and Wales in 1931. The professionals included insurance managers (1.5 per cent of the preachers), chartered accountants (0.7 per cent), works or store managers (4 per cent), and dealers or retailers (11.7 per cent).

work on the heads of large UK businesses.[7] Hopefully it will serve to reduce the persistent hagiographical tendency in religious (and secular) biography.

Some idea of the extent of Nonconformist involvement in big business can be gleaned from the pre-adult and adult religious associations of the heads of the largest businesses in the UK. If schooling is used as a proxy for pre-adult religious association, the profile conveyed in Table 1 is the result.

Out of approximately two hundred individuals heading the hundred largest employers in the UK at four dates across the century, the proportion receiving some kind of Nonconformist education fell from seven or eight per cent in the first half of the century to four per cent in the 1950s and to under 3 per cent in the 1990s. Adult Nonconformist associations among the same business elite, seen in Table 2, stood at around 10 per cent until the 1930s but in the century's middle quartile stood at about 6 per cent and by the 1990s was probably much less. The discrepancies are more or less consistent because it would take twenty-to-thirty years for classrooms to be exchanged for boardrooms.

If Tables 1 and 2 are merged, and if individuals rather than elite posts are counted, then the absolute numbers of those with Nonconformist connections in the business elite emerge as 17 out of 201 in 1907, 15 out of 203 in 1935, 11 out of 212 in 1955, and a very small number, at least three, in 1998.[8]

In short, Nonconformity in England and Wales had a major impact on the lives of about ten per cent of the UK business elite before 1914, a proportion which dropped to around 6 per cent by the 1930s, steadied until the 1960s and thereafter fell to one or two per cent by the 1990s. Two points should be noticed. First, the Quakers far outperformed all other denominations when their representation in the UK business elite is compared to their religious density. Second, counting heads is not the same as estimating influence, either received or exerted.

---

7   See David J. Jeremy, *Capitalists and Christians: Business Leaders and the Churches in Britain, 1900–1960* (Oxford: Clarendon Press, 1990), on which much of the rest of this essay is based.

8   Jeremy, *Capitalists and Christians*, pp. 115-17; *idem* (ed.), *Religion, Business and Wealth in Modern Britain* (London: Routledge, 1998), p. 15.

What have Nonconformists Contributed to Twentieth-Century Business?

The Relationship between Business and Religion in the Twentieth Century

First, how far were Christian views and influence admitted into business? Proprietors owning a majority share of their own business ostensibly had little trouble in doing as they pleased, imposing religious preferences with mixed positive and negative effects. Directors and managers of limited companies, the spreading business form since the 1860s, were stewards (and agents) of their shareholders. Theirs was a different position.

In the last quarter of the nineteenth century businessmen *qua* businessmen were distancing themselves from religion and church. Religious neutrality was seen as essential for the efficient functioning of the market. The 1890 edition of George Rae's influential text for managers of banks, pronounced, 'It is hardly necessary to suggest that in your dealings with the public there must be a total absence of bias— religious, political or social. When a man brings you his banking account, you do not require to know whether he goes to church or chapel, nor how he voted at last election, nor who his grandfather was.'[9] Large businesses, once entwined with church and chapel by the tentacles of family and tradition, worried about religious bias after they converted the family firm into a limited company.

By the First World War the centralized professional managements of the large railway companies and the giant combines of the first merger wave of the 1890s–1900s were establishing the dominant business ethos of the future. It was one in which the role of religion was increasingly circumscribed. When, in 1909, the directors of the Bleachers' Association, a textile finishing combine employing 12,000 mostly in north-west England, received appeals from religious bodies for funding places of worship or schools, they minuted their decision that 'The various religious denominations should have no favouritism shewn as between one and the other, but that attention should rather be paid as to the interest of the workpeople at any particular [bleach]works have in the undertaking for which assistance is asked.'[10] The corporation, having roused so much ire by its centralizing commercial policies, was anxious to minimize impositions of other kinds on its local works and communities.

---

9   George Rae, *The Country Banker: His Clients, Cares, and Work: From an Experience of Forty Years* (1st edn, 1885; London: John Murray, 8th edn, 1890), p. 2.

10   Quoted in David J. Jeremy, 'Survival Strategies in Lancashire Textiles: Bleachers' Association Ltd to Whitecroft plc, 1900–1980s', *Textile History* 24.2 (1993) pp. 183, 188.

A strongly capitalist view was expressed by Sir Josiah Stamp, well-known executive and Methodist. He adhered to the sort of advice Rae published about the separation of business and faith. He avoided high ethical themes when chairing the Abbey Road Building Society (of which he was president through his friendship with its secretary Harold Bellman). He declined to develop religious views when discussing economic matters in the *Methodist Recorder*. However, in three books, which started as lectures, he did stake out his opinions on the interactions between business and religion.[11] 'Stamp's main concern was to distance the church from economic institutions and to place a new onus on the individual Christian to work out social redemption... [he] questioned whether the morality required of individuals was identical to that demanded of individuals acting in groups: "in what precise sense can...the National Union of Railwaymen love the Railway Stockholders' Union"' he asked.[12]

Since the 1930s the view that economics and business should be subordinated to religion and ethics has gained ground. Chiefly this has come from church leaders and bureaucrats, but not entirely.

Nonconformist Contributions to Twentieth-Century Business

So, what difference have Nonconformists made in twentieth century business? I suggest that in at least five respects they have made distinctive contributions. First, they have been responsible for part of the education of numbers of business leaders, some national, many more local figures. Second, particular individuals with Nonconformist roots have made outstanding contributions to business enterprise. Third, Nonconformity has provided institutional bases for the networks of trust which are essential to business. Fourth, Nonconformists have offered challenges and alternatives to aspects of the modern business system. Last, Nonconformity has reinforced several important business values.

EDUCATING PEOPLE IN BUSINESS
While the Church of England had many times more elementary/primary schools in England and Wales than the Nonconformists,[13] the latter did

---

11   The books were: *The Christian Ethic as an Economic Factor* (1926); *Motive and Method in a Christian Order* (1936); and *Christianity and Economics* (1939).

12   Stamp, *Motive and Method*, p. 40; Jeremy, *Capitalists and Christians*, p. 182.

13   Nonconformist day schools numbered less than 7 per cent of all schools in England and Wales in 1900 and under one per cent in 1960s, compared to the Church of England's 52 per cent of such schools in 1900 and nearly 33 per cent in 1960. See A.H. Halsey (ed.), *British Social Trends since 1900: A Guide to the Changing Social Structure of Britain* (London: Macmillan, 1988), p. 238.

better when it came to Sunday Schools. In the first decade of the century over half the five-to-nineteen-year-olds in England and Wales attended Sunday School and of those nearly 60 per cent went to Nonconformist Sunday Schools. Even when that proportion of youngsters going to Sunday School fell to 44 per cent in 1930 and 21 per cent in 1960, the Nonconformists' share remained at 50-60 per cent.[14] (See Table 3.) From the 1970s and 1980s traditional Sunday Schools, held on Sunday afternoons, were transmuted or disbanded. In their day, however, they were a powerful influence on people in all walks of life. Anecdotal evidence shows that Nonconformity offered a major formative training for those going into business in the first half of the century. Reading, writing, public speaking, chapel-taught skills and the values projected by Bible stories and oft-sung hymns, equipped many an individual starting out as shop assistant, clerk, or engineering apprentice.

Sir Harold Bellman, recalled with affection and insight his upbringing in Trinity Wesleyan Church on Fernhead Road, Paddington, in the 1890s:

> I owe a special debt to the old chapel. It was there in the Bible class and Guild I was encouraged to speak. I started by reciting at an early age, and later read the lesson in church on anniversary day. I think that early experience gave me some degree of immunity from nervousness on a public platform. I was never taught elocution, but critics in the family circle were severe enough then, as they are now, to impress upon me the essentials, which I believe to be clarity in articulation, and the necessity of so controlling the voice as to ensure that the most distant member of an audience can hear distinctly without feeling he is being shouted at. The old chapel attracted in those days a great company of youth, some of whom possessed a mental equipment much above the average. Some of them won distinction in the Civil Service, the professions, and in business.[15]

Bellman was describing a vital piece of training for the budding business person: rehearsal of the skills of presentation.[16] In the chapel setting he clearly received the formative shaping of the publicity and marketing skills essential in his creation of the largest building society in the country (the Abbey Road).[17] There was more that Sunday Schools provided potential business men and women. The classic Protestant codes

---

14   Figures calculated from Robert Currie, Alan Gilbert and Lee Horsley *Churches and Churchgoers: Patterns of Church Growth in the British Isles since 1700* (Oxford: Clarendon Press, 1977), pp. 175-92, and B.R. Mitchell, *British Historical Statistics* (Cambridge University Press, 1988), p. 15.

15   Bellman, *Cornish Cockney*, pp. 40-41.

16   To which today (2000) an element in of all undergraduate degrees in business studies is dedicated.

17   See Esmond J. Cleary, 'Sir Charles Harold Bellman', in David J. Jeremy and Christine Shaw (eds), *Dictionary of Business Biography* (6 vols; London: Butterworths, 1984–86), I, pp. 273-79; hereafter cited as *DBB*.

of the work ethic and responsible individualism were there transmitted to underpin the attitudes and behaviours of generations of people in business.

Some were specially privileged. They attended the private schools set up for the sons (mostly) of Nonconformists. The Congregationalists' Mill Hill School, north of London, was patronized by the Wills family, the Bristol tobacco manufacturers and Congregationalists, who sent William Henry Wills (later Lord Winterstoke) there in the 1840s and his second cousin George Alfred Wills in the late-1860s. Laurence Cadbury, son of George and father of Sir Adrian, was sent to Leighton Park School, Reading, which had been established in 1890 for the sons of wealthier Quakers who were destined for Oxford or Cambridge. At Leighton Park, Laurence Cadbury imbibed a strong interest in maths, science, and music, antipathy towards the classics (or at least the classics master), and a pleasure in reading the Bible which he first learned from his parents.[18]

Sons of Methodist ministers since Wesley's day had been sent to Kingswood, first in Bristol then in Bath. Among the distinguished businessmen to be educated there was Sir Robert Perks, solicitor, railway company director, organizer and chairman of the pressure group of 185 Nonconformist MPs who were returned in the Liberal landslide of 1906, initiator of Methodist union, and first Vice-President of the Methodist Church in 1932: ecclesiastical as well as political strategist and schemer.[19] Of his religious education at Kingswood, Perks had unflattering recollections: occasional revivals meant suspension of classes and games. But, he recalled, 'Kingswood certainly turned out a body of hard-working, self-reliant, well-educated lads who knew that they had to face the struggles of life with courage. Most of us have done so.'[20]

The Leys School, Cambridge, set up by the Wesleyan Methodist Conference of 1875 specifically to educate the sons of Methodist businessmen, achieved a remarkable record. Never larger than 200 boys in its first three decades, under the Reverend Dr William Fiddian Moulton (1835–98), a Wesleyan version of the Arnoldian vision of godliness and good learning unfolded. By 1907 they had sent 250 boys to Cambridge alone where they gained fifty first class degrees and six fellowships. Two pupils gained London University BSc degrees while still at school. Religious achievements were similarly outstanding. The *Old Leysian Directory* of 1908 recorded the religious mission of the school: 'The Leys has failed of its sovran purpose if it has failed to foster a high moral

---

18   Sir Adrian Cadbury, *Laurence John Cadbury, 1889–1982* (privately printed, 1983).

19   Charles E. Lee, 'Sir Robert William Perks', *DBB* IV, pp. 628-32; Stephen Koss, *Nonconformity in Modern British Politics* (London: Batsford, 1975), *passim*, Appendix.

20   Sir Robert Perks, *Sir Robert William Perks, Baronet* (London: Epworth Press, 1936), pp. 16 and 20.

tone, or even a definitely religious one, to wield and influence in the broadest and deepest sense evangelical'.[21] To counter what may well have been a hot-house atmosphere, the school in 1886 set up the Leysian Mission to channel boys and old boys into evangelistic and social work among London's poor. Whether the businessmen patronizing the school were satisfied with the school's output is unknown. Well over a third of old boys in 1934 (627/1,642) and again in 1956 (766/2,067) were pursuing business careers.[22] We need quantitative estimates of the occupations of Leys' pupils' fathers.

PRODUCING OUTSTANDING INDIVIDUAL BUSINESS LEADERS

As noted, the quantitative data show that Nonconformity helped to shape the lives of ten per cent of heads of big business before the First World War, a proportion falling to six per cent by the 1930s and remaining at that level until the late-1950s.[23] At the top of the business pyramid in the first half of the century we may note two names: Josiah Charles Stamp (1880–1941) and William Hesketh Lever (1851–1925).

Stamp was among the best known Methodist laymen of the inter-war years and possibly the most distinguished professional manager produced by Nonconformity. In the 1930s he was president of the Midland & Scottish Railway Company executive, managing 220,000 employees. Raised as a Baptist, he became a staunch Wesleyan Methodist after his marriage. Starting in the Inland Revenue and a brilliant part-time degree at the LSE, during the First World War he devised Excess Profits Duty. He then joined the board of Nobel Industries and introduced from the USA the accounting techniques which allowed dozens of subsidiaries to be integrated into the parent company. This paved the way for the adoption of the crucial multi-divisional form of corporate organization when Nobels and three other chemical firms merged as Imperial Chemical Industries in 1926. By then Stamp had moved to the chief executive position on the LMS Railway where he stayed until his death in 1941. A Germanophile, he and some of his family died in a German air-raid, three years after being raised to the peerage as 1st Baron Stamp of Shortlands.[24]

Few twentieth-century entrepreneurs have been as overwhelmingly successful as Lever who was brought up as a Congregationalist and ended his days in 1922 as 1st Viscount Leverhulme of the Western Isles.

21 Quoted in Jeremy, *Capitalists and Christians*, p. 91.

22 Jeremy, *Capitalists and Christians*, p. 93.

23 For a roll-call, substantial but not exhaustive, see David J. Jeremy, 'Religious Links of Individuals Listed in the Dictionary of Business Biography', in David J. Jeremy (ed.), *Business and Religion in Britain* (Aldershot: Gower, 1988), pp. 188-205.

24 Michael Bywater, 'Josiah Charles Stamp', *DBB* V, pp. 260-73; Jeremy, *Capitalists and Christians*, pp. 178-83.

Whatever is surmised about Lever's motives, there is no denying the magnitude of his creative impulses and the energy with which he directed them. In business he built an organization that straddled the world with a network of factories supplied with oils and fats from plantations as far flung as the Pacific and the Congo, a business empire comprising 160 subsidiary and associated companies and employing 20,000 to 30,000 worldwide at his death. The hub of his empire was Port Sunlight village on the Cheshire side of the Mersey. Lever made five journeys round the world to inspect his works and frequently visited continental Europe. In private he relished building and rebuilding all but one of the thirteen houses (and their gardens) he and his wife occupied. At Rivington, near Bolton, he created a fine Japanese garden. He avidly (if not always tastefully) collected pictures, sculpture, tapestries, furniture, porcelain and pottery much of his adult life. He built and endowed five Congregational churches. He was elected to Parliament (as Liberal MP for the Wirral, 1906–09) on his fifth attempt, and returned to Westminster in 1917 when he was raised to the peerage.

However, Lever was not simply a super-energetic entrepreneur. Success inevitably brought power. And power he learned to enjoy. His village as much as his business gave scope to feed his megalomaniac tendencies. In the double-edged words of the Reverend Dr J.D. Jones, chairman of the Congregational Union addressing Lever's memorial service at the City Temple, a pastor who knew him well enough: 'There was something Napoleonic about him'.[25] Napoleon indeed was one of Lever's heroes, after whom he named a room in his Lady Lever Art Gallery at Port Sunlight. The trait worried him at times, hence the contradictions between his public avowals and his less visible actions in the affairs of Port Sunlight village.

CREATING INSTITUTIONAL BASES FOR NETWORKS OF TRUST IN BUSINESS

Networks and the trust they generate and convey are essential for the operation of modern business.[26] Until the 1960s, Nonconformity offered business extensive institutional bases for networking. We have mentioned Sunday Schools and schools. The local chapel or meeting; the regional circuit, synod, or association; the national conference: all represented institutional opportunities for building trust and networks between

---

25   *Progress* 25 (July 1925), p. 116.

26   Francis Fukuyama, *Trust: The Social Virtues and the Creation of Prosperity* (London: Hamish Hamilton, 1995); Mark Casson, *Information and Organization: A New Perspective on the Theory of the Firm* (Oxford: Clarendon Press, 1997).

individuals from the local to the national level. In addition there were family connections forged in the chapel context.[27]

By their nature, networks and trust are difficult to detect. Quantitative evidence may show individuals attending the same school or chapel but the quality and extent of their relationship may not be wholly positive, indeed, given human nature, sometimes the reverse.

Networks comprise nodes and links, with the simplest social network formed by two nodes (people) and one link. Bellman and Stamp, already encountered, illustrate this sort of network in the inter-war business community. Closer inspection reveals that the links between the two men were more complex than their shared Wesleyanism. Stamp was six years older than Bellman. They first met at the meetings of the Royal Statistical Society in 1914, when Stamp was thirty-four and, having gained a first-class degree at the LSE three years earlier, was moving to the secretariat of the Board of the Inland Revenue. Bellman left the Civil Service in 1920, shortly after Stamp joined Nobels. While Bellman became secretary of the Abbey Road Building Society then facing the post-war boom in demand for housing, Stamp was enjoying a meteoric rise. He sat on the Royal Commission on Income Tax in 1919 and for his public work his CBE of 1918 was advanced to KBE in 1920. The fathers of Bellman and Stamp, coachbuilder and cheesemonger respectively, were both members of the Abbey Road Building Society, which started with a group of Nonconformists in 1874. This paternal connection, renewed by the involvements of both men in the affairs of London Wesleyan Methodism,[28] led Bellman in 1925 to invite his titled acquaintance to become president of the Abbey Road. In this capacity, Sir Josiah Stamp regularly addressed the Abbey Road's annual meetings held in the Queen's Hall, London, in the late-1920s.[29] Presumably he received a fee for his services. Bellman became the best-known publicist and pioneer of the building society movement and the individual who did most to turn the British population into a home-owning society. His connection with Stamp, an influential champion, illustrates how, in the first half of the century, the chapel could be an important institutional setting for

---

27   For some late-nineteenth Wesleyan Methodist business networks, see David J. Jeremy, 'Late-Victorian and Edwardian Methodist Businessmen and Wealth', in Jeremy (ed.), *Religion, Business and Wealth*, pp. 76-78.

28   The Stamps at this time were members of Twickenham Wesleyan Methodist Church; the Bellmans were at Finchley Wesleyan Methodist Church, but both men were elected to their District Synods and would have met again when they were elected to the Wesleyan, after 1932 Methodist, Conference. Bellman, *Cornish Cockney*, pp. 44 and 225.

29   Bellman, *Cornish Cockney*, pp. 75-78, 221-26. Sir Josiah C. Stamp, *Criticism and Other Essays* (London: Ernest Benn, 1931), pp. 271-88, reprints his addresses to the Abbey Road annual meetings.

significant commercial networking, in this instance supplemented by the linkages of parentage and intellectual interest, to say nothing of an assumed cash nexus.

Several points about Nonconformist networks may be made. By resting business structures and goals on religious institutions, these networks sooner or later invited conflicts of interest between the economic and the non-economic.[30] Did chapel-based networking operate in favour of rational economic behaviour or in favour of religious altruism? Did the former bring charges of hypocrisy and, in causing a rejection of ethical considerations, accelerate unbelief?

Then, in unravelling networks, which linkage layer had primacy? At Port Sunlight, Lever installed some of his managers and directors on the governing Committee of Christ Church.[31] Was Christianity subservient to and serving commerce, or was faith advancing into capitalist territory?

Last, if chapel-based networking helped to develop trust in commercial relations, what was the effect of this on commercial relations outside chapel networks? Did chapel networks promote a higher degree of trust in the wider society and, if so, how? Linkages were layered. One important network allied to Nonconformity in places, about which we know too little (due to the movement's secretiveness), was freemasonry. William Lever was not alone among leading Nonconformists in his masonic participations. When William Henry Hawthorne, Burslem tile manufacturer and Primitive Methodist Vice-President in 1929, died in 1932, his funeral service at Wolstanton in the Potteries, involved masonic brethren. They included the Primitive Methodist superintendent of the Newcastle-under-Lyme circuit and a line of freemasons who cast sprigs of acacia into the grave.[32]

OFFERING CHALLENGES AND ALTERNATIVES TO ASPECTS OF THE MODERN BUSINESS SYSTEM

Laying out ideals, at which the Nonconformist pulpiteers were well-practiced, was one thing, implementing them was another. Angus Watson, addressing the meetings of International Rotary at Edinburgh in 1931, cited the profit-sharing scheme of Theodore Cooke Taylor (also a Congregationalist) at Batley, Yorkshire. Taylor, Watson reported, 'has distributed no less than a million pounds among his employees under his

30   Robert A. Pollak, 'A Transaction Cost approach to Families and Households', *Journal of Economic Literature* 23 (June, 1985), pp. 581-608.

31   Six out of fourteen members of this committee in 1900 were senior executives of Lever Bros. See David J. Jeremy, 'The Enlightened Paternalist in Action: William Hesketh Lever at Port Sunlight before 1914', *Business History* 33.1 (January, 1991), p. 71.

32   *Evening Sentinel* 22 February 1932; *Pottery Gazette and Glass Trade Review* 1 April 1932.

profit-sharing scheme during the last forty years'.[33] Profit sharing was a nineteenth-century attempt to reconcile the conflict between capital and labour. Pioneered by a Unitarian Yorkshire colliery owner,[34] the scheme gave employees a fixed percentage of corporate profits in addition to wages and salaries. Historians have debated whether it was anything more than a capitalist device to seduce workers away from trade unions and lock their loyalty into the interests of corporate proprietors and managements. Ironically, at Batley the autocratic Taylor arranged his corporate finances so that the bumper wartime profits of the First World War years were reinvested in gilt-edge securities to the disproportionate advantage of Taylor and his managers vis-à-vis his 1,500 employees,[35] a fact presumably unknown to Angus Watson. More consistently self-appraising were the Quakers.

Between the wars, and after, the Quaker employers met every decade (1918, 1928, 1938, 1948) at Woodbrooke (George Cadbury's former home near Selly Oak) to discuss their common industrial problems in the light of Quaker principles. Around a hundred individuals met on each occasion, with the Cadbury's, Rowntree's, Reckitt's being the most strongly-represented firms. What is remarkable is the range of thorny issues with which they grappled. Worker control of industry, unemployment, the allocation of surplus profits were some. These were reviewed in the light of contemporary Quaker principles of social responsibility, in particular, the dignity of work, frugality, and service; egalitarianism; abhorrence of conflict; and avoidance of exploiting fellow human beings. Their most radical conclusion, perhaps, was that the employer's prime duties were first to provide a living wage (defined precisely by Benjamin Seebohm Rowntree at the 1918 conference) for all employees; and second to attain higher efficiency in order to have more profits to distribute to both capital and labour. Presented by William Wallace of Rowntree's, this view was adopted in the final report of the 1928 conference and repeated again in the 1938 report.[36]

Out of the Quaker firms came another, wider, result. Between the 1930s and 1950s, 'Quaker employers' concepts played an important role in the ready acceptance by British managerial thought of its most recent modern inspiration—the ideas of the Harvard so-called "human relations in industry" school.'[37]

---

33   Watson, *Faith of a Business Man*, p. 156.

34   Henry Currer Briggs.

35   Sidney Pollard and Robert Turner, 'Profit-sharing and Autocracy: The Case of J.T. & J. Taylor of Batley, Woollen Manufacturers, 1892–1966', *Business History* 18 (1976), pp. 4-34.

36   Jeremy, *Capitalists and Christians*, pp. 162-73.

37   John Child, 'Quaker Employers and Industrial Relations', *Sociological Review* new series 123 (1964), p. 308.

One of the more radical departures taken by a Nonconformist business figure was Ernest Bader's foundation of Scott Bader in 1951. Bader (1890–1982) was a Swiss-born plastics manufacturer who moved emigrated to England in 1912, became a strong pacifist, and left the Baptists for the Quakers at the end of the Second World War. A domineering personality, with much turbulence he followed the logic of his idealism and effectively gave his company over to his employees, represented by a form of trust, the Scott Bader Commonwealth Ltd (a company limited by guarantee). In this he emulated the John Lewis Partnership (1928) and much earlier in Germany, the Carl Zeiss Foundation at Jena (1896). Bader's example was cited at length and with admiration by Fritz Schumacher in his influential *Small Is Beautiful: A Study of Economics as if People Mattered* (1973). At any rate, Bader's initiative at Wellingborough gave a fillip to the wider movement for industrial democracy, presenting a clear alternative model to the professional managerial capitalism which, however, remains the dominant paradigm for business organization.[38]

A major modification of the UK business system came with the co-operative movement. Nonconformists amongst others played a part in promoting the movement in the nineteenth century; and although the co-operative principle was not much copied elsewhere in British industry, the Co-operative Wholesale Society and local co-operative retail societies made a very considerable impact in improving the standard of living of working class consumers. At the beginning of the twentieth century there were 1.7 million members in over 1,400 co-operative societies.[39] Their main supplier, the CWS, was chaired in the first decade of the twentieth century by the venerated John Shillito, a Unitarian. From his Manchester headquarters, he managed a multi-national, vertically-integrated empire of 17,000 employees, twenty-seven factories, a small fleet, and a clutch of depots and warehouses.[40] The mutual and democratic model of the co-operative societies offered a striking alternative to the joint-stock limited company of private enterprise. Their major defect has been the failure to reconcile democratic governance with managerial control.

A recent innovation in the business system for which Nonconformists claim credit is the movement for ethical investment. In principle this goes back to the eighteenth and early-nineteenth centuries and the struggle against slavery. Quakers and evangelical Anglicans combined to defeat within imperial bounds first the iniquitous trade, then the iniquitous

---

38   Susanna Hoe, *The Man Who Gave His Company Away: A Biography of Ernest Bader, Founder of the Scott Bader Commonwealth* (London: Heinemann, 1978).

39   G.D.H. Cole, *A Century of Co-operation* (London: George Allen & Unwin, 1944), p. 371.

40   Percy Redfern, *The New History of the CWS* (London: Dent, 1938); *CWS Annual* (1908), pp. 11-13.

institution; they campaigned against it in other empires from the 1870s. Additional causes involving business interests followed. The temperance crusade from the 1830s brought battles with brewers. Gambling attracted Nonconformist opposition in the 1880s; Sunday trading at the end of the nineteenth century; and the arms trade, fought by Nonconformists in the mid-nineteenth century and again between the world wars, has been consistently opposed by the Quakers since their seventeenth-century beginnings.[41]

Modern ethical investment emerged in the USA. It grew out of the anti-Vietnam War movement; Ralph Nader's consumer activism; Rachel Carson's environment alarms; and, building on the domestic black struggle, protests against South Africa's policy of apartheid. Apartheid, commenced in 1948 and massively extended after the South African republic was constituted in 1961, led in Britain to Harold Wilson's arms embargo (1964) and popular boycotts of South African products like fruit.[42]

In England, Charles Jacob (b. 1921) found himself in a position to do something to encourage ethical investment. He had been on the Investment Committee of the Central Finance Board of the Methodist Church for a many years as a stockbroker when he was forced into retirement through ill health (and told he would never work again) in 1969. Three years later, however, he was persuaded by the Methodist Central Finance Board to return to the City as the board's first professional investment manager. Already an ethical policy operated within the board with the exclusion of investments in the armaments, alcohol, tobacco, and gambling industries.

During his three years absence from the City, Jacob had been studying the growth of ethical investment in the United States, particularly in the retail sector. This he found to be solely negative in approach. He was anxious to produce an ethical unit trust in this country but with more positive attributes.[43] His return to the City gave him this opportunity. With assistance from Jeremy Edwards of First Investors (later managing director of Henderson Administration) and Richard Rowntree of the

---

41 For these campaigns see David W. Bebbington, *The Nonconformist Conscience: Chapel and Politics, 1870-1914* (London: George Allen & Unwin, 1982).

42 For some historical background, see Russell Sparkes, *The Ethical Investor* (London: HarperCollins, 1995), pp. 114-29 and *passim*.

43 For example, the positive criteria for a company to be supported by an ethical investment trust included excellent products and services; good customer relations; strong community involvement; operations which conserve energy or natural resources. Negative criteria included involvement in environmental harm; unnecessary animal exploitation; trade with oppressive regimes; production of pornography, weapons, alcohol or tobacco. Kenneth Noble, 'Investing with Principle', *For a Change* (June–July, 1996), pp. 16-17.

Rowntree Social Services Trust, in 1973 he submitted a scheme for an ethical unit trust to the Department of Trade. It was rejected, on grounds of a conflict of interest between ethics and profits. Jacob was stung but not defeated. In 1976 Jacob and Edwards again submitted their proposal but it was again turned down by the Department of Trade.

Charles Jacob concentrated on Methodist and charitable funds for more than a decade. As a member of the Methodist Ethics Committee he helped to bring Methodists and the Church Commissioners to further solidly responsible investment within the churches. A Church Investors meeting on ethics was set up and was later widened to cover all denominations of investors. It continued to publicize Jacob's cause for an ethical unit trust. The breakthrough came in 1979 when he gained the support of Nicholas (later Sir Nicholas) Goodison, chairman of the Stock Exchange. His approach to the Department of Trade on behalf of Jacob's ethical unit trust succeeded.

After more hiccups in settling arrangements for its administration and management, the first ethical fund, named the Stewardship Unit Trust (with plain biblical connotations), was eventually established by the Friends Provident group (where Quakers dominated the board) in 1984. Charles Jacob joined the Stewardship Unit Trust, first on its Committee of Reference, later on the board of the first Ethical Investment Trust, retiring in 2000. His work as Investment Manager of the Central Finance Board of the Methodist Church continued for fifteen years during which period the assets under his management expanded a hundred-fold. A suitable management structure and offices were set up. He was succeeded by his assistant Bill Seddon.

It is of interest to note that not only were the ethically managed Methodist Funds the beneficiaries of above-average performance and considerable expansion but the growth of the ethical unit trust movement exceeded the most optimistic of forecasts. Original estimates of investment demand ranged from £2.5 million to £5 million. However, the yearly growth, now outstripping demand for standard unit trusts, has led to a £2.5 billion market. Of this the Stewardship Unit Trust, which Jacob originated, now contributes £1.3 billion, in a market with over forty other ethical funds.[44]

---

44   The preceding material on the ethical trust movement is derived from correspondence and a telephone conversations (5-17 July 2000) with Charles Jacob, to whom I am indebted for information and copies of articles; Sparkes, *Ethical Investor*; John Hancock, *The Ethical Investor* (London: Financial Times, 1999); Friends Provident, *Stewardship, a Decent Investment: The Stewardship Investment Trusts* (1994); *Professional Investor* (July–August, 1994); Frank Blighe, 'Making a Decent Return', *UK CEED Bulletin* 46 (November–December, 1994); Noble, 'Investing with Principle'; Charles Jacob, 'Ethical Investment: From Birth to Puberty', *UKSIF Events Reports* (January, 1997).

This of course has to be set in the context of a unit trust sector managing over £40 billion in 1994.[45] In brief, however, this innovative, theologically-informed financial instrument has spread from the churches to major institutions like the Co-operative Bank which under Terry Thomas, later Lord Thomas of Macclesfield, in 1992 adopted a wide-ranging ethical policy.[46]

REINFORCING KEY BUSINESS VALUES

Behind educational influences, enterprising individuals, trust networks, and reformed business systems lay Nonconformist values. However we define these, they were all developed by exposure to a Bible-informed faith centred on the founder of Christianity. Leaf through the biography of any convinced Nonconformist and you will almost inevitably find the youthful influence of Bible, of Sunday School, of chapel, of a point of commitment to Christ. In adulthood there followed the experience of learning and accumulating religious knowledge, through Sunday School teaching, lay preaching, or acting as chapel organist. We cannot precisely measure the impact of this culture. Opponents would say that it nurtured narrow outlooks and heavy guilt complexes; sympathizers, that it brought a fuller awareness of the human condition, hope for redemption, transcendent accountability. Whether George Eliot's Adam Bede or William Hale White's Mr Snale the draper was the truer model, we cannot tell. Particular values were certainly emphasized by Nonconformists. Distinguishing them from wider Christian values is not easy, perhaps impossible. Indeed, within Nonconformity, some denominations emphasized values which other Nonconformists did not. The selection of allegedly distinctive Nonconformist values offered here is therefore subjective.

Writing in the *Methodist Recorder* in 1934 shortly after Methodist Union and against a background of global economic depression and national economic slump, the Reverend Ernest Barrett, MA (Leeds) offered a full-page piece under the title 'Can a Business-Man Be a Good Christian?'.[47] He made some perceptive remarks on this question, drawing on three years' experience as Primitive Methodist, and then Methodist, General Book Steward (managing director of the Church's publishing house).

He distinguished between business morality, what he called 'prudence-morality'—'the morality of keeping contracts...even when not written',

---

45   *Annual Abstract of Statistics* (1996), Table 17.20.

46   Sparkes, *Ethical Investor*, pp. 149-55.

47   *Methodist Recorder* 5 July 1934, p. 15. For Ernest Barrett (1872–1955) see *Methodist WW 1910*; *WW Methodism 1933*; *Minutes of the Methodist Conference* (1957), p. 179; Frank Cumbers, *The Book Room: The Story of the Methodist Publishing House and Epworth Press* (London: Epworth Press, 1956), pp. 26 and 106.

and Christian morality. The latter was superior because 'Christian morality transcends not only business but every part of man's complex worldly interests'. The 'rough and tumble of the crowded market-place' was where Christian principles were tested.' 'The real danger which confronts the Christian in business is that of ceasing the struggle and accepting the lower standard of life—of becoming a business-man and nothing more. It is the peril of losing the loftier ideal and being satisfied with the commonly accepted level of unsanctified commercial life. Many succumb. That is the tragedy.'

Thus, Christians in business in the 1930s could be expected to subject their business norms to the higher standards of the Christian moral code. In doing so they would seek consistency across all areas of their life. Though he did not explicitly advocate a Christian Socialist position, the timing of Barrett's article may have been significant. It appeared in the *Methodist Recorder* of 5 July 1934, less than two weeks before the Methodist Conference met and, among many other issues, considered adopting the 'Declaration of the Methodist Church on a Christian View of Industry in Relation to the Social Order'. So, Barrett's article may have been intended to reduce capitalist opposition to a leftish resolution inspired by the socialist-sympathizing bureaucrats in the Methodist Church's Temperance and Social Welfare Department.[48] Whatever the circumstances, Barrett offered an ideal for Christians in business command.

Second, having won the battle to remove most of their legal disabilities in the nineteenth century, Nonconformists preserved a high respect for the law and their rights under the law. The Primitive Methodist solicitor Edmund Charles Rawlings wrote a standard work on their legal rights, *The Free Churchman's Legal Handbook: Including a Summary of Laws Particularly Relating to Social Questions* (London: National Council of the Evangelical Free Churches, 1902). In it he covered not only rites of passage, charities, ministers, street preaching, and Sunday observance, but also liquor licensing, prostitution, gambling, cruelty to children, the poor law, education, the franchise, and slander and libel, all as they affected Nonconformists. Law, and the property rights it upholds, is of course fundamental to the effective functioning of capitalist society.

Some reflection of the regard Nonconformists had for the law is seen in their memberships of Parliament, the magistracy, and city, county, urban district, and parish councils. Up to the 1930s the *Methodist Recorder* printed lists of 'Methodist Lord Mayors and Mayors for the Coming Year'.[49] Of thirty-one businessmen who were Vice-Presidents of the Primitive Methodist Church between 1900 and 1932, sixteen were JPs

---

48   Jeremy, *Capitalists and Christians*, pp. 176-78.
49   For example, *Methodist Recorder* 8 November 1934.

and a further six were aldermen, mayors, or councillors. While this may be interpreted as part of the middle class hegemony in a class-structured society, it nevertheless chimes with the historic Nonconformist concern for minority legal rights. But that was not all. Nonconformists respected a law higher than that enacted by Parliament. Hence their passive resistance to the 1902 Education Act or their protests against South African apartheid.

Despite their ideals, Nonconformists had no monopoly on righteousness or on righteous causes. Were those in business any more, or less, honest than Anglicans, or Catholics, or co-operative or trade union officials? That sort of study of ethical business behaviour has yet to be written. Meantime, we can be reminded of the most spectacular cases among Nonconformist business figures who fell by the wayside. In 1900 Jabez Spencer Balfour, former building society executive and property developer, former mayor of Croydon, former MP for Burnley, and a Congregationalist, was languishing in Parkhurst Prison, having been extradited from Argentina whence he fled in 1892. His crimes included forgery and conspiracy to obtain money by false pretences from the Liberator Building Society (established 1868) which had made many loans for house and chapel building in Nonconformist and temperance circles before crashing in 1892 leaving nearly 12,000 shareholders with losses, a tenth of them widows and spinsters.[50] Harold Morland, brilliant mathematician, partner in Price Waterhouse the accountants, and a devout Quaker was implicated with Lord Kylsant in the collapse of the huge Royal Mail shipping business in 1931. Kylsant, who was convicted of issuing misleading accounts and a false prospectus, went to prison for twelve months. Morland, who escaped that fate because he had a better defence counsel than Kylsant, retired under a cloud.[51] In the 1960s John Poulson, architect and property developer, raised as a Methodist and educated at Woodhouse Grove School, abandoned his spiritual inheritance and spread a web of bribery and corruption among politicians, civil servants, and local government officials, mostly in North East Labour-controlled authorities. He went to prison.[52]

These were examples of gross misconduct. Until unbridled mammon took hold of the City in the 1980s, it is likely that the generality of business people felt obliged to live honourably. Barrett, the Methodist Church's publishing executive, was probably right when he observed in

50   Esmond J. Cleary, 'Jabez Spencer Balfour', *DBB* I, pp. 129-34.

51   Edwin Green and Michael Moss, *A Business of National Importance: The Royal Mail Shipping Group, 1902–1937* (London: Methuen, 1982); Edgar Jones, *True and Fair: A History of Price Waterhouse* (London: Hamish Hamilton, 1995).

52   John Poulson, *The Price: The Autobiography of John Poulson, Architect* (London: Michael Joseph, 1981); Alan Doig, *Corruption and Misconduct in Contemporary British Politics* (Harmondsworth: Penguin, 1984).

the 1930s, 'The typical businessman may be as keen as a razor, he may drive a bargain sharply, but he is on the whole as clean as he is keen. He lives up to the standard morality of his profession or business-circle, delivers the goods, and pays his way. If he goes under, it is usually because he is caught in a network of adverse circumstances from which his most strenuous struggles cannot extricate him. It is rarely folly, and still more rarely anything discreditable, which brings him down. Rotters there are, one must admit, but the unfortunate men who are genuinely the victims of circumstances must not be classed with them.'[53] There were such victims among Nonconformists. Sir Joseph Pease, head of the great North East Quaker dynasty and family conglomerate, was unwittingly pulled down into insolvency in 1902. In a measure, which would scarcely be repeated later in the twentieth century, the local Quaker Monthly Meeting investigated Sir Joseph's culpability and exonerated him.[54]

Third, almost by definition, Nonconformists have displayed independence of mind and spirit. In their quaint speech (and earlier their dress), the Quakers maintained a distinctly independent lifestyle which had teeth when pitted against issues such as the slavery detected in the cocoa plantations supplying Cadbury, Rowntree, and Fry in the 1900s;[55] or labour relations between the wars, as seen above.[56] This independence of spirit was not confined to the Quakers. For example, the Primitive Methodists, quietly or vigorously, maintained their rights. Thus Alderman Adam Adams, grocer of Lowestoft and the century's first Vice-President of the Primitive Methodist Connexion, insisted on using his Nonconformist chapel, rather than the parish church, for civic worship during his two mayoral terms.[57] Of Councillor Albert Shaw JP, mineral water manufacturer of Cradley Heath, Staffordshire, another Primitive Methodist Vice-President, it was reported in the denominational press in 1916, 'he wrested a seat on the Staffordshire County Council from a brewer when the odds were tremendous, and in this capacity, amongst lords and squires, is the match of the acutest in many a controversy, even his enemies acknowledging his skill and prowess.'[58]

---

53   *Methodist Recorder* 5 July 1934.

54   Maurice W. Kirby, *Men of Business and Politics: The Rise and Fall of the Quaker Pease Dynasty of North-East England, 1700–1943* (London: George Allen & Unwin, 1984); *idem*, 'The Failure of a Quaker Business Dynasty: The Peases of Darlington, 1830–1902', in Jeremy (ed.), *Business and Religion in Britain*, p. 158.

55   Jeremy, *Capitalists and Christians*, pp. 145-52.

56   T.A.B. Corley, 'How Quakers Coped with Business Success: Quaker Industrialists, 1860–1914', in Jeremy (ed), *Business and Religion*, pp. 164-87, isolates the following characteristics of Friends in business: individualistic; diligent; democratic; conflict-avoiding.

57   *Primitive Methodist Leader* 14 June 1900, p. 381.

58   *Primitive Methodist Leader* 22 June 1916, p. 388.

Nonconformists, being a minority, exhibited the psyche of the outsider, the underdog, the person habituated to doing things differently, the individual alert to threats (and opportunities). It is tempting to believe that in business this made Nonconformists more entrepreneurial, more innovative. It may have done, but all kinds of other minorities not subscribing to the Protestant ethic or theology have had a similar experience. So this, the Weberian hypothesis, remains tantalisingly attractive but not wholly convincing.[59]

Independent of spirit Nonconformists may have been. Over a single career and over generations, however, they were not immune from worldliness. We know about Quaker lapses among Quaker businessmen. Some stayed 'plain'; some became 'worldly' (with private pleasures turning deeply held faith into a comfortable, hereditary loyalty, in some cases to the detriment of their workforces); some resigned, in pursuit of social status and political power.[60]

Something akin to the gentrification phenomenon affected belief and churchgoing.[61] As business success allowed them to move up the social scale, Nonconformists moved up the respectability scale of churchgoing, sometimes crossing the great divide and becoming members of the Anglican Church. With this came a more relaxed view of wealth and work. Examples from my business elites of 1907 and 1935 offer anecdotal glimpses of both the frugal, industrious founder and the spendthrift inheritor. In the 1907 elite William Carnelly, chairman of John Rylands & Sons, and a Wesleyan who wrote two books about the Bible, in fifty years never took a full week's holiday from work. He retired just before his ninety-fourth birthday, dying shortly afterwards.[62] David Davies, 1st Baron Davies of Llandinam, chairman of the Ocean Coal Co founded by his grandfather, was a benefactor of the Calvinistic Methodists (Presbyterians).[63] Under recreations, his *Who's Who* entry read 'much interested in sport, including hunting, and has foxhounds at Llandinam'. Another inheritor, this time in the 1935 elite, was John William Beaumont Pease (later 1st Baron Wardington), chairman of Lloyds Bank, who came from a North East Quaker dynasty. Educated at Marlborough and Oxford, Pease had no known Quaker connections in

59   See David J. Jeremy, 'Introduction', and W.D. Rubinstein, 'The Weber Thesis, Ethnic Minorities, and British Entrepreneurship', in Jeremy (ed.), *Religion, Business and Wealth*, pp. 170-81.

60   Corley, 'How Quakers Coped with Business Success', pp. 164-87.

61   For a summary of which see David J. Jeremy, *A Business History of Britain, 1900–1990s* (Oxford: Oxford University Press, 1998), pp. 501-503.

62   *Manchester Guardian* 27 July 1916.

63   *The Times* 17 June 1944.

adult life and, rather than as a banker, was 'probably better known to the general public as an amateur golfer'.[64]

The Debit Side of Nonconformists in Business

Lest the impression is given that Nonconformists in business had an unblemished record in pursuing these Christian ideals, legal rectitude, and independent mindedness, mention must be made of several episodes where Nonconformist employers fell below the expectations set before them.

In contrast to the Quaker employers, Methodist business leaders declined the opportunity to engage in collective, theologically-grounded debate about business policy or business ethics. Only two of Methodism's big businessmen were on the denomination's Temperance and Social Welfare Committee who at the 1934 conference secured the passage of a 'Declaration...on a Christian View of Industry in Relation to the Social Order', drafted by Henry Carter, a former Wesleyan minister of Christian Socialist convictions. Those two were Sir Luke Thompson MP, member of a Sunderland firm of coal merchants, and Lord Rochester (Ernest Henry Lamb), retired transport contractor, National Labour MP, and Paymaster General in Ramsay MacDonald's coalition government. Lords Wakefield and Marshall, the Ranks, father and son, Stamp, and Bellman were all conspicuous by their absence from this attempt to subordinate business and industry to theology and ethics—a position established a decade earlier by the interdenominational Conference on Christian Politics, Economics and Citizenship (COPEC), under the leadership of William Temple (then Bishop of Manchester). The idea that 'industry ought therefore to be an instrument for establishing the Kingdom of God on earth' evidently threatened Methodist magnates. Anything smacking of socialism certainly offended Sir Robert Perks, the most venerable capitalist in the counsels of 1920s Wesleyan Methodism.[65]

If the new professional managers, including an eminent Nonconformist like Josiah Stamp, were moving the boundaries of religion outside the firm, William Lever, before the First World War at any rate, was busy utilizing the agencies of religion inside the firm for his own ends. The social commentator, William Lionel George, who investigated Port Sunlight in 1909, concluded, 'It is not too much to say that at Port Sunlight Mr W.H. Lever's ideal "to socialize and Christianize business

---

64   Kirby, *Men of Business and Politics*, pp. 121-22 and 125.
65   Jeremy, *Capitalists and Christians*, pp. 62-65, 176, 186-88.

relations" has been attained'.[66] Elsewhere,[67] I have presented the evidence to show that Lever (in what turned out to be a rearguard strategy) pursued every opportunity to use religious devices to shape the shared values, the group culture, of the inhabitants of his company village at Port Sunlight, on the Wirral side of the Mersey, during the two decades before 1914. Ensuring the corporate virtues of loyalty, conformity, teamwork, punctuality, diligence, as much as the personal virtues of self-discipline, cleanliness, respect for authority, became his goal.

He cut a master-stroke in 1900 when he appointed a Wesleyan Methodist clergyman with Christian Socialist sympathies as the first minister to the village and welfare officer to the company—the tactic was not unique for that year Rowntree's recruited a Congregational minister as welfare officer for their boy employees.[68] Lever failed. His company church attracted less than ten per cent of the adult population of Port Sunlight into church membership. Eventually he came to pin more faith in freemasonry, his second ideological strategy for securing managerial trust and loyalty.

In retrospect the most reprehensible of twentieth-century Nonconformist enterprises may have been a family firm of Rochdale Methodists, the Turners. For decades, they and their successors generated and preserved a culture of denial to conceal the occupational hazards of asbestos manufacture, which they pioneered in the late nineteenth century. Despite the medical confirmations of links between asbestos and lung disease, clearly established between the 1920s and the 1960s (asbestosis, causal link published in 1927; lung cancer, link published in 1955; and mesothelioma, link published in 1960), the company persisted in their cover-up and in badly compensating victims and their families. This story has now been told and the scandal exposed.[69]

How could these Nonconformist employers reconcile the Christian ethic of the good neighbour with the emerging evidence of the harm their business was causing their employees? Other eminent businessmen in Rochdale besides the Turners were Methodists, like Sir James Edward Jones, a Manchester merchant who also worshipped at the Turners' Baillie Street Chapel, and Sir James Duckworth, business associate of Jesse Boot. In this company the Turners would imaginably have been careful to conform to the high moral code of sectarian Methodism. Indeed the

---

66   W.L. George, *Labour and Housing at Port Sunlight* (London: Alston Rivers, 1909), p. 185.

67   David J. Jeremy, 'The Enlightened Paternalist in Action: William Hesketh Lever at Port Sunlight before 1914', *Business History* 33.1 (January, 1991), pp. 58-81.

68   This was D.S. Crichton. See Robert Fitzgerald, *Rowntree and the Marketing Revolution, 1862–1969* (Cambridge: Cambridge University Press, 1995) p. 225.

69   Geoffrey Tweedale, *Magic Mineral to Killer Dust: Turner & Newall and the Asbestos Hazard* (Oxford: Oxford University Press, 2000).

second Sir Samuel Turner, perhaps a less pious individual than his father and uncles, in 1932 acknowledged that the issue was 'a moral issue, the health of the workers'.[70] I have argued, with no direct evidence, that the Turners' stance of denial was rooted in their faith and paternalism: it was unthinkable that 'the springs of their wealth were poisoned' and all they could do was engage in denial.[71] But other extenuating arguments might be advanced, at least for the early years when knowledge of the problem was scanty: given the dominant norms in early twentieth-century industrial society, asbestos seemed no worse than cotton; the Turners and their fellow directors compartmentalized religion and ethics from economics and business; employment of the many seemed worth the sacrifice of the health of the few, especially in depression years; ill health in the long term seemed an acceptable trade-off for employment and higher wages in the short term.

Business in the Nonconformist Denominations: Quantitative Measures

How pervasive was the influence of business in Nonconformity in the twentieth century? Again, quantitative and qualitative impressions may be offered, beginning with the former—estimates of numbers and proportions.

Clive Field's estimates of the occupational profile of Methodist local preachers in 1934 have already been cited. So, shortly after Methodist Union, perhaps as many as one in five local preachers was a business proprietor or manager. Of its kind, *The Methodist Local Preachers' Who's Who 1934* is unfortunately a unique source. Therefore other ways to measure business influence in the life of the churches have to be found. Local and regional studies offer one means. In his work on south London, Jeffrey Cox noticed the roles of business patrons in local churches: the Spicers, paper merchants, among the Congregationalists; the Higgs, builders, among the Baptists; and Sir Henry Tate, sugar refiner, a Unitarian who moved to the Congregationalists. Tate was an example of mobility between Nonconformist denominations. His second wife diverted him from the Unitarian cause and into the pews at Brixton Independent Church where he could enjoy a much more eloquent, though still liberal, pulpit prince, the Reverend Bernard Snell. However, Cox sees his businessmen merely as bounteous brethren, having little influence after the turn of the century, and the impact of religion on the

---

70   Tweedale, *Magic Mineral*, p. 31.
71   Jeremy, 'Corporate Responses', p. 264.

businesses of these important entrepreneurs is beyond his interest.[72] Simon Green's study of religion in Halifax and Keighley, ending in 1920, is concerned with collective behavioural trends within the life of the churches, rather than the roles of lay individuals and the interplay of personalities.[73] In fact we need serious local studies, which will examine business and religion from both sides of the fence.

Here we are forced to return to national lay leaderships in Nonconformity. It must be emphasized that the result is confined to the apex of these major religious structures and social institutions. To get at lay (including business) leaders in Nonconformity I have used two familiar historical sampling methods: the cross-sectional; and the longitudinal. For cross-sectional views of national lay leaderships I have chosen four benchmark dates: 1907, 1935, 1955, and 2000. Data for the first three, which derive from business sources,[74] were assembled a decade ago.[75] For the fourth I did a postal survey of (national) council members of the Methodist Church, the United Reformed Church, and the Baptist Union. The results are baldly stated in Table 4.

As can be seen, by the objective measure of membership of the Institute of Directors (or in 2000, being a director), the Wesleyan Methodists in 1907 and the Methodists in 1935 and 2000 had the consistently highest business involvements, at 37-39 per cent in each of those three years. Then came the Baptists (21, 18, and 46 per cent), followed by the Congregationalists (16 and 11 per cent in 1907 and 1935 respectively, and 29 per cent in 2000). Noticeably, for all three denominations, their proportions of company directors sharply dipped in 1955. Presumably this was not unrelated to the presence of the nationalized industries and the eclipsing of entrepreneurialism in the century's middle decades. The pattern, perhaps, suggests, on the one hand, a greater supply of entrepreneurial men (relatively few women) in business in the first half of the century and at century's end, than in the 1945–79 period. On the other hand, it may indicate appropriate responsiveness by the churches to the country's changing economic and business conditions.

For a longitudinal method, I have identified all the holders of the highest lay office in Methodism, the Vice-Presidency. Before union in 1932 only the Primitive Methodist Connexion had such an office. From 1932 the Conference of the Methodist Church annually elected a Vice-President to be for a year 'the first layman of the Methodist Church', as

---

72   Jeffrey Cox, *The English Churches in a Secular Society: Lambeth, 1870–1930* (New York: Oxford University Press, 1982), pp. 116-20.

73   Simon J.D. Green, *Religion in the Age of Decline: Organisation and Experience in Industrial Yorkshire, 1870–1920* (Cambridge: Cambridge University Press, 1996).

74   Namely the Censuses of Production.

75   Jeremy, *Capitalists and Christians*, pp. 295-393.

headmaster George Dymond told Lloyd's underwriter Edmund Lamplough when passing the Vice-Presidency to the latter at Conference in July 1935.[76] In juxtaposing Primitive Methodists and post-1932 Methodists there is one distorting distinction. The Primitive Methodists were a lay-dominated denomination while the Methodist Church, in which Wesleyans outnumbered the rest by 10:7, was much more clerically-controlled.[77] Furthermore, after the First World War, Britain's wealth-based class society, with its broad distinctions between the landed, capitalist, and working classes, was beginning to give way to what Harold Perkin has called 'the triumph of the professional ideal'.[78] That triumph tarried until after 1945. By then, certainly, professionalism, resting on career hierarchies, trained expertise, and the notion of service, was in the ascendant.

So, after 1932 we might expect to see some weakening of the links between church lay leadership and capitalist enterprise, and the office of Methodist Vice-President to move into more professional domains. That is, not only would the office be rotated through the Church's constituent connexions (Wesleyan, Primitive, United Methodist), but also a wider social mix would be tapped when electing to the Vice-Presidency. Did this happen?

In a hundred and one years (1900–2000 inclusive) there have been 102 slots for Vice-President, there being two holders (Primitive Methodist and Methodist) in 1932. I have been able to identify the occupations of all but one of the thirty-three Primitive Methodist and all of the sixty-nine Methodist holders of the office. It may be noted that three individuals were elected to the office both before and after 1932: James Gray, Moses Bourne, and A. Victor Murray. For the purposes of analysis I double count each of these since it is office holders rather than individuals that are considered in this aggregation.

Findings emerge as follows. Under the Primitive Methodist Conference 91 per cent of their Vice-Presidents came from business backgrounds. Twenty of these thirty-three men were proprietors, i.e. they owned their firms. Only two were identified as directors of a limited company, though of course many of the proprietors may have been directors as well as owners of their businesses. Four were managers. As for the industries they spanned, Table 5 shows that a third were engaged in manufacturing

76   *Methodist Recorder* 18 July 1935, p. 4.

77   See, for example, remarks in Kenneth D. Brown, *A Social History of the Nonconformist Ministry in England and Wales, 1800–1930* (Oxford: Clarendon Press, 1988), pp. 143-54. For a contemporary statistical statement, see W.A. Sturdy, *Methodist Finance: Past, Present and Future* (London: Epworth Press, 1932), p. 66. This is very close to the figure in Currie, Gilbert and Horsley, *Churches and Churchgoers*, p. 143.

78   Harold Perkin, *The Rise of Professional Society: England since 1880* (London: Routledge, 1989).

and nearly 50 per cent were in services (including one solicitor). In short, Primitive Methodists consistently recognized the successful businessmen who emerged in their midst. Or, from a more sceptical viewpoint, the lay leadership of the Primitive Methodists was consistently captured by capitalists.

In aggregate, a different picture of the business people elected to the Vice-Presidency emerges under the Conference of the Methodist Church, from 1932 until 2000. First, the business group radically shrinks from 91 per cent to 45 per cent. The manufacturers plummet to 12 per cent, the distributive trades people collapse to 6 per cent, and there is a movement from financial services to professional services (mostly solicitors). Outside the business group, school teachers, academics, medical practitioners, and, more recently, social workers, and non-ministerial church-related employees emerge to reflect the triumph of professionalism.

Two quantitative questions remain. Was the Primitive Methodist experience untypical of Methodism or, more broadly, Nonconformity as a whole? Second, when did the shift from capitalists to professionals among Nonconformity's lay leaders take place?

The benchmark studies, cited earlier, suggest that lay leadership in the major Methodist denomination, the Wesleyans, at the beginning of the twentieth century was equally, if not more, rooted in the capitalist class of the day. In 1907 some seventy-six Wesleyan laymen (no women) held 31 per cent of their Connexion's 1,671 national committee posts. Of these seventy-six men, 70 per cent (53) were in business. If the six legal professionals are included the proportion rises to 78 per cent.[79] This does not sound as high as the Primitive Methodists' involvement in business but it is a benchmark, not a flow of election results. The chances are that the Wesleyans would also have elected as their Vice-President one of their business figures. The manipulative doyen of the Wesleyan business network, Robert Perks (made a baronet in 1908), would have seen to that.

When did the shift in the Methodist Vice-Presidency from capitalists to professionals occur? The 1932–2000 record of office-holders' backgrounds indicates fairly precisely when this happened. Between 1932 and 1950, in nineteen years, fourteen businessmen held the office of Vice-President of the Methodist Church. That number of business people was not accumulated in the Methodist Vice-Presidency again until 1997, a passage of forty-eight years. So the swing from plutocrats to professionals begins in 1950 when the first of four professionals consecutively became 'first layman (person) of the Methodist Church'.

---

79   Jeremy, *Capitalists and Christians*, pp. 295-306; *idem*, 'Late-Victorian and Edwardian Methodist Businessmen and Wealth', in Jeremy (ed.), *Religion, Business and Wealth*, ch. 4.

As for other Nonconformist denominations, the comparable longitudinal evidence is more difficult to assess because clergy and laity competed to hold the figurehead office, or it was closed to the laity, or such an office did not exist. The Congregational Union's highest office open to lay people was chairman of the Union. Annually elected, they could be either a minister or a layman. In the seventy-three years before the Congregationalists merged with the Presbyterian Church in 1972, only fifteen lay people held the office. Of these, four had business backgrounds: Sir J. Compton-Rickett, coal company chairman; Sir Arthur Haworth, cotton merchant; John Claxton Meggitt, timber importer; and Angus Watson, fish processor. Since 1972 the highest office in the United Reformed Church has been that of Moderator of the General Assembly. In the period 1972–2000 only four lay people have held the office, one man and three married ladies, three certainly not in business, one unknown.

The Baptist Union had a similar arrangement. Their record in choosing lay people was similar to the Congregationalists': twenty-six lay persons in 101 years. Sixteen of the twenty-six were elected in the first half of the twentieth century. Of the sixteen, twelve were in business. Two (Herbert Marnham and John Chown) were London stockbrokers. Two (Henry Ernest Wood and Robert Wilson Black, father of Sir Cyril) were London property dealers. One (James Seymour Price) was a London insurance company general manager; and one (Arthur Newton) was Chief Financial Officer of the Metropolitan Water Board. Alfred Ellis, a London solicitor of Ellis & Co., acted for the early Soviet Russian government in London. From outside London came (Sir) George White, Norwich shoe manufacturer; Sir George Watson Macalpine, Accrington colliery and brickworks owner; Thomas Stubbs Penny, a Taunton timber merchant; and Arthur Robert Doggart, Darlington drapery store chain owner; and Harry Langford Taylor, director of E.S.&A. Robinson, the Bristol paper manufacturers.

Casting the net wider than figureheads, I have been able to survey the current lay leaderships of the Methodist, URC and Baptist churches, capturing some idea of their occupational compositions. Good response rates mean that we can have confidence in these data. The salient findings, in Table 6, are that about half the lay leaders of the Methodist Church and the Baptist Union have or have had some experience of business. In the United Reformed Church under 20 per cent were in this category. By century's end the mainline Nonconformist churches were tapping into the growing pool of retired people, with about 40 per cent of all three denominational councils coming from this source.

In addition, because of the Methodists' greater transparency, it was possible to perform a geodemographic analysis of their postcodes. This showed a very significant bias towards high-income families (29 per cent of lay leaders, compared to 9.9 per cent nationally). There were lesser biases in lay leaders' residential patterns towards the accommodation of 'stylish singles' and country dwellers.[80] Some 38 per cent lived in London and the South East, a higher proportion than the general population (30.4 per cent) in this region.

Business People in the Life of the Nonconformist Churches

Within the connexional structures of Methodism, businessmen with wealth emerged as denominational strategists at the beginning of the twentieth century. Sir Robert Perks, solicitor and railway company director and Liberal politician, among the Wesleyans, and Sir William Hartley, Liverpool jam maker, among the Primitive Methodists, were the most striking examples. Their schemes, their pump-priming munificence, their tireless campaigning were not only inspirational but crucial for denominational development. Church headquarters, ministerial training colleges, denominational periodicals, to say nothing of their critical commercial eye on the conduct of home and foreign missions (which they liberally funded), all served to improve the effectiveness of church bureaucracy, the education of the ministry, the strength of connexional identity. This, in sociological terms, transformed sects into denominations.[81]

The successors of the pre-1914 generation remained institutionally invaluable between the wars when Perks's scheme for Methodist Union at last reached fruition. Union in 1932 imposed two enormous challenges. One was to achieve organizational integration. The other was to merge the diverse ecclesiastical cultural traditions of the three constituents, the Wesleyan, the Primitive, and the United Methodist Churches.

Simplified, the organizational challenge was to integrate the financial and property resources of the three churches and the legal instruments on which they were based.[82] At the local church level, trustees were responsible for church buildings and leaders for raising money for pooling in circuit finances to pay circuit ministers. Trust income came from pew rents and anniversaries, circuit leaders' funds from class ticket money and non-hypothecated collections. Communion collections were dedicated to the Poor Fund. By the 1920s here and there an all-in

---

80   I am most grateful to John Byrom, graduate student in Manchester Metropolitan University Business School, for subjecting my postcode data to geodemographic analysis using a MOSAIC package.

81   David Martin, *Sociology of English Religion* (London: Heinemann, 1967). For notice of headquarters formation, see Jeremy (ed.), *Business and Religion in Britain*, pp. 11-12, and for Perks's activities, see Jeremy, *Capitalists and Christians*, pp. 314-24.

82   Sturdy, *Methodist Finance*.

envelope system was replacing the traditional forms of fund raising. Complementing this was circuit assessment by which local churches paid proportionate sums for the support of circuit ministers, who now totalled around 3,500. All of this needed to be brought under a uniform system of finances, a common financial structure and practice.[83]

The major task at the national level was to merge the three groups of connexional funds (nine Wesleyan, eight Primitive, and nine United). These paid for the training and retirement support of ministers, for new church building schemes, and for home and foreign missions. Financial, legal, and managerial skills were clearly required and here the Methodist Conference naturally turned to experienced men from the business world.

Sir Josiah Stamp was appointed chairman of the Finance Board: with his experience of integrating subsidiaries of Nobel Industries a decade earlier, there could hardly be a more appropriate person inside or outside the Methodist Church. He was supported by William Arthur Sturdy, a civil servant and auditor of the Indian Home Accounts, and also Leslie Farrow, a London School of Economics graduate, accountant, and in 1935 director of twenty companies.[84] The board's task, however, was neither easy nor quickly done. The conference of 1932 gave them five years in which to complete their work. In 1935 Stamp was thanking circuit officials for returning 'his troublesome schedules and enquiries' but he hoped next year to have a 'comprehensive view of the changes and movements in financial strength from year to year.' Clearly he was seeking some sort of moving average which would permit the kind of financial forecasting familiar to company accountants. In addition, not only had they to find out the details of current practice but also they had to consolidate the contributions to three sets of connexional funds to assessments and collections across the country into one set.[85]

The Methodist Church in the 1930s was much indebted to people in business for skills needed to effect organizational and financial merger, not just at the top but also down at circuit and local church levels. Their story has yet to be told. Despite the obligations they incurred, businessmen at the top of the Methodist Church were not as popular as their contributions might suggest. This becomes evident if we examine the voting patterns for elections for the Vice-President of the Methodist

---

83   In 1932 at the local church level there were over 16,000 trusts (15,000 for chapels, the rest for manses). Trust income amounted to over £2.1 million on properties valued at £36.7 million in 1914. Debt on these properties was just over £2.1 million. Jeremy, *Capitalists and Christians*, p. 347, quoting the *Minutes of the Uniting Conference* which differs slightly from Sturdy, *Methodist Finance*, p. 66.

84   Jeremy, *Capitalists and Christians*, pp. 339, 342, 346.

85   *Methodist Recorder* 25 July 1935, p. 4; *Minutes of the Methodist Conference 1935*, pp. 73-78.

Church in the 1930s. Held at the beginning of the Representative (as opposed to the Ministerial) Session of Conference each July, these elections also reveal who among the Methodist Church's laity was willing to stand and how to some extent the problem of melding the three church cultures was approached at the national leadership level of the post-union Church.

In summer 1932 when the three Methodist Conferences (Wesleyan, Primitive, and United) met separately for the last time they voted for the first President and Vice-President of the new Methodist Church.[86] About the choice of first Vice-President, a layman of the Methodist Church 'designated by ballot without nomination and by a clear majority of the votes cast at the preceding Conference',[87] there was no doubt. All three Methodist conferences in summer 1932 were 'unanimous in acclaiming Sir Robert Perks as the mastermind of the movement [for unity]' and elected him as their first Vice-President.[88] The old Wesleyan campaigner, then in his eighty-fourth year, was well-known in early twentieth-century Methodism for his legal and political skills, sharpened in railway property rights work and in the House of Commons, as well as at the Wesleyan Conference. The Uniting Conference hailed him as one who 'has always pleaded for the rights and privileges of laymen... He is as capable in the committee room as in the Conference. He has often been invaluable to our Committee of Privileges, and has always placed at its disposal his unique knowledge of those legal technicalities and precedents which must be observed if chaos is to be avoided. That knowledge is encyclopaedic.'[89]

While the selection of Vice-President for the first year was clear-cut, a unanimous choice was never made again in the 1930s. Indeed, in all but one year the election for Methodist Vice-President went to a second ballot. Some interesting features emerge if we look at all the candidates, whose names were put into the ballot for the Vice-Presidency from 1932 until 1939 inclusive, excluding Perks. In these eight years thirty-two men's names were presented. For every one of them we know their occupation and their pre-1932 Methodist affiliation. We also know the votes they attracted in first and second ballots. From this information we can make some deductions about businessmen in Nonconformity in the 1930s.

---

86   The election for President, always a Methodist minister, was contested in the Wesleyan Conference, where it went to a second ballot between the Revd Dr John Scott Lidgett, CH, and the Revd Frederick Luke Wiseman, both ageing giants of the Wesleyan pulpit. Scott Lidgett won. *Methodist Recorder* 21 July 1932, p. 21.

87   Methodist Church, Standing Orders, recorded in *Minutes of the Annual Conference of the Methodist Church* (1935), p. 250.

88   *Methodist Recorder* 15 September 1932, p. 17.

89   *Methodist Recorder* 15 September 1932, p. 17.

As noted earlier, the 1930s was still the heyday of businessmen in Methodist leadership. Of the thirty-two Vice-Presidential candidates, twenty-eight were businessmen: fifteen in manufacturing and the rest in services (including three solicitors). All twenty-eight were proprietors, partners, directors, or senior managers. Many indeed were national figures: Sir Harold Bellman, of the Abbey Road Building Society; Sir Charles Bird, chemical manufacturer of Cardiff; Isaac Foot, Plymouth solicitor, Liberal MP for Bodkin, and short-stay member of Ramsay MacDonald's second National government; Sir Henry Lunn, travel company founder; Sir Harold Mackintosh, toffee manufacturer; Joseph Rank, the miller, and his son J. Arthur Rank, not yet synonymous with films; Lord Rochester (Ernest Henry Lamb), transport contractor, National Labour MP, and Paymaster General in Ramsay MacDonald's two coalition governments of 1931–35; and Sir Josiah Stamp. Only four of the thirty-two candidates were not in business: George Diamond, Plymouth headmaster; Victor Murray, academic; Arthur Richards, evangelist; and W. Sydney Walton, journalist. So, seven out of eight candidates for the Vice-Presidency of the Methodist Conference in the 1930s were businessmen. With the background of the Thirties Depression, cynics might well conclude that the respectable end of the Nonconformist spectrum had been captured by capitalism.

Voting patterns show that it was not quite like that. Not one of the great and the good, except Isaac Foot, was elected to the office of Methodist Vice-President in the 1930s. Of these rejected national public figures, Bird averaged most, 102 votes in three ballots, which was still not very high since the whole conference of 450 ministers and 450 lay persons could vote.[90] Poor Stamp: his name went forward every year from 1934 to 1938 but until 1937 he collected no more than eighty-two votes in any one ballot. In 1937 he gained 173 votes but this pitched down to fifteen in the first ballot the following year. Joseph Rank the miller, probably the greatest benefactor of Methodism (who gave over £3.5 million to Methodist causes between 1922 and his death in 1943 alone[91]) received an ignominious eleven votes in 1936 and his son, J. Arthur Rank, a similarly humiliating twenty-six votes in 1938. Lord Rochester, the National Labour politician, mustered no more than an average of twenty-one votes in the three ballots his name was entered, 1934–39.

These humbling results compared to the 1,028 votes cast for Moses Bourne in two ballots which took him to the Vice-Presidency in 1933, or the 1,355 votes in six ballots for Isaac Foot, which culminated in the second ballot of 1936 when, against three returning contenders, he

---

90   Methodist Church, Standing Orders, recorded in *Minutes of the Annual Conference of the Methodist Church* (1935), pp. 247-50.

91   Jeremy, *Capitalists and Christians*, pp. 348-52.

secured an overwhelming 607 votes. How can the unpopularity of the really big business figures be explained?

One consideration in the minds of delegates must have been a concern to uphold some sort of balance between the three former Methodist bodies, the Wesleyan, the Primitive, and the United Methodist Churches. Preserving this would establish a leadership example so important for helping to create a new, shared, post-union Methodist culture.

On the whole, representativeness seems to have been achieved through the 1930s. In nine years, the former Wesleyans provided five Vice-Presidents, the former Primitive Methodists three, and the former United Methodists one. The members of the three churches at union in round figures had been 500,000 Wesleyan to 200,000 Primitive, to 141,000 United Methodists.[92] The ratio of 5:3:1 is reasonably close to 5:2:1.4. The former Primitives benefited most, but not by much. Eighteen of the thirty-two names put up for balloting between 1932 and 1939 were former Wesleyans. Of these eighteen, seventeen were businessmen, including all the big capitalists. Voting in the interests of harmony may help to explain why they were largely rejected.

Political considerations may well have entered voting preferences at Methodist conferences in the 1930s when economic depression polarized party political differences. If, as the 1934 adoption of the Methodist Declaration on a 'Christian View of Industry in Relation to the Social Order' hinted, conference was going to the Left, it was not surprising that capitalist businessmen and National Labour members of the coalition government were out of favour. On the other hand, it was perhaps surprising that the conference forgot the backing Lord Rochester gave to that resolution.[93]

Clearly there was the relative attractiveness of the winners, compared to the losers, in the Vice-Presidency elections. Moses Bourne, Methodist Vice-President after Perks, was in his sixties and widely known as a Primitive Methodist layman. Secretary and commercial manager of the Moira Colliery Co. and the Donington Sanitary Pipe & Fire Brick Co., he was consistently recalled as a preacher, least of all a commercial man. In 1912 the *Primitive Methodist Magazine* profiled him as 'one of our stalwarts', distantly related to Hugh Bourne, one of the founders of Primitive Methodism. Then in his forties, 'To Moses Bourne preaching is a supreme delight. He preaches because he must preach... When men and women are being converted Moses lives in a heaven of delight.'[94] His obituary in the *Methodist Recorder* in 1941 recalled this characteristic: 'A man of dignity, both in bearing and address, Mr Bourne commanded

92   Sturdy, *Methodist Finance*, p. 66.
93   Jeremy, *Capitalists and Christians*, pp. 179-80.
94   *Primitive Methodist Magazine* (1912), p. 551.

a polished and weighty style of utterance. He took his preaching very seriously, regarding the call as the chief purpose of his life.' Though a coal master, he was in a relatively safe coal region where unemployment was lowest in the industry in the 1920s.[95] His companies were not large and Bourne was not one of the tyrants of the industry. In 1926, 'immediately before the great coal strike, he preached to a congregation composed chiefly of miners and asked them to pray for him during his year in office [as Primitive Methodist Vice-President]. The pledge was at once given'.[96] Nor was Bourne one of the seriously big capitalists. He left just over £17,000 when he died in 1941: not much compared to the £164,000 estate of Lord Stamp, who died the previous month in an air-raid; or the Rank family's millions.[97]

Very different was Edmund Sykes Lamplough. He and his brother Williamson (and their three sisters) were well known benefactors of Wesleyan Methodism. One time shipowner and for more than fifty years an underwriter in Lloyd's the insurance market, where he rose to be deputy chairman, Lamplough was given a rather vague and effusive profile by Leslie F. Church when he was elected Vice-President in 1935. His obituary in 1940 is a little more informative. At Sunfields Methodist Church, Blackheath, where he spent much of his life, he was circuit steward and organist. A bachelor, he was 'married to his Church'. His great generosity was directed into the support of the Methodist Overseas Missionary Department and the Ministerial Training Fund, and their Wesleyan predecessors. He was a founder of the Laymen's Missionary Movement. His hobbies included collecting stamps and logbooks and Wesleyana. During his year in office he was instrumental in installing a statue of John Wesley in the forecourt of the New Room, Bristol. 'A man of winsome personality, gentle in speech and conduct, successful in business but mainly occupied with the "things which belong to the Spirit", Mr Lamplough presented to the world a Christian character known and esteemed by all men. He "walked with God" even during the busiest hours of his well-ordered life.'[98]

Compared to Bourne and Lamplough, Joseph Rank was a difficult character. His sympathetic biographer described him as 'dictatorial' and, within his business, 'apt to make inordinate demands.'[99] He was much

---

95   Barry Supple, *The History of the British Coal Industry: Volume 4. 1913–1946: The Political Economy of Decline* (Oxford: Clarendon Press, 1987), pp. 180-81.

96   *Methodist Recorder* 8 May 1941, p. 4.

97   *Leicester Evening Mail* 5 September 1941, p. 6 (my thanks to Mr Aubrey W. Stevenson of Leicester Record Office, for this reference); Michael Bywater, 'Josiah Charles Stamp', *DBB*.

98   *Methodist Recorder* 18 July 1935, pp. 3, 4, 19; 24 October 1940, p. 7.

99   R.G. Burnett, *Through the Mill: The Life of Joseph Rank* (London: Epworth Press, 1945), p. 192.

the same in the Methodist Church. Stupendously generous with his millions, he required as much frugality in the deployment of his wealth as he had exercised in its creation. In his eighties he bluntly told the Secretary of the Methodist Chapel Committee, 'I have seen too much money wasted in Methodism. I have had to work hard all my life and to deny myself of many things so that I might be in a position to do good, and I do not agree with wasting money to carry out the views of some people who do not mind how much they spend so long as they do not have to provide the money.'[100]

If Rank did not endear himself to the fraternity of ministers, Stamp would also have been problematic as Vice-President. A rapid speaker with a prodigious output, he was simply too busy. Bellman, his friend, recalls how he spent his time travelling around the LMS Railway network in his chairman's coach, dashing from one stationmaster's meeting to another.[101] In 1937, when Stamp's name topped the first conference ballot for Methodist Vice-President, with 173 votes, he withdrew because it was 'quite impossible for him to take the position at the present time.'[102] Other particularities might have precluded specific individuals. Sir Walter Essex, for example, wallpaper manufacturer and former United Methodist, was known as an opponent of Methodist union.[103] Without a lot more detailed work, we cannot wholly explain why the Methodist conferences of the 1930s rejected the men of capital who had served them so well.

Since the Second World War the involvement of business people in Nonconformity has been rather more muted than earlier. Major changes in society, church, and business arrived with force. The searing experience of depression in the 1930s swung the country to the Left in 1945. In the Methodist Church this strengthened the position of ministerial leftwingers, especially of those in the Temperance and Social Welfare Department set up in 1933 just after union.[104] While temperance was the abiding focus, as it had been in its three predecessor departments, its remit was all manner of social questions. The relation of industry to

---

100 Quotation, cited in Jeremy, *Capitalists and Christians*, p. 349, is from the correspondence of the Joseph Rank Benevolent Fund, the John Rylands University Library, Manchester. His generosity increased after 1933, when he converted his business into a public company with a capital of £7.295 million and thereafter set up his Benevolent Fund.

101 Bellman, *Cornish Cockney*, p. 223.

102 *Methodist Recorder* 22 July 1937, p. 7.

103 *Methodist Recorder* 2 October 1941, p. 7.

104 Men such as the Reverends Henry Carter and E.C. Urwin, and their mentor Samuel Keeble. For a good survey of the Methodist Church's social witness, see George Thompson Brake, *Policy and Politics in British Methodism, 1932–1982* (London: Edsall, 1984), pp. 433-579.

the social order figured among them. The left-wing declaration of 1934 stated 'Industry ought therefore to be an instrument for establishing the Kingdom of God on earth.'[105]

As seen, big business opinion voiced by the Methodist Sir Josiah Stamp, adhered to the political economy of Adam Smith: the market best ruled commercial organizations; religion, the individual's heart and mind. Stamp's view was widely accepted in the business community. Proprietors of their own businesses could pick and choose but self-interest suggested that religion be separate from trade, as bank managers taught. Moreover, industrial concentration and its separation of ownership and control meant that shareholders demanded maximum profits, undiluted by charitable giving: the antithesis of the Methodists' 1934 Christian view of industry in which 'Service for the common good must be a dominant motive'.[106] The growing corporate hierarchies of professional managers, responsible to shareholders, would have found it difficult to agree with the Methodist Conference when it called for 'the admission of workers to a larger share in responsibility for and direction of industry'.[107]

Executives in the new post-1945 nationalized industries might have agreed in theory but by the 1960s they too were having to concern themselves with financial targets.[108] Between the 1940s and the 1960s many Nonconformist princes of purse-strings and pulpit passed from the scene. In an era of state control of industry, J. Arthur Rank, now in films as well as flour milling, belonged to an increasingly rare species, the Nonconformist magnate. Nationalization and its new ethos of management as service diminished the pool of big entrepreneurs.

Post-war, faith ebbed. Old standards and values in British society began collapsing in the 1960s when rising standards of living heralded an unprecedented consumer society. Faith was marginalized more perhaps than ever, in sharp contrast to the USA. While the Methodist Department of Christian Citizenship, the new name adopted in 1950, issued and proclaimed its declarations on alcohol, peace, gambling, use of leisure, sex and marriage, its message on one occasion at least was compromised by a business baron of the past. Harold, now Baron Mackintosh, who had done so much in promoting wartime National Savings, scandalized many fellow Methodists and upholders of the Protestant work ethic in 1956 by supporting the introduction of Premium Bonds.[109] Ecumenism across the

---

105 Methodist Church, *Declarations of Conference on Social Questions* (London: Methodist Church, 1959), p. 25.

106 Methodist Church, *Declarations of Conference on Social Questions*, p. 25.

107 Methodist Church, *Declarations of Conference on Social Questions*, p. 33.

108 Jeremy, *Business History of Britain*, p. 139.

109 Harold Mackintosh, *By Faith and Work: The Autobiography of the Rt Hon the First Viscount Mackintosh of Halifax* (London: Hutchinson, 1966), pp. 132-38.

Established–Nonconformist churches dividing line also helped to broaden, and perhaps weaken, Nonconformity's Puritan social standards on issues like drink.

After three-and-a-half decades of the dominance of state-run industries, the business climate changed once more. In 1979 Mrs Thatcher, daughter of a Methodist grocer, and the Conservatives were returned to government. Entrepreneurship was in again. People in business were back. But now they operated without the kind of ethical code which had previously restrained modern business behaviour. The culture of London's capital markets, following Big Bang in 1986, saw golden handshakes, annual bonuses, and raw competitive aggression displace the old, albeit cosy, code of gentlemanly honour. Law and regulation were therefore applied to achieve equitable markets. Despite this, huge financial scandals in the 1980s and 1990s left pensioners and savers nigh destitute and Lloyd's names impoverished and suicidal. More broadly, the gulfs between rich and poor, and between London and the South East and the rest of the country have widened. On the other hand it has been argued that in the enterprise society of the last two decades business has become more socially responsible.[110] Where were Nonconformist business people in all this?

The end of the century is too close for a definitive appraisal. The impression I have is that, in contrast to the 1930s, few heads of large firms (by employment measure) are involved in Nonconformity, or any other church. Brian Souter, head of Stagecoach Holdings Ltd, which employed nearly 22,000 in 1998 and just gets into the UK's top hundred employers, is highly exceptional. However, his business is based in Perth and he cannot be considered here.

Perhaps the Methodists, the largest mainline Nonconformist denomination, offer the most challenging examples of business people on the national church scene. We have already noted the impact of Conference and Methodist investment managers in pioneering ethical investments. On another front, earlier, and following the Church of England, the Revd William Gowland, a factory chaplain in the 1940s and 1950s, realized his vision of founding an industrial college. It opened at Luton in 1957, as a department of the Methodist Home Missions Department, offering courses for shop-stewards, managers, youth, clergy, and others. Lord Rank (J. Arthur) and Rank family trusts funded £30,000 of the £45,000 of new buildings.[111] By 1976 over 10,000 people had attended courses at Luton Industrial College. Gowland retired as Principal

---

110 M. Marinetto, 'The Historical Development of Business Philanthropy: Social Responsibility in the New Corporate Economy', *Business History* 41.4 (October, 1999), pp. 1-20.

111 David Gowland and Stuart Roebuck, *Never Call Retreat: A Biography of Bill Gowland* (London: Chester House Publications, 1990), p. 137.

in 1987 and died in 1991. The Methodist Conference in 1996 decided to close the college, not least because of the post-1990 explosion in higher education.[112]

Then there is the work of Methodist Homes. Founded by the Revd Walter Hall in 1943, Methodist Homes for the Aged, a charity responsible to the Methodist Conference, opened its first residential home in 1945. With the elderly proportion of the population (aged 65 and over) in England and Wales rising from 4.7 per cent in 1901 to 9.2 per cent in 1939 and 15 per cent in 1981,[113] the needs of the elderly mushroomed. By 1998 Methodist Homes managed thirty-eight residential homes. A shift in activity occurred when in 1976 (with thirty-four homes open) it was decided to develop sheltered accommodation: a response to the increasing numbers of retired people able to manage largely by themselves, but encountering the frailties of old age. Methodist Homes Housing Association was formed for this purpose and by 1998 thirty-three sheltered housing developments were functioning. Special care homes, one offering nursing care and five dementia care, were added between 1989 and 1998 and 'live at home' schemes were started in 1987, with thirty-one in operation in 1997. Open to all on the basis of need, Methodist Homes were highly popular among Methodists, who of course were long familiar with their work.

State regulation and competition from the private sector complicated the challenges of managing the expansion and new initiatives of Methodist Homes, not least the move of headquarters from London to Derby in 1990. For much of the period when the major policy changes occurred, the Chief Executive of Methodist Homes was David Wigley. He joined them in 1982 after leaving Procter & Gamble in the USA, having earlier been director of product development at that multinational's Italian subsidiary. His managerial skills, especially organizational and HRM skills, were essential to the smooth running of Methodist Homes which in 1997 was the equivalent of a medium sized firm, with a staff of over a thousand and a budget of £20 million.[114] The pattern of its recent developments indicates that Methodist Homes were making policies appropriate to changing market conditions.

Perhaps too much attention has been paid to the Methodists. They, however, have been the largest, most socially concerned, and most

---

112   E.H. Lurkings, 'The Origins, Context, and Ideology of Industrial Mission, 1875–1975' (PhD thesis, University of London, 1981), pp. 201-202; Gowland and Roebuck, *Never Call Retreat,* pp. 154, 168; *Methodist Recorder* 30 May 1991, 20 June 1996.

113   Halsey (ed.), *British Social Trends,* p. 106.

114   All information in the preceding two paragraphs, unless otherwise footnoted, comes from David Wigley, *The Person, Not the Problem* (Derby: Methodist Homes for the Aged, 1997).

transparent Nonconformist denomination. A few words must be added about the activities of two other outstanding business figures on the Nonconformist scene.

Although he saw himself primarily as a non-sectarian evangelical Christian, John (later Sir John) Laing, founder of the eponymous building and civil engineering firm and a leader among the Brethren, must surely be mentioned in any survey of twentieth-century Nonconformity and business.[115] A veritable dynamo, who needed only four hours sleep[116] and who daily divided his twenty waking hours between church work and business,[117] Laing was instrumental in organizing and building the London Bible College. In this his associate was the much less well-known Philip Henman, a Baptist minister's son and the self-made entrepreneur behind the Transport Development Group.[118] Laing was also one of a group of wealthy laymen who sponsored the Billy Graham Crusade of 1954.[119] In all this he was following in the steps of men like Perks and Hartley who could see that evangelism was properly complemented by a trained ministry.

Conclusion

So, what in twentieth-century England and Wales, has Nonconformity contributed to business and what have business people contributed to the Nonconformist churches? First, the limits of coverage must be noted. I have written too much about Methodists and nothing about business and religion in Wales. The latter is complicated by the migration of Welsh entrepreneurs to London and Liverpool, Bristol, and Birmingham, and the steel districts, in search of opportunities and fortunes. It demands another study to complement E.T. Davies, *Religion in the Industrial Revolution in South Wales* (Cardiff: University of Wales Press, 1965). Furthermore, this paper has not touched the subject at regional and local levels, nor, at any level, the old and new charismatic groups and sects.

One finding, hardly unexpected, is that the century seems to break into two halves with respect to Nonconformity and business. Before 1950 when Methodism still had around three-quarters of a million members,[120] about the same as in 1900, business and a few big business people sat in the highest councils of the mainline Nonconformist denominations. In

---

115 Roy Coad, *Laing: The Biography of Sir John W. Laing CBE* (London: Hodder & Stoughton, 1979).

116 Information from Mr Ernest C. Uren, interviewed 14 July 1980.

117 Coad, *Laing*, pp. 117, 131.

118 David J. Jeremy, 'Philip Sydney Henman', *DBB* III, pp. 158-64.

119 Jeremy, *Capitalists and Christians*, pp. 397-410.

120 Halsey (ed.), *British Social Trends*, p. 524.

the second half of the century they were increasingly conspicuous by their absence. This shift, it would seem, was related to broader economic and social changes, not least the replacement of a class society with a professional one. After 1945 socialist-sympathizing Nonconformist ministers and bureaucrats, as much as trade unionists, wanted a voice in the workplaces and boardrooms of big business. Outside the nationalized industries, entrepreneurs and executives were usually anxious to keep the door closed, especially the one leading into the boardroom.

Nonconformist contributions to the twentieth-century capitalist system have been multiple. Nonconformist churches contributed to the education of generations of business people in the first half of the century, through their Sunday Schools especially, imbuing them with biblical knowledge, the Protestant ethic of work and responsible individualism, and literacy and public speaking skills. Nonconformist chapels produced outstanding individuals in business, like Josiah Stamp or J. Arthur Rank or John Laing. They provided extensive institutional bases for networks of trust in business. They offered challenges and alternatives to components of the prevailing business system, like profit sharing, industrial democracy or ethical investment. They contributed values derived from the Bible, stressing the importance of law, and prizing independence of mind and spirit. Yet some of their boldest entrepreneurs created business arrangements which cramped independence of mind and ruined employee health. The record is mixed.

In the other direction Nonconformists in business played a crucial role in the life of their churches. In the language of the sociologist, until the late-nineteenth century most Nonconformist groupings were still sects, lacking national bureaucracies, headquarters, and professional educational institutions. The financial, legal, and organizational underpinning for these centralized institutions helped to transform sects into denominations. Rich men, invariably in business, provided the resources necessary for this shift. Ironically, by their very efficiency the resultant bureaucratic organizations, as Weber predicted, tended to stifle the individualism, enthusiasm, and self-reliance essential to growth, and in the secular sphere, entrepreneurship.[121] Reliance on a few wealthy individuals hazarded a dependency which was likewise stultifying for the larger body of the local or national church. Hartley's example, and that of John Mackintosh the Halifax toffee manufacturer and New Connexion Methodist,[122] suggest that rich men were keenly aware of the danger.

So, at every level, from national to local, Nonconformists of wealth and community standing gave their money, time, managerial and financial

---

121 H.H. Gerth and C. Wright Mills (eds), *From Max Weber: Essays in Sociology* (London: Routledge, 1948), ch. 8.

122 David J. Jeremy, 'Chapel in a Business Career: The Case of John Mackintosh (1868–1920)', in Jeremy (ed.), *Business and Religion in Britain*, pp. 95-117.

knowledge and skill, political influence, and beyond their business competencies, their musical talent, their public speaking and preaching abilities to their churches. These resources were keenly needed by the denominations down to the 1930s when they were preoccupied with declining growth rates, the organization of national institutional structures, and schemes for merger. To reverse sagging growth rates, Wesleyan businessmen backed the central halls; the Ranks mobilized funds for church extensions. To develop national structures, Perks drove forward the Twentieth Century Fund and raised a million guineas, a quarter of which was used to build Westminster Central Hall, London, the Wesleyans' headquarters. In Primitive Methodism, Hartley was Perks's counterpart. To secure merger of the Methodist denominations, Perks campaigned long and hard; Stamp and other businessmen implemented organizational, financial, and legal aspects of union. With much less publicity, professional managers, who after 1950 succeeded the men of capital in the Nonconformist denominations, faced the continuing problems of shrinking and ageing congregations. They, and the Nonconformist charitable foundations established earlier in the century, directed their efforts at improving financial investments, introducing the churches to the new means of mass communication like film, providing church-linked accommodation for the elderly: generally striving to make the church more responsive to the changing needs of late twentieth-century society while relating those needs to the unchanging Christian gospel. On the conservative evangelical wing John Laing backed the Billy Graham Crusades.

In terms of church teaching about business and faith, Stamp's 1930s view, that individuals not systems are capable of being redeemed, has remained one orthodoxy among Nonconformist industrialists on the Right of the political spectrum. On the other hand, both church and business bureaucrats in mainline Nonconformist denominations, as well as some academics, followed the lead of the Methodist 1934 declaration on industry and the social order (which in turn reflected an earlier Christian Socialist influence among Anglican Churchmen running from F.D. Maurice through to William Temple).[123] The subject needs proper

---

123 In the 1960s H.F.R. (now Sir Frederick) Catherwood, a leader in the small Fellowship of Independent Evangelical Churches, who had moved from the Conservatives to Labour, placed most faith in the new National Economic Development Council, a tripartite forum between government, business and unions, rather than any firm-level structural solutions. The hierarchical managerial corporation he saw as the 'necessary way of organizing large-scale enterprise among fallible men'. By the mid-1970s he was accepting the need for worker directors. H.F.R. Catherwood, *The Christian in Industrial Society* (London: Tyndale Press, 1964), pp. 35, 37, 101; *idem, A Better Way: The Case for a Christian Social Order* (Leicester: Inter-Varsity Press, 1975), p. 122. His endeavours to improve industrial relations at a national strategic level continued with

study. What is certain is that the Thatcher years have made many Christians, Nonconformists among them, very dissatisfied with the pure market economics encapsulated in Milton Friedman's famous phrase, 'the social responsibility of business is to increase its profits'.

There were debits to the close relationship between Nonconformity and business in the first half of the century. By unintentionally fostering a climate of dependence on the economic resources of a tiny minority, business people with wealth and power might diminish the commitment of the mass of church laity. Another defect perhaps: compared to their Catholic and Anglican counterparts, Nonconformist business leaders were not great patrons of the arts in religion. Lever seems to have been exceptional in this respect. Perhaps this was hardly surprising given their Puritan heritage. Three other questions come to mind. Did Rank's involvement in films and Lord Mackintosh's in Premium Bonds have any impact on ethical standards? What efforts have Nonconformist businessmen made to bring women into senior management and achieve greater gender equality? What have Nonconformist entrepreneurs and managers done to train and invest in business people in the immigrant black churches?

Whether Nonconformity or business benefited more from their symbiotic relationship is a question beyond measurement. I maintain my former view that 'at leadership levels, the impact of business on the churches has on balance been more substantial than the impact of the churches on business'.[124]

---

his chairmanship of the British Institute of Management. More radical, but rather isolated, was the evangelical Anglican George Goyder whose wide view of stakeholding inspired Bader. See Jonathan Boswell and James Peters, *Capitalism in Contention: Business Leaders and Political Economy in Modern Britain* (Cambridge: Cambridge University Press, 1997).

124   Jeremy, *Capitalists and Christians*, p. 418.

Table 1
Religious links of schools attended by chairmen and managing directors of the hundred largest firms in the UK, 1907, 1935, 1955 and 1998

	1907	1935	1955	1998
Baptist				
chairmen		1		
md				
Congregational				
chairmen	2			
md	2			
Methodist				
chairmen	1	1	3	1
md	1	3	1	1
Quaker				
chairmen	1	2	1	1
md	2	1	1	
Others				
chairmen	2			
md				
TOTAL	11	8	6	3
chairmen	100	100	100	100
md	101	103	116	100
Total in cohort	201	203	216	200
Known cases	142	115	153	110
Nonconformist share of known cases	8%	7%	4%	2.7%

Sources:
Jeremy, *Capitalists and Christians*, pp. 80-83; Financial Times Information (comp.), *The Times 1000, 1998* (London: Times Books, 1998); *Who's Who, 1998.*

Table 2
Adult religious links of chairmen and managing directors of the hundred largest firms in the UK, 1907, 1935, 1955 and 1998

	1907	1935	1955	1998
Baptist				
chairmen		2		
md				
Brethren				
chairmen			1	
md			1	
Congregational				
chairmen	4	1	1	
md	3	1		
Methodist				
chairmen		1	2	
md	1	3	2	
Quaker				
chairmen	3	2	1	
md	1	1	1	
Unitarian				
chairmen	2			
md		1		
Others				
chairmen			2	
md		1	1	
TOTAL	14	13	12	
Total in cohort	100	100	100	
chairmen	101	103	116	
md	201	203	216	
Known cases	145	171	160	N/A
Nonconformist share of known cases	9.7%	7.6%	7.5%	

Source:
Jeremy, *Capitalists and Christians*, p. 111.

Table 3
Sunday School scholars, 1900–1960

	1900	1910	1930	1960
Wesleyan	967,046	980,165	763,075	
Primitive	460,632	470,839	368,782	
United	311,188	309,649	224,767	
Methodist Church				587,276
Congregationalists	687,068	697,509	512,592	201,192
Baptists	525,136	572,686	477,929	259,742
Presbyterians	81,078	86,394	55,283	30,125
Quakers				
Presbyterian Church of Wales	177,172	187,024	145,294	62,641
Nonconformity	3,209,320	3,304,266	2,547,722	1,140,976
Church of England	2,302,000	2,437,000	1,802,000	1,039,000
Total in Sunday School	5,511,320	5,741,266	4,349,722	2,179,976
Nonconformist share	58%	58%	59%	52%

Population (census years) England and Wales

	1900	1910	1930	1960
5 to 9	3,487	3,697	3,323	3,262
10 to 14	3,342	3,500	3,207	3,725
15 to 19	3,246	3,337	3,435	3,201
Total	10,075,100	10,533,100	9,964,400	10,188,200
Proportion in Sunday School	55%	55%	44%	21%

Sources:
Currie, Gilbert and Horsley, *Churches and Churchgoers*, pp. 175-92; Mitchell, *British Historical Statistics*, p. 15.

Table 4
Business people among the core lay leaders in the Nonconformist denominations: percentages of company directors (and absolute figures)

	1907	1935	1955	2000 (5)
Methodists				
Wesleyan (1)	38.2 (29/76)			
Primitive (1)	23.1 (3/13)			
United Methodist Free Churches (3)	33.3 (3/9)			
Methodist New Connexion (2)	33.3 (3/9)			
Bible Christians (3)	0 (0/3)			
Methodist Church (1) for 1935 and 1955; (4) for 2000		37.2 (16/43)	17.4 (4/23)	38.8 (71/183) [278]
Congregational Union (4)	15.8 (27/171)	11.2 (19/169)	1.4 (3/217)	
United Reformed Church (4)				29.2 (7/24) [29]
Baptist Union (4)	21.3 (10/47)	18.2 (12/66)	8.6 (5/58)	46 (13/28) [81]
Quakers (1)	3.2 (1/31)	16.7 (4/24)		

Notes:
(1) Key lay leaders are defined as holders of 5 or more national committee posts.

(2) Key lay leaders are defined as holders of 4 or more national committee posts.

(3) Key lay leaders are defined as holders of 3 or more national committee posts.

(4) Key lay leaders are defined as members of all national committee posts.

(5) The denominator in the fractions in this column is the number of those national lay leaders responding to my lay leadership postal survey (May–June 2000). In the far right column, figures in square brackets indicate the number of lay persons on the respective denominations' councils in the year 2000.

Sources:
Jeremy, *Capitalists and Christians*, pp. 303, 324, 360; *Directory of Directors* 1907, 1935 and 1955.

Table 5

Business associations among Methodist Vice-Presidents, 1900–2000

Business backgrounds	1900–1932 (Primitive Methodists)		1932–2000 (Methodist Church)	
Primary industries	3	9%	2	3%
Manufacturing	11	33%	8	12%
Services				
Transport and communications			3	4%
Distributive trades	9	27%	4	6%
Financial services	5	15%	7	10%
Legal services	1	3%	7	10%
Miscellaneous services	1	3%		
Total in business/ ex-business		**91%**		**45%**
Non-business backgrounds				
Education			12	17%
Academia	1	3%	7	10%
Medicine			5	7%
Church	1	3%	8	12%
Miscellaneous			6	9%
Unknown	1	3%		
Total	**33**	**100%**	**69**	**100%**

Table 6

Lay leaderships in Nonconformity in 2000: Business Links

	Methodist Church	United Reformed Church	Baptist Union of Great Britain
Number of lay national committee posts	344	29	82
Number of holders of these posts	278	29	81
Known cases	183	24	47
Response rate	66%	83%	58% (1)
Number in business (current or past) (2)	101	4	25
Percentage	55%	17%	53%
Number retired (all occupations)	81	9	19
Percentage	44%	38%	40%

Sources:
Author's survey of responsive council members, April–June 2000; conducted with the support of the Revd Nigel T. Collinson, Secretary of the Conference of the Methodist Church; the Revd Anthony Burnham, General Secretary of the United Reformed Church in the United Kingdom; and Mr Philip Putman, Head of Administration and Finance, the Baptist Union of Great Britain. To these officials and to all those responding to my questionnaire I wish to express my thanks.

Note (1):
Just 29 members of the Baptist Union Council returned my questionnaire. The occupations of another 18 have been identified by Mr John Barfield, formerly of the Baptist Union Council.

Note (2):
Business is defined as having a business occupation or the holding of at least one directorship.

ACKNOWLEDGEMENTS

My thanks are due to my university for customary research supprt and to the staff of the John Rylands University Library of Manchester for facilitating my use of the Methodist Church Archives.

CHAPTER 11

Some Aspects of the History of French-Speaking Protestantism in the United Kingdom

Hugh R. Boudin

Introduction

In order to establish the limits of this paper, may I specify that I am only dealing with French-speaking Protestantism: churches (excluding the bilingual French–German Swiss Church in Endell Street, London, and the Eglise Protestante Evangélique de Bayswater, which had no refugee origin) and institutions with French Protestant connections.

Apart from the Union Chrétienne de Jeunes Gens de langue française de Londres (UCJG) and the Huguenot Lodge No. 2104 which are examined here, there exists also: La Providence, L'Hôpital pour les Pauvres François Protestants et leurs descendants résidents dans la Grande Bretagne in Rochester, Kent, with its newly opened Huguenot Museum; the French Protestant Church of London and charities connected therewith; the Huguenot Society of Great Britain and Ireland with its rich library in London; the now closed French Protestant Schools; and the Anglo-French Christian Fellowship.

L'Eglise Protestante Française de Brighton

One of the three French-speaking protestant churches still in existence today (2003) in the United Kingdom is situated in Brighton. This congregation cannot look back to an uninterrupted existence since the Reformation,[1] but presents a remarkable example of a response to meet the needs of French-speakers on the south coast of England.

---

1   The congregation experienced what might be termed an ecumenical peregrination around Brighton holding services in different venues: Queen's Road (Presbyterian Church), St Margaret's Church Hall (Church of England), Church Road (Old Presbyterian Church), Union Street (Congregational Church), Cannon Place ('Little Vic')

It has a dual origin. First in 1858, a French-speaking Congregation held services of worship in the Union Street chapel, a Frenchman from Nîmes César Pascal being called to serve there.

At about the same time an English lady Mrs E. Hayes opened her home at 18 Montpellier Villas for the embryo of a community. A local committee was formed, the Revd J.G. Gregory being president, the Revd E.L. Roxby secretary, and the Revd W. Fraser, treasurer.[2] Soon, Alphonse Gonin, a French-speaking pastor from the Lyons area was called to minister to the small congregation. This 'Mission aux Etrangers' was serving French- and German-speakers, who were then numerous in Brighton, employed as teachers or governesses. So Brighton, for a period, had the unusual privilege of having two Francophone congregations: l'Eglise Réformée Française, meeting in the Newbury Rooms and l'Eglise Protestante Française meeting in Union Street. In 1877 these two groups merged and adopted the title Eglise Protestante Réformée Française.

An increase in rent for the Newbury Rooms forced the Conseil presbytéral to plan for its own church building. In 1887 the first stone of the chapel was laid in Queensberry Mews. These historical details show how missionary zeal was vigorous in nineteenth-century Brighton to reach the foreigners residing in the town. The church had now an operating council, le Conseil presbytéral, which quite clearly adopted the structure of presbyterian government.[3]

The widow of the Revd H. Migot, Mrs Gladys E. Migot, remained in Brighton and became the pivotal element of the congregation welcoming new foreign pastors and helping them to adapt to their surroundings. She died in 1984, and the present pastor conducted her funeral.

In 1914 the Conseil presbytéral asked to contribute to a fund for Belgian refugees organized by the Roman Catholic Church of Portslade-on-Sea declined because the work was deemed 'sectarian and exclusively catholic'. Each individual was free to participate as he/she thought appropriate. The following year a collection was held by invitation of the Mayors of Brighton and Hove in favour of victims of war in France. Zeppelin incursions were taken so seriously that the Conseil insured the church building against damage by air raids.

The 1916 children's Christmas tree brought together in a joyful gathering the Sunday School pupils, the other children of the congregation, and refugee children living in the vicinity. In July 1917

---

before settling in 1887 in the present location in its own church building at Queensbury Mews, off Regency Square, near the sea front, tucked away behind the Hotel Metropole.

2   H. Migot, *The French Protestant Church of Brighton and Hove* (Brighton, 1928), p. 7.

3   The church now has the legal status of a charity, No. 1.063.644.

another collection was made for the inhabitants of reconquered regions of France.

During WWII in 1941 the French church of Southampton showed its solidarity by a gift of £25 to its sister church in Brighton. A few days later the chapel of the Holy Rood at Southampton was completely destroyed by enemy action. The Brighton pastor expressed his deepest sympathy at this wanton destruction. The war exerted a negative influence on the church's life. As a consequence of the hostilities, the Conseil met rarely: six times from 1939 to 1945. Trustees were difficult to recruit. Because of the blackout the evening service was moved from 6.30 pm to 3.15 pm, and finally amalgamated with the 11 pm morning worship. This was indeed a time of testing. Some members left Brighton for fear of bombing. Nevertheless the annual sale of work was held in 1942 and opened by Princess Despina Karadja. The amount gathered was £100 19s 2d. Unfortunately the stipend of £200 was not paid in full to the pastor. Various repairs had to be undertaken after the conflict, but no war damage could be claimed.

The difficulty of recruiting members for the Conseil presbytéral accelerated the inevitable evolution of electing female members. Mrs Gladys Migot, Miss Rickman, and Mrs Louise Thiébaud (of Bognor Regis) elder of the churches in London and Dijon joined the consistory. Rationing and food restrictions did not prevent Mrs Migot in organizing the sale of work in June 1945. In 1947, the Conseil acknowledged that its meetings were rare, but the members being dispersed there were no urgent matters to be dealt with. On the whole, apart from modified hours, services had been conducted as in peace time, but transport difficulties had much impeded regular attendance.

Soon a tradition developed: the Institut Emmaüs—a biblical training centre in the Canton de Vaud (Switzerland)—furnished a number of students who gained an opportunity of practising what they had learned by staying one year in the service of the Brighton church. A more permanent situation arose when the Revd F.J. Orna-Ornstein took over the pastoral responsibility for Brighton. In fact his parish extends beyond Brighton and Hove. He conducts the annual French Service at St Julien's Church in Southampton each year during July.[4] He also chairs the annual martyr's commemoration in Lewes at the monument, Cliffe Hill, and the Corn Exchange.[5] Being a Fellow of the Huguenot Society, he preached at the commemorative service for the Revocation of the Edict of Nantes at Soho Square in 1985. Also, in 1993, he preached in the Tercentenary Service of the Orange Street congregation in London which started life as the Huguenot congregation of Leicester Fields.

4   *Eglise Protestante Française de Brighton*, 1993, No. 1, p. 2; 1994, No. 1, p. 3.
5   *Eglise Protestante Française de Brighton*, 1996, No. 1, p. 3.

In Brighton during the Sunday service, Pastor Orna-Ornstein gives a brief talk in English. Originally a children's address, it has it become a liturgical feature for adults, because unfortunately, the number of young participants has dwindled

The French church in Brighton can be interpreted as a ministry to many single persons without family. They appreciate the warmth of a small community and have become regular attenders. Work of this kind has a value of its own. Even if the regular congregation is small, individuals or groups appear unexpectedly at Sunday services, such as a party of students from French-speaking Gabon who came to improve their English in order to teach it more efficiently in their home country. In fact the visitors impart a multinational mixture to the Brighton congregation expanding its range to other continents. A weekly French conversation group is an outreach which the church offers to those who love the French language.[6] Frequently the French church takes part in the Mid-Sussex Bible Convention at Hove, where fellowship is experienced and excellent preaching is heard.[7] The French church is affiliated to the Brighton and District Evangelical Alliance keeping in touch with several churches and Christian organizations in Brighton and Hove.[8]

In 1988 a century had elapsed since the building of the present church. The centenary was duly celebrated by the Revd Dr Marc-François Gonin, the grand-nephew of Alphonse Gonin, one of the pioneers, who travelled from south-west France to preach the commemorative sermon.[9]

On 5 May 1995, after Sunday service, the Brighton congregation travelled to Canterbury coupling attendance at the afternoon service of the French church with a tour of the cathedral and the precincts: a happy reunion of two of the French-speaking congregations of Great Britain.[10] Opportunities for fraternizing between the three churches occur when a new minister is installed in one of the congregations. The other two rally and consider it a duty to be present.[11]

6   *Eglise Protestante Française de Brighton*, 1993, Nos 3-4, pp. 2-3.
7   *Eglise Protestante Française de Brighton*, 1990, No. 1, p. 3; 1991, No. 4, p. 4; 1993, No. 1, p. 2; 1993, No. 2, p. 4; 1993, Nos 3-4, p.4; 1996, Nos 3-4, p. 4.
8   *Eglise Protestante Française de Brighton*, 1994, Nos 3-4, p. 2.
9   The Revd F. Orna-Ornstein kindly provided valuable information on the history of French-speaking Protestantism in Brighton. I am grateful for his help.
10   *Eglise Protestante Française de Brighton*, 1996, No. 2, p. 3.
11   Pastor changes, *Eglise Protestante Française de Brighton*, 1991, Nos 2-3, p. 3.

Rôle pastoral de l'Eglise Protestante Française de Brighton

César Pascal 1858–76
Merging of both French churches
Alphonse Gonin (French) 1861–d.1883
Jacques Massis (French) 1884–92
S.J. Knatz (Swiss) 1890–93
Jean-François Koeune (Belgian) 1893–d.1910[12]
Désiré J. Joye (French) 1911–d.1921[13]
Honoré Migot (French) 1921–d.1947
Several students and pastors on short stay: 1947–80
Samuel Stauffer (Swiss) 1952–53
Claude Brocqueville (French, later Swiss) Sept. 1954 - 1955[14]
Paul Petter (Swiss) 1956–57[15]
Philippe Cherix (Swiss) 1958
R. Racine (French) 1962–65
A. Bernadel (French) 1965–67
Jacques de Reland (French) 1967–68
Frank J Orna-Ornstein (British/French) 1980—current[16]

---

12   Whilst studying at the *Ecole préparatoire de l'Oratoire* in Geneva, J.-F. Koeune (4 May 1885 Chenogne in the Belgian province of Luxemburg d.1910 Brighton) formed in June 1859 with his compatriot Henri Thomas Wautier and with P. Estrabaud and J.-J. Charpiot the first international team helping military wounded in Northern Italy. This was the response of young theology students to the appeal made by Henry Dunant after the battle of Solférino. Cf. H.R. Boudin, 'Répertoire des étudiants originaires de Belgique ayant fréquenté les Ecoles préparatoire et de Théologie de l'Oratoire de Genève (1839–1919)', *Analecta Theologiæ Facultatis Bruxellensis II, 1976–1985* (Brussels: FUTP, 1987), pp. 137-38.

13   D. Joye's final dissertation to obtain his BD was entitled 'Théorie du Cardinal Newman sur le développement du dogme chrétien'.

14   C. Brocqueville (previously Brocquevielle) was a student at L'Institut Emmaüs. After his stay in Brighton, he completed his national service in the French Army in Algeria during two years, before becoming pastor of the Methodist Church in Alès (France). *Missionary Notes. The French Protestant Church of Brighton* (New Series, No. 28, 1955), p. 2.

15   P. Petter also studied at the same institute. However, before coming to Brighton, he attended a Scottish Bible School to become familiarized with English. Later, afer his marriage he toured the USA and returned to Switzerland. *Missionary Notes. The French Protestant Church of Brighton* (New Series, No. 29, 1956), p. 2.

16   F. Orna-Ornstein, though British born, lived in France until the age of seventeen. Whilst on national service, he became a committed Christian. He studied French and History at the University College of Wales, Aberystwyth. There he met his future wife Pamela Lucas, with whom he spent two years at the European Missionary Fellowship School of Biblical Studies. The couple joined this fellowship for work in Metz (France), moving later to Montauban and then to London where he served the Swiss

L'Eglise Protestante Française de Cantorbéry[17]

During the twentieth century five ministers have successively discharged pastoral duties in the cathedral crypt: Jean Reglaine Barnabas from 1898–1946; Alfred G. Tucker from 1943–49; Albert J. Garnier 1949–67; François Dubois 1975–91; and Hugh Robert Boudin from 1991–2001.

The Canterbury church has been victim of what has been called 'The Magpie Tendency'—which is simply a euphemism for theft.[18] Francis Bennett Goldney, mayor of Canterbury from 1905 till 1910, was planning a trip to the USA. Mentioning to the consistory the North American interest in antiques, he said that the church's 1632 communion cups would be a valuable asset in an exhibition to further public relations for church and city. He received two cups on loan. Months passed and no silver was returned. When challenged the mayor showed surprise. In a gesture of grand generosity he handed over instead the purported proceeds of the sale and an enamelled dish bearing his name. Nothing could have been further from the intention of the consistory than the disposal of their sacramental silver. Today the two communion cups are in the Metropolitan Museum of Art in New York as part of a bequest given in 1968 by Judge Untermeyer.

The Revd J.R. Barnabas was endowed in a large measure with showmanship. He reported to the consistory that travelling in 1906 in North America, as soon as he had crossed the Canadian–USA border, he had sent a letter to the President of the United States of America, expressing sincere thanks to the supreme authorities of the country for the kind welcome that they always extended to the Huguenots, and expressed his admiration for the high positions the descendants of the Huguenots were occupying in the public affairs of the nation. As pastor of the oldest Protestant church in the British Isles, as he modestly wrote, he thought that it was within his province to do this. A suitable reply was received from the President.

Barnabas also addressed the Huguenot Society of America about Canterbury. His appearance there was not devoid of ulterior motives, namely a financial campaign towards the building of a manse and the founding of a language college, where young continentals could be

Church before going to Brighton in 1980. Orna-Ornstein is author of *France: Forgotten Mission Field* (Watford: EMF; n.d.).

17   Miss Anne M. Oakley, Senior Research Archivist, Canterbury Cathedral, very kindly read the original text and made pertinent suggestions, for which I am very grateful indeed.

18   A. Bateman, *The Magpie Tendency* (Whitstable: A. Bateman, 1999), p. 85. This section is based on M. Peters, *The Chalices of the Church in the Crypt at Canterbury Cathedral* (Canterbury: EPFC, 1992), p. 4 .

initiated into the difficulties and idiosyncrasies of the English language. This dream never came true, although linguistic tuition is still an aspect of modern Canterbury educational life.

A modest outcome of the World Conference of Life and Work at Stockholm in 1925—one of the milestones in modern ecumenical history—was the invitation extended to the Revd Wilfred Monod of the Oratoire du Louvre in Paris to address the Canterbury cathedral congregation. George Bell, Dean of Canterbury at the time, had met him in Sweden and invited him to preach. It was the first time, since the Reformation, that a French Reformed pastor had occupied the pulpit in the nave of the cathedral, though every Sunday a French Reformed liturgy was being performed in the Black Prince's Chantry downstairs in the crypt.[19]

Apart from the regular Sunday worship and the biennial communion service, the Canterbury church held two special services every year: the Reformation Memorial Service and the Annual Youth Service.[20]

The church was keen to invite important leaders of French Protestantism, for example, the Revd Paul Conord, secretary-general of the Eglise Réformée de France.[21] Dr Marc Boegner, président de la Fédération protestante de France, was one of the star preachers.[22] Among the congregation gathered to hear him was the French Consul of Folkestone, Maurice Ducros, the mayor of Folkestone, John F. Moncrieff, and the bishop of Chichester, Dr G. Bell, with whom Boegner could renew his ecumenical friendship of old.[23]

A change in the hymns books, which can be traumatic for certain parishioners, was the passage from *Hymnes et Cantiques* to *Louange et Prière*.[24]

When John Reglaine Barnabas' mental health failed, he was certified in the hospital at Chartham. There he died aged eighty-eight on 29 July

---

19   K. Robbins, 'The Twentieth Century 1898–1994', in P. Collinson, N. Ramsey and M. Sparks (eds), *A History of Canterbury Cathedral* (Oxford: Oxford University Press, 1993), p. 311.

20   The pupils of the highest classes of secondary schools in and around Canterbury were invited to the *Assemblée de la Jeunesse* which, due to its success, was held twice annually.

21   P. Bolle, 'Conord, Paul', in André Encrevé (ed.), *Dictionnaire du Monde religieux dans la France contemporaine*. Volume 5: *Les Protestants* (Paris: Beauchesne, 1993), pp. 137-38.

22   P. Bolle, 'Boegner, Marc', in Encrevé (ed.), *Dictionnaire du Monde*, pp. 77-79.

23   A.J. van der Bent, 'George Allen Kennedy Bell 1883–1958', in I. Bria and D. Heller (eds), *Ecumenical Pilgrims: Profiles of Pioneers in Christian Reconciliation* (Geneva: World Council of Churches, 1995), pp. 32-36.

24   *Louange et Prière. Psaumes Chorals, Cantiques Répons liturgiques adoptés par les Eglises Evangéliques de France et de Belgique* (Paris-Bruxelles: Beauchesne, 1938), containing 536 items.

1947.[25] The delicate question then arose as to whether the pastor, as a Romanian dictator, was appointed for life. This had a direct financial implication. The French Episcopal Church of the Savoy Act of Parliament 1925 had on the capital of this dissolved church, granted £150 to the Canterbury pastor. Had this to be paid when there was a pastoral vacancy? Ouvry and Co., a solicitor's firm with Huguenot background, dealt with the legal aspects.[26] The outcome of this action was very satisfactory. The consistory received £900, that is six years' salary (1 January 1945–31 December 1950). The half yearly payment from the Savoy Trust was payable only to the consistory until the appointment of a pastor, when it was to be made to him.[27]

In July 1948 Albert J. Garnier from Hayes, near Bexley, was appointed pastor. He travelled down each week to take the Sunday service, whilst Alfred G. Tucker had been recognized as a lay reader on 26 July 1944.

Making the first visit of an Archbishop of Canterbury to France for 400 hundred years, Dr Michael Ramsey crossed the channel in 1967. The French Television, ORTF, capitalizing on this event, scheduled a programme about Canterbury.[28] Among the features shown were interviews with Tucker and Garnier and the French service in the Black Prince's Chapel.[29]

The future of the pastorate, and linked with it the very existence of the church, was an ongoing concern which the consistory had to face at this time. Being of advanced years and failing health, A.J. Garnier was worried about the succession. His intention was to resign as soon as a new pastor was appointed.[30] The consistory entrusted Tucker with the mandate of finding suitable candidates. Through correspondence and visits to London and Paris, he sought to ensure the necessary recruitement.[31]

---

25   The Dean of Canterbury Dr Hewlett Johnson officiated at his burial, Register of Canterbury Consistory Meetings (RCCM), p. 2.

26   RCCM, p. 13.

27   Letter of Ouvry and Co. to Hon. Sec. Eglise wallonne Huguenot (sic) Française. H. Ovenden, 9 January 1951, RCCM, p. 5.

28   'Vendredi, 1ère chaîne Georges Brassens et l'archevêque de Canterbury à "Panorama"', in *Paris-Soir* 21 April 1967. The programme was composed by Jean Lanzi and Marc Pasquette.

29   RCCM, p. 99.

30   RCCM, p. 102.

31   All enquiries having started positively, unfortunately came to nothing. Dr Samuel Jacques, a medical missionnary on the point of leaving Africa, the retired pastor of the French Reformed Church in Dieppe, Roger Dieny, a researcher in biblical archaeology, Jean Sapin, a student and A. Bernadel, a candidate first for Brighton then for Canterbury, all expressed interest, but finally declined.

Meanwhile the London church did not to leave her sister in Canterbury in the lurch. During the interregnum active laymen from London travelled to the cathedral city in order to ensure that the crypt church was not deprived of ministry and the services of worship continued. Foremost among visitors was Yves Jaulmes, a lay preacher, who many a time negotiated railway travel despite the habitual Sunday engineering works on the South East network. He rendered similar assistance to the Brighton church when no pastor was available. Without such a commitment both congregations would have withered away and disintegrated.

Pastor François Dubois presented a provisional rota of pastors for Soho and for the crypt ensuring a monthly service in Canterbury. This arrangement developed into a plan for the appointment of a second pastor in London who would also have responsibility for the Kent church. Finally Dubois found a solution. He retired from his post in London and he and his wife came to stay permanently in Canterbury and offered to take care of the church. The consistory accepted this rather unexpected proposal with great eagerness. The situation had reverted to normal with a residential pastor in the city. This arrangement lasted for sixteen years until François Dubois retired for a second time.

With the enthronment of each new Archbishop of Canterbury, the French Protestant minister is invited to take part in the procession, marking the special relationship that the See of Canterbury maintains with the Refugee Congregation.[32] This connexion goes back to the 'Lettres Patentes'granted by King Edward VI to the Strangers Churches. He created the office of Superintendent of the Foreign Congregations, which was first filled by a Polish nobleman Johannes a Lasco.[33] As time went by, the post passed to the local Anglican bishop, but not every Archbishop of Canterbury is aware of this historic responsibility. The French church is always eager to invite each successive Archbishop to preach in the Black Prince's Chantry and emphasize this link with the Anglican Church. Ecumenically this connection can take unexpected forms. The French pastor also took part in the Procession of the Canterbury Gospels, Laity and Clergy when Pope John Paul II visited Canterbury cathedral in May 1982.[34]

---

32 Liturgy: *The Inauguration of the Ministry of The Most Reverend Father in God Robert as Archbishop of Canterbury Primate of All England on the Feast of the Annunciation of the Blessed Virgin Mary at 3.00 o'clock Tuesday 25th March 1980 in the Cathedral and Metropolitical Church of Christ, Canterbury*, Canterbury, 1980, p. 6.

33 H. Jürgens, *Johannes a Lasco 1499–1560. Ein Europäer des Reformationszeitalter*, Veröffentlichungen der Johannes a-Lasco-Bibliothek (Wuppertal: Foedus, 1999).

34 Liturgy: *The Cathedral Church of Christ, A Celebration of Faith to welcome Pope John Paul II on the Eve of Pentecost, Saturday 29th 1982*, Canterbury, 1982, p. 4.

In 1991 a new pastor of the French Protestant Church was installed[35] and the continuity of its history maintained.[36] In May 1995 the church hosted the 'Xme Colloque européen des Musées Protestants'. Many of the staff of the different cathedral departments gave valuable addresses making the conference a success. Its theme being 'Le Guide, un témoin d'histoire et de foi' enabled 100 participants from Belgium, France and Germany to share in the accumulated experience in the fields of competent guiding and crowd management. This includes the deft handling of large numbers of school children all year round. The French congregation is happy to participate in the 'Open Cathedral Evening' every autumn when hundreds of visitors explore every corner of the buiding and in the yearly 'Cathedral Schools Day' which each November is not only a valuable educational experience, but also turns into an enjoyable day full of interesting things to do.[37]

Nowadays two questions frequently asked about the French church in the crypt are: 'Is the service still in French?', and 'Is it sixteenth-century French?' The answer to the first question is 'Yes!' , to the second it is 'No. Unlike some churches we do not practise any kind of liturgical archaeology. The worship is conducted in modern French, and the Bible is read in "français courant"'.[38]

Among the numerous visitors to the cathedral, some are quite astonished to find this remnant of the sixteenth century migration of religious refugees. There are those who think that this movement was exclusive to England and particularly to Kent. On the contrary, it was a demographic explosion of worldwide scale. From Gothenburg in Sweden to Drakensteyn in South Africa, from St Petersburg in Russia to Constantinople in Turkey, from Berlin in Prussia to Charleston in South Carolina, more than 650 localities have been identified where a

---

In this liturgy the Revd F. Dubois is identified as 'The Pastor of the French Church in the Crypt'.

35   Liturgy: *Installation du pasteur H.R. Boudin. Dimanche 2 février 1992 à 15 heures dans la Chapelle du Prince Noir. Cathédrale de Cantorbéry.*

36   Robbins, 'Twentieth Century 1898–1994', p. 339.

37   *Xème Colloque 'Musées Protestants' 5ème Rencontre Européenne 28 Avril au 1er Mai 1995 à Cantorbéry—Kent "Le Guide: Témoin d'Histoire et de Foi". Cette brochure a été réalisée par l'Eglise Réformée de France. Coordination nationale Témoigner & Servir en collaboration avec la Société de l'Histoire du Protestantisme français et l'Eglise Protestante Française de Cantorbéry* (Paris: ERF, 1996).

38   H.R. Boudin, 'The French Protestant Church of Canterbury...fidèle à ses origines', in *Canterbury Cathedral Chronicle 1996* No. 90 (March, 1996), pp. 20-23.

congregation of expatriates was founded at some time or other by Flemings, French, Waldensians, Walloons and English.[39]

Four groups compose the sociological make up of the church. The hard core are the families of French citizens or French-born and individuals fully aware of their Walloon or Huguenot ancestry maintaining this family tradition.[40] A second group are people interested in the French language, who want to practise it and choose to worship in the Black Prince's Chantry. The third group is composed of active Christians who know French and who are conscious of the historical and spiritual significance of the continuing refugee tradition in Canterbury. By offering their support they are eager to ensure the prolonged existence of the congregation. The fourth group are tourists and other visitors who come across the church by chance and join the service. Their origins are surprisingly far-flung: a couple with two sons from Dour in Hainaut near where Vincent van Gogh worked as an evangelist among the coal-miners, a teenager from South Africa, the grandson of the organ builder, an Australian back-packer seeking her roots, a teacher from Alsace on an exchange programme, a young Finn studying astronomy at the University of Kent. They all seem to find their way to the chapel.

The life of the Canterbury congregation flows at a regular weekly rhythm with a monthly communion service when the communicants sit around the table. The liturgical pattern is interspersed with baptisms, marriages and special services highlighting events of the Walloon or Huguenot past.

On 5 November 1995, exercising an ancient right, the first part of a service was held in the main crypt—the largest Norman crypt in England—where for centuries the refugees and their descendants had worshipped. During the course of the service, members of the consistory carried the different liturgical elements such as Bible, communion cup, flagon, orders of service, the 1561 Belgic Confession of Faith and hymn books from the crypt into the Black Prince's Chantry for the last part of the service. In a symbolic gesture the Dean, Dr John A. Simpson, handed the large key of the chapel to the pastor reconfirming its use by the French congregation since 1895 and marking the hundredth anniversary of the transfer of the French service from the main crypt adjoining.[41]

---

39   H.R. Boudin, *Le Refuge ou La Diaspora des persécutés. Liste provisoire des Eglises anglophones, flamandes, huguenotes, vaudoises et wallonnes*, 5me édition, (Canterbury: EPFC, 5th edn, 1995).

40   Typical is the Peters (previously de la Pierre) family of whom a member is presently *secrétaire consistorial*. The thrilling research for the family roots is aptly described in J. Peters, *A Family from Flanders* (London: Collins, 1985).

41   Liturgy: *Culte commémoratif du Centenaire du transfert de l'Eglise Protestante Française de Cantorbéry de la Crypte de la Cathédrale vers la Chapelle du Prince Noir 1895–1995*, Canterbury, EPFC, 1995.

In 1998 a bilingual communion service offered sacramental hospitality to a delegation of the Huguenot Society of South Carolina, travelling between London, Paris, and Amsterdam, 'Sur la route des Refuges'. Bread from Flanders and wine from the Cévennes were used to prepare the Lord's Supper, symbolizing the dual origin of the Canterbury congregation.[42]

The Canterbury church is sometimes called upon to extend its sphere of service, including Huguenot marriage in the Netherlands or Walloon baptisms in Sweden. On the same basis La Société charitable des François protestants réfugiés founded in Dublin in 1719 was eager to renew the Irish refugee tradition. On 16 May 1999 a Reformed French service was held by the Canterbury pastor at the Unitarian church at St Stephen's Green in central Dublin.[43] It was exactly 185 years since a similar worship service had been held in Ireland.[44] A congregation 150 strong was present to sing the traditional psalms of Goudimel and Marot. A CD-Rom was made of the event.

The autocephalic character of the Refugee Church, of which the Canterbury congregation is very proud, constitutes nevertheless a weakness. Having no synodical structure to fall back on, no national commission of the ministry to check academic credentials or vet the pastoral qualities of possible candidates, the independant church has to fend for itself and exercise a sort of ecclesiatical DIY.

In this respect the relations between Canterbury and the Commission des Eglises Evangéliques d'Expression Française à l'Extérieur are not satisfactory. The Fédération protestante de France is not a presbyterian church. It is rather more a conglomerate of members of very differing natures. As well as traditional Lutheran and Reformed churches, it comprises hospitals, mission to the gypsies, scouts, YMCA's, old people homes, psychiatric wards and missionary societies. Added to the problems of structure, the geography of Europe places the English Channel as a substantial barrier between the Canterbury church and the natural pastoral recruiting grounds of the French-speaking Reformed churches in France, Belgium and Switzerland.

A solution was found in article forty of the Constitution of the United Protestant Church of Belgium which stipulates that a congregation of

---

42   Liturgy: *Culte de Sainte Cène. Visite d'une délégation de la Huguenot Society of South Carolina fondée en 1885. Dimanche le 25 octobre 1998 à 15.00 heures*, Canterbury: EPFC, 1998.

43   Liturgy: *Culte réformé 16 mai 1999 15.00 heures. Dublin Eglise unitarienne, Saint Stephen's Green. Texte bilingue de la liturgie Français-Anglais. Société Charitable des François protestants réfugiés à Dublin Anno Domini 1719. The French Huguenot Fund Dublin*, Canterbury: EPFC, 1999.

44   H.R. Boudin, 'Un silence de 185 ans est rompu' in *INFO, Mensuel de l'Eglise Protestante Unie de Belgique* 6 (June, 1999), p. 13.

Belgian origin, but which for a major reason—such as those just mentioned—cannot become a full member of the UPCB, has the right to apply for the status of an affiliated member. Since 1998 the Canterbury church has been an affiliated member of the UPCB and shares in the fellowship of the French-speaking congregation of Francophone Brabant. The affiliation document was officially signed by the Revd Daniel Vanescote, President of the UPCB, the Revd Léon-Alexis Rocteur, president of the District of Francophone Brabant of the UPCB and Mr Michael H. Peters, secretary to the consistory.[45] The Belgian Embassy in London showed its interest by sending the Minister-Counsellor Francis de Sutter and a message was received from H.M. Albert II, King of the Belgians.[46]

The latest special service was held in March 2000. A strong delegation from Soho joined the Canterbury congregation in an act of thanksgiving. Flowers were laid in front of the statue of King Edward VI standing next to the main entrance of the cathedral[47] and then a service was held in the crypt to commemorate the 450th anniversary of the granting by this monarch of Letters Patent to the Church of the Strangers composed of refugees from religious persecution in the Low Countries and France.[48]

Living in the cathedral of Canterbury, the French church has been privileged to follow the progress made by the Association mondiale des Anglicans et Episcopaliens d'expression française and to witness the emerging consciousness of two million French-speaking Anglicans the world over, dispelling the incorrect assumption that Anglican invariably means English-speaking. The resulting oppurtunities for the collation of French language Anglican literature and the translation of important documents are helpful in the dissemination of knowledge.

An African outreach is the link with the Faculté de Théologie protestante de Butare in Rwanda where the Anglicans, Baptists, Methodists and Presbyterians train their ministers.

---

45 Liturgy: *Culte d'actions de grâce à l'occasion de l'affiliation de l'Eglise Protestante Française de Cantorbéry à l'Eglise Protestante Unie de Belgique-Verenigde Protestantse Kerk in België*, Canterbury: EPFC, 1999.

46 Liturgy: *Culte d'actions de grâce à l'occasion de l'affiliation de l'Eglise Protestante Française de Cantorbéry*, 25 March 2000, p. 12.

47 'Flowers for a King—Prayers for a Queen', in *BELPRO, Agence protestante d'information et de communication de l'Eglise Protestante Unie de Belgique*. Also *Belgian Events. A publication of the Embassy of Belgium in London* (May–June, 1999), p. 8.

48 Liturgy: *Ordre du Culte commémoratif célébré à l'occasion du 450ième anniversaire de l'octroi des Lettres patentes aux Eglises des Etrangers par le roi EDOUARD VI en présence d'une délégation de l'Eglise Protestante Française de Londres le samedi 25 mars 2000*, Canterbury: EPFC, 2000.

The French church in Canterbury has tried to express its mission in a triple motto: 'Fidèle à ses origines—En prise sur le présent—Ouverte vers l'avenir'.

L'Eglise Protestante Française d'Edimbourg

Two more congregations in the north of the United Kingdom gave ecclesiatical expression to the Auld Alliance: the Franco–Scots communities in Edinburgh and Glasgow.

Both had the same characteristics. Their services of worship were conducted only between October and May. This was owing to the fact that the ministers in charge were French, Belgian and Swiss theological students pursuing their studies at the local university. Like a phoenix rising from its ashes, the pastorate resurrected each autumn with a new incumbent. Without a local committee covering the interregnum these congregations would have disappeared. Both pulpits were occupied by students who later became prominent churchmen and theologians. All bear witness to the value of their study and sojourn in Scotland.

Let us mention a few: Jean de Saussure, who became pastor of the St Pierre Cathedral in Geneva and professor of Dogmatics at the Free Faculty of Theology in Lausanne, was a distinguished leader of the neo-Calvinist revival movement.

Jean G.H. Hoffmann, whose ministry in the French Church of Stockholm from 1936 to 1947 and again from 1964 to 1978 was significant especially during WWII.[49] Hoffmann was entrusted by the Revd Marc Boegner with several delicate missions, for example, to prepare the French intervention at Narvik in Norway. Preparing for the post-war period in the spring of 1944, he met William Temple, the Archbishop of Canterbury, and Dietrich Bonhoeffer at the home of the Lutheran bishop of Stockholm. He also intervened to prevent Polish and Balt refugees being handed over to the Soviets. André Philip helped in his endeavours.[50]

René Lovy, who as a military chaplain in WWI, was decorated with the *Croix de Guerre*, repeated the feat in WWII. In July 1942 with three other colleagues, he chaired a clandestine meeting of the Protestant youth

---

49   The Swedish government, which was very touchy about its neutral attitude, asked Hoffmann to minister to the crews of three Polish submarines interned in Swedish ports instead of letting Polish Roman Catholic priests do their pastoral work.

50   H. Dubief, 'Les Protestants français hors de France. La Suède', in *Les Protestants français pendant la seconde guerre mondiale: actes du Colloque de Paris, 19-21 Novembre 1992* (Paris: Société de l'histoire du protestantisme français, 1994).

leadership at Bois de la Thure near Etobon[51] in Montbéliard country, where Protestants are numerous. As they left, the youth leaders were given two typical Huguenot motto's: *Résistez* and *En Dieu mon appuy*.[52]

Other names to be mentionned are Georges Lauga,[53] André Boegner,[54] and André Monod,[55] Max Dominicé, one of the outstanding preachers from Switzerland.

In 1946 the French Church of Edinburgh launched a modest periodical, *Le Huguenot*, on the absorption of the sister church in Glasgow the subtitle *Eglise Protestante Française d'Ecosse* was added.

Amongst Edinburgh's oldest communion plates are two solid silver communion cups made in 1685—a significant date for French Protestantism—by James Penman, an established Edinburgh silversmith bearing the inscription *'Pour l'Eglise Françoise d'Edimbourg'*. After disapearing for almost a century, these cups were rediscovered in 1875 and handed over to Trinity College. In December 1949 they were entrusted to the French pastor Gérard Moscheroche. When not in use they were exhibited in the National Museum of Antiquities.[56]

On 8 May 1950, a Franco–Scots service of worship was held in the High Church of St Giles in Edinburgh using the French Reformed liturgy. Several hundred faithful sang English psalms and hymns to Huguenot tunesettings. Both ministers, the Revd Dr Warr and Pastor Moscheroche, spoke in their own language without translation. In his sermon, Moscheroche stressed that the service was not only a prestigious ceremony, but it took its significance as an act of worship directed towards God. It was possible because of a mutual recognition of brotherhood deriving from the honour paid to Almighty God our Father.[57]

---

51   Etobon became a martyred village: forty inhabitants were shot against the wall of the Protestant Church.

52   R.J. Lovy has left unpublished notes, *1939-1944. Souvenirs d'un pasteur.*

53   G. Lauga intervened in an appeal for clemency for French Protestant conscientious objectors: Jacques Martin and Philippe Vernier, in *Les Protestants*, p. 66.

54   Revd André Boegner, brother of Marc, was the Chairman of the *Fédération Protestante de France en Afrique* (Alger) which was founded at the end of 1943 in liberated North Africa. Although anti-Gaullist feeling was rampant in French North Africa after the raid on Mers-el-Kébir where thirty Protestant sailors were killed by Royal Navy gun fire A. Boegner and F. Christol corresponded in friendly terms in *Les Protestants*, pp. 555, 609 and 666.

55   André Monod was responsible for the Army Chaplain Service in Paris and for relationships with the French prisoners of war in Germany and Austria, see *Les Protestants*, p. 561.

56   'City's French congregation Gets Communion Cups Back', *Edinburgh Evening News*, 10 December 1948.

57   J.R.P., 'Ancient link with France. Edinburgh Church Congregation', *The Scotsman*, 22 January 1949.

In 1956, pastor Frank Christol from London conducted a communion service in the Chapel of the Central Office of the Church of Scotland at 121 George Street.[58]

Rôle pastoral de l'Eglise Protestante Française d'Edimbourg

Charles Freundler (Swiss), October 1914–June 1915
Henry Berthoud (Swiss), October 1915–June 1916
Frank Reymond (Swiss), October 1916–June 1917
Philippe Daulte (Swiss), October 1917–June 1918
Paul M. Hugret (Swiss), November 1919–May 1920
Marc Chalamet (Swiss), November 1920–May 1921
Eugène Ferrari (—), November 1921–May 1922
Charles Westphal (French), October 1922–May 1923
Roger Rombeau (—), October 1923–May 1924
Jean de Saussure (Swiss), October 1924–May 1925
Eric Barde (—), October 1925–May 1926
André Chatoney (Swiss), October 1926–May 1927
Max Dominice (Swiss), October 1927–May 1928
W. Benignus (French), October 1928–May 1929
Jean G.H. Hoffmann (French), October 1930–May 1931
Michel Du Pasquier (Swiss), October 1931–May 1932
Charles Ed Chassot (French), October 1937–May 1938
René Lespinasse (French), October 1938–May 1939
Vacant 1940–49
Gérard Moscheroche (—) October 1949–May 1950

L'Eglise Protestante Française de Glasgow

More than forty student-pastors served this church. The first venue was Park Parish Church Hall, Woodlands Road. The congregation amounted up to eighty and sometimes one hundred participants: a very heterogeneous group composed of French teachers, male and female; cooks; hairdressers; milliners; wine merchants; the Chancellor of the French Consulate; and even Breton sailors—an ever-changing congregation entrusted to very young ministers, who were only completing their theological studies. For most of them it was an arduous training with hard disillusions and unexpected encouragments. The presence of Scotsmen and women who remembered the historic ties

---

58   Information given by Ms Norma Armstrong, Central Library, George IV Bridge, Edinburgh, 16 January 1990. Ed/AJB/HB.

between France and Scotland gave a certain endurance to the group. First attracted by the language, they stayed on for the worship.

WWI left its aftermath. It became increasingly difficult to recover after the armistice of November 1918. The old mainstays had faded away and a younger generation was not forthcoming. The services had to be moved to St Matthews Blythewood in Bath Street. The downward trend accelerated after WWII. The congregation dwindled to an average of fifteen. The question was raised: 'Did the church still have its *raison d'être*?'. A church where each year means a new beginning. A church where the minister did not have the time to get to know each of his parishioners before he left. A church where the members themselves showed a big turnover. Was it really a church worthy of the name?

From the point of view of the student-pastor it represented an enrichment and an important part of his training. To the faithful it gave the opportunity to hear God's word in French in an international atmosphere.

However the inevitable took place in 1959, when the local committee decided upon the dissolution of the French Protestant Church of Glasgow. The last regular service was held by Revd Mr Marty.[59]

L'Eglise Protestante Française de Folkestone

Climbing the stairs to the Local Heritage Room in Folkestone Central Public Library, the visitor is confronted by a huge oil painting which covers almost a whole strair wall. It is called *'The Landing of the Belgian Refugees. August 1914'*.[60] Painted by the Italian artist Fredo Franzoni, it is reminiscent of the engravings showing Huguenot refugees landing on the Kent beach beneath the White Cliffs of Dover. It was a gift from the painter to the Folkestone Borough Council as a token of gratitude for the welcome he and his family received at the beginning of WWI.[61] The event shown is the landing of destitute Belgian refugees fleeing the German

---

59   F. Dubois, 'Il y avait une Eglise Protestante Française à Glasgow', in *Le Lien, Eglise Protestante Française de Londres*, October 1959, No. 249, pp. 4-5. This article was based on notes by M.G. Brown, the last secretary of the Glasgow Church.

60   *The Folkestone Express*, 13 September 1916.

61   The people appearing on the painting are: 1. Nurse Wilson with the two Franzoni daughters; 2. The Very Revd Monsgr C. Coote; 3. A.F. Kidson, Esq., Town Clerk; 4. Sir Stephen Penfold, Mayor of Folkestone; 5. Mr Alderman Spurgen, Deputy Mayor of Folkestone; 6. Monsieur A. Peterson, Belgian Vice-Consul; 7. Mr Alderman E.J. Bishop; 8. W.H. Routley, Esq., Borough Treasurer; 9. Dr Tyson, JP; 10. Canon Tindall, Vicar of Folkestone; 11. Dr J.C. Carlile, DD; 12. Mr Councillor T.S. Frank; 13. Chevalier Cl. van Outryye d'Ydewalle. Heritage Room, Central Library Folkestone, F WW1 82.

invasion of their country. The composite and artifical nature of the painting is immediately perceptible. All the persons of distinction such as the vicar of Folkestone, Canon Tindall, and Alderman Spurgen, Deputy Mayor of Folkestone, are standing on the quay side having turned out in all their finery. Next to the Mayor, Sir Stephen Penfold, wearing gown and chain of office, stands a uniformed gentleman sporting a rapier at his side. This is the Revd Adolphe Peterson in his apparel of Consul of the Kingdom of Belgium. This is without doubt the only instance of a Protestant minister being a member of the Belgian Consular Service. This is how it came about.[62]

Seeing the immediate and generous response of the Folkestone population towards the refugees, Peterson officially founded a Belgian Committe for Refugees on the premises of the French Protestant Church, at Victoria Grove on August 24 1914.[63] This group was to organize local good-will and coordinate individual initiatives. Its main task was to give useful addresses, find suitable lodgings, furnish travel instructions for those moving on to London. Soon it was found practical to merge with the Central Refugee Committee of the Mayor of which Peterson was also member.

Folkestone was the first port of call for the fleeing Belgians. During the first week of September 1914, 20,000 individuals landed, and during the three weeks ending October 10 1914, 54,000 refugees disembarked. The population rose to this momentous occasion and put in place an efficient organization to welcome such increasing numbers of hapless exiles. No other town in England has such an impressive record of war work as Folkestone.[64]

With a Belgian flag displayed outside, St Michael's Hall became the new headquarters for all help to the refugees. Peterson was very busy dealing with their settling in.[65] With the help of the headmaster of the

---

62   The complete story is told in H.R. Boudin, *Pastorat, consulat et espionnage. La vie insolite de Adolphe Frédéric Peterson* (Brussels: Pro Doc, 2002).

63   A. Varlez, the author of *Les Belges en Exil* (Brussels: Librairie moderne, 1917), got his information muddled when he attributed the founding of the Belgian Committee to a Huguenot Charity in London. It was, in our view, a local initiative of the French Church of Folkestone spearheaded by Peterson.

64   Carlile, *Folkestone*, p. 4.

65   An incident Peterson was confronted with was the story of Belgian children whose hands had been cut off by the Germans. A surgeon who had devized new artifical limbs was anxious to offer his services and searched in vain for some of these innocent victims. Even an 'American' promised £1,000 for any child produced with mutilated hands. Later on, this was uncovered as a ploy to discredit gruesome stories and the 'American' seemed to be none other than an alien agent. As Folkestone was not only a civilian port, but also a harbour for the passage of troops, espionage was present. Some spies mascaraded as refugees whom Peterson had to unmask. Counter-intelligence was also present. Proof of this is the security pass of a Belgian detective, Ernest Theodore H.

Grammar School, H. Froggatt, he marshalled volunteer French speaking pupils to act as guide in the town. Who said school French does not come in handy? He made provision for the changing of Belgian currency into pounds sterling, intervened to smooth over any difficulties arising from mainly language problems and different habits. He helped his compatriots, who refused to live on charity, to find work as hop-pickers and in the Kent orchards. During this busy time Peterson continued to assure the French services in Victoria Grove. He was helped by Ruben Saillens, the French evangelist, and by Pierre Blommaert, who was to become Chief Protestant Chaplain to the Belgian Armed Forces.[66]

Sir Charles Allom, representative of the London Refugee Committee, suggested to the Belgian Legation in London that it would be helpful to have an official representative in Folkestone because of the thousands of exiled nationals staying or passing through the Kentish Coast Town.[67] He ventured to propose the pastor of the local Huguenot church, Revd Adolphe Peterson. Although he had no consular training for the proposed office, he brought 'considerable gifts of insight and administrative skills and a fine quality of eloquence' to this function. Already he had proved valuable help in dealing with the influx of refugees.[68] In London, this proposal was met with a positive response and the pastor of the French-speaking church in Folkestone became Agent consulaire pour le Royaume de Belgique à Folkestone.[69]

A few months later the Home Office sent official notification of the appointment of Peterson as vice-consul to the Folkestone council asking for his recognition in that capacity. At the council meeting Councillor

Godefroid, permitting admission to the harbour installations day and night found in the Archives of the Folkestone Library. This document was validated by Captain P. Ackroyd, RN, and A. Peterson, the Belgian Consul, and marked by an identity photograph and fingerprints. File 'Belgian Refugees', Folkestone Heritage Room, Central Library, Folkestone.

66   On 15 September 1914, P. Blommaert had been recognized as the first Protestant volunteer chaplain in the Belgian army. Evacuated from Ostend he spent some time in Folkestone. Strangely enough it was A. Peterson who delivered him his temporary demobilization papers. Later he rejoined the Belgian army. H.R. Boudin, 'Aumôniers protestants militaires et civils au service des militaires, prisonniers de guerre et internés belges pendant la Guerre mondiale 1914–1918', in *Biographies Protestantes Belges* (Brussels: Pro Doc, 1990), L-21, pp. 9, 37-38.

67   Carlile, *Folkestone*, p. 24.

68   Article, 'Belgian Refugees. Many arrivals at Folkestone. Sympathy and ready help. The Money difficulty', a clipping from the *Folkestone Herald*, August 1914, East Kent Archives, Whitfield, FO/AC2/1.

69   The Belgian Consulate was situated 50 Sandgate Road, Folkestone. *Parson's Directory and Year Book, Folkestone and District, 1915*, p. 48. The staff of the Belgian Consulate comprised: Ancion; Andries; L. Beauduin, secretary: Bruyaux, treasurer, and Collinet.

Wambach, who—as elder of the French Church—had known Revd Peterson for many years and frequently worked with him, commented on this appointment saying he was well fitted for the job. The Chief Constable had been informed and the press took note. To perform his new function, Peterson had the use of an office in the town hall. When the refugees arrived in great numbers, he managed to conduct more than a hundred interviews a day with the most needy and sent out a daily average of fifty letters. Someone even said 'He was one of the discoveries of the war!'[70]

Peterson was faced with a balancing act. His consular duties had in no way to overshadow his pastoral activities, which, considering the size of his congregation, were limited in scope. Nevertheless, his new function enabled him to take part in numerous official and social events of which he would have been excluded as the minister of a small foreign church. Fortunately his wife helped him. She brought together a group of people of social influence who formed a working party to provide comforts for men at the front.

In his consular capacity, Peterson was duly present when Belgian dignitaries visited Folkestone. In September 1914, he welcomed Mesdames Aloïs Vandevyvere and Armand Hubert respectively spouse of the Minister of Finances and of the Minister of Industry and Labour who had come to confer with the refugees at the Technical Institute, one of the Folkstone buildings used as a shelter.

An exceptional event in November of the same year—a highlight in the life of Peterson—was the visit of Léopold, the Belgian Crown Prince, accompanied by his aunt Henriette, duchess of Vendôme. The royal guests visited Manor House, the Military Hospital at Shornecliffe Camp, and the Bevan Home at Sandgate, three wards for Belgian wounded.[71]

After the hectic years of the World War, the Belgian Consulate continued its work until 1926, when it was closed. Peterson's consular career seems to have come to an end.[72]

How had this all started? What had given rise to this unususal pastoral–consular combination?

At the turn of the century, the consistory of Canterbury felt called to establish mission work in a town of the Kentish coast. Should it be

---

70   Carlile, *Folkestone*, p. 24.

71   The Royal visitors were received at the Central Station by the Mayor; M. Hubert, the Belgian Minister; M.A. Peterson; Captain Brandreth Gibbs; M. Bennet Goldney, MP, and Colonel Baron van Zuylen van Nyvelt, the Belgian Town Major of Folkestone.

72   By royal decree of 21 July 1919, A. Peterson was decorated as *Chevalier de l'Ordre de Léopold*, Belgium's highest Order of Chivalry.

Folkestone or Ramsgate?[73] Canon Freemantle and Revd Emmanuel Christen (1892–95) persuaded their consistory colleagues to choose the former.[74] In 1894, the consistory allocated £10 to the pastor to cover his expenses for the services in Folkestone. Revd Eugène Burnat (1895–97) maintained this outreach at the coast with the help of a Folkestone resident C. Beauvard.[75] This active layman occasionally took the services in the Canterbury crypt when the pastor was absent.

In 1902 the Folkestone group was in need of help and asked the consistory of Canterbury for assistance.[76] The consistorial members were not moved, they even disavowed the paternity of the Folkestone nucleus and refused to extend a helping hand, although C. Beauvard had given them 'valuable assistance'.

The following year Adolphe Peterson, the son of a Reformed pastor at work in the industrial city of Seraing near Liège,[77] where he was born on 30 December 1872, came to Britain and was put in charge at Folkestone.[78]

Research in different archives has not produced many records, mere snippets of information dealing with the activities of the French-speaking church. So we still do not know how church life developed, if a consistory was operating and what financial sources were available.

Today in Victoria Grove, near Guildhall Street, the Church of the Good Shepard still stands empty covered in sheeting of corrugated metal and slowly being taken over by shrubs and weeds. Here was the site of the French-speaking services in Folkestone. What we do know is that Pastor

---

73   Minutes of the Canterbury Consistory, Register No. 3, Meeting 22 October 1892, p. 58.

74   F.W. Cross, 'History of the Walloon & Huguenot Church at Canterbury', *Proceedings of the Huguenot Society of London* 15 (1898), p. 181.

75   'Le Dimanche à six heures un quart du soir le service sera fait par M.E. Burnat, pasteur protestant à Cantorbéry', in *Pike's Folkestone, Hythe and Sandgate Directory, Blue Book 1900-1901* (Brighton: Robinson and Pike), p. 35.

76   'Notre œuvre est un peu la vôtre. Ne sont-ce pas vos pasteurs qui l'ont créée et continuée?'. Letter dated 3 January 1902. Minutes of the Canterbury Consistory, Register No. 3, p. 117.

77   Adolphe-Fréderic was the son of Reindert Peterson and Marie Léopoldine Saenge, born 30 December 1872 at Seraing where his father was pastor of the local parish of the *Union des Eglises Evangéliques Protestantes de Belgique*. Adolphe studied at the *Ecole préparatoire* (1890–91) and at the *Faculté de l'Oratoire* of Geneva (1893–94). He was ordained on 16 January 1900 in the *Eglise du Musée-Chapelle Royale* in Brussels in presence of all the pastors of the Union. H.R. Boudin, 'Répertoire des étudiants originaires de Belgique ayant fréquenté les Ecoles préparatoire et de Théologie de l'Oratoire à Genève', in *Analecta Theologiæ Facultatis Bruxellensis II 1976–1985* (Brussels: Pro Doc, 1988), p. 150.

78   'Le service sera fait par M. Ad. Peterson, pasteur', in *Pike's Folkestone Hythe and Sandgate Directory, Blue Book, 1902-1903* (Brighton: Robinson and Pike), p. 50.

Adolphe Peterson pursued his ministry throughout the war years, with the aforesaid developments, probably until the twenties. He rose to the challenge that world events had laid at his doorstep and made a significant impact in the life of Folkstone serving his compatriots and his country and working towards Belgo–British understanding.

L'Eglise Protestante Française de Londres[79]

For the French Protestant Church of London the twentieth century began in 1893. The present church was erected in that year in the middle of Soho, which was then predominantly a French neighbourhood. The church was built in the Franco–Flemish Gothic style with Romanesque elements by Sir Aston Webb, the architect of the front of Buckingham Palace. Its interior has simple terracotta walls and a barrel vaulted roof. At the front a dome covers the organ and semi-circular stalls.[80] Inside are several remnants of its past: a roll of pastors since 1550, a memorial tablet to the fallen of both world wars (see Appendix A to this section), a bell from the now closed French School, and a facsimile of the charter given by King Edward VI in 1550. The consistory room is lined with glass panelled cupboards where the church library, rich in incunabula, is stored. A series of previously unknown sermons by John Calvin was rediscovered there recently.[81] A complete catalogue is now being compiled.

During the twentieth century seven pastors served the Soho church:

Léon Degremont 1894–1912
Vacant 1913–26
Jean Autrand 1926–27
Frank Christol 1928–52
François Dubois 1952–75
Claude Vanderlinden 1975–78

---

79   Mr Michael H. Peters, secrétaire du Consistoire de l'Eglise Protestante Française de Cantorbéry, very kindly read our original text and made pertinent suggestions, for which we are very grateful indeed.

80   Howard Willows (ed.), *A Guide to Worship in Central London: Compiled by the London Central Y.M.C.A. Place of Worship Research Team* (London: Central YMCA, 1988), pp. 321-22.

81   M. Engammare, *Les sermons de Calvin sur Esaïe conservés à Londres* was published in a translation by H.R. Boudin, 'Calvin Incognito in London: The Rediscovery in London of Sermons on Isaiah', *Proceedings of the Huguenot Society of Great Britain and Ireland* 26.4 (1996), pp. 453-62.

Vacant 1979–81[82]
Pierre Simon 1982–91
Leila Hamrat 1991–continuing.[83]

Two personalities, a layman and a minister, towered above the Eglise Protestante Française de Londres during the eventful years 1939–45. They were André Philip,[84] a leading layman, who escaped from occupied France in July 1942[85] and Frank Christol, Pastor of the French Church since 1928.[86]

Christol could not avoid drawing a parallel between the present situation and the original plight of the refugees. He felt all the more lonely, because his wife and his three sons were in occupied territory. When speaking on the BBC French service, his name could not be mentioned, as reprisals might be taken. Once an absent-minded speaker said: 'Voici le pasteur Frank Christol qui vous parle'. Luckily the German and the Vichy French monitoring departments were snoozing. Five years passed before the London pastor learned that his eldest had crossed the Sahara with General Leclerc, that Jean-Claude had been killed in the maquis of the Yonne, and that Michel had spent long years as a PoW in Germany.[87]

Christol's frame of mind was shared by the members of his church. They also saw a striking similarity between the cause of the Huguenots and the aims of the Free French. Past and present encountered each other dramatically. In days gone by, Reformed refugees had left their country in search of a safe haven, where liberty prevailed, enabling them to worship according to their consciences. Now the Free French volunteers the world over, but especially in the United Kingdom, had gathered to

82   During this time no officially appointed pastor was in charge. Help was forthcoming from the *Eglise Protestante Unie de Belgique* whose pastors came for short or longer periods totalling more than fifty-two Sundays. They were: H.R. Boudin, F. Hoyois, J.-L. Ravet, J.-L. Seban, M. Van Den Steene and J. Verlinden.

83   Y. Jaulmes, *The French Protestant Church of London and the Huguenots from the Church's Foundation to the Present Day* (London: Eglise Protestante Français de Londres, 1993), p. 37.

84   It is believed that the English spelling of his surname results from the stay of his Huguenot ancestors in England, before going back to France.

85   J. Poujol, 'André Philip, les années de guerre 1939–1945', *Bulletin de la Société de l'Histoire du Protestantisme Français* (1992), pp. 181-241.

86   F. Christol bequeathed his archives to the Bibliothèque de la Société de l'Histoire du Protestantisme Français. *Les papiers du pasteur Frank Christol, aumônier des Forces Françaises Libres à Londres* being in Paris, the London church archives are depleted concerning WWII and therefore we wish to acknowledge our grateful indebtedness to M. Yves Jaulmes for sharing his personal archives with us.

87   F. Christol, 'Quelques souvenirs de guerre (1939–1946)', *Bulletin de la Société de l'Histoire du Protestantisme Français* (January–February–March, 1977), p. 133.

pursue the fight for freedom. It was akin to a crusade, prompted by reminiscences of how a royal tyrant had dealt harshly with their ancestors. They very easily transposed the understanding of the past into the present. Again they were fighting evil forces intent on submitting everyone to the power of a dictator. The slogan: 'Un roi, une loi, une foi!' received a new translation: 'Ein Reich, ein Volk, ein Führer!'

Epitomizing this attitude and wanting to create a tangible sign of recognition, Pastor Christol conceived a badge for distribution among his civilian and military parishioners. Its symbolism draws a striking parallel between the Huguenot past and the Free French present. This insignia contains three graphic elements which were well known to French Protestants. As a shield it was divided in three horizontal sections: at the top on a blue field the motto 'Résistez' in golden letters; in the middle on a white field the silhouette of the Tower of Constance in golden outline;[88] at the bottom on a red field a golden Huguenot Cross. The blue, white and red backgrounds composed the colours of the French Republican Flag. Part and parcel of French Protestant imagery, these three symbols immediately strike a chord in the historical memory and spiritual pride of the French and even among the West European Continental Reformed fellowship. In a stone on the battlement of the Tower of Constance the verb 'Résistez' has been scratched. Tragically this inscription of the eighteenth century could be matched with the prison graffiti in the walls of Gestapo prisons all over France.

Five hundred badges were made by the firm Cartier Ltd in London.[89] Recently I enquired at the same address in New Bond Street. An elderly gentleman assured me that as no diamonds were used in this badge,

---

88   In 1717, the Tower of Constance situated at Aigues-Mortes on the old coastline of the Mediterranean became a state prison for Protestant women caught attending clandestine services called 'assemblées'. Their numbers varied. In 1745, thirty-three female prisoners were registered. The best known among them is Marie Durand, the sister of Pierre Durand, a pastor hanged for this faith. Some letters which she wrote in prison during her stay of thirty-eight years have recently been published. *Lettres de Marie Durand 1711–1776, prisonnière à la Tour de Constance de 1730 à 1768*. Texte revu, annoté et présenté par Etienne Gamonnet. Préface de Fréderic Mayor, (Montpellier: Les Presses du Languedoc, 1st edn 1986, 2nd edn 1998).

89   A facsimile of the Cartier invoice for 500 badges dated 27 November 1941 appears in H. Dubief, 'Londres' which is part of *Les Protestants français hors de France: Londres, Empire français, Déportés, Prisonniers de guerre de 1940 à 1945* in *Les Protestants français pendant la seconde guerre mondiale. Actes du Colloque de Paris. Palais du Luxembourg, 19-21 novembre 1992 réunis par André Encreve et Jacques Poujol*, Supplément au *Bulletin de la Société de l'Histoire du Protestantisme Français* 3 (July–August–September, 1994).

production had been stopped and would not be resumed. This badge has become what the British call a collectable.[90]

The team Philip–Christol set their energies to create an efficient channel of information for disseminating Free French Protestant news. *Le Lien*, until then a useful parish news sheet, went through a metamorphosis and developed into a periodical with a worldwide readership. Its subtitle was clear: '*Organe protestant de la France combattante*'; its Huguenot motto unequivocal: 'Plus à me frapper on s'amuse, tant plus de marteraux on use'. In editions of the time are recorded the many activities of the minister, the relations with other churches, information about the situation in France received via the USA and from clandestine emissaires slipping into Spain or Switzerland. The Geneva secretariat of the World Council of Churches, still being formed, and the various mission fields—Africa, the Pacific Islands, and Madagascar—also provided news items.[91] With the help of André Philip's subsidy of £25 a month, *Le Lien* was widely distributed. Just as de Gaulle's initiative put France back in the camp of the Allied Nations, so also Philip's work meant that French Protestants were again taking part in the fight for freedom.[92]

One of de Gaulle's problems was to establish his republican legitimacy, bridging the political vacuum between the Third Republic and the Vichy regime. As a quirk of history, the only person in London, and in the United Kingdom for that matter, who could boast of having this legal approval in republican terms, was Pastor Christol. Before June 1940 he had been appointed as Protestant Chaplain to the French Expeditionary Force to Norway.

A few days after the France's capitulation in June 1940, Christol met a parishioner in Oxford Street, who asked him if that evening he was going to the Central YMCA to hear a French general. Unfortunately he had to visit wounded soldiers back from Dunkirk, but later he realized this was the first time he had heard about de Gaulle without the mention of his name.

The necessity of joining the Free French Forces dawned on him. At Carlton Gardens, their London HQ, he was interviewed by de Gaulle's Chief of Staff and the Roman Catholic chaplain, who assured him there were no Protestants among the Free French. His offer was declined. On 27 December 1940, Christol returned to the charge and was seen by de

---

90   A colour reproduction of the badge is to be found on the back cover of *Les Protestants*, p. 4.

91   In *Le Lien*, No. 123 (October, 1943) an extract from an anonymous letter from a French PoW was published 'D'un artilleur au Col du Faïd', which was written by Yves Jaulmes, one of the future long-standing leaders of the Soho Church.

92   P. Bolle, 'Philip, André', in A. Encreve (ed.), *Dictionnaire du monde religieux contemporain, Les Protestants* (Paris: Beauchesne, 1993), pp. 386-87.

Gaulle himself. The General was eager to know what the stand point of the faithful of Soho Square really was. The pastor was adamant that as Huguenot descendants they were on his side in the fight for liberty. Contrasting with this attitude was the pro-Vichy opinion of the Roman Catholic parish of Notre-Dame de France, near Leicester Square. Consequently during their stay in Britain, Yvonne and Charles de Gaulle worshipped only in an English Roman Catholic Church in South Kensington.

In 1942, Christol was invited to address the General Assembly of the Church of Scotland. Allotted fifteen minutes, he painted a large fresco of Huguenot history and modern French Protestantism in occupied territory and in the free world. In conclusion he handed over to the Moderator a few sixteenth-century méreaux, the passport to clandestine meetings and the Free French Protestant badge, a present day token to the future.[93] Thunderous applause ensued.

After the war, a most memorable event in the life of the Soho Church was the 1550 celebration. It was exactly, 400 years since King Edward VI had granted the Charter to the Strangers Churches. A special thanksgiving service was held[94] at the conclusion of which M. Gabriel Puaux, Président de la Société de l'Histoire du Protestantisme français, unveiled a monument over the porch commemorating the arrival of the refugees in England and the welcome given by the King. The sculptor of the striking bas-relief was John Prangnell. Later an Exhibition 'Les Huguenots et le Refuge en Grande-Bretagne' was openend at the Institut Française de Londres by the French Ambassador M. René Massigli— incidentally a Protestant—in presence of Major-General C.T. Beckett, President of the Huguenot Society of London and M.G. Puaux.[95]

When in 1952, after the eventful ministry of Frank Christol, François Dubois was called, the consistory followed the time-honoured procedure: election and submission of the choice to the approval of the reigning

---

93   Free French Protestant badges were given to Wilhelmina, Queen of the Netherlands, Sir Winston Churchill and General Charles de Gaulle.

94   Liturgy: *Service d'actions de grâces en souvenir du Quatrième Centenaire de la Charte Royale du Roi Edouard VI en faveur des Huguenots réfugiés en Grande-Bretagne. Dimanche 23 juillet 1950 à 11 heures à l'Eglise Protestante Française de Londres, 8-9 Soho Square, Londres W.1..* The Pastors Frank Christol, Claude Reverdin, and Marc Boegner took part. The benediction was given by the Bishop of Chichester, the Very Revd Dr G.K.A. Bell.

95   Among the exhibits were the actual Charter of King Edward VI, a group of wax medalions and black silhouettes by Isaac Gosset lent by King George VI from his collections in Windsor, rare books from the Soho Library and several artefacts from 'La Providence'. René Varin, Cultural Attaché of the French Embassy, had offered great assistance in bringing this valuable and interesting collection of Huguenot memorabilia together.

monarch. With rare exceptions the archives of the Soho Church contain the autographs of all the Kings and Queens of the realm since the sixteenth century.[96]

Among the foreign language churches in London, Dubois maintained the prominent position of his church, one of the older, if not the oldest in the capital. In a Thames Televison programme this was well apparent, when interviewer Brian Cullingford talked to him about the historical background and present parish life.

Having served the French Church in Glasgow as a pastor-student (where he met his future wife), he appreciated the *raison d'être* of foreign language churches. After the end of Dubois's ministry, the consistory encountered difficulties in filling the pastoral post. The pastor in such a church has to have a particular profile requiring adaptability, insight, a capability to answer the specific needs of expatriates and to forge links with the indigenous churches.

Finally Pierre Simon, a pastor of the Eglise Réformée de France, was called. He discovered that the number of French families permanently residing in London was decreasing and being replaced by individuals or households remaining on short term assigments for French or multi-national firms.[97] Taking stock of the congregation, he noticed that the French members of the consistory were not in the majority: a Swiss lady, an Italian lady, a Belgian industrialist, an American businessman and some Britons were present next to Mauritian and Malagasy Christians. Indeed, the Soho Church was still a French-speaking church, but quite diverse in the origin of its people. Reflecting on his relationships with the English churches, he gives a disgruntled view admitting they were practically nil, but confessing that his English was also absent. Once a year a cup of tea at Lambeth Palace was his official contact with the Church of England. With the United Reformed, the Methodists, and the Salvation Army, it was not any better.[98]

The Soho church considers it as a duty to send a representative to the annual Remembrance Ceremony organized by the French Embassy at its national plot in the WWII Allied Military Cemetery at Brookwood, Surrey. Several members of the Soho Church are buried there.

The Congregation's Charitable Trust, which is a registered charity, undertakes various activities, such as bursaries for theological students. An association with the Embankment Mission helps needy French individuals.

---

96   A facsimile of the Royal Approbation of Leila Hamrat, the first female pastor of the Soho Church signed by Queen Elizabeth II in 1992 is to be found in Jaulmes, *French Protestant Church of London*, p. 16.

97   Jaulmes, *French Protestant Church of London*, p.16.

98   P. Simon, *Parle-moi de Soho. Témoignage sur l'Eglise Protestante Française de Londres* (London: Le Lien, 2000), p. 37.

London has the advantage of having two French-speaking churches: a Roman Catholic and a Protestant one. Ecumenical relations have slowly developed especially through the dual Chaplaincy at the Lycée Charles de Gaulle. A joint Bible study group and an ecumenical annual retreat brings members of both churches into physical and spiritual contact.

Nowadays the European Union multiplies the opportunities of moving around. It is forseeable that the vocation of the French Church will remain: an entry to British society for those who stay and a staging post for those who leave.[99]

The present incumbent is a young dynamic female pastor, Leila Hamrat, intent on making an impact on the French colony. She is very positive about her contact with British churches, which have made her very welcome. She finds it easy to collaborate with their representatives because—in a pragmatic way—they do not centre their attention on fundamental differences. In France Christians tend to enjoy the debate—at times rather sterile—that emphasizes theological disagreements. Here collaboration extends very widely: Irish and French Roman Catholics, Baptists, Methodists, Presbyterians, Pentecostals, Church of England. There are often common services with many churches. It is a way of giving space to other people and accepting their difference in religious language. Analyzing her London experience the pastor declares: 'From a religious point of view, the British...are very tolerant. I have learnt a great deal from them.'[100]

L'Eglise Française de Southampton

An important event took place on 20 December 1915, when the president of the Huguenot Society of London Sir William Portal of Laverstoke, one of the trustees of the local church, presented some church silver to the Southampton French Congregation. This was a flagon in the form of a tankard and two communion cups hallmarked 1711 and bearing the inscription: 'This belongs to the French Church of Southampton'. This plate was handed over to the Anglican Bishop of Southampton who consecrated them.

To explain this particular episcopal consecration, and even more basically, the conformist character of the French Southampton Church, one must reach back to the eighteenth century. Indeed the Southampton congregation had then written to the Walloon Church of London to request their advice on passing from the Reformed Confession of old

---

99   D. Levesque, *ibid.*, p. 28.

100   M. Walker, 'The French Protestant Church of London' in the *French Protestant Industrial Mission. Mission Populaire Evangélique de France. Newsletter of the British Committee* No. 129 (Spring, 2000), p. 2.

over to the Anglican Communion. The London Walloons answered that they thought that by this move their brethren in Southampton would add affliction to the brethren elsewhere and scandalize many good souls. Southampton nevertheless persevered in their intention, and the first baptism according to the rites of the Church of England was performed on 21 April 1712. Thus a conformist French-speaking church continued the tradition of the Reformed Walloon and Huguenot Congregation by holding regular worship services in Southampton according to the Book of Common Prayer in a French translation.

A rapid perusal of the lives of the last four priests reveals their rather chequered pastoral career. The Revd Frederick M. Vincent, of whom we know very little, served the French Episcopal congregation of God's House in Southampton from about 1846 until 1855.[101] In 1852, during his ministry, the elders of the French Church applied to the Charity Commissionners for the status of a charity. A new constitution was drawn up and a Board of Trustees formed, which exercised the function of appointing the minister.

Vincent was followed by Hubert Napoléon Dupont in 1856 who was minister of the St Julien's French Conformist Church until 1876.[102] Alphonse Auguste Dupont had undertaken university studies in France at the Collège de Valogues in 1860. He then went to the Theological School in Coutances. In 1854 the Bishop of Coutances ordained him as a Roman Catholic priest. He decided then to become Anglican and was received by the Anglican Bishop of Central New York in 1876, and later by the Bishop of Winchester two years later. Becoming Perpetual Curate of the Eglise française anglicane de St Julien in Southampton in 1878, he remained there until 1905.[103]

Auguste Bellet started his training at the State University in Paris and obtained there a Baccalauréat-ès-Lettres in 1869. The Roman Catholic Bishop of Grenoble ordained him as a priest. Wanting to pursue his vocation in the framework of the Church of England he benefited in 1892 from the Sanction of the Archbishop of Canterbury under the Colonial Clergy Act of 1819.[104] This enabled him to enter the service of the French Church of the Holy Rood Chapel in Southampton. Bellet remained faithful to French-speaking congregations taking up the

---

101 'Huguenot Clergy List 1548–1916' compiled by W.H. Manchee, in *Proceedings of the Huguenot Society of London* 11 (1915–1917) p. 292. *Crockford's Clerical Directory* (1853), p. 272.

102 *Crockford's Clerical Directory* (1876), p. 272.

103 *Crockford's Clerical Directory* (1879), p. 289.

104 We thank the Deputy Librarian and Archivist of the Lambeth Palace Library, Melanie Barber for having sent us the text of the Act.

ministry of the St John the Evangelist in Shaftesbury Avenue in Westminster in 1908.[105]

On 10 October 1905, the Trustees appointed a new minister, Revd Jules Toussaint Costa. The formal recognition and acceptance took place on 19 October, when the Bishop of Southampton agreed to conduct the necessary formalities. He was the incumbent at the time when Sir William Portal of Laverstoke had responded positively to the need of the congregation for sacramental plate. Before coming to Southampton, this theologian pursued a rather circuitous career. In 1902 he took a degree of Bachelier en théologie at the State Protestant Theological Faculty of Montauban, in the South of France, which remained a state institution until the 1905 separation of Christian churches and the French Republic. He seems to have served in the Anglican Holy Trinity Church in Ajaccio in Corsica. Benefitting by the Colonial Clergy Act, on 14 November 1905 he was enabled to take charge of the French Church of St Julien in Southampton

In 1935 the combined efforts of the Queen's College, Oxford[106] and the Trustees of the church restored and beautified the Maison de Dieu. The cost of the improvements were met by the College, whilst the Trustees of the Chapel bore the expenses for the new organ. On 15 February 1935, Dr A.B. Kearney, Bishop of Southampton, performed the dedication of the organ, altar and furniture. Among the dignitaries taking part in the procession were the Provost, Canon B.H. Streeter from Queen's and its Bursar, the Hon. A.H. Stafford Cripps, and from the local church, the Revd E.G. Molyneux, Chaplain's of God's House, and the Revd J.T. Costa. The liturgy in English comprised the prayer of dedication by the Bishop, who laid his crozier on the new altar and special prayers in French by the minister J.T. Costa

In his address the Provost thanked the Trustees for presenting the new organ, which not only ensured dignified and harmonious divine worship, but equally benefited other congregations especially the inmates of God's House. This co-operation succeeded in making the ancient sanctuary more worthy of the purpose to which it was dedicated. The Provost further recalled that in 1185 Gervaise le Riche, an Anglo–Norman marchant had founded the *Domus Dei* and that his College had given permission in 1567 to the refugees to hold services in the Chapel. Later the congregation included other French-speakers from the

---

105 *Crockford's Clerical Directory* (1885), p. 359.

106 The Wardenship of the Hospital of God's House was conferred in 1344 by Edward III upon the Provost and Scholars of Queen's College, Oxford. In their corporate capacity of Warden they still own and administer God's House and its Chapel of St Julien. The College gave permission to the French Church to use the Chapel in 1567 and this permission has continued to the present. Information kindly given by M.J.M. Kaye, Keeper of the Archives, Queen's College, Oxford.

continent, and the Channel Islands. Canon Streeter also declared: 'That two groups of people speaking different languages and inheriting different national and racial traditions should have succeeded in getting along together for 3 1/2 centuries is—in view of the infirmity of human nature—a rare and I venture to think commendable achievement'.[107] Through the Provost, the College renewed the permission—already confirmed in 1864—for the use of its chapel by the French Church.

The Revd J.T. Costa died on 29 December 1937.[108]

Later on the number of members decreased, so that in 1939 the Trustees decided to suspend regular French services, only to have an annual service in St Julien's Chapel to maintain a historical reminder of the existence there of the Southampton French Church,[109] which was used for the work of the parish of St James' Dock. French worship resumed in 1948.

A welcome addition to the events held during the 1957 Southampton French Fortnight was a service entirely conducted in French in St Julien by the Revd J.O.C. Alleyne of St Mary's Church.[110] The service was preceded by the laying of wreaths at the Cenotaph by the Mayor Aldeman, Mrs K.E. Cawte, JP, on behalf of the Borough and by Major P.V. Stannard of the Southampton Branches of the British Legion. These floral tributes 'were tokens of remembrance and repect for the dead of our French Allies'.[111]

The commemorative service is held yearly in the setting of the small church in Winkle Street, close to the Town Quay.[112]

In 1960 the Revd Roger Bellant, from the Eglise Réformée de Dieppe, preached the sermon, whilst Angela Berger of the Grammar School for Girls and Roger Scallon of King Edward VI School read the Lessons.[113]

Nowadays, the pastor of the French Church in Brighton, the Revd F. Orna-Ornstein, is responsible for this event every July.

107 'New Altar and Organ dedicated in Ancient St Julien's Church at Southampton', *Southern Daily Echo* 16 February 1935.

108 J.T. Costa lived at 7 Howard Road, Southampton. He was Officier d'Académie et de l'Instruction publique. *Crockford's Clerical Directory* (1911), p. 325; (1915), p. 332; (1923), p. 327; (1930), p. 277; (1936), p. 282; (1937), p. 282; (1938), p. 282.

109 Minutes of the French Church Southampton 1701–1939. Southampton Archives Services, Southampton.

110 John Olpherts Campbell Alleyne in *Crockford's Clerical Directory* (1957–58), p. 16.

111 'Service in French continued an Anglo-French tradition', *Southern Daily Echo* 10 November 1957.

112 Folder: 'God's House. Southampton' kindly sent to us by Revd Belinda Searl-Burns.

113 In the congregation were the French Vice-Consul M. Joseph Chiari and Madame Chiari, the Trustees of St Julien's, representatives of the *Alliance Française* and the Franco–British Society, the University, and local schools.

Rôle pastoral de l'Eglise Française de Southampton

Frederick M. Vincent 1846–55
Hubert Napoléon Dupont 1856–72
Alphonse Auguste Dupont 1878–1905
Auguste Bellet 1905–06
Jules Toussaint Costa 1906–38
Frank Orna-Ornstein 1980–continuing

Conclusion

Can we formulate some concluding remarks after this rapid overview? Indeed every church is maintained by the untiring commitment of volunteers such as secretaries, organists, treasurers, cleaners, archivists, trustees, and other advisers, who often working behind the scenes and in combination with the professionnals, keep the congregation going. The faithfulness of the Christians in the pews turning up every Sunday is the life line of the church.

However, what is particular to the long existence of the surviving refugee churches? It was made possible by the input of numerous individuals over many years. Nevertheless these people were surrounded by a multitude of English-speaking churches, where spiritual nurture was readily available. So apart from the spiritual aspect, one has to stress the linguistic, cultural and national attractions to explain their historical continuity. Let us not underestimate the fact that praying and singing hymns learned at an early age in one's own mother tongue remains an important element of a person's identity. This remark is valid especially for expatriates.

What about the descendants of the refugees? A strong sense of history, an allegiance to family living traditions, a pride in the courage and faith of past generations and a feeling of spiritual aristocracy prevails among them making them identify with the refugee churches, thus ensuring their continuity. Prolonged existence to the present day has been achieved only by the old well-established refugee congregations. No attempts to found new groups as a missionary outreach have survived. Pastoral activity alone was not sufficient to maintain Eastbourne, Folkestone or Dover without the suppport of longstanding faithful parishioners. Trying to impose or introduce a congregation where a well-defined local need was not present, was doomed to failure.

One can surmise that the long-term survival of the London church is mainly due to four factors:

a) The presence in the metropolis of a considerable number of French-speakers from whom a Protestant minority could be recruited.

b) A continuing pastorate attracting members enthused by a diversified urban ministry and whose needs as expatriates were cared for.

c) A sound financial foundation resulting from the fruitful investments of the Walloons and Huguenots enabled activities to be driven and an adequate stipend to be paid to the minister.

d) The existence of a vast building comprising sanctuary, manse, consistorial room, office and meeting rooms with catering facilities in the centre of town.

In Canterbury the continued existence of the church can be attributed to four factors:

a) The presence of a nucleus of descendants of the refugees of the sixteenth and seventeenth centuries proud of their ancestry and willing to give expression to their origins by identifying with the congregation and to sustain it by their commitment.

b) The incorporation of the chapel in the fabric of the metropolitical church and cathedral of Canterbury, the mother church of Anglicanism. This material advantage created and continues to provide the adequate physical conditions for a prolonged presence.

c) Over the years the help of the London church was important in maintaining the services by sending preachers—lay and clerical—at least once a month to the pastorless Kent church.114

d) The sympathy of the Anglican authorities, especially the dean and chapter of Canterbury, who although respecting the independance of the congregation are eager to see this international link and ecumenical relationship preserved. The Walloon and Huguenot congregation is a constant, albeit modest, reminder in their very midst of the disunity of the church and the imperative necessity of working towards reunion.

As far as we have been able to ascertain no serious attempt has ever been made to merge or unite or even simply come closer in some kind of loose connection with the Presbyterian or United Reformed Church in England or in Wales or with the Church of Scotland. This is due for the most part to the fact that the refugee churches are very jealous of their autocephalic nature and their independance from Anglicanism. Free from all ties with the Church of England, the French-speaking congregations were not going to abandon this cherished freedom by entering into a relationship with the churches of their own confession in Great-Britain. It is important not to jump from the frying pan into the fire!

Any links are with the churches in France or Belgium: on the one hand, with the Commission des Eglises Evangéliques d'Expression

---

114 Although one has to remember that in the nineteenth century, the London Trustees tried in an attempt of rationalization to close Canterbury and absorb the remaining finances. Thanks to the intervention of Archbishop Archibald Campbell Tait (1868–82) in the House of Lords, Canterbury was saved from the London asset strippers.

Française de l'Extérieur de la Fédération Protestante de France and, on the other, with the United Protestant Church of Belgium.

One can note that in a wider sense theological literature has not produced any substantial handbook or treatise about foreign language churches. Here lies a barren no man's land. Is it because everybody thinks their situation is absolutely unique and cannot be found elsewhere that no systematic treatment or general guidelines exist?

Representatives of the Aussenamt of the Evangelische Kirche Deutschlands, the Dutch Kerk Overzee, the Church of Scotland and the Anglican Diocese of Europe, including the European parishes of the Episcopal Church of the United Sates of America, have come together at irregular intervals to discuss the problems of their congregations in foreign parts. The only text which was produced is the so-called 'Statement of Brussels' which attempts to define in broad terms the mission of these expatriate churches and their duties towards the other Christian congregations in the host countries (see Appendix B).

For some observers the churches of descendants of the sixteenth-century French- and Dutch-speaking refugees can appear to be small and even largely irrelevant groups and as such they are unlikely to have have ever shaped twentieth-century history. However, political circumstances have made their contribution meaningful and this should not be minimized by intellectual patronizing.

Historiography has often been inspired by theological and ecclesiastical triumphalism. As unusual remnants of a glorious past and historical anomalies in the present, these tiny congragations have, nevertheless, played a substantial and tangible role.

We hope we have not slipped into hagiography or over-indulged in a taste for anecdotes or used commemorative rheroric to excess in trying to convey something of the life and faith of French-speaking Protestantism in the United Kingdom during the twentieth century.

Appendix A

Plaque commémorative
1914–1918

Auguste Charleron
Adrien Cornu
Aspirant Georges Devaux
Richard Reymond
Sergent Yves Ramette
Marcel Thouvenet

1939–1945

Millet
Aviateur Aubry de Tahiti
Lieutenant Edouard Barzilai
Capitaine Parachutiste C. Boissonnas
Sergent pilote Maurer
Coutenceau de l'Ile Maurice
Matelot Patan Demene de la Nouvelle Calédonie
Capitaine Lucien Fatoux
Aviateur Ernest Courmac de Tahiti
Aviateur Kainuku de Tahiti
Aviateur Francis Lille
Chef d'escadrille Jacques Schloesing
Sous-lieutenant Charles Witt de la Nouvelle Calédonie

CIVILS
Mademoiselle Berthoud
Mademoiselle Antoinette Christol
Monsieur Robert L. Cru
Mademoiselle Marguerite Grellet
Madame Yvonne Jaulmes
Monsieur Emile Jezep
Mademoiselle Klenrett
Monsieur Thibaut

Appendix B

The Brussels Statement

Foreign-language and/or Expatriate Congregations:
Their Role and Responsiblity

Statement from the 9th Conference of Church Executives Responsible
for the Foreign-language Congregations of the Churches of Europe held
at Brussels, Belgium, October 1-3, 1973

I

1. The mission of the Church in any place is to be God's intrument in witnessing to his love for the world, and to help men and women to realize and respond to his love.

2. The many people moving between countries today are increasingly important for the life and mission of the Church. Churches in the 'sending' and 'receiving' countries have a common responsiblity for those who migrate between them.

3. Foreign-language and/or expatriate congregations have a particular function in the fulfilment of this responsibility. They minister to these Christians, who, bcause of language and other cultural characteristics have difficulty of sharing fully in the life of the indigeneous churches. They also have a missionary responsibility to those expatriate who have lost contact with the Church.

4. Since expatriates tend to be isolated, their congregations should as fully as possible seek visible links and common witness and service with the indigeneous churches, and encourage their members to participate as much as possible in indigeneous churches and church activities.

The indigeneous churches should take the initiative to encourage foreign-language and/or expatriate congregations to enter into the closest possible fellowship with them.

II

1. In the light of the foregoing considerations, a foreign-language and/or expatriate congregation should not be established or supported
   a) to serve the self-interest of a national, racial or social group;

b) without prior consultation with the Council of Churches, or the national church of the same confessional family, in the country where the establisment of such a congregation is proposed;

c) without prior consultation with the churches of other countries of that language which may be concerned;

d) until full consultation with the churches of the country has shown that they cannot provide for the ministry such a congregation should perform;

e) which is not integrated into a indigeneous church, or, if this is not possible, which is not related to a Council of Churches or similar ecumenical body wthin the country where the establishment of such a congregation is proposed;

f) by a church of its own country without prior consultation with the Councils of Churches, or the national churches of the same confessional family which may be concerned.

2. The Churches adopting this document will encourge existing foreign-language and/or expatriate congregations to abide by the principles set out above.

III

1. Churches and church agencies in the 'sending' countries should co-operate in the orientation and training of people going abroad in secular occupations and their families for their responsibility as Christians. So far as a Church in a 'receiving' country is able to conduct such an orientation and training programme, the churches adopting this document will support it in every way possible.

2. Ministers should only be appointed to foreign-language and/or expatriate congregations after a period of orientation and/or with the assurance of a period of orientation in the country in which they are appointed, preferably under the responsibility of the indigenous Church.

Appendix C

L'Union Chrétienne de Jeunes Gens
de langue française de Londres

The Association which catered for the needs of the young men of the three French-speaking churches in London: the Huguenot church in Soho, the Swiss Protestant church at Endell Street, and the Eglise Evangélique Française de Bayswater was l'Union Chrétienne de Jeunes Gens de langue françasie de Londres founded in 1883 by two Swiss young men: A. Brauen[115] and W. Gardy, freshly disembarked in London.[116]

It had also a missionary outreach for the French, Swiss, and Belgian youths, who were spending some time in London on apprenticeship or study. The French YMCA offered a congenial meeting place for the young people who could feel quite lonely in the British capital. For many a young fellow unfamiliar with his new surroundings, the association acted as a substitute for parents, friends and country. Many members were able to rekindle and strengthen their faith and others discovered a new living relationship with their Saviour.[117]

First using Exeter Hall,[118] that Evangelical shrine which provided the venue for so many religious societies, the Union moved in 1907 to The Strand waiting for the completion of the Central YMCA building on Tottenham Court Road, where it still stands today. The new meeting rooms were a welcome oasis in the bustle of London life.

Launched in October 1903 a periodical, *Le Trait d'Union. Organe mensuel de l'UCJG de langue française de Londres*, aimed at publicizing

---

115 A. Brauen was an active member of the Swiss Church of London. He entered the Consistory in 1898, which he chaired for twenty-two years. On 22 June 1952, the church gave a reception in his honour celebrating his ninetieth birthday. See C.I. Reverdin, *L'Eglise suisse de Londres. Notice historique d'après les procès-verbaux des séances du Consistoire, 1891–1952* (London: Eglise suisse de Londres, 1952), p. 106.

116 'Fête annuelle et vingt-cinquième anniversaire de notre Union', in *Le Trait d'Union* (March, 1908), pp. 4-6, with photographs of the founders.

117 Odilon Vansteenberghe, the future leader of the 'Belgian Gospel Mission' expressed his gratitude to the UCJG where he had learned to study God's Word, in *Le Trait d'Union* (March–April, 1930), p. 3. Cf. M.J. Blok, 'Odilon Aimé Marie Vansteen-berghe', in *Belgische Protestantse Biografiëen* (Brussels: Pro Doc, 1991). Also Ph. Thompson, *Firebrand of Flanders* (Chicago: Moody Press, 1960).

118 As the association was allocated Room 16 in Exeter Hall, its meeting place was known as 'the Sixtine Chapel'.

the association's activities among the whole French-speaking community in London.

In the summer months, leaders and members adopted a very English institution which is Speaker's Corner at Hyde Park. French was the medium used. Hecklers did not hesitate to tackle the young orators pouring scorn on the French people in general.

The development of the association called for the appointment of a general-secretary.[119]

Renowned speakers from the continent were invited: such as Ruben Saillens, the fiery French evangelist, pasteur Vautier of the Mission Romande and Casalis of the Mission de Paris, both experts on missionary topics. Baron de Béthune, a Belgian ex-benedictine monk, spoke about the necessity of evangelism in Belgium. More than 500 were in the audience when the talented speaker Frank Thomas from Geneva occupied the rostrum. Before each talk, a prayer meeting with the three London pastors: Degrémont, Brændli and Rayroux was held.

George Williams, the founder of the London YMCA, was a faithful contributor to the Union's work.

During 1903 more than 9,000 people were noted at the various activities. The members of the Union fraternized with those of the Ramblers Club of Central YMCA learning to practice their English and visit historical and industrial sites in the outskirts of London. Contact was maintained with the German YMCA, which had a special branch, 'The Christian Waiters Home', helping the numerous young Germans in the catering trade. The French and German YMCA's held each November the international week of prayers sponsored by the World Alliance of YMCAs.

The leadership of the association was well aware of the importance of foreign language YMCA's in large cities. Encouraging news was received from the French YMCA of New York having taken possession of a new building in 1904. Another French-speaking YMCA was founded in Charleroi, Pennsylvania. So London was not a unique phenomenon. G. Birde, member of the London committee, left the capital for Stuttgart where he founded a francophone Union. An offspring of the association was the Spanish group which valiantly strived to gather Hispanic-

---

119 The rapid turnover of the secretaryship makes the following list of secretaries incomplete, the records do not give systematicaly each replacement: E. Marcault; A. Reymond; J. Sauvain; Charles Guillot, 1908; W. Bourquin, 1909–13; W. Bunter; René Fiaux, 1914–16; Emmanuel Morax, 1916–17; Joseph Savels, 1917–18; Alfred Renoux, 1921–23; Pierre Jacot, 1929; Ed. Jeanneret, 1930; E. Steck, 1930; Steinmann; G. Pash, 1930. After his work during WWI, J. Savels, a former Roman Catholic *Père de Scheut*, left London for the 'American Presbyterian Congo Mission' post at Luebo in the Kasai province of Belgian Congo. H.R. Boudin, *Savels, Joseph August* in *De Léopold Ier à Jean Rey. Les Protestants en Belgique de 1839 à 1989* (Brussels: FUTP, 1990), p. 96.

speaking young men in London. Unfortunately their secretary, Jimenez, left for Bolivia.

In 1905, the London YMCA lent its secretary to the organizing staff of the World Conference in Paris helping with the celebration of the fiftieth anniversary of the World Alliance.

Combining the leaving of the premises at Exeter Hall with the celebration of Bastille Day, a special meeting was held with comte Jacques de Pourtalès and Emmanuel Sautter.[120] The latter was a YMCA leader of distinction who became general-secretary of the National Committee of the French UCJG and later was responsible for setting up the vast network of YMCA soldiers' huts for the French Armed Forces during WWI, 'Les Foyers du Soldat de l'Union franco-américaine'.

WWI made a deep impact on the association. For a time it was disorganized, suspending the publication of *Le Trait d'Union*. Its members were dispersed among the allied armies in Europe, where they exerted themselves to live as Christians capitalizing on the meaingful experience made in London. The available records reveal a more definite *Sitz im Leben* in the war than the minutes of the churches which only have fleeting hints to the conflict. As soon as the Belgian refugees gathered in great numbers, the French YMCA organized 'Les lundis belges' at Notting Hill Gate.[121] The secretary visited the wards of all Belgian military hospitals of Greater London. This work was sustained financialy by Paul Hymans, Belgian Minister Plenipotentiary in Great-Britain.[122]

A typical week of the association activities comprised a social evening on Monday; opening of the library—one of the best French language libraries of the capital—on Tuesday before the Bible study; scout troop meetings on Wednesday and Saturday; 'Les conférences de l'Union', a talk for the general public on Friday; and Football on Saturday. A diversified progamme of talks on political science kept the members abreast of new developments in the world.[123] Every day except Sunday, the secretary was available from 10.30 to 12.30 am and from 6.30 to 9.00 pm. He remained a pivotal element of the Union helping new

---

120 J. Valyseele, 'Sautter, Emmanuel', in *Dictionnaire du Monde religieux compemporain* (Paris, 1933), p. 441-42. E Sautter wrote *Une Œuvre de guerre. Les Foyers du Soldat de l'Union franco-américaine*, Société des Foyers de l'UFA (Paris, 1919).

121 *Le Trait d'Union* (September–October, 1915), p. 3.

122 P. Mahillon, 'Hymans, Paul', in *De Léopold*, p. 66.

123 Here are some titles: L.P. Valat talked about *'Scènes vécues de la guerre en Belgique'*; R. Hoffmann-De Vismes: *'La Belgique héroïque'* and *'La Finlande et le Bolchévisme'*; Shoran Singgh, *'India today'*; Colonel Luxmoore:*'Yougoslavia'*; W.H. Rainey: *'Le Vénézuéla et l'Orénoque'*, and G. Thoumarian, ex-representative of Armenia in the Turkish Parliament: *'Armenia and Europe'*, in Jean Rey, *Les protestants en Belgique de 1839 á 1989* (Brussels: FUTP, 1990).

arrivals to settle in and bridge the installation period. In 1921, for example, he received some 700 letters requesting information about accomodation, work, tutorships, and apprenticeships. More than a 1,000 visits were made by newcomers as well as old timers.

A visit of a group of *'Eclaireurs Unionistes de France'* (French YMCA scouts) inspired the UCJG, which decided to found its own unit, the only French-speaking scout troop in London.[124]

With their coming and going, soon the association had members scattered all over the world. Often they corresponded remembering the joyous and fruitful time they had enjoyed thanks to the YMCA.

A blow which could have been its death knell, hit the association in 1925. For some obscure reason, probably financial, the Central YMCA turned the UCJG out of its rooms.[125] The Committee recalled with sadness its wholehearted participation in the campaign to erect the building to the sum of 200,000 francs. As no written contract existed and the committe did not wish to recur to legal action, the expulsion took place. However, another YMCA offered a replacement venue at 186 Aldergate Street. The members rallied and after some time moved in to satisfactory accomodation near Russell Square, 15 Upper Bedford Place. The crisis was averted.

Le Trait d'Union, with a 1,000 copies at each run, was a link—not entirely free from a whiff of nostalgia—between members.[126] After WWI, the president A. Brauen, walked up memory lane by visiting France, Belgium and Switzerland to make contact with 'old Londoners' who kept cherished memories of their association days.[127]

---

124 *Le Trait d'Union* (October–November, 1920), p. 3; (December 1920–January 1921); (April–May, 1921), p. 2; (June–July, 1921), p. 3.

125 R.Hoffmann–De Vismes, pastor of the Swiss Church of London, 'A tous les "Anciens" et tous les amis de l'UCJG de Langue française de Londres', in *Le Trait d'Union* (April–May, 1925), pp. 1-2.

126 'Je dois avouer que quand je lis "Le Trait d'Union", je ressens le cafard', in *Le Trait d'Union* (September–October, 1923), p. 4.

127 *Le Trait d'Union* (July–August, 1923), p. 3.

Appendix D

The Huguenot Lodge No. 2140
English Constitution

Interest in Huguenot history has been revived at certain moments in time when the anniversary of important events have come up for celebration. This was not only a boon for historians who could then delve into archives and produce learned papers, but a series of associations were founded to perpetuate the memory of bygone days. In the wake of the commemoration of the Revocation of the Edict of Nantes, the Hugenot Society was founded in 1885. At the same period the so-called Huguenot Lodge was created by the directors of the French Hospital.

At an informal meeting of these members held on October 1885 an agreement emerged that a Lodge of Freemasons be founded to recall the momentous happenings of the Revocation in view of celebrating its bi-centenary. The founders were conscious of placing the founding of this group in the setting of history, but not only of the Huguenot history, in the framework of the events they saw unfolding before their very eyes. The political situation in Europe was disquieting. The Austro–Prussian and the Franco–Prussian wars had ravaged the continent altering the political nature of nations. France was now a republic and Germany had proclaimed its empire. The Zulu war and the Boer war had shed blood on African soil. In America Abraham Lincoln had been assassinated. In the same period several peaceful events had, however, taken place. By the opening of the Suez Canal, frozen beef from Australia and frozen mutton from New Zealand were circumnavigating the globe; gold was discovered in South Africa. Communications and transport were helped by Bell's telephone, Pelton's hydraulic and Parson's steam turbines, Daimler's motor engine and Carl Benz's motor car.

In 1887 Queen Victoria's jubilee was celebrated and the Prince Albert monument was built. In this sequence of events the directors of the French Hospital were keen to further fellowship and progress in their midst through the working of a Huguenot Lodge.[128]

In the official petition sent to the Grand Secretary of the United Grand Lodge of England, the signatories asked to form a lodge named after Ruvigny, the General of the French Army, Henri de Massue de Ruvigny, Earl of Galway, Lord Justice of Ireland. In December 1885 an alteration

---

128 *Notes on the History of the Huguenot Lodge No. 2140. Prepared for the Centenary of the Lodge May 1986* (unpublished MS, 1986), n.p., but pp. 9-10.

was brought in the denomination Ruvigny was replaced by Huguenot. This modification could only be accepted by introducing a new application. Presumably the founders had thought that they could organize their four yearly meetings on the premises of the French Hospital. They discovered more Masonic red tape, when it became clear that it was not permitted to hold lodge meetings in a private institution. The venue was chosen as Masonic Hall, 8a Red Lion Square at High Holborn.

As the recently formed Huguenot Society of London held its meetings at the Criterion Restaurant, the leaders of the lodge decide to adopt the same location after long discussions and abundant correspondance about the respective qualities of the Holborn and Criterion Restaurants.

No self-respecting masonic lodge can operate without a banner. The emblem of the Huguenot Lodge No. 2140 was an exhibit at the exhibition 'The Quiet Conquest. The Huguenots 1586–1985' held at the Museum of London from May to October 1985. This textile is embroidered in gold thread on a cotton base. Its description is as follows: 'On a shield azure, a candlestick or, with a lighted candle proper surmounted by seven stars figurative of "The Light that shineth in Darkness" and the seven liberal arts and sciences, namely grammar, rhetoric, logic, arithmetic, geometry, music, and astronomy'.[129] One must remark that the emblem is not a Huguenot one, nor even a French one. In fact the motto is in Latin on a ribbon: 'Lux lucet in tenebris'. They are distinctively Waldensian emblems: the lighted candle, the stars and the motto which the Church of the Valdese has had in use for many years. It is the native Protestant Church of Italy, which goes back to the evangelical movement set in motion by Valdo in the twelfth century and still has its headquarters in the high valleys of Piedmont in the Alps.[130] One could speculate why they chose pre-Reformation symbolism as the banner explicitly states on a wavy ribbon 'Founded to commemorate the Bicentenary of the Revocation of the Edict of Nantes 1685–1885'. Was it because they seemed to go even further back than the sixteenth-centrury Reformation? The other inscription on the banner would confirm this supposition it says 'Antiquissima insignia'.

The original banner—a gift from Bro. Major George Lambert—was burned beyond retrieval in a fire of the Criterion Restaurant in January 1918. On 20 June 1973 a new banner was presented and dedicated by Bro. Revd Joe Crompton.

---

129 *The Quiet Conquest. The Huguenots 1685-1985. A Museum of London exhibition in association with the Huguenot Society of London 13 May to 31 October 1985.* Catalogue compiled by Tessa Murdoch (London, 1985), exhibit 472, p. 318.

130 S. Prescot, 'The Waldensian Church', *The Waldensian Reviw* 97 (Summer, 1999), p. 16.

Another exhibit at the aforesaid Exhibition was a Past Master's Jewel depicting the candelestick motive suspended from a special ribbon of red and white symbolizing 'the purity of our Protestant martyrdom stained by the blood of the persecution'.[131]

---

131 *The Quiet Conquest*, exhibit 473, p. 318

CHAPTER 12

Protestant Nonconformists and Ecumenism

John A. Newton

Granted the traditional dissidence of Dissent, it might be thought that Protestant Nonconformists would have found it hard to come to terms with the ecumenical movement of the twentieth century. Yet there is within the history of Nonconformity a positive ecumenical strand, which, while not predominant, is by no means negligible, and which has commanded the allegiance of notable leaders. The representative Puritan, Richard Baxter (1615–91), was ardent for church unity, and deplored the fact that, 'The ministers of England are sadly guilty of...*undervaluing the unity and peace of the whole church*'. He was convinced that a closer unity was possible: 'Is the distance so great that Presbyterian, Episcopal and Independent might not be well agreed? Were they heartily willing and forward for peace they might—I know they might... If we could not in every point agree, we might easily find out, and narrow our differences, and hold communion upon our agreement in the main'.[1]

Again, though John Wesley insisted that his Methodist followers were not Dissenters, he proved quite unable to keep his preachers and societies within the Church of England, and so unwittingly gave rise to a new denomination of Protestant Nonconformists. Yet Wesley remained a consistent advocate of Christian unity. He greatly admired Baxter and recommended his writings, including the eirenical *Reformed Pastor*, to his preachers and people. Wesley's own eirenicon, his *Letter to a Roman Catholic* of 1749, has been twice republished within the last forty years, as a stimulus to Protestant–Catholic understanding. In 1968, Michael Hurley, an Irish Jesuit, edited the *Letter* and in 1987, the Revd. Sam Burch, a Belfast Methodist, together with Fr. Gerry Reynolds of Clonard Monastery, Belfast, jointly produced another edition. Wesley stresses the fundamental truths which separated Christians hold in common. He is clear that unity does not exclude variety and diversity in a range of secondary matters—forms of worship, patterns of church order, traditions

---

1   Richard Baxter, *The Reformed Pastor* (ed. J.T. Wilkinson; London: Epworth Press, 1955 [1656]), pp. 101-102.

of spirituality, systems of theology. He also distinguishes between ecumenism and proselytizing, assuring his Roman Catholic correspondent, 'My dear friend, I am not persuading you to leave or change your religion, but to follow after that fear and love of God without which all religion is vain'.[2]

Coming nearer to our own time, Sir Henry Lunn (1859–1939), a Wesleyan Methodist who was also confirmed as a member of the Church of England, was a notable Free Church advocate of unity. In 1891, despite the unpropitious climate of nineteenth-century sectarianism, he founded *The Review of the Churches*, a journal devoted to the cause of Christian reunion. From 1892, he organized annual conferences for Anglican and Free Church leaders at Grindelwald, Switzerland, with the same ecumenical end in view. Yet these ecumenical pioneers, if not voices crying in the wilderness, were certainly not widely representative of Protestant Nonconformists. The Oxford Movement, stimulating a Catholic revival in the Church of England, had hardened Anglican attitudes towards Nonconformists, and increased the already strong fear of Roman Catholicism in Victorian England. As the twentieth century dawned, there were major barriers to be surmounted before ecumenism could develop on any significant scale among Free Church people. The barriers included: the ancestral memories of the Great Ejection of Nonconformist ministers in 1662; the long history of civil disabilities which Protestant Dissenters had shared with Roman Catholics; the late nineteenth-century battles over education; and the deep-seated fear of Rome.

In this chapter, an attempt will be made to look at the response of the Free Churches to the major events of the twentieth-century ecumenical movement, beginning with the World Missionary Conference at Edinburgh in 1910; to examine ecumenical relations among the Free Churches themselves; and to highlight the contribution to the ecumenical movement made by a number of leading Free Church men and women.

By common consent, the modern ecumenical movement takes its origin from the Edinburgh Conference of 1910.[3] Behind that gathering lay two seminal movements. There was, first, the eighteenth-century Evangelical Revival, which influenced not only the British Isles, but also Europe and North America; and secondly, the overseas missionary expansion of the nineteenth century, ending in 1914, and constituting

---

2   John Wesley, *A Letter to a Roman Catholic*, reprinted in A.C. Outler, *John Wesley* (London: Oxford University Press, 1964), p. 496. On Wesley's ecumenism, see Herbert B. McGonigle, 'John Wesley—Exemplar of the Catholic Spirit', in Anthony R. Cross (ed.), *Ecumenism and History: Studies in Honour of John H.Y. Briggs* (Carlisle: Paternoster Press, 2002), pp. 50-68.

3   On the conference, see Brian Stanley, 'Edinburgh 1910 and the *Oikoumene*', in Cross (ed.), *Ecumenism and History*, pp. 89-105.

what Kenneth Scott Latourette has termed the 'Great Century' of modern Christian missions.[4] There had been earlier missionary conferences, but Edinburgh 1910 was the first to be organized on a world scale. The 1,355 representatives of the 120 missionary societies who came together were full of hope, based on the solid achievements of the previous century. Their confidence was encapsulated in the slogan: 'The evangelization of the world in this generation', since they held it now possible—granted vastly improved communications and the spread of Christianity into every continent—for every human being on the planet to hear the offer of the gospel.

Another significant mark of this world gathering was the presence of outstanding leaders from the younger churches, such as Samuel Azariah of Dornakal (1875–1945), who in 1912 was to become the first Indian Bishop of the Anglican Church. Though only eighteen in number, these church leaders from Asia made their own distinctive contribution to the conference, not least in their criticism of the western churches' denominational differences, which they saw as a serious hindrance to mission in largely non-Christian cultures. There were no Roman Catholic nor Eastern Orthodox Christians present, but the conference brought together an unprecedented representation of Protestant, Anglican and Free Church Christians.

The Edinburgh Conference, in its resolve to maintain the impetus of its co-ordinated missionary endeavour, set up a permanent organization to continue its work. Its Continuation Committee issued in 1921 in the formation of the International Missionary Council, in which the missionary societies of the Free Churches were fully involved.

Another development stemming from the conference was the Faith and Order movement. The Edinburgh consultation had only been possible on the strict understanding that there should be no discussion of doctrine or organic union, but only practical questions of missionary policy. In the event, however, it proved impossible to exclude theological questions, since these were often at the root of different practices in mission. With the development of Faith and Order, which held the first of its ten-yearly meetings at Lausanne, Switzerland, in 1927, doctrinal issues, and their bearing on Christian unity, could be explicitly addressed. The third strand of inter-church concern, in addition to mission and Faith and Order, was that of Christian service, expressed through the Life and Work movement. Here the leading pioneer was Nathan Söderblom, Lutheran Archbishop of Uppsala, Sweden. Its first international conference, held at Stockholm in 1925, attempted to address the huge social, economic and political problems facing the nations in the aftermath of the First World

---

4   Kenneth S. Latourette, *A History of Christianity* (London: Eyre and Spottiswoode, 1954), pp. 1061-1345.

War. The conference slogan declared 'Doctrine Divides, Love Unites', but it proved impossible to separate theology and Christian action in this way. Significantly, the conference message to the churches affirmed, 'The nearer we draw to the Crucified, the nearer we come to one another, in however varied colours the Light of the World may be reflected in our faith. Under the Cross of Jesus Christ we reach out hands to one another'.[5] Faith and Order and Life and Work were eventually brought together in 1938 in the Provisional Committee of the World Council of Churches (WCC), which was formally inaugurated at Amsterdam ten years later. The three-fold strand was completed in 1961, when the International Missionary Council was integrated into the WCC.

How did the Free Churches stand in 1910, on the brink of these ecumenical developments? In that very year, they had achieved virtual parity with the Church of England in terms of communicant members, numbering 2,125,000 as against the Anglican total of 2,232,000. They were confident and forward-looking, but in the long perspective of history, it is clear that they had already passed their peak in terms of their influence on the life of the nation. Sir Denis Brogan (1900–74), writing in 1943, observed: 'It is probable that Nonconformity reached its height of political power, was most representative of the temper of the English people, round the beginning of the [twentieth] century'.[6] Some Free Church leaders clearly sensed a need for renewal and looked to the possibility of closer union among the Free Churches themselves. On paper, such a proposal might seem eminently straightforward; in practice, it was far from being so. As to any wider unity—with Anglicans, for example—that was even more problematic. In the 1880s, Dr R.W. Dale (1829–95), the minister of Carr's Lane Congregational Church, Birmingham, was thoroughly sceptical about the likelihood of any ecumenical advance, much as he desired it. He recognized 'the spiritual unity of Nonconformists with those from whom we are most widely separated', but believed that any organic unity was a remote possibility. He could not even envisage any kind of federation among Nonconformists. During a holiday in Wales, Dale wrote to Sir Percy Bunting (1836–1911), a notable Wesleyan advocate of Free Church federation:

> I was at Barmouth yesterday. We Congregationalists have a wooden church, holding perhaps 150 people; the Baptists, three years ago, opened a church— stone, however—holding about as many; your people [Wesleyan Methodists] also

5   G.K.A. Bell, *The Stockholm Conference 1925: Official Report of the Universal Christian Conference on Life and Work held in Stockholm, 19-30 August 1925* (London: Oxford University Press, 1926), pp. 715-16.

6   D.W. Brogan, *The English People: Impressions and Observations* (London: Hamilton, 1943), p. 21.

have a church. The Baptists and Wesleyans conduct English service only in the season; it is the same with the Presbyterians. In the winter, I believe, they are all with us. It is no use saying that such a policy as this is hateful—I could swear when I think of it. It exists. It is far too strong to be suppressed. Even the different Methodist communities—with a common creed, common institutions, a common ethos, a common history, and with the causes of the original divisions gradually disappearing—can neither combine nor confederate; how can we dream of a more general confederation?[7]

Yet some did dream, nevertheless; and in 1910, the Revd J.H. Shakespeare (1857–1928), Secretary of the Baptist Union, pleaded passionately for a United Free Church of England. He was a central figure in his own denomination, and in 1905 had been largely responsible for the first meeting of the Baptist World Congress in London, which led to the formation of the Baptist World Alliance in that same year. Yet his vision was wider than the consolidation of the bonds uniting Baptists across the world. He sought also a union of the Free Churches of England and Wales, and was deeply disappointed when it failed to materialize.

Why did Shakespeare's proposal evoke so little response? There were, first of all, major differences of theology and church order among the Free Church denominations. Again, the denominational bureaucracies, of which Shakespeare may be seen as an untypical representative, may well have feared that his plan would threaten their own positions, as big fish in relatively small ponds. In addition, it would seem that there was as yet no general ecumenical vision, and without that, such schemes were destined to perish. Yet Shakespeare remained a convinced advocate of church union, as his later publication, *The Churches at the Cross-Roads* (1918) clearly evidences; and though his call for a Free Church Federation fell largely on deaf ears, he was instrumental in securing, in 1919, a representative and consultative body, the Federal Council of Evangelical Free Churches. Nearly thirty years earlier, in 1892, the National Free Church Council had been formed, and in 1939 the two councils came together to form the Free Church Federal Council, (recently renamed the Free Churches Council). The discussions leading to the formation of the 1919 Federal Council issued in a further step towards Free Church unity, in the form of an agreed statement of faith, which included a shared doctrine of the Church.[8]

---

7   A.W.W. Dale, *The Life of R.W. Dale of Birmingham* (London: Hodder & Stoughton, 4th edn, 1899), p. 396, the letter is dated 14 August 1889.

8   This common Free Church statement of faith is printed in John W. Grant, *Free Churchmanship in England 1870–1940* (London: Independent Pres, n.d. [1955]), pp. 209-10.

In *The Churches at the Cross-Roads*, Shakespeare's bold proposals for a wider church union, reaching beyond the Free Churches, surprised and alarmed many of his fellow-Nonconformists. Writing in 1918, after the carnage of the First World War, he roundly declared that 'Our modern world will not even listen to a divided Church',[9] and looked to a union with the Church of England, which would involve the Free Churches in acceptance of a form of epsicopacy. He argued that Nonconformists would have their own weighty contribution to make to such a United Church, and he urged that 'If in the united Church the essential elements of Congregationalism and Presbyterianism are included, it is not unreasonable to crown the edifice with that principle of government which is so dear to the Episcopal Church'.[10] This proposal interestingly anticipates features of the scheme which led to the United Church of South India in 1947, in its inclusion of episcopal, presbyterian and congregational elements in the proposed union. Needless to say, it did not find favour with many Free Churchmen in 1918. Some of Shakespeare's fellow-Baptists, like Dr John Clifford (1836–1923), were appalled, and the general alarm the scheme provoked may well, in the medium term, have set back any Baptist moves towards greater church unity.[11] There seems little doubt that Shakespeare, though a leading Baptist, and courageous in his inititiative, was hardly representative of the great majority of the members of his denomination, or of Free Church people at large. That, it has to be said, was to be a recurring experience of twentieth-century ecumenical leadership in the Free Churches. Too often, the generals were so far ahead of the troops as to be almost out of sight.

After Edinburgh 1910, the next major ecumenical initiative in Britain came from the Lambeth Conference of Anglican Bishops in 1920, which issued its 'Appeal to All Christian People', as a way of moving nearer to 'the goal of a reunited Catholic Church'. The bishops spelled out their hopes as follows: 'The vision which rises before us is that of a Church genuinely Catholic, loyal to all Truth, and gathering into its fellowship all who "profess and call themselves Christians", within whose visible unity all the treasures of faith and order, bequeathed as a heritage by the past to the present, shall be possessed in common, and made serviceable to the

---

9   J.H. Shakespeare, *The Churches at the Cross-Roads: A Study in Church Unity* (London: Williams and Norgate, 1918), p. 12. On Shakespeare, see Peter Shepherd, *The Making of a Modern Denomination: John Howard Shakespeare and the English Baptists 1898–1924* (Studies in Baptist History and Thought, 4; Carlisle: Paternoster, 2001), especially pp. 93-138 and 182-85 on his ecumenical convictions and work.

10   Shakespeare, *Churches at the Cross-Roads*, p. 186; see also Grant, *Free Churchmanship*, pp. 263-64.

11   On Baptists and ecumenical developments, see Anthony R. Cross, *Baptism and the Baptists: Theology and Practice in the Twentieth Century* (Studies in Baptist History and Thought, 3; Carlisle: Paternoster, 2000), especially pp. 42-97, 127-81 and 244-318.

whole Body of Christ'.[12] The Lambeth Appeal proposed a union on the fourfold basis of scripture, the Nicene Creed, the two gospel sacraments and an episcopal ministry, 'exercised in a constitutional manner'. While the distinguished Baptist scholar, T.R. Glover, promptly repudiated the proposal in his *The Free Churches and Reunion* (1921), the initial response of the Free Churches was cautiously favourable. It would appear that the Anglican initiative struck a chord with many people, inside and outside the Free Churches, who shared the widespread hope for a better state of society following the devastating impact of the First World War.

Sir Henry Lunn, the Wesleyan Methodist ecumenical pioneer, went so far as to address the bishops, as they were about to assemble, in a tract entitled, *Reunion and Lambeth: John Wesley's Message to the Bishops in Conference, July 1920* (1920). Writing under the persona of John Wesley, Lunn pointed out that he was, untypically, a Methodist who was also a member of the Church of England, like Wesley himself. He claimed that, 'For over forty years the question of Christian Reunion [has] been my constant study, and the advance of this sacred cause my steady endeavour'.[13] He longs for reunion, but at the same time refuses to deny the work of God's grace in the ministry of his own church and those of the historic Free Churches: 'I can never take up a position which would necessarily involve any expression of doubt as to the validity of my own ministry in the past, or of the present validity of those excellent representatives of the Free Churches who have worked with me in this movement'.[14] Lunn was gratified that, after the Lambeth gathering, a joint conference took place between representatives of the Church of England and the Federal Council of Evangelical Free Churches. These conversations were to continue until 1925, but foundered on the issue of the validity of Free Church ordinations. The Free Churches could not accept a conditional ordination of their ministers, and the Anglicans could not agree to a simple form of episcopal commissioning or authorization as an alternative. Moreover, the Malines Conversations, between Anglicans and Roman Catholics, which were begun informally in 1921, and continued officially from 1923, sowed new doubts in Free Church minds. Many Nonconformists were alarmed at this new ecumenical development, which confirmed their fears that Anglicans were more interested in reunion with Rome than with the Free Churches. Even J.H. Shakespeare was so discouraged that he withdrew from any further active participation in the movement for reunion. It is hardly surprising

---

12 'The Lambeth Conference 1920: *1. An Appeal to All Christian People*', in G.K.A. Bell (ed.), *Documents on Christian Unity (1920–4)* (London: Oxford University Press, 1924), pp. 2-3.

13 H.S. Lunn, *Reunion and Lambeth: John Wesley's Message to the Bishops in Conference, July 1920* (London: Epworth Press, 1920), p. 11.

14 Lunn, *Reunion and Lambeth*, p. 30.

that, after this loss of confidence, the 'Outline of a Reunion Scheme for the Church of England and the Free Churches in England',[15] produced by the conversations which followed the 1930 Lambeth Conference, failed to elicit Free Church support.

If Anglican–Free Church reunion failed to carry in this period, there were positive moves towards unity within Nonconformity itself. As we have seen, R.W. Dale in 1889 had lamented that the various groups of Methodists, despite all they held in common, could 'neither combine nor confederate'. The 1930s were to prove that Methodist union was possible, though it was not easily or swiftly achieved. As early as 1908, the redoubtable Dr John Scott Lidgett (1854–1953) outlined his view of his own, Wesleyan Methodist, church's ecumenical task: 'Where there are no differences, our watchword must be union; where they are comparatively light, federation; where they are serious, yet not destructive of the fundamental agreement of Christianity, co-operation in order to defend the supreme interests and applications of our common Christian life'.[16] It was an ambitious programme, but its firstfruits may be seen in the Methodist Union of 1932.

That union proved to be a long time in gestation. As early as 1917, a group of leaders from the three denominations involved, Wesleyan, Primitive and United Methodists, met to discuss ways of bringing the three branches together. In 1920, an outline scheme was submitted to the three Conferences, but no binding vote was to be taken. In 1922, the scheme was sent down to the Circuit Quarterly Meetings, where it had a mixed reception. The three sticking points were: finance; the proposed separate Ministerial Session of the Conference, which the Wesleyans insisted on in return for agreeing to drop the Legal Hundred, the 100 permanent members of the Conference, all ministers, which had given a heavy clerical weighting to the combined lay-ministerial membership of their Conference; and the doctrinal basis of a united church. The opposition was not all on one side. On the one hand, the Primitive Methodists were very loath to accept a separate Ministerial or Pastoral Session of the Conference, alongside the combined lay–ministerial Representative Session, as smacking too much of what they saw as Wesleyan clericalism. On the other hand, though agreement had been virtually reached by 1926—in terms eventually finalized in 1932—the Union was held up by the determined opposition of a group of convinced High Wesleyans, led by Dr J.E. Rattenbury, Sir Kingsley Wood, and Sir Henry Lunn, who were strongly opposed to aspects of the proposals which, in their judgment, would weaken the doctrine of

15   Printed in G.K.A. Bell (ed.), *Documents on Christian Unity: Thirrd Series 1930–48* (London: Oxford University Press, 1948), pp. 71-101.

16   R.E. Davies (ed.), *John Scott Lidgett* (London: Epworth Press, 1957), p. 196.

ordained ministry and make it harder to achieve any future Anglican–Methodist union. In particular, they objected to the provision, in special circumstances, for lay presidency at the Lord's Supper, which Wesleyan Methodism, unlike the other two Methodist churches, did not allow.

Yet in the end, despite the various opposition groups, the union carried, since there were powerful forces in its favour. One contributory factor was the idealism and desire to shape a new and better society in the aftermath of the 1914–18 war. John Kent goes so far as to claim that, 'The catalyst which brought popular opinion into the issue on the side of union was the emotional aftermath of the first World War'.[17] Again, in the 1920s and 1930s liberal theology was very much the vogue in the English-speaking world. The Barthian reaction had hardly yet made any general impact, so that the doctrinal basis for the union eschewed detailed dogmatic statement, in favour of a certain studied vagueness and flexibility. Clause 30, the doctrinal clause of the Deed of Union, merely stated that the newly-formed Methodist Church, 'rejoices in the inheritance of the Apostolic Faith and loyally accepts the fundamental principles of the historic creeds and of the Protestant Reformation'.[18]

Another influence in favour of the union was a shared desire among the participants to arrest and reverse the membership loss from which each of the three churches was suffering. In the period 1907–21, the Wesleyans experienced a net loss of 35,000 members; the Primitive Methodists, 10,000; and the United Methodists, 9000.[19] By today's standards, these may not seem exorbitant figures, but they were deeply shocking to churches which had been accustomed to growth and expansion. The hope was that, with a united church, involving rationalization and redeployment of resources, cutting out waste and overlapping, membership would begin to rise again. Sadly, however, redeployment was slow in coming in many local situations, and there was no major reconstruction throughout the Connexion, so that unity without reform and renewal produced no increase in membership, though union may in some areas have slowed down the rate of decline.

Undoubtedly, Methodist Union did not fulfil many of the high hopes of those most keenly committed to it. It did not staunch the haemorrhaging of the membership. Indeed, in a slight measure it increased it, since the research of Geoffrey Nuttall has traced an accession of strength to some of the Congregational churches in the North of England, as a result of their being joined by ex-Primitive and ex-United Methodists, unable to accept union with the Wesleyans, who historically stood much closer to the Anglicans. For some, this disappointment led to

---

17   J.H.S. Kent, *The Age of Disunity* (London: Epworth Press, 1966), p.8.

18   *The Constitutional Practice and Discipline of the Methodist Church*, Volume 2 (Peterborough: Methodist Publishing House, 2000), pp. 2-3.

19   Kent, *Age of Disunity*, p. 4.

jaundiced views about later schemes of reunion, and a tendency to assert that, in the light of the 1932 amalgamation, unity solves nothing. It is true that unity by itself is not enough; but the moral may rather be—to adapt Chesterton's dictum on the alleged failure of Christianity—not that union has been tried and found wanting, but that it has been found difficult and not tried, at least in a thoroughgoing sense. Genuine unity must involve costly renewal, serious restructuring and imaginative replanning of resources. Without these, simply reshuffling the denominational packs of cards has little long-term result; but given them, as the experience of the Church of South India suggests, unity may bring renewal and new life.

As the Lambeth Appeal of 1920 came hard on the heels of the First World War, so another Anglican ecumenical initiative was launched soon after the end of World War II. In 1946, the Archbishop of Canterbury, Geoffrey Fisher, in a Cambridge sermon, invited the Free Churches to achieve intercommunion with the Church of England by 'taking episcopacy into their systems'. This invitation led to the publication of a joint Anglican–Free Church document, *Church Relations in England* (1950), which invited the various Free Churches to enter into bilateral conversations with the Church of England, with a view to closer unity. It is important to stress that Archbishop Fisher had in mind from the beginning not organic union, but intercommunion. In the event, the Methodist Church proved the only Free Church ready to enter into conversations, when in 1955 its Conference overwhelmingly voted to accept the Anglican invitation.

In 1958, the joint Anglican–Methodist committee published the result of its deliberations, in a discussion document entitled, *Conversations between the Church of England and the Methodist Church: An Interim Statement*. The report went beyond Fisher's aim of intercommunion, declaring forthrightly that, 'Organic union, whatever form it may take' must be the 'final goal'.[20] Instead of the South India pattern of unifying the ministries of the two churches, consisting of mutual acceptance rather than anything resembling re-ordination, the document proposed a formal rite of unification of ministries as part of the inauguration of the union. In other respects—the consecration of selected Methodist ministers as bishops and the agreement that all future ordinations in the United Church would be episcopal in character—there was correspondence with the South India scheme.

In 1963, the definitive *Report of the Conversations* set out in detail the order for unification of ministries, in a Service of Reconciliation. The rite featured a deliberate ambiguity, since it was designed to accomodate those High Church Anglicans who believed it was essential that the

20   *Conversations between the Church of England and the Methodist Church: An Interim Statement* (London: SPCK/Epworth Press, 1958), p. 41.

Methodists should be episcopally ordained to enter the United Church; and also to be patient of interpretation as an extension of commission rather than ordination, to satisfy Methodist consciences. The report was not unanimous, since four of the Methodist members of the conversations, all from the non-Wesleyan traditions within the Methodist Church, could not with integrity sign it. Their scruples were echoed and amplified by an association, The Voice of Methodism, formed specifically to combat the proposals. There was also opposition from both ends of the Anglican spectrum: from High Church Anglicans, who sought explicit re-ordination of the Methodist ministers, and from Evangelical Anglicans, who contended for a simple acceptance of Methodist orders and dismissed the Service of Reconciliation as a gratuitous slur upon them.

In 1965, both the Methodist Conference and the Anglican Convocations gave approval in principle to the scheme, and a new joint commission was appointed to work out detailed proposals. In 1967, the commission published its report, *Towards Reconciliation: The Interim Statement of the Anglican-Methodist Unity Commission*, and after further study and debate in the churches, the scheme in its final form was published in 1968. The following year, the Convocations and the Conference voted simultaneously on the understanding that a 75% on both sides was needed for the scheme to be implemented. The Methodist Conference approved by 78%, but the Convocations' vote (69%) failed to attain the required majority. Another attempt to secure agreement was made in 1972 when the General Synod, which comprised both clergy and laity, having replaced the clerical Convocations in 1970, voted on the proposals, but its final vote fell below the previously recorded 69%.

Many on both sides were saddened by the outcome. Some took this reverse of their hopes as a challenge to redouble their ecumenical efforts. Why the scheme failed is a large question, but some answers can be ventured with reasonable confidence. First, although among the leadership of the two churches there had grown up strong bonds of personal friendship and trust, the same could not be said, to anything like the same extent, of clergy and people at parish and circuit level. The infrastructure of local ecumenism, which was to develop so markedly later in the century, was all too often rudimentary or non-existent. Again, there were longstanding differences, in culture and ethos, between 'church' and 'chapel', and these 'non-theological factors' cannot be discounted. The divisions within the Church of England also played a part, since the Anglican vote failed to carry not least because of what ecumenists termed the 'unholy alliance' of recalcitrant Anglo-Catholics and Evangelicals.

All was not loss, however. Before the final voting in 1972, there had been several new initiatives aimed at forwarding ecumenical activity at local level. In 1964, the first British Conference on Faith and Order, meeting at Nottingham University, with its ringing call for 'One Church, Renewed, for Mission', helped stimulate local joint Christian activity. In 1969, the Shared Churches Act opened the way for the joint use of buildings, and the British Council of Churches gave strong support to local Areas of Ecumenical Experiment. After the 1972 vote, an Anglican–Methodist Liaison Committee was set up, specifically to encourage local ecumenism through a Consultative Commission for Local Ecumenical Projects (LEPs). At another level, the failure of Anglican–Methodist union meant that Methodists felt free to ordain women to the presbyteral ministry. The Conference had held back from doing so, during the Conversations, for fear of alienating the Anglicans; but in 1973 it voted overwhelmingly that women should be ordained.

1972 proved a pivotal year for Nonconformist efforts towards greater Christian unity in another, more positive sense. It saw the union of the Presbyterian Church of England with the churches of the Congregational Union, which came together to form the United Reformed Church (URC).[21] That union led directly to the next ecumenical initiative in England, when in 1973 the URC invited all the English churches to make a fresh effort to achieve visible unity. Those which responded included all the main churches, including the Roman Catholic Church, and a Churches' Unity Commission was formed to further the proposal. In 1976, the commission produced a report, entitled *Visible Unity: Ten Propositions*. This document outlined the possibility of the mainstream churches signing a covenant of unity.

In the event, five churches agreed to pursue the covenant idea: the Church of England, the Methodist Church, the Moravian Church, the Disciples of Christ and the United Reformed Church. They appointed representatives to a churches' Council for Covenanting, which in due course produced a major document, *Towards Visible Unity: Proposals for a Covenant* (1980). Churches who signed the covenant would commit themselves thereby to recognize each others' members and ministries; commit themselves to full intercommunion; accept common ordinations for the future; and pledge themselves to seek fuller visible unity. In 1982 the proposals were put to the vote. The Methodists, Moravians, Disciples of Christ and URC voted to accept the covenant, but the Anglicans narrowly failed to achieve the necessary two-thirds vote in the House of Clergy of their General Synod. Lesslie Newbigin, who had previously served as a Bishop of the Church of South India, was a member of the URC team on the Churches' Council for Covenanting, and wholly

---

21   In 1981, the URC was joined by the Re-formed Association of Churches of Christ, which brought 200 churches and 16,000 members into the union.

committed to its success. Reflecting on the failure of the Anglican vote, he wrote in his later autobiography:

> The whole exercise and the character of many of the debates in which I was involved exposed in a painful way the lamentable fading of the ecumenical vision in the minds of English church people. I began to realize how great was the loss which had been inflicted on the Church by the virtual eclipse of the SCM [Student Christian Movement]. I belonged to a generation which had been given their formative vision of the Christian life and received their Christian calling in an ecumenical setting. But now the majority of those in the Churches had been shaped either in a conservative evangelical setting where visible unity was not seen to be important, or in a merely denominational setting which had deprived them of the opportunity to form deep and trustful friendships outside of that setting.[22]

Bishop Newbigin had begun his ministry in the English Presbyterian Church, but served for many years (1936–59; 1965–74) in India, where he became one of the architects of the united Church of South India (CSI). When the CSI was inaugurated in 1947, Newbigin was appointed bishop in Madurai and Ramnad and so became a leader of a communion which included Christians from the Anglican, Methodist, Presbyterian, Congregational, Lutheran and Reformed traditions. After his retirement and his return to England in 1974, he served as the minister of a small URC church in inner city Birmingham and was elected Moderator of the URC in 1978. Thanks to his service in India, and his long personal experience of working in the united church there, he brought to his ecumenical work in Britain a strong sense of urgency. It was an urgency rooted in the gospel imperative for unity—that Christians might be truly and visibly one in Christ, but also an urgency inspired by the needs of the Christian mission in India. He sought not unity for its own sake, but 'so that the world might believe'. He was an influential author in the fields of apologetics, missiology and ecumenism, and in his later writings he was seized by the urgent need of the church's mission not only in India, but in secularized, post-Christian Britain. Hence his stream of books in this field, including, *The Other Side of 1984* (1983), *Foolishness to the Greeks* (1986) and *The Gospel in a Pluralist Society* (1989). His ecumenism was imbued throughout his life by an overriding concern for the church's universal mission to proclaim and embody the gospel of reconciliation in Christ, as is clear from his earlier publication, *The Reunion of the Church* (1948; rev. edn 1960). There he argues: 'Surely it is clear that no pattern of missionary strategy can meet the needs of the world in which we live save one in which men everywhere can recognize the lineaments of one universal fellowship, transcending the divisions that

---

22   J.L. Newbigin, *Unfinished Agenda: An Autobiography* (Geneva: World Council of Churches, 1985), pp. 249-50.

scar our world, and holding out to all men the secret of reconciliation with God. And men will not see that except in a Church which has dealt far more seriously than it yet shows signs of doing with its denominational divisions.'[23]

Newbigin was not alone among Nonconformist ministers who, having served in the Church of South India, were eager to share their ecumenical experience with their co-religionists when they returned to England. Some did so through their writings, and alongside Newbigin we may mention the Methodist, Marcus Ward, whose *The Pilgrim Church* (1952) gives a vivid, personal account of the first five years of the CSI. Others, like Bishop Norman Sargant and Bishop Kenneth Gill, both formerly Methodists, bore their ecumenical witness through their continuing ministry of preaching, teaching and pastoral care. Part of the value of the contribution these men could make to the English ecumenical scene was their ability to speak concretely from experience of a united church. They could help dispel some of the fears and illusions about what closer unity might mean. To Free Church people who feared that unity must inevitably mean absorption and loss of what was most distinctive and precious in their traditions, they were able to testify that, although the CSI was an episcopal church, it had incorporated strong Congregational and Presbyterian elements. Moreover, the episcopacy itself had been distinctly modified from the received Anglican pattern. Lesslie Newbigin, typically of the CSI bishops, was bishop 'in', not 'of' Madurai or Madras, his two successive dioceses. What may seem a trivial verbal difference actually signified a genuine change. The bishop was not the lord bishop, exalted over his diocese and elevated above clergy and people. He was now the bishop in council, surrounded by his clergy and representative lay people, in all his planning and pastoral care of the diocese.

Moreover, when challenged as to whether the CSI union had in practice made much difference to the life, worship and mission of the church, Free Church ministers who had served in it were able to give a positive response. The CSI eventually produced from its common life a new *Book of Common Worship* (1963), which was much admired by other churches. Part of its merit was its deliberate effort to bring together some of the treasures of early Christian devotion, as well as drawing on both Eastern and Western traditions of prayer and praise. It was able, for example, in its 'Order for the Lord's Supper or the Holy Eucharist', to incorporate the Eastern Christian celebration of the joy of the resurrection, to complement the sometimes overwhelming Western emphasis on the cross and the sin that made it necessary. As to the wider fruits of the union, when Bishop Newbigin was pressed to say what precisely these were and

---

23   J.L. Newbigin, *The Reunion of the Church* (London: SCM Press, rev. edn, 1960 [1948]), p.xxxvi.

whether they related at all to the renewal of the church, as against its mere enlargement by amalgamation, he was in no doubt as to the answer he should give. He would refer first to the inbuilt conservatism which ecclesiastical bodies all too often share with secular institutions. Each denomination, when considering questions of worship, education, mission or evangelism, would tend to be guided by its own tradition, with a weighting towards the 'But we've always done it this way' syndrome. When, however, five or six denominations come together, vital questions of the church's life and mission cannot be settled in such an easy, traditional manner. Newbigin testified that, in the united CSI, confronted by a variety of traditions, they were forced to face more fundamental questions, and had to ask over and again, 'What course of action is nearest to the mind of Christ and in accordance with the leading of the Spirit; and what will best serve the needs of India today, as we seek to minister to it in mission and service?' Insofar as the church was driven to face these questions honestly, unity could be said to be a means of renewal, and might approximate to a response to the Nottingham Faith and Order Conference's challenge to seek 'One Church, Renewed, for Mission'.

If Lesslie Newbigin was an outstanding ecumenist from the Presbyterian tradition, and Marcus Ward equally prominent from the Methodist Church, Dr Ernest Payne (1902–80) may represent the very significant contribution made to ecumenism from the Baptist Union. In a recent article in the *Baptist Quarterly*, Anthony R. Cross has made a comprehensive survey of Baptists, ministerial and lay, who have given signal service to the ecumenical movement.[24] Under the title of 'Service to the Ecumenical Movement', he brings together a most impressive roll call of Baptists who have served with distinction in the National Council of Evangelical Free Churches, the Free Church Federal Council, the British Council of Churches, the World Council of Churches and its Faith and Order Commission, and in the Ecumenical Instruments inaugurated in 1990 as the fruit of the Inter-Church Process. Of the many listed, none gave longer or more devoted service to the cause than Ernest Payne.[25] It might be taken as a portent of Baptist involvement that the British Council of Churches, formed in 1942, came into being in the Council Chamber of Baptist Church House, London. Ernest Payne, who was General Secretary of the Baptist Union (1951–67), served as Vice-President of the Council (1960–62) and chaired its Executive Committee (1962–71). Nor did he confine his ecumenical labours to the British scene. He was a Baptist representative to the First Assembly of the World

24   Anthony R. Cross, 'Service to the Ecumenical Movernent: The Contribution of British Baptists', *Baptist Quarterly* 38.3 (July, 1999), pp. 107-22.

25   See W.M.S. West, *To Be a Pilgrim: A Memoir of Ernest A. Payne* (Guildford: Lutterworth Press, 1983), *passim*.

Council of Churches at Amsterdam in 1948, and served as Vice Chair of the WCC Central Committee, and as one of the Presidents of the Council until his retirement from office in 1975. Dr Payne had considerable influence, both within and beyond the Free Churches, in getting Christians to face up to 'non-theological factors' in the making and un-making of Christian union. He also contributed to ecumenical thinking through his writings, and more especially in his *The Free Church Tradition in the Life of England* (1944, 4th edn 1965), *Free Churchmen, Unrepentant and Repentant and Other Papers* (1965) and his *Thirty Years of the British Council of Churches, 1942–72* (1972).

The member churches of the Baptist Union have certainly not been equally zealous for closer Christian unity; but as a denomination the Baptists have produced an outstanding succession of ecumenical leaders, out of all proportion one might think to their size as a denomination. Another prophetic Baptist voice on the British scene is that of Alec Gilmore. As clearly as Lesslie Newbigin, he has seen the interrelation between Christian unity and the renewal of the church. As early as 1963, in a Baptist symposium he edited, entitled *The Pattern of the Church: A Baptist View*, he argues forthrightly that 'Denominational reform and movement towards church union in England are but two sides of a single coin', and 'Reform and reunion belong together' since both involve a drastic shake-up of established patterns of church life. He is clear that it is unity, not uniformity, that should be the goal; diversity in unity, reflecting the many-coloured wisdom of God and the riches of the denominational traditions. He writes, of course, before the inauguration of the United Reformed Church, or he would not, perhaps, have been so scathing in his dismissal of any merely Free Church union. He states categorically: 'The time for Free Church union has long since passed. The curious inheritance of division with intercommunion, of co-existence without cost, has sanctified the scandal and dried up the springs of healing'.[26] He therefore calls for conversations with the Church of England, as well as the Free Churches, though aware that difficult issues must then be faced, notably the meaning of tradition, Christian initiation,[27] *episcope* and the establishment of the Church of England. On the last, it may be said that Free Church anti-establishment feeling has, in the latter twentieth century, somewhat abated, while many Anglicans have become critical of the current form of establishment, and eager either for reform or the severance of the ties with the state.

A propos of Alec Gilmore's contention that church reform and Christian reunion are bound together, it is interesting to note that in the

---

26   Alec Gilmore (ed.), *The Pattern of the Church: A Baptist View* (London: Lutterworth Press, 1963), ch. 5 'Towards Church Union', pp. 163-64.

27   See, e.g., A. Gilmore's *Baptism and Christian Unity* (London: Lutterworth Press, 1966).

long list of Baptist ecumenists just cited, which runs to over a hundred names, covering the twentieth century, there are only five women. Moreover, these women appear in ecumenical leadership roles almost entirely in the last two decades of the century. The leadership is overwhelmingly masculine, and there is no reason to think that the Baptists were alone in this heavily male bias. In the Free Churches at large, women ecumenical leaders such as the Methodist Dr Pauline Webb, are far to seek. Webb was a participant in the Anglican–Methodist conversations of the 1960s, and the first woman to be elected as an officer of the Central Committee of the World Council of Churches. Her ecumenical activity was accompanied by a concerted effort to persuade the Methodist Church to accept the ordination of women. This issue had remained dormant in the Methodist Conference for some years, but Webb re-opened it in the Conference of 1959 and was thereafter a consistent advocate of women's ordination. Thus for her, true to Alec Gilmore's thesis, denominational reform and Christian reunion were cognate causes. Pauline Webb's engagement in the Anglican–Methodist conversations would have brought home to her the general unwillingness of the Methodist leadership to proceed to the ordination of women, even though by the 1960s there was a strong consensus in favour of it, lest such action might prejudice the successful outcome of the union negotiations.

It is interesting, therefore, to note the views of Constance Coltman (1890–1969), the first woman to be ordained to the Christian ministry in England. She trained at Mansfield College, Oxford, for the Congregational ministry, was ordained in 1917, and shared a pastorate with the Revd Claud Coltman, her husband. She too saw the link between church reform and reunion, but she did not favour the delaying tactics of the Methodists, who were later to plead inopportunism in face of their conversations with the Church of England. On the contrary, in an article she wrote in *The Free Catholic*, Constance Coltman explicitly rejected the view that the question of the ordination of women should not be raised until the church was reunited. She argued: 'Only as each Church, according to its own light, draws nearer to Him who is the Truth, will the Churches find themselves side by side. Those who shrink from acting on the truth they themselves have glimpsed because others have not yet seen it, are committing the real sin of schism by separating themselves from the Truth, who is Head of the Church. They are denying the operations of the Holy Ghost.'[28]

The Methodist Conference, after the second failure of a scheme for Anglican–Methodist union in 1972, decided to act on its own convictions, and duly ordained its first women ministers in 1974, so that the last

---

28   Elaine Kaye, 'Constance Coltman—A Forgotten Pioneer', *Journal of the United Reformed Church History Society* 4.2 (May, 1988), p. 146.

quarter of the twentieth century saw the Methodist churches—like the Baptist and United Reformed Churches before them—greatly enriched by the gifts and leadership of women ministers.

In the last fifteen years of the century, another ecumenical initiative was launched, known as the Inter-Church Process (ICP). It was wider in scope than any previous attempt at closer unity, but at the same time more modest and realistic in its programme and aims. It was first mooted at the Spring 1984 Assembly of the British Council of Churches and formally inaugurated in the following year. The churches accepting the invitation to take part in the process were both numerous and diverse, comprising the Anglican, Baptist, Black-led Pentecostal and Holiness Churches, Congregational, Lutheran, Methodist, Orthodox, Roman Catholic and United Reformed Churches. Their representatives met at The Hayes Conference Centre, Swanwick, Derbyshire, in 1987, and on Friday 4 September, agreed a ringing declaration of their commitment to the ICP as a means to greater unity:

> We now declare together our readiness to commit ourselves to each other under God. Our earnest desire is to become more fully, in his own time, the one Church of Christ, united in faith, communion, pastoral care and mission. Such unity is the gift of God. With gratitude we have truly experienced this gift, growing amongst us in these days. We affirm our openness to this growing unity in obedience to the Word of God, so that we may fully share, hold in common and offer to the world those gifts which we have received and still hold in separation. In the unity we seek we recognise that there will not be uniformity but legitimate diversity.

> It is our conviction that, as a matter of policy at all levels and in all places, our churches must now move from co-operation to clear commitment to each other, in search of the unity for which Christ prayed and in common evangelism and service of the world.[29]

In 1990, a series of new 'Ecumenical Instruments', so-called, was launched. Churches Together in England (CTE) replaced, for the English churches, the former British Council of Churches; ACTS (Action of Churches Together in Scotland) and CYTUN (Churches Together in Wales), provided similar agencies for co-operation for other national groupings of churches. The Council of Churches for Britain and Ireland (CCBI) enabled wider joint working together of churches across the British Isles. The inclusion of the Roman Catholic Church and a number of Black-led Holiness and Pentecostal Churches made the new instruments more widely inclusive than any previous councils of churches. The mention of CYTUN, the co-ordinating body for the Welsh churches, provides an opportunity to look at ecumenical developments

---

29 *Churches Together in Pilgrimage* (London: British Council of Churches/Catholic Truth Society, 1989), pp. 7-8.

among the Protestant Nonconformists of Wales, where the Free Churches are numerous and have deep roots in the history and culture of the Principality.

In 1975, a significant group of Welsh churches signed a covenant of unity. Their action in so doing was an appropriate response to the challenge issued to the British churches by the 1964 Nottingham Faith and Order Conference, inviting them, in appropriate groupings such as nations, to covenant together to work and pray for the inauguration of union by a date to be agreed amongst them. The Welsh churches duly formed a Joint Covenant Committee, which produced in 1971 specific proposals in a document entitled, *Covenanting for Union in Wales*. When it came to the signing of the covenant, the churches involved proved to be the Church in Wales, the Methodist Church, the Presbyterian Church in Wales, the United Reformed Church, and a number of individual Baptist churches. They prefaced the terms of their covenant with the following affirmation of faith: 'Confessing our faith in Jesus Christ as Lord and Saviour, and renewing our will to serve his mission in the world, our several churches have been brought into a new relationship with one another. Together we give thanks for all we have in common. Together we repent the sin of perpetuating our division. Together we make known our understanding of the obedience to which we are called.' The covenant then spelled out the churches' mutual acceptance of all their members and ministries as 'within the one Church of Jesus Christ', and their resolve to serve and witness together in obedience to the gospel and for the good of the people of Wales. They pledged themselves to strive, with the help of the Spirit, 'to overcome the divisions which impair our witness, impede God's mission, and obscure the gospel of man's salvation, and to manifest that unity which is in accordance with Christ's will'. The covenanting churches acknowledged that they were only just setting out on a new pilgrimage to greater unity. They intended 'to seek an agreed pattern of ordained ministry which will serve the gospel in unity', and also 'a mode of Church government which will preserve the positive values for which each has stood'. They concluded the covenant in forward-looking, hopeful mode: 'We do not know the form union will take. We approach our task with openness to the Spirit. We believe that God will guide his Church into ways of truth and peace, correcting, strengthening, and renewing it in accordance with the mind of Christ.'[30]

Given the sectarian tensions which have at times marred the history of Christianity in Wales, the covenant marked a genuine resolve, not least on the part of the major Nonconformist churches, to seek a more excellent way of living and working together.

---

30   *Churches Together in Pilgrimage*, pp. 74-75.

The new inter-church relationships established by the Welsh covenant proved an admirable preparation for the wider association of churches in CYTUN, which added to the signatories of the covenant new groups of Christians, namely, The Union of Welsh Independants, the Salvation Army, the Religious Society of Friends and the Roman Catholic Church.

Wales is the smallest of the countries whose groupings of churches form the membership of the CCBI, yet it is one which has a deep-rooted, lively and variegated Christian presence. It may, therefore, appropriately serve to introduce the remaining part of this study, which focuses on the varied patterns of involvement of Protestant Nonconformists at local and regional levels. The twentieth century saw no significant breakthrough in terms of a union between the Anglicans and Free Churches. As far as Free Church unions are concerned, the century saw a union of Methodist Churches in 1932, and forty years later, the creation of the United Reformed Church. Yet although ecumenical progress towards national unions was relatively limited, there was a great and increasing development of Christian unity and co-operation in the regions and localities. Nonconformists, along with fellow-Christians of other communions, began to take seriously, in the latter part of the twentieth century, the call of the Lund (1952) World Conference of Faith and Order, that Christians should do nothing separately that they could do together, unless strong conscientious scruples prevented such joint action.[31]

At the regional level, one of the prime examples of such growing co-operation is Merseyside, with its centre in the international port of Liverpool. For generations, the city was marked by intense Protestant–Catholic rivalry, and by a sectarianism which challenged comparison with Northern Ireland at its worst. Yet in 1990, when the CCBI was inaugurated, the service of thanksgiving and commitment was held in Liverpool's two cathedrals, Anglican and Roman Catholic, joined appropriately by Hope Street, along which thousands of Christians processed in a walk of witness as part of the celebration. Liverpool was chosen by the officers of CCBI, not primarily because of its geographical position—close to Wales, within easy reach of Ireland, and not far from the border with Scotland—but because by 1990 it had become a byword for Christian unity.

In 1976, a joint Church Leaders Group was formed in Liverpool, which was serviced by the full-time ecumenical officer, at that time the Revd David Savage, a Baptist minister. The leaders—Roman Catholic, Anglican and Free Church—met regularly for prayer, study and planning. David Sheppard, the then Anglican Bishop of Liverpool, and his colleague,

---

31   *Faith and Order: The Report of the Third World Conference at Lund, Sweden, August 15-28, 1952* (London: SCM Press, 1952).

Derek Worlock, the Catholic Archbishop, played a key role in bringing the leadership of the churches together in this way. They have described, in their joint account, what a demanding agenda the church leaders set themselves:

> From the beginning there was determination that this group should be more than a talking-shop. Items included in its agenda in the first few years reflect this and give some of the flavour of our discussions: planning a two-day conference on ministry; arranging an annual Shrove Tuesday party for mayors, civic officials and their partners; responding to the government's inner areas study; making the Liverpool Industrial Mission an ecumenical enterprise; planning the Queen's visit to the Church in Liverpool; leading a youth pilgrimage to Taizé; establishing a World Development Centre; supporting a new pastoral counselling project called COMPASS [Counselling on Merseyside and Pastoral Support Service]; launching a joint clergy orientation course; involvement with the Roman Catholic National Pastoral Congress in Liverpool; a score of other items listed in the agenda and including police liaison, episcopacy, marriage and family life, and a joint pastoral letter to all the Churches at Pentecost.[32]

The two bishops, both nationally known, were increasingly expected, by the media and government departments, to speak on behalf of the Merseyside churches. Given the close relationships between the church leaders, the absence of an accompanying Free Church voice became more and more apparent, and the Merseyside Churches Ecumenical Council proposed that the Free Churches should appoint their own Moderator for Merseyside, who would be 'a recognised spokesman to stand with Bishop and Archbishop in the corporate witness of the Churches'.[33] In 1985, an appointment was made, and the Revd John Williamson, then Moderator of the Mersey Province of the United Reformed Church, became Free Church Moderator for Merseyside. The church leaders that same year signed a covenant of unity, sealing their growing co-operation, and the Merseyside and Region Ecumenical Assembly (MARCEA) was constituted. Within the Assembly, there was a Free Church Sector, which met, under the chairmanship of the Moderator, for specifically Free Church matters, but the overwhelming majority of concerns were dealt with jointly in the full Assembly.

From the work of the Assembly, a number of new joint Christian initiatives sprang. CARE (Churches Action for Racial Equality), with a full-time director and a team of volunteers, had a dual role. It sought to work on behalf of Liverpool's black community, whose members were often disadvantaged in terms of housing and employment. It also had a wider remit—to train church members and others in racial understanding

---

32   David Sheppard and Derek Worlock, *Better Together: Christian Partnership in a Hurt City* (London: Hodder & Stoughton, 1988), pp. 84-85.

33   Sheppard and Worlock, *Better Together*, p. 87.

and a concern for racial justice, using biblical materials and the resources of the Christian Faith. Again, the churches jointly sought to respond the impressive redevelopment of Liverpool's waterfront, the Albert Dock complex, which with its shops, art gallery and maritime museum, attracted over six million visitors a year. The churches jointly raised money to rent a property in the middle of the shopping area of the Dock, designated The Churches' Anchorage and serving as a pastoral advice and information centre for all who cared to take advantage of it. The work of the church leaders and the activities of the ecumenical assembly did not stand alone. They were given local shape and form through shared church agreements, Local Ecumenical Partnerships, and joint service and witness at parish and congregational level.

Liverpool is, of course, only one among many examples of regional ecumenism which might be cited, and in which Protestant Nonconformists have taken their full part. It is striking, however, in that its marked ecumenical progress stands out against the experience of bitter sectarianism which for so long marked the life of the city. A different and more recent example may be taken from Milton Keynes, home of the Open University and a prime instance of a successful New Town development. The Development Corporation, at the request of all the churches of Milton Keynes, granted them a prime site for the building of a central church, to be used jointly by all the mainstream churches, and dedicated to Christ the Cornerstone, as the foundation of all Christian unity. The church was duly opened and dedicated in 1992 and is used for worship by Roman Catholics, Anglicans, Baptists, Methodists and United Reformed Church Christians. The church incorporates a baptistery for baptism by immersion, a Fairtrade shop, meeting rooms for church and community use, and a flat where people with disabilities may learn how to cope with independent living. The ministers and clergy work as an integrated team, under the leadership of a Moderator for Milton Keynes, the first one to occupy that office being the Revd Hugh Cross of the Baptist Union.

One final example of local co-operation, in a very different setting, comes from Swindon Old Town, Wiltshire, where the Anglican, Methodist and United Reformed Churches have formed themselves into an ecumenical parish. A 1977 report on this experiment in ecumenism describes it as follows:

> The staff of the three churches act as a team and the Ecumenical Synod of 30, under a lay chairman, organizes the work of the Parish in detail. There is a system of Parish Stewards, laypeople who cover the whole Parish by being each responsible for one street and all the families in it (and also for the Christian Aid collection). Twenty or thirty Lenten house groups, comprising 350 people, have operated each year since the inauguration of the Parish, and all meet together for an Agape Meal and Holy Communion on Maundy Thursday. Considerable social outreach is carried out

together, and Christian education, with many experiments, takes place in an ecumenical setting. Worship continues separately for the most part in the participating Churches, and an increase in joint worship is not felt to be a matter of great urgency. But, apart from this, it has become inconceivable to ministers and laypeople alike that they should do anything in separation which can be done together.[34]

These examples of practical ecumenism at local level may be paralleled by the more than 600 Local Ecumenical Partnerships scattered across England and Wales, by the numerous covenants signed by local groups of churches, by church-sharing agreements and by the common authorization of a minister of one denomination to have pastoral responsibility for members of another, as for example the Methodist Conference annually grants to Anglican, Baptist and URC ministers the additional status of being Recognised and Regarded (RR) as a Methodist minister.

In conclusion, it is clear that over the twentieth century the churches of England and Wales have made considerable progress in their pilgrimage to fuller unity, though there is clearly a long way yet to go before any general organic unity may be realized. In this ecumenical progress, Protestant Nonconformists have played a distinct, in some cases a notable, part. In point of fact, the twentieth-century unions of churches have taken place among the Free Churches themselves, rather than between Free Churches and Anglicans, though that is not to deny the greatly improved relations between those two streams of Christian faith and life. The failure of Anglicans to unite with other churches does, however, prompt the question whether, given serious internal divisions within a denomination, it is capable of reaching a sufficiently common mind to enter into a union. Certainly, the Church of England is at present experiencing serious tensions within its own ranks, over a number of major issues— both ethical and theological. Those tensions are certainly not helpful in the context of the renewed talks begun in 1999 with the Methodist Church, with a view to exploring a closer unity. On the other hand, since the earlier attempts at Anglican–Methodist union, there has been a considerable growth in trust and joint working at local level. A further new development is the presence at these talks of official observers from Methodism's sister-churches of CTE, including other Free Churches. Whatever the result of these particular conversations, we may be reasonably confident, given the public commitment of the churches, that the pilgrimage towards deeper visible unity in Christ will go on. Not all share the same ecumenical vision, of course. Yet whether we see the goal as close co-operation and sharing, a loose form of federation,

---

34   L. Vischer and D. Gill (eds), *In Each Place: Towards a Fellowship of Local Churches Truly United* (Geneva: World Council of Churches, 1977), pp. 87-88.

intercommunion or full organic unity, the call to unity has been heard, and Protestant Nonconformists in England and Wales have not been slow to respond to it. The ecumenical climate may currently seem rather unfavourable to any striking progress towards unity, but the Free Church leaders who were the last century's ecumenical pioneers, together with those who follow them today, might well want to say Amen to the word of Dr Visser 't Hooft, the first General Secretary of the WCC: 'We are not fair weather ecumenists!'

Index

Christen, E. 333
Christian initiation 102, 116, 121
Christian Science 143
Christian Socialism 109
Christian Unions 209
Christian, E. 159
Christie, K.S. 146, 147, 149, 151, 152, 155, 157, 158, 159
Christol, F. 327, 328, 334, 335, 336, 337, 338
Church in Wales 375
Church of Christ the Cornerstone, Milton Keynes 132, 133, 170, 378
Church of England 2, 39, 51, 52, 54, 55, 56, 57, 59, 62, 66, 70, 71, 76, 87, 97, 104, 127, 128, 195, 202, 214, 215, 231, 254, 260, 261, 268, 283, 339, 340, 357, 358, 359, 362, 363, 366, 367, 368, 372, 373
Church of Scotland 113, 120, 144, 345, 346
Church of South India 114, 127, 362, 366, 368, 369, 370, 371
Church of the Peace of God, Oxted 134, 135, 136, 138, 171
Church, L.F. 296
church-state 51, 52, 53, 54, 55, 56, 57, 65, 66
Churches of Christ 102
Churches Together in England 374, 379
Churches Together in Wales 374, 376
Churches' Council for Covenanting 368
Churches' Unity Commission 368
Churchill, W. 235, 338
City Temple, London 38, 39, 138, 141, 184, 191, 192, 237, 272
Clarendon Code 66
Clark, A. 146, 150, 151, 152, 155, 157
Clark, H.W. 53
Clark, J. 70
Clark, N. 103
Clarke, S. 104
Cleary, E.J. 269, 281
Cleaves, R.W. 211
Clement 110
Clements, K.W. 47, 192, 242, 261
Clements, R.E. 11, 19, 20
clerical dress 103
Cliff College 196, 205
Clifford, J. 63, 164, 190, 191, 222, 224, 243, 245, 252, 362

Cline, C.A. 234
Coad, R. 301
Coates, G. 210, 212, 213
Coggan, D. 30, 31
Cole, G.D.H. 276
Coleg Coffa, Swansea 95
Coleridge, S.T. 46
Colet, J. 66
Coll, A.R. 239
Collinet 331
Collins, L.J. 239
Collinson, N. 257
Collinson, N.T. 311
Collinson, P. 319
Coltman, Claude 373
Coltman, Constance 103, 373
commissioning service 102
communion 106, 108, 109, 110, 111, 112, 113, 114, 116, 118, 119, 121, 123, 124, 125, 126, 127, 128, 129, 130, 131
Compton-Rickett, J. 290
Conder, E.R. 35, 36, 47, 62
confirmation 107, 116
Congregational Church 116
Congregational Church Order Group 113
Congregational Church Service Society 108
Congregational Federation 117-18
Congregational Historical Society 70
Congregational Literature Committee 111
Congregational Liturgical Committee 115
Congregational Memorial College, Brecon 35, 87, 95
Congregational Union of England and Wales 35, 55, 63, 114, 191, 193, 203, 254, 255, 260, 261, 290, 368
Congregationalism 38, 51, 57, 61, 89, 91, 96, 97, 98, 103, 120, 130, 134, 135, 136, 139, 142, 145, 199, 272, 362, 365, 370, 373, 374
Congregationalists 1, 4, 33, 34, 38, 39, 42, 47, 54, 56, 60, 73, 78, 81, 95, 102, 103, 105, 106, 108-15, 117, 134, 135, 138, 143, 156, 167, 168, 188, 191, 193, 194, 198, 199, 200, 206, 209, 235, 252, 260, 270, 271, 274 285, 286, 287, 290, 369
Conord, P. 319
Cook, C.T. 203

Haworth, A. 255, 290
Hawthorne, W.H. 274
Hay, D.M. 29
Hayden, R. 261
Hayes, D. 236
Hayes, E. 314
Headingley Methodist College 37, 43, 60
Heller, D. 319
Henderson, A. 231, 232, 233
Henman, P.S. 301
Herbert, P. 148
Hertford, C.H. 86
Hick, J. 48, 49, 50, 58
high churchmanship 54
Hill, C. 211
Hilton, B. 192
Hinsley, F.H. 223
Hipper, K. 162, 165, 167
Hippolytus 128
Hoare, S. 234
Hocking, S. 222
Hodge, C. 209
Hodgkin, H. 226
Hodgson, L. 59
Hoe, S. 276
Hoffmann, J.G.H. 326, 328
Holiness Churches 374
holiness teaching 196
holiness tradition 208
Hollowell, J.H. 52
Holscher, G. 20
Holy Trinity, Brompton 213
Hone, D. 126
Hook, N. 154
Hooke, D.B. 260
Hooke, S.H. 18
Hooker, M.D. 28
Hope Street Unitarian Chapel, Liverpool 244, 262
Horn, R 209
Horne, C.S. 63-67, 69, 70, 70, 71, 72, 73, 76
Horsley, L. 269, 307
Horton, R.F. 187, 228, 262
Hosti, K.J. 216
Houghton, A.M. 97
Howard, F. 127
Howard, W.F. 31
Hoyois, F. 335
Hubert, A. 332
Hubert, M. 332
Hughes, H.P. 76, 187, 190, 221

Hughes, J. 80
Hughes, R. 236
Hughes, S. 84
Hugret, P.M. 328
Huguenots 313-56
Hunter, J. 103, 105, 106, 108, 109, 111, 113, 118, 128
Hunter, T. 132, 133
Hurley, M. 357
Hurst, L.D. 7
Huxtable, J. 56, 103, 113
hymn-books 102, 103, 116, 125

Ibberson, H.G. 143 166, 168, 177
immanentism 109
inclusive language 103, 116, 117
Independency 91, 98, 99
Independent Baptist churches 74
Independent Methodists 125, 130
Independents 58, 83, 95, 96, 201, 260, 357
infant baptism 105, 111, 112, 116, 118, 119
infant dedication 105, 106, 116, 119, 120, 121, 122, 124, 130
Inter-Church Process 371, 374
Inter-Varsity Fellowship 209, 210
International Congregational Council 58
International Holiness Mission 196
International Missionary Council 359, 360

Jacks, L.P. 59, 246-50, 254
Jackson, G. 37, 192, 193, 195
Jacob, C. 278
Jacob, H. 277
Jacques, S. 320
James, J.C. 52
James, J.S. 80
Jarman, M. 207
Jaulmes, M.Y. 321, 335, 337, 339
Jeffery, R. 142
Jeffreys, G. 196
Jenkins, C. 97
Jenkins, D. 77, 113
Jenkins, D.E. 92
Jenkins, D.T. 47
Jenkins, G.H. 80, 84, 95, 95, 96, 98, 101
Jenkins, R. 64